1992

Platonism in Late Antiquity

Christianity and Judaism in Antiquity

Charles Kannengiesser, Series Editor

Volume 8

Platonism

in

Late Antiquity

Edited by

STEPHEN GERSH

and

CHARLES KANNENGIESSER

UNIVERSITY OF NOTRE DAME PRESS
Notre Dame, Indiana

Library of Congress Cataloging-in-Publication Data

Platonism in late antiquity / edited by Stephen Gersh and Charles
Kannengiesser.
    p.   cm. — (Christianity and Judaism in antiquity ; v. 8)
    English, French, and Italian.
    Includes bibliographical references.
    ISBN 0-268-01513-9
    1. Platonists. 2. Plato—Influence. 3. Philosophy, Ancient.
4. Christianity—Philosophy—History. I. Gersh, Stephen.
II. Kannengiesser, Charles. III. Series.
B517.P56   1992
184—dc20   91-43920
                                            CIP

The authors and editors of this volume dedicated their work as a homage to Père Édouard des Places, S.J., for his ninetieth birthday on July 23, 1990.

Contents

Édouard des Places

Bibliography 1980-1989

(Suite de la bibliographie 1929-1979 in *Études platoniciennes 1929-1979* = *Études préliminaires aux religions orientales dans l'Empire romain*, t. 90, Leiden, E.J. Brill, 1981, p. XI-XIX).

• • • • •

1980

Eusèbe de Césarée, *La Préparation évangélique*, Livres v, 18-vi. (Sources chrétiennes, 266). Paris, Éd. du Cerf, 1980, 291 pages.

"Chronique de la philosophie religieuse des Grecs (1977-1980)," in *Bulletin de l'Association Guillaume Budé* (1980): 420-437.

1981

Études platoniciennes (V. p. 1, début), XX-416 pages.

"Les Oracles chaldaïques et Denys l'Aréopagite," in *Les Cahiers de Fontenay*, nos. 19-22: *Néoplatonisme*. Mélanges offerts à Jean Trouillard, Fontenay-aux-Roses, Éc. norm. sup. (1981): 291-295.

"Le Pseudo-Denys l'Aréopagite, ses précurseurs et sa postérité," in *Dialogues d'histoire ancienne*, 7 (1981): 323-332.

"Chronique de la philosophie religieuse des Grecs (1978-1981)," in *B.A.G.B.* (1981): 315-331.

1982

Eusèbe de Césarée, *La Préparation évangélique*, Livre XI. Introd., trad. et comm. de Geneviève Favrelle. Texte grec révisé par E. d. Pl. (Sources chrétiennes 292). Paris, Éd. du Cerf, 1982. 406 pages.

Eusebius Werke, VIII. 1: *Die Praeparatio evangelica*, I-X. 2. bearbeitete Aufl. herausg. von É. d. Pl., Berlin, Akademie-Verlag, 1982; Nachträge und Berichtigungen, 615-623.

Eusèbe de Césarée commentateur. Platonisme et Écriture Sainte. (Théologie historique 63). Paris, Beauchesne, 1982. 196 pages.

Porphyre, *Vie de Pythagore, Lettre à Marcella.* (Coll. des Univ. de France). Paris, Les Belles Lettres, 1982. 200 pages (34-127 doubles).

"Maxime le Confesseur et Diadoque de Photicé," in *Maximus Confessor*, Symposium Fribourg, 2-5 Sept. 1980, Fribourg, Éd. univ. (1982): 29-35.

"La théologie négative du Pseudo-Denys, ses antécédents platoniciens et son influence au seuil du Moyen Age," in *Studia patristica*, 18 Oxford, Pergamon Press (1982): 81-92.

"Éléments de sotériologie orientale dans le platonisme à la fin de l'antiquité," in *La soteriologia dei culti orientali nell'impero romano.* Atti di colloquio internazionale, Roma, 24-28 sett. 1979 (= *Études préliminaires.* 92). Leiden, E.J. Brill (1982): 243-255.

"Chronique de la philosophie religieuse des Grecs (1979-1982)," in *B.A.G.B* (1982): 421-436.

1983

Eusèbe de Césarée, *La Préparation évangélique*, Livre XII-XIII. Introd., trexte grec, trad. et annotation. (Sources chrétiennes 307). Paris, Éd. du Cerf, 1983. 493 pages.

Eusebius Werke, VIII. 2: *Die Praeparatio evangelica*, XI-XV, bearbeitete Aufl. herausg. von É. d. Pl., Berlin, Akad.-Verlag, 1983; Nachträge und Berichtigungen, 587-496.

"La préparation évangélique d'Eusèbe a-t-elle eu deux éditions? Rédactions longues et rédactions courtes," in *Orpheus*, 4 (1983): 108-112.

"Notes sur quelques oracles chaldaïques," in *Mélanges Édouard Delebecque*, Marseille, Laffitte (1983): 321-329.

"Chronique de la philosophie religieuse des Grecs (1980-1983)," in *B.A.G.B.* (1983): 399-473.

1984

"Les Oracles chaldaïques," in *Aufstieg und Niedergang der römischen Welt* II. 17. 4, Berlin/New York (1984): 2299-2335.

"Le platonisme moyen au IIe s. ap. J.-C.: Numénius et Atticus," in *Koinônia*, 8 (1984): 7-15.

"Platonisme moyen et apologétique chrétienne au IIe s. ap. J.-C.: Numénius, Atticus, Justin," in *Studia patristica*, 15 (Oxford, 1975), 1, Berlin (1984): 432-441.

"Chronique de la philosophie religieuse des Grecs (1982-1984)," in *B.A.G.B.* (1984): 408-425.

1985

"La seconde sophistique au service de l'apologétique chrétienne: le *Contra Hiéroclès* d'Eusèbe de Césarée," in *Comptes rendus de l'Académie des Inscriptions et Belles Lettres* (1985): 423-427.

"Chronique de la philosophie religieuse des Grecs (1983-1985)," in *B.A.G.B.* (1985): 395-412.

1986

Eusèbe de Césarée, *Contre Hiéroclès.* Introd., trad. et notes de Marguerite Forrat. Texte grec établi par É. d. Pl. (Sources chrétiennes 333). Paris, Éd. du Cerf, 1986. 237 pages.

"Le sort de l'homme après la mort chez Platon et dans le platonisme du II⁰ s. ap. J.-C.," in *Energeia,* Études aristotéliciennes offertes à Mgr. Antonio Jannone. Paris, Vrin (1986): 293-302.

"Les citations profanes de Clément d'Alexandrie dans le *IIIe Stromate,*" in *Revue des études grecques,* 99 (1986): 54-62.

"Chronique de la philosophie religieuse des Grecs (1984-1986)," in *B.A.G.B* (1986): 408-423.

1987

Eusèbe de Césarée, *La Préparation évangélique.* Livres XIV-XV. (Sources chrétiennes 338). Paris, Éd. du Cerf, 1987. 451 pages.

"Chronique de la philosophie religieuse des Grecs (1985-1987)," in *B.A.G.B.* (1987): 395-411.

1988

"Quelques progrès récents des études sur Michel Psellus en relation surtout avec les Oracles chaldaïques," in *Orpheus* 9 (1988): 344-349.

"Chronique de la philosophie religieuse des Grecs (1986-1988)," in *B.A.G.B.* (1988): 379-393.

1989

Jamblique, *Protreptique.* (Coll. des Univ. de France). Paris, Les Belles Lettres, 1989. 172 pages (p. 36-153 doubles).

"Chronique de la philosophie religieuse des Grecs (1987-1989)," in *B.A.G.B.* (1989): 406-426

Contributors

Ysabel de Andia
CNRS, Paris

A. Hilary Armstrong
Ludlow

H.J. Blumenthal
University of Liverpool

Frederick E. Brenk, S.J.
Pontificio Istituto Biblico,
Rome

Ugo Criscuolo
University of Naples

John Dillon
Trinity College, Dublin

Pierluigi Donini
University of Turin

Antonio Garzya
University of Naples

Stephen Gersh
University of Notre Dame

Miroslav Marcovich
University of Illinois at
Urbana

Raoul Mortley
Bond University,
Queensland

Jean Pépin
CNRS, Paris

David T. Runia
Free University, Amsterdam

Hervé D. Saffrey
CNRS, Paris

John Whittaker
Memorial University of
Newfoundland

About the Editors

STEPHEN GERSH is a Professor of Medieval Studies at the University of Notre Dame. He has published three other books, including *Middle Platonism and Neoplatonism: The Latin Tradition* (Notre Dame Press, 1986). CHARLES KANNENGIESSER is the Catherine F. Huisking Professor of Theology at the University of Notre Dame. Among other projects, he is the co-editor of *Origen of Alexandria: His World and His Legacy* (Notre Dame Press, 1988).

Introduction

STEPHEN GERSH

In coupling the words 'Platonism' and 'late antiquity' one characterizes a major period in the history of western philosophy. The Platonic tradition—ideas derived from Plato's own thought or at least from an interpretation of his writings—had suffered an eclipse in the early Hellenistic period. Engulfed or superseded by other traditions and especially by the Stoa, it was reduced to the level of a purely literary memory, only to re-emerge from the first century B.C. onwards. Yet this fresh incarnation of the Platonic spirit was destined to be its most dramatic and spectacular, and also to be of exceptionally long duration. Two phases may be distinguished. In the first century B.C., Platonism was combined with Stoic and Pythagorean influences, a tendency documented in the extant fragments of writers like Antiochus of Ascalon and Varro and in the indirect testimonies of Cicero and others. The combination with Pythagorean doctrines is interesting since, although Plato himself was clearly much influenced by the most ancient form of Pythagoreanism, the Platonism of the first century B.C. had these aspects set in relief. This is because Pythagoras' legacy was itself subject to renewed debate at this period. The second phase of the Platonic revival was from roughly the first to third centuries A. D. This philosophy was truer to the original intentions of its founder in that the materialism of the Stoa grafted onto the main Platonic stem by earlier generations was pruned to reveal the strict notion of metaphysical transcendence. However, other aspects of Stoic thinking—particularly the pantheism and vitalism—remained in a loose alliance with original Platonism to be stressed to varying degrees during the centuries which followed. When he surveys this later Platonic tradition stretching from Philo of Alexandria through Plutarch of Chaeronea and Albinus (or Alcinous) to Numenius of Apamea among the Greek speakers, or from Apuleius of Madaura through Censorinus to Calcidius among the Latins, the modern scholar is impressed by a kind of branching of the tradition. On one side are those thinkers who are more Pythagorean in their approach. These are often characterized by the expression of religious feelings, by an interest in problems of mathematics and numerology, and sometimes by astrology. The other side exhibits these tendencies less or not at all. Another branching is based on reaction not to Pythagoras but to Aristotle. On one side the Platonists are eager to assimilate the dynamic concepts of Aristotelian physics and also the noetic, whereas the other side desires a purer kind of legacy. The history of the Platonic tradition from the first to third centuries is an arborescence of contributions by individualistic thinkers who presumably had small groups of disciples. This tendency culminated in the work of the greatest of the late ancient Platonists Plotinus and in that of his student Porphyry. After this time, the complicated tradition was gradually reduced to a duality at most, represented by the great philosophical schools of Athens and Alexandria: the former led by men like Proclus and Damascius and concentrating on the exegesis of Plato's dialogues, the latter by those like Ammonius Hermeiou who emphasized the 'Platonic' commentary on Aristotle. By the fourth and fifth centuries A.D., Platonism had achieved in the hands of such exponents a thorough domination of the philosophical scene. However, from an ideological and institutional viewpoint the territory to be held had itself been reduced by the triumphant march of Christianity.

To this brief sketch of philosophical traditions may be added some compelling reasons for assembling a collection of essays on Platonism in late antiquity. In the first place, the sheer abundance of the written record makes definite claims on the modern historian of ideas. Some of the important Platonic thinkers of the later ancient world are now represented in pathetically small bodies of fragments, for example the Middle Platonists Atticus and Numenius and the Neoplatonists Porphyry and Iamblichus. In reading such authors, we are faced with all the problems attendant on the reconstruction of major themes from minimal evidence which has bedevilled—cynics might say bewitched—Presocratic studies. Yet other late ancient Platonists have bequeathed complete works of philosophical or partly philosophical character, thus permitting a soundly based as well as critically sophisticated reading of their doctrine. Examples would be the Middle Platonists Philo of Alexandria and Plutarch of Chaeronea and the Neoplatonists Plotinus, Proclus, Damascius, and Simplicius. Another justification for publishing a volume like this lies in the enormous influence of many of the late ancient Platonic writers. That owing to the profound ideological and social transformation whereby the ancient world became medieval such influence was mostly indirect does nothing to diminish its historical significance. During the patristic period, pagan Platonic thought was assimilated with the requisite mixture of love and hate by the most intelligent and creative Christian writers. In this way, the teachings of Plotinus reappeared in Augustine, those of Porphyry in Boethius, those of Proclus in pseudo-Dionysius the Areopagite, and so on. During the twelfth and thirteenth centuries, the same Platonism—together with more of Aristotle—was transmitted to the Schoolmen through the intermediary of Arabic and Jewish philosophers. Important documents of this transmission are the pseudo-Aristotelian *Liber de Causis* and various works of Avicenna and Avicebron.

Happily, the prejudices which for a long time hampered the study of late ancient philosophy now seem on the wane. Those historical interpretations which sought unrealistically clear demarcation lines between 'Biblical' and classical cultures or between pure and 'eclectic' philosophies brought with them an insensitivity to the true nature of intellectual developments in the first to fifth centuries A.D. In the former case, a true perception that Christian writers were frequently borrowing from pagan Platonic sources often led to the false deduction that characteristics like monotheism, religiosity, or exegetical preoccupations were not idiomatic in the classical world at all but only in its Christianization. In fact, the three features were prevalent in Graeco-Roman thought of the second century B.C. if not earlier. In the second instance, an even less defensible view that writers like Plato and Aristotle exemplified some pure activity of philosophy whereas a Numenius, a Plotinus, or a Iamblichus simply the process of distilling earlier material led to the relegation of the latter group to the periphery of historical interest. Yet all philosophers use an inherited language of concepts, in Plato's case that formed by the Pythagoreans, Heraclitus, Parmenides, and others. In conjunction with these historical prejudices there is also the anti-metaphysical viewpoint typical of twentieth-century philosophy to contend with. It has always been possible to read the Platonic dialogues and minimize their speculative and metaphysical content—as evidenced by the 'New Academy' itself—whereas Plotinus' *Enneads* or Proclus' writings are noticeably resistant to such a procedure. For this reason, the late ancient phase of the Platonic tradition seems unwelcome or irrelevant to some. Yet this reaction is hardly the only one possible in the circumstances. Even granting that the metaphysics of transcendence is no longer viable for us, the examination of its impact upon so many people for so long must be about the most extraordinary case-study in the history of European culture.

The editors have great pleasure in dedicating this volume to Édouard des Places who has done so much during his long scholarly career to promote the study of ancient philosophy together with its final phases. The papers here presented are of two main types. Some of the contributors have chosen to trace an idea or theme through a succession of Middle Platonic or Neoplatonic writers. Runia, Brenk, and Whittaker proceed in this way with pagan philosophical material, whereas Criscuolo considers the interrelation of the pagan and the Christian. Other contributors have concentrated on a topic within a single representative of the Platonic tradition. Thus, Donini, Armstrong, Dillon, Gersh, Saffrey, and Blumenthal examine specific Middle Platonic or Neoplatonic thinkers, Marcovich, Mortley, Pépin, Garzya, and de Andia some Christian ones together with their pagan sources. It may be useful now to provide the reader with a foretaste of what is to come, summarizing these papers in chronological order of topic within our rough classification.

Runia's paper traces the development of a theme through the non-Christian Platonic tradition: that of applying superlatives to things like the world, Paradigm, and Demiurge. As the author points out, this topic originates in Plato's cosmology and continues through the Middle Platonists to Plotinus. Three specific tasks are set: first, to tabulate Plato's use of the superlative; secondly, to examine the structure of the argument in the *Timaeus* applying the superlative—where Runia finds evidence that Plato's terminology is designed to permit a rigorous logical deduction about the nature of the universe. The third task is to investigate the continuation of this theme in Middle Platonism and Neoplatonism. Among later writers, Philo, Plutarch and Plotinus employ similar superlatives in a more overtly theocentric context. In Plotinus' case, however, the usage is clearly at variance with the logical form of argument attributed earlier in the essay to Plato.

Brenk and Whittaker also follow a single topic through the late ancient philosophical tradition. In Brenk's case the subject is the vision of God. Proceeding in historical sequence, he asks whether Plato makes this vision—as opposed to one directed to the Forms—a philosophical *telos*, and concludes in the negative. He finds the notion also absent from Numenius, Atticus and Plotinus. In Philo and Plutarch the situation is more ambivalent, while in Alcinous the goal of beatific vision begins to emerge. Whittaker's contribution deals with the topic of *katachresis*—defined specifically as 'the deliberate misuse of a word in order to represent a meaning for which no correct word is available'—as applied to God. Replying to an earlier essay by Runia where such a usage was attributed to Philo, he concludes that there is no evidence for such a concept either in Philo or in other writers of late antiquity like Porphyry and Simplicius. In passing, however, he discuses the more problematic theory of divine naming devised by the Gnostic Basilides.

Criscuolo's paper traces the elaboration of a theme through both the pagan and Christian Platonic traditions. His starting-point is the accusation of Hellenism made by opposing parties in the Byzantine dispute about icons and especially during the second period of iconoclasm (815-43 A.D.). Noting that reference was made to the reading of Plato's *Laws* and to Porphyry, the contributor studies the philosophical notion of image presented by Plotinus, Porphyry, Iamblichus, Julian and Proclus—author of the first really systematic account. Several general conclusions are drawn: that the influence of Greek philosophy makes the Byzantine controversy very different from comparable disputes in Judaism and Islam; that the Neoplatonic notion of theurgy is an important feature of the intellectual background; and that the need to accommodate the Incarnation reorientates the Christian handling of traditional questions.

The other essays in this collection deal with topics not in a succession of writers but in individual ones.

With Donini, the subject is that of God's transcendence according to Plutarch. Transcendence or immanence of divinity was a major philosophical problem for the Middle Platonists, and Plutarch's position on the question is not absolutely clear. Donini especially studies a section of *De Facie in Orbe Lunae* where a hierarchy of divine principles is postulated as in the writings of Numenius and Albinus. However, there are difficulties of interpretation owing to the allusive and quasi-mythical presentation in Plutarch. Examination of parallel passages in *De E apud Delphos* and *De Procreatione Animae in Timaeo* permits the conclusion that a radically transcendent deity is envisioned together with certain mediating principles. Armstrong's topic is Plotinus' thought considered in relation to the viewpoint of a hypothetical Christian. Comparing the two approaches, he notes that the Neoplatonist and the Christian would agree on the spirituality of the first principle and on its identification with Being—in a special sense of that term; they would disagree on the nature of the first principle's freedom and on the manner of its immanence in the visible cosmos. Dillon's topic is Plotinus' doctrine viewed in relation to the non-hypothetical *Chaldaean Oracles*. He challenges the received opinion that Plotinus made no use of these pagan religious writings not only by underlining the Byzantine testimony to his citation of them in one instance but also by noting various terms and phrases in the *Enneads* uniquely paralleled by this source. However, the traditional interpretation may stand to the extent that Plotinus' debt is a literary rather than philosophical one.

With Gersh's essay, the scene shifts to the successors of Plotinus in the pagan tradition. Since Porphyry's *Commentary on the Harmonics of Ptolemy* has escaped the attention of most earlier scholars, Gersh provides a summary of this work together with notes on points of philosophical interest. In some places, the commentator deviates considerably from the base text by incorporating other material from Plato, Aristotle, various Pythagoreans and the *Chaldaean Oracles*; or by introducing digressions on the specifically Neoplatonic notions of Intellect, the Forms and Soul. A general characteristic of Porphyry's commentary emerges: the reinforcement of technical terms in harmonic theory with further metaphysical connotations. Saffrey's subject is Iamblichus' doctrine of first principles as expressed in *De Mysteriis* VIII. 1-5. This text is of particular interest in documenting a controversy between Iamblichus and Porphyry over the interpretation of Egyptian or 'Hermetic' theology. Iamblichus sets out his own teachings especially regarding the two principles prior to Intellect and the nature of the Demiurge in the language of the Hermeticists. In his view, Porphyry has falsely construed the Egyptian doctrine through reading popular writings speaking of nothing beyond the sensible realm. Blumenthal's subject is the theory of the human soul's vehicle in Simplicius. In the first systematic study of this problem as it appears in the Aristotelian commentator's writings, a group of interrelated questions are addressed: how many vehicles has each soul?; what constitution is indicated by the terminology applied to the vehicles?; what is the function of those vehicles in Simplicius' cosmology and psychology?; and how long does each vehicle endure after earthly incarnation?

The contribution of Marcovich is a group of short notes on Athenagoras and Hippolytus unified by the theme of reaction by Christian writers to Plato or the pagan Platonic tradition. Athenagoras refers to the distinction of two Zeuses: the Great and the Earthly, and Marcovich traces this idea right back to the Old Academy of Xenocrates. In Hippolytus' case, he shifts his attention to the discussion of God, the Logos and the Ideas where Middle Platonic theory has been modified under Old Testament influence. Further fragments of Hippolytus give evidence of a polemic with the pagan

Platonic tradition and a treatment of the latter's theories regarding the origin of soul. With Mortley's paper, we turn to Arius' Trinitarian doctrine and especially to the seemingly extreme subordinationism implicit in the Father's alienation from his Son. Noting that the usage of such language is without obvious parallel in the pagan Neoplatonic tradition, Mortley concludes that it represents an innovative attempt to formulate a negative theology in which even the application of analogy is questionable. However, since Arius otherwise preserves the normal balance of identity and difference between hypostases, perhaps the divergence from philosophical norms is more verbal than real. Pépin's essay studies passages in Gregory of Nyssa where various aspects of the relationship between man and God are described with the comparison of a mirror. Of the two basic uses of this analogy, the first applies it to human intellect or soul which can thereby receive an image of the divine, the second to God who provides himself as a medium through which man's self-knowledge becomes possible. Pépin finds parallels to these usages in both pagan and Christian writers of late antiquity, Porphyry the Neoplatonist and Zosimus the alchemist providing striking testimony to the human and divine mirrors respectively. The contribution of Garzya deals with various aspects of Synesius' *Epistola* CXL. Among topics discussed are the methodological differences between epistolary and didactic writing apparent in the later ancient world, the duality of higher and lower forms of friendship or love—a notion traditional since the time of Plato—, and the relationship between the epistolary genre and the ethical ideal of friendship. Garzya also includes some discussion of Synesius' presentation of the Porphyrian hierarchy of virtues.

The final essay is by de Andia and investigates pseudo-Dionysius the Areopagite's concept of an experience of God. After tracing the history of the contrast between experiencing and knowing in the earlier philosophical tradition from Aristotle onwards, she concludes that pseudo-Dionysius' version is remarkable in positing not simply a contrast between the two terms but a subordination of the one to the other. This version also raises the subtle question of reconciling experience of God and the spiritual goal of impassibility. The paper ends with observations on the *Nachleben* of such ideas in the Greek and Latin commentators on the Dionysian corpus.

Short Bibliography
of
Secondary Material

Aujoulat, N. *Le néoplatonisme alexandrin, Hiéroclès d'Alexandrie*, Leiden 1986.

Baltes, M. *Die Weltentstehung des platonischen Timaios nach den antiken Interpreten* I-II, Leiden 1976, 1978.

Beierwaltes, W. *Proklos, Grundzüge seiner Metaphysik*, 2. Auflage, Frankfurt a. M. 1979.

Bregman, J. *Synesius of Cyrene, Philosopher-Bishop*, Berkeley-Los Angeles 1982.

Charles, A. *L'Architecture du divin. Mathématique et philosophie chez Plotin et Proclus*, Paris 1982.

Charrue, J.-M. *Plotin, lecteur de Platon*, Paris 1978.

Deuse, W. *Untersuchungen zur mittelplatonischen und neuplatonischen Seelenlehre*, Wiesbaden 1983.

Dillon, J. *The Middle Platonists, A Study of Platonism 80 B.C. to A.D. 220*, London 1977.

Festugière, A.-J. *La révélation d'Hermès Trismégiste* I-IV, Paris 1944-54.

Gersh, S. *From Iamblichus to Eriugena*, Leiden 1978.

——————. *Middle Platonism and Neoplatonism, The Latin Tradition*, Notre Dame, Indiana 1986.

Hadot, I. *Le problème du néoplatonisme alexandrin. Hiéroclès et Simplicius*, Paris 1978.

Hadot, P. *Porphyre et Victorinus*, Paris 1968.

Invernizzi, G. *Il Didaskalikos di Albino e il medioplatonismo* I-II, Roma 1976.

Kobusch, T. *Studien zur Philosophie des Hierokles von Alexandrien*, München 1976.

Krämer, H.-J. *Der Ursprung der Geistmetaphysik*, Amsterdam 1964.

Larsen, B.D. *Jamblique de Chalcis, Exégète et philosophe*, Aarhus 1972.

9

Merlan, P. *From Platonism to Neoplatonism*, 3rd edition, The Hague 1968.

O'Meara, D. *Pythagoras Revived*, Oxford 1989.

Pépin, J. *Théologie cosmique et théologie chrétienne*, Paris 1964.

Rist, J.M. *Plotinus, The Road to Reality*, Cambridge 1967.

Romano, F. *Porfirio di Tiro*, Catania 1979.

Sheppard, A. *Studies on the 5th and 6th Essays of Proclus' Commentary on the Republic,* Göttingen 1980.

Smith, A. *Porphyry's Place in the Neoplatonic Tradition*, The Hague 1974.

Steel, C. *The Changing Self, A Study on the Soul in Later Neoplatonism*, Brussels 1978.

Theiler, W. *Die Vorbereitung des Neuplatonismus*, Berlin 1934.

------. *Forschungen zum Neuplatonismus*, Berlin 1966.

Trouillard, J. *L'Un et l'âme selon Proclus*, Paris 1972.

Wallis, R.T. *Neoplatonism*, London 1972.

Witt, R.E. *Albinus and the History of Middle Platonism*, Cambridge 1937.

The Language of Excellence in Plato's *Timaeus* and Later Platonism

DAVID T. RUNIA

There has been a strong tendency in recent years to keep the study of Platonic and Platonist thought in separate compartments, as if the interpretation of the dialogues by the later Platonist commentators is only of marginal interest for the understanding of what Plato meant to say in them. This emphatically has not been the policy of Father des Places in his long and illustrious scholarly career. I hope, therefore, that he will be pleased to accept this article as a tribute to the generous scope of his learning, for it will move back and forth between Plato and his later followers, concentrating on the theme of the 'language of excellence' which has its origin in Plato's *Timaeus*.

I

My starting-point is a thinker who in strict terms should not be regarded as a Platonist, but certainly stands in close relation to the incipient Platonist tradition, Philo of Alexandria. In one of his expositions of Mosaic scripture Philo tells a παλαιὸς λόγος, the source of which is disputed, but which is clearly at least partially indebted to the cosmological tale of the *Timaeus*.[1] When the creator (ποιητής) had finished the task of creating the entire cosmos, he asked one of his subordinates whether anything was still lacking. The reply was that every part was complete, except the speech (λόγος) required to report their perfection. The Father of the universe (πατέρα τοῦ παντός) praised this reply, and soon thereafter the family of the Muses came

---

[1] *Plant.* 127-131. On this passage and the problem of its source see D. T. Runia, *Philo of Alexandria and the* Timaeus *of Plato* (Leiden 1986²) 114-115.

into being. The lesson of the tale, Philo continues, is that it is God's task to confer benefits (εὐεργετεῖν), while the only appropriate response on the part of created being (γένεσις) is to give thanks (εὐχαριστεῖν):[2]

μαθόντες οὖν, ὡς ἓν ἔργον ἡμῖν ἐπιβάλλει μόνον ἐν τοῖς πρὸς τιμὴν θεοῦ, τὸ εὐχάριστον, τοῦτο ἀεὶ καὶ πανταχοῦ μελετῶμεν διὰ φωνῆς καὶ διὰ γραμμάτων ἀστείων καὶ μηδέποτε ἐπιλείπωμεν μήτε λόγους ἐγκωμιαστικοὺς μήτε ποιήματα συντιθέντες, ἵνα καὶ ἐμμελῶς καὶ χωρὶς μέλους καὶ καθ' ἑκατέραν φωνῆς ἰδέαν, ᾗ τὸ λέγειν καὶ τὸ ᾄδειν ἀποκεκλήρωται, ὅ τε κοσμοποιὸς καὶ ὁ κόσμος γεραίρηται, ὁ μέν, ὡς ἔφη τις, ἄριστος τῶν αἰτίων, ὁ δὲ τελειότατος τῶν γεγονότων.

The final words are an inaccurate quote of the well-known words at *Tim.* 29a5-6, where Plato describes the cosmos and its maker as ὁ μὲν γὰρ κάλλιστος τῶν γεγονότων, ὁ δ' ἄριστος τῶν αἰτίων.[3] It is apparent that Philo was fond of this Platonic formula. Not only does he quote it elsewhere,[4] but he also adapts it for other purposes. For example when he says that the Mosaic creator (just like the Platonic demiurge) commences his creative work with the heaven and ends it with man, he describes them as ὁ μὲν γὰρ ἀφθάρτων τελειότατος, ὁ δὲ θνητῶν ‹ἄριστος›.[5] And elsewhere in Philo there are numerous examples of his use of the characteristic phraseology used in the *Timaeus* to describe the excellence of the cosmos.[6]

Let us turn to a second author, whose life just overlaps that of Philo, Plutarch. The Platonist from Chaeronea starts his controversial interpretation of the cosmogony of the *Timaeus* with the following words:[7]

---

[2]*Plant.* 131; text Cohn-Wendland, except that I have deleted the incorrectly used quotation marks (on which see Runia *op. cit.* 370).

[3]In this study I shall consistently render καλός by 'fair' and κάλλιστος by 'fairest'. A problem is posed by the adverb, since 'in the fairest way' can give rise to wrong associations. I shall therefore render κάλλιστα by 'in the finest way'.

[4]*QG* 1.6.

[5]*Praem.* 1. Some mss. read ὁ δὲ θνητῶν φθαρτός, others simply ὁ δὲ θνητῶν. It is to be agreed with P. Shorey, *CPh* 7 (1912) 248, that a final adjective is needed, but his suggestion φέρτατος does not agree with Philonic usage. If we correlate the parallel passage *Opif.* 82, the emendation I suggest looks attractive.

[6]See further texts given at Runia *op cit.* 118.

[7]*Mor.* 1014A; text H. Cherniss, *Plutarch's Moralia*, vol. 13.1, LCL (Cambr. Mass. 1976) 180, who fails to note the remarkable parallel in Philo.

'κόσμον τόνδε' φησὶν Ἡράκλειτος 'οὔτε τις θεῶν οὔτε ἀνθρώπων ἐποίησεν', ὥσπερ φοβηθεὶς μὴ θεοῦ ἀπογνόντες ἄνθρωπόν τινα γεγονέναι τοῦ κόσμου δημιουργὸν ὑπονοήσωμεν. βέλτιον οὖν Πλάτωνι πειθομένους τὸν μὲν κόσμον ὑπὸ θεοῦ γεγονέναι λέγειν καὶ ᾄδειν 'ὁ μὲν γὰρ κάλλιστος τῶν γεγονότων ὁ δ' ἄριστος τῶν αἰτίων' τὴν δ' οὐσίαν καὶ ὕλην, ἐξ ἧς γέγονεν, οὐ γενομένην ἀλλὰ ὑποκειμένην ἀεὶ τῷ δημιουργῷ εἰς διάθεσιν καὶ τάξιν αὐτὴν καὶ πρὸς αὐτὸν ἐξομοίωσιν ὡς δυνατὸν ἦν ἐμπαρασχεῖν.

In two ways Plutarch's remarks remind us of the Philonic passage quoted just above: he cites the same words from *Tim.* 29a5-6 (though more accurately), and he says we should 'chant' (ᾄδειν) them. A few lines later Plutarch goes on to say that the god took both principles— vague and obscure matter and confused and unintelligent (preexistent) soul—and ordered and organized and harmonized them, producing from them the *fairest* and *most perfect* living being (τὸ κάλλιστον ἀπεργασάμενος καὶ τελειότατον ἐξ αὐτῶν ζῷον).[8] Elsewhere, in answering a question that arose at an erudite dinner-party, namely what Plato meant when he says that god is always doing geometry, Plutarch says we should recall the three-fold division of first principles in the *Timaeus*: matter as the *most unordered* of substrates, form as the *fairest* of models, god as the *best* of causes (ἡ μὲν οὖν ὕλη τῶν ὑποκειμένων ἀτακτότατόν ἐστιν, ἡ δ' ἰδέα τῶν παραδειγμάτων κάλλιστον, ὁ δὲ θεὸς τῶν αἰτίων ἄριστον).[9] The final phrase is evidently based on the words from the *Timaeus* cited earlier; the second phrase takes its cue from *Tim.* 30d1 (τῷ τῶν νοουμένων καλλίστῳ); the first phrase is Plutarch's own adaptation of Plato's language to the Middle Platonist doctrines of the three principles with matter as substrate.

Finally we turn to one of the best known passages of Plotinus. In the opening chapter of the treatise *On the descent of the soul*, *Enneads* 4.8, a contrast is made between a pessimistic and an optimistic strain in Plato's thinking on the cosmos. Elsewhere (*Phaedo*, *Republic*, *Phaedrus*) Plato's are negative, Plotinus affirms, but in the *Timaeus* he praises the cosmos and calls it a blessed god and affirms that it receives its soul from a good demiurge.[10] The characteristic phraseology of *Tim.* 29a5-6 is not found here. But it does emerge elsewhere in the same treatise. Matter is said there to participate in goodness to the

---

[8]*Mor.* 1014C.

[9]*Mor.* 720B.

[10]*Enn.* 4.8.1.41-44.

extent that it can accept it, so that that which is *fairest* in the sense-perceptible realm is a demonstration of the *best* in the intelligible realm and of their power and goodness (δεῖξις οὖν τῶν ἀρίστων ἐν νοητοῖς τὸ ἐν αἰσθητῷ κάλλιστον, τῆς τε δυνάμεως τῆς τε ἀγαθότητος αὐτῶν).[11] The cosmos, he says in another treatise, is the *best* of things that have a body (τῶν μετὰ σώματος ... ἀρίστῳ).[12] But it is necessary to distinguish between it and its source: intellect is beautiful and the *fairest* of all things; the cosmos is its shadow and image, though it has no darkness in it and leads a blessed life (τοῦ δὴ νοῦ καλοῦ ὄντος καὶ πάντων καλλίστου..., οὗ καὶ ὁ καλὸς οὗτος κόσμος σκιὰ καὶ εἰκών, ὅτι μηδὲν ... σκοτεινὸν ... ἐν αὐτῷ, ζῶντος ζωὴν μακαρίαν).[13]

It has become somewhat of a scholarly platitude to describe the *Timaeus* as a prose hymn in honour of the cosmos, celebrating in the well-known words of Arthur Lovejoy 'a peculiarly exuberant this-worldliness'.[14] Or, as Pierre Hadot has aphoristically affirmed with a calculated play on words, 'seule la *poiesis* du langage humain peut essayer d'imiter la *poiesis* divine'.[15] What struck me, however, in reading the extracts from the three authors in the Platonist tradition was their perception that Plato has used a distinctive kind of phraseology in order to depict the excellence of the cosmos. This phraseology involves the *deliberate and extensive use of the superlative*, and the most striking example of its usage is in the passage 29a5-6 cited by both Philo and Plutarch (and partially recapitulated in 92c7-9, the final lines of the work). My intention in this paper is to examine this characteristic phraseology, and in so doing to take a somewhat more hard-headed look at the so-called lyrical or hymnic language employed by Plato on the subject of the coming into being of the cosmos. I shall commence by examining Plato's use of the superlative, the chief stylistic device which Plato uses in the *Timaeus* to give expression to what I shall call his 'language of excellence'. Thereafter I turn to Plato's actual argument, and it will emerge that the two phrases in *Tim.* 29a5-6 form an excellent avenue of approach to the more philosophical aspects of my theme. Finally I shall very briefly

---

[11]*Enn.* 4.8.6.23-24. (text Henry-Schwyzer[2]).

[12]*Enn.* 3.2.3.2.

[13]*Enn.* 3.8.11.26-29; the final phrase is based on *Tim.* 34b8, 36e5 etc.

[14]A. O. Lovejoy, *The Great Chain of Being* (Cambr. Mass. 1935, 1982[15]) 45; cf. also the passages cited by Hadot at the beginning of his article cited in the next note.

[15]'Physique et poésie dans le *Timée* de Platon', *RThPh* 115 (1983) 113-133.

return to the Platonist authors with which I started, in order to observe whether there are any changes in emphasis in comparison with Plato's original approach.

II

Let us commence with an inventorization of those objects which Plato describes by means of the superlative, taking them in order of appearance in the dialogue.[16] I ignore those examples which are merely *elative* (i.e. for heightened effect, e.g. 20a2 εὐνομωτάτης πόλεως τῆς ... Λοκρίδος, which Cornford translates 'the admirably governed city Locris'),[17] those which are *culminative* but only within a limited range of comparison (e.g. the fourteen examples used at 55e1-56b2 in order to indicate the various relations between the atomic bodies of the four elements), and, in general, all those examples which are of no significance for the dialogue's philosophical thematics.

A. We start with the superlatives which are to be regarded as *positive culminative*, i.e. indicating the highest degree of a particular quality or characteristic.

1. The *ideal city*, both in Socrates' fictional account (reminiscent of the *Republic*) and in the distant past as related by Critias: 17c2 περὶ πολιτείας ... οἵα ... ἀρίστη; 23b7 τὸ κάλλιστον καὶ ἄριστον γένος ἐπ' ἀνθρώπους; cf. also 18d7, 21d4, 23c5-7, 24c7-d1. Without doubt the excellence of ancient Athens was to play a crucial role in the trilogy as

---

[16]There does not appear to be a strict terminology for the diverse types of superlative. I have based my analysis to some degree on H. Thesleff, *Studies in the Greek Superlative* (Helsingfors 1955), but have felt free to adapt the terminology to my own requirements. It can be represented by the following division:

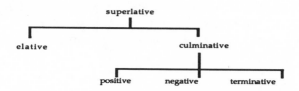

The basis on which the division has been made will emerge in the text.

[17]F. M. Cornford, *Plato's Cosmology* (London 1937) 12 (I use Burnet's text).

Plato originally conceived it (the city as another microcosm, parallel to man). But in the *Timaeus* the theme remains peripheral.[18]

2. The *cosmos* as ζῷον consisting of soul and body: 29a5 ὁ μὲν γὰρ **κάλλιστος** τῶν γεγονότων; 68e1-4 ὁ τοῦ **καλλίστου** τε καὶ **ἀρίστου** δημιουργὸς ἐν τοῖς γιγνομένοις..., ἡνίκα... τὸν **τελεώτατον** θεὸν ἐγέννα; 92c7-8 θεὸς αἰσθητός, **μέγιστος** καὶ **ἄριστος κάλλιστος** τε καὶ **τελεώτατος**; cf. in more general terms 46c8, 48a3.

3. The *demiurge*: 29a5 ὁ δ' **ἄριστος** τῶν αἰτίων; 30a6-7 θέμις δ' οὔτ' ἦν οὔτ' ἔστιν τῷ **ἀρίστῳ** δρᾶν ἄλλο πλὴν τὸ **κάλλιστον**; 37a1 τῶν νοητῶν ἀεί τε ὄντων ὑπὸ τοῦ **ἀρίστου**.

4. The *model*: 30d1-3: τῷ γὰρ τῶν νοουμένων **καλλίστῳ** καὶ κατὰ πάντα **τελέῳ μάλιστα** αὐτὸν ὁ θεὸς ὁμοιῶσαι βουληθείς; cf. 30c7 on the similarity of the cosmos to the model, 'to this [the model], above all things, let us say it [the cosmos] is *most_similar* (**ὁμοιότατον**).

5. The proportional relation between the quantities of the *four elements*: 31c2-4 δεσμῶν δὲ **κάλλιστος** ὃς ἂν αὐτὸν καὶ τὰ συνδούμενα ὅτι **μάλιστα** ἓν ποιῇ, τοῦτο δὲ πέφυκεν ἀναλογία **κάλλιστα** ἀποτελεῖν.

6. The *body* of the cosmos, which receives a spherical shape: 33b6 σφαιροειδές... κυκλοτερὲς αὐτὸ ἐτορνεύσατο, πάντων **τελεώτατον ὁμοιότατόν** τε αὐτὸ ἑαυτῷ σχημάτων, νομίσας μυρίῳ κάλλιον ὅμοιον ἀνομοίου.

7. The *soul* of the cosmos: 37a2 **ἀρίστη** γενομένη τῶν γεννηθέντων; cf. the description of the rational circuits of the soul of the cosmos, 39c2 day and night as 'the period of the single and *most intelligent* revolution' (ἡ τῆς μιᾶς **φρονιμωτάτης** κυκλήσεως περίοδος), 40a4-5 'he places it [the genus of the heavenly beings] in the intelligence of the supreme [i.e. the outermost sphere of heaven]' (τίθησίν τε εἰς τὴν τοῦ **κρατίστου** φρόνησιν).

8. The *celestial beings*: 40a2-3 the form of the divine kind the god made for the most part of fire, so that it would be **λαμπρότατον** ἰδεῖν τε **κάλλιστον**; cf. 40c2-3, the description of the earth as **πρεσβυτάτην** θεῶν ὅσοι ἐντὸς οὐρανοῦ γεγόνασιν.

9. The kinds of *motion*: 40a7-b4 the celestial beings receive two of the seven motions, but with respect to the five others they are motionless, ἵνα ὅτι **μάλιστα** αὐτῶν ἕκαστον γένοιτο ὡς **ἄριστον**; cf.

---

[18]Though the introduction as a whole should not be divorced from the rest of the dialogue, as P. Donini has recently shown in 'Il *Timeo*: unità del dialogo, verisimiglianza dell discorsó, *Elenchos* 9 (1988) 5-52.

also 34a2 and 89a1-2 on the best kind of motion in relation to both the cosmos as a whole and to man as one of its parts.[19]

10. On the creative task of the 'young gods' as secondary creators see below 19f.

11. Man: 42a1 ζῴων τὸ θεοσεβέστατον.

12. Man's *structure* (i.e. above all his rational part and its location): 44d5-6 τοῦτο ὃ νῦν κεφαλὴν ἐπονομάζομεν, ὃ θειότατόν τέ ἐστιν καὶ τῶν ἐν ἡμῖν πάντων δεσποτοῦν; 45a1 τὴν τοῦ θειοτάτου καὶ ἱερωτάτου... οἴκησιν; cf. also 70b8, 71a1, 73a7, 85a6, 88b23, 90a2.[20]

13. Man's *telos* (the philosophic life): 46e7-8 τὸ δὲ μέγιστον αὐτῶν [τῶν ὀμμάτων] εἰς ὠφελίαν ἔργον; 47b1 φιλοσοφίας γένος, οὗ μεῖζον ἀγαθὸν οὔτ' ἦλθεν οὔτε ἥξει ποτὲ τῷ θνητῷ γένει δωρηθὲν ἐκ θεῶν; 90d5-7 τέλος ἔχειν τοῦ προτεθέντος ἀνθρώποις ὑπὸ θεῶν ἀρίστου βίου πρός τε τὸν παρόντα καὶ τὸν ἔπειτα χρόνον; cf. also 42d1-2, 47a2, 47b3, 47c7.

14. The *primary atomic bodies*: 53e1 κάλλιστα σώματα; 54a1-6 of the endless number of scalene triangles it is necessary to take the *fairest* (a3, a6 κάλλιστον).

15. Of the constituent parts of the human body we note especially the marrow: 82d5-7 as καθαρώτατον γένος τῶν τριγώνων λειότατόν τε καὶ λιπαρώτατον it filters through the close texture of the bones (cf. also 73b7).

B. At the opposite end of the scale we also note a number of *negative_culminative* superlatives that play an important role in the *Timaeus*:

16. *Disease*: 44c1 ignorance as τὴν μεγίστην νόσον, also at 88b5 (cf. 69d1 pleasure as μέγιστον κακοῦ δέλεαρ.)

Motion: 89a4-5 the worst kind, χειρίστη [κίνησις] δὲ κειμένου τοῦ σώματος καὶ ἄγοντος ἡσυχίαν δι' ἑτέρων αὐτὸ κατὰ μέρη κινοῦσα.

Sub-rational animals: 92a5-8 of land animals the gods made the *most stupid* (τοῖς ἀφρονεστάτοις) footless and attached to the earth;

---

[19]The superlatives used to describe the chaotic movements of a baby in 43c7-8 πλείστην καὶ μεγίστην ... κίνησιν are probably elative, but stand in clear and deliberate contrast to the above-mentioned passages.

[20]Note also 75e1, where the gods are described as devising the mouth as τὴν μέν εἴσοδον τῶν ἀναγκαίων μηχανώμενοι χάριν, τὴν δ' ἔξοδον τῶν ἀρίστων·... τὸ δὲ λόγων νᾶμα ἔξω ῥέον καὶ ὑπηρετοῦν φρονήσει κάλλιστον καὶ ἄριστον πάντων ναμάτων). This is a rare instance in the *Timaeus* in which Plato is being genuinely hyperbolic. As Ps. Longinus remarked long ago (Περὶ ὕψους 32.4ff), he wants to enliven the long descriptive passages in the final part of Timaeus's speech.

92a8-b2 'the fourth, aquatic sort came into being ἐκ τῶν μάλιστα ἀνοητοτάτων καὶ ἀμαθεστάτων.[21]

C. A further category of superlatives that should not be ignored in our context is that of *terminative culminatives*, which give expression to the highest possible degree of a quality in a given situation. Important examples of these can be mostly subsumed under headings set out so far (a number have in fact already surreptitiously been cited):

19.a. 29e3 the *demiurge* 'wished to make all things *as closely resembling himself as possible*' (πάντα ὅτι μάλιστα ἐβουλήθη γένεσθαι παραπλήσια ἑαυτῷ)—cf. 3. above.

b. 30b5 the *cosmos* made by the demiurge as fair and excellent a work as possible (ὅτι κάλλιστον κατὰ φύσιν ἄριστόν τε ἔργον)—cf. 2. above.

c. 31c3 on the role of *geometrical proportion*—already cited above no. 5.

d. 38b8 time came into being with the cosmos, so that it might resemble the model of the eternal nature as closely as possible (καὶ κατὰ τὸ παράδειγμα τῆς διαιωνίας φύσεως, ἵν' ὡς ὁμοιότατος αὐτῷ κατὰ δύναμιν ᾖ)—cf. 4. above.

e. 40a3, 40b4-5 on the nature and motion of the *celestial beings*—already cited above in 8. and 9.

f. 42e2 on the task of the 'young gods' ὅτι κάλλιστα καὶ ἄριστα τὸ θνητὸν διακυβερνᾶν ζῷον; also 71d6-7 the father's command, ὅτε τὸ θνητὸν ἐπέστελλεν γένος ὡς ἄριστον εἰς δύναμιν ποιεῖν—see above 10.

g. 89d4-7 on the educating part of man (i.e. the νοῦς), παρασκευαστέον εἰς δύναμιν ὅτι κάλλιστον καὶ ἄριστον εἰς τὴν παιδαγωγίαν εἶναι.

D. Finally, for the sake of completeness, one can point out a number of *comparatives* which contribute to the theme of excellence

---

[21]Note also the reversal of values on the part of the Atlantids (*Crit.* 121b, καὶ τῷ δυναμένῳ μὲν ὁρᾶν αἰσχροὶ κατεφαίνοντο, τὰ κάλλιστα ἀπὸ τῶν τιμιωτάτων ἀπολλύντες, τοῖς δὲ ἀδυνατοῦσιν ἀληθινὸν πρὸς εὐδαιμονίαν βίον ὁρᾶν τότε δὴ μάλιστα πάγκαλοι μακάριοί τε ἐδοξάζοντο εἶναι, πλεονεξίας ἀδίκου καὶ δυνάμεως ἐμπιμπλάμενοι), which forms a pendant to the excellence of the ancient Athenians at the beginning of the *Timaeus*.

by contrasting a better and a worse state of affairs.[22] These too can be subsumed under the earlier headings.

20.a. 30a5-6 *order* as ἄμεινον than disorder; 30b2 a visible cosmos possessing reason is κάλλιον than one without—cf. 2. above.

b. 33b7 uniform shape as κάλλιον than non-uniform; 33d2 a self-sufficient animal as ἄμεινον than one dependent on others—cf. 6. above.

c. 41b5 the bond of the demiurge's will as μείζονος καὶ κυριωτέρου than the one the heavenly beings were bound with at birth—cf. 8 (and 5.) above.

d. 45a3 man's front as τιμιώτερον καὶ ἀρχικώτερον than his back, 75a4-7 nonrational parts of man have lots of flesh, rational parts (i.e. head) are covered less (ἧττον).

So much for our inventory, and it surely amounts to an impressive list. Thesleff in his study on the Greek superlative observes that Plato's use of the superlative is in general terms quite frequent, though not occurring as often as in his contemporary Xenophon.[23] It is a deliberate stylistic device, invoked in order to add elevation and/or pathos. The over-zealous use of the superlative to such ends is clearly parodied in Agathon's well-known speech in the *Symposium*.[24] In fact Plato's use of the superlative in the *Timaeus* is not much less extreme. Needless to say, not all the examples that we have collected should be placed on the same level. To some extent they may be meant to contribute elevation to the high-flown and somewhat ponderous style of the *Timaeus*. But there is more to it than that. I would wish to argue that the deliberate and extensive use of the superlative in the dialogue has a clear philosophical motivation.[25]

---

[22]It should be borne in mind that there is no absolute distinction between superlatives and comparatives, and the latter can be used to convey excellence in the same way as the former. In the romance languages the comparative and superlative are distinguished only by the article (in Italian the old 'Latin' superlative is only used in an elative sense).

[23]Thesleff (*op. cit.* n. 16) 71.

[24]*Symp.* 194e-197e.

[25]H. Thesleff, *Studies in the Styles of Plato* (Helsinki 1967), regards the superlative as a stylistic marker of what he calls the rhetorical style and the pathetic style, and not of the intellectual and onkos styles considered predominant in the *Timaeus* (cf. 82, 85, 144). He does not note the marked frequency of the superlative in this dialogue.

Because the heavy exploitation of the superlative is quite beyond doubt, it seems useful to give it an easily recognizable label. My suggestion, put forward some years ago,[26] is that we speak in more general terms of Plato's use of the 'language of excellence' in the *Timaeus*. This title would appear to be appropriate for at least two reasons. Firstly the dominant superlatives are evidently ἄριστος and κάλλιστος, indicating functional and aesthetic excellence respectively (but in fact nearly always two sides of the same coin).[27] Secondly the word 'excellence' we associate especially with that crucial Greek word, ἀρετή.[28] ἀρετή is in fact what beings described in superlative terms possess. Plato is at pains to indicate that both the cosmos and its soul possess ἀρετή to a preeminent degree:

34b4-9 ... καὶ κύκλῳ δὴ κύκλον στρεφόμενον οὐρανὸν ἕνα μόνον ἔρημον κατέστησεν, δι' ἀρετὴν δὲ αὐτὸν αὐτῷ δυνάμενον συγγίγνεσθαι καὶ οὐδενὸς ἑτέρου προσδεόμενον, γνώριμον δὲ καὶ φίλον ἱκανῶς αὐτὸν αὐτῷ. διὰ πάντα δὴ ταῦτα εὐδαίμονα θεὸν αὐτὸν ἐγεννήσατο.
34c4-35a1 ὁ δὲ καὶ γενέσει καὶ ἀρετῇ προτέραν καὶ πρεσβυτέραν ψυχὴν σώματος ὡς δεσπότιν καὶ ἄρξουσαν ἀρξομένου συνεστήσατο...

It is worth noting, however, that there is no mention of the ἀρετή of the demiurge (or, for that matter, of the model).

III

If the list of superlatives which chiefly constitute Plato's language of excellence is recalled to mind, it is apparent that the more important objects or persons to which they are applied are the following: cosmos, demiurge, model, cosmic body, cosmic soul, celestial beings, man (structure and *telos*), primary bodies (in that order of appearance in the discourse). Primacy in this list can be given, I submit, to the triad cosmos, demiurge, model. This for two reasons. They are the first to

---

[26]Cf. Runia *op. cit.* (n.1) 114, while studying Philonic adaptation of Plato's language.

[27]It should be noted that ἀγαθός and ἄριστος indicate value of a functional rather than a moral kind in earlier Greek thought; cf. J. Rist, *Human Value: a Study in Ancient Philosophical Ethics* (Leiden 1982) 11ff.

[28]'Excellence' rather than 'virtue' is happily becoming the standard way to render the word in English, e.g. M. Nussbaum, *The Fragility of Goodness; Luck and Ethics in Greek Tragedy and Philosophy* (Cambridge 1986) 6. There is etymologically, of course, a direct connection between ἄριστος and ἀρετή. One would assume that Plato was aware of this, but he does not exploit it at *Crat.* 415d.

occur in Timaeus' argument. All the others are, in one way or another, parts of the cosmos, and so can be 'subsumed' in its excellence. The only other entity which cannot be included in the cosmos is the receptacle, in relation to which the language of excellence is not used.

But even among this triad there is a distinction to be made. The excellence of the *cosmos* and the *demiurge* are emphatically announced in *Tim.* 29a5-6. On the excellence of the *model* we are only informed later at 30b-c, after Plato has begun his account of the transition from disorder to order in 30a2-6. The famous phrase cited by both Philo and Plutarch—the cosmos as ὁ κάλλιστος τῶν γεγονότων, the demiurge as ὁ ἄριστος τῶν αἰτίων—is the first instance of the language of excellence (leaving aside the dialogue's introductory part),[29] and can be said to lay the foundation of Plato's theme. To this phrase we now turn.

First of all it is most important to note the location of the phrase. It belongs to what Plato himself calls the προοίμιον of Timaeus' speech (29d5). The purpose of this short section (about 60 lines of text) is to set out as succinctly as possible the general principles on which the entire account is based. It can be divided, for our purposes here, into four parts.[30]

1. 27d5-28b2 affirmation of three fundamental philosophical *principles*:
(i) division into the realm of being and the realm of becoming (27d5-28a4);
(ii) whatever comes into being does so through some cause (28a4-6);
(iii) the degree of excellence of the product is determined by the model to which the maker looks (28a6-b2).
2. 28b2-4 the cosmos, as *object of inquiry*, is introduced (the name it is given is not important—call it οὐρανός or κόσμος or something else).

---

[29]See above n. 18.

[30]I have dealt with the structure and status in an article entitled 'Observations on Plato, *Timaeus* 27c-29d' (forthcoming), to which the reader is referred. In that paper I give a seven-fold structure of the entire prooemium; but in the context of this article a simpler structure is sufficient.

    3.   28b4-29b1 *application* of the three fundamental philosophical principles to the cosmos as object of inquiry:
        (i) the cosmos has come into being (28b4-c2);
        (ii) it has a cause, the maker and father (or demiurge) (28c2-5);
        (iii) the maker must have looked to an eternal model (28c5-29b1).
    4. 29b1-d3 the epistemological *status* of the account that can be given of the cosmos: it is an εἰκών, so the λόγος can be no more than εἰκώς.

The sequence of principles, introduction, application and methodological discussion is clear enough. It is less immediately clear, however, what the precise epistemological status of the argument in the προοίμιον is. I would wish to argue that the entire passage outlined above is the result of an (implicit) exercise in Platonic dialectic. One might compare similar passages at *Phdr.* 245c-e, *Laws* 892d-894b. We note that in the second of these passages the speaker is explicitly given permission to carry on a (dialectical) argument with himself, because it is beyond the strength of the partners in the conversation (cf. also *Gorg.* 506cff.). Similarly Timaeus is giving a speech, and so dispenses with the responses required in the true dialectical situation.[31] The same method, in effect, is also used at *Tim.* 48e-52e, where at 49a6 Plato says εἴρηται τἀληθές with reference to the earlier passage 27d-28b, and a little later in 52c1 ἐγερθέντες διοριζόμενοι τἀληθές λέγειν. Such διορίζειν is without doubt the task of dialectic. Moreover the reference to truth evidently picks up the crucial distinction between ἀλήθεια and πίστις used to summarize the methodological discussion at 29c3.

It is further worth pointing out that the three philosophical principles can be interconnected in a kind of academic diaeresis. Concerning each thing one can say that it is or it has come into being. That which has come into being did so through a cause. Depending on how the cause acts the result is either fair or not fair. Schematically we can represent the chain as follows:[32]

---

[31]See the final section of the article cited in the previous note.

[32]Once again for further discussion see the article mentioned in the two previous notes.

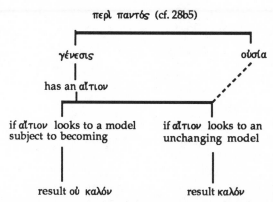

The diaeresis, one hardly needs to say, is one of the chief dialectical instruments in Plato's later philosophy. The schema is presented in the *præmium* of the Timaeus as if it would be valid for any existent (later it is qualified, for it emerges in 49a that the receptable as τρίτον γένος does not fit in the first division). Plato here applies it to the very special case of the cosmos. The diaeresis between καλόν and οὐ καλόν amounts to the distinction between the third and fourth sections of the divided line in *Republic* VI (and applied in the distinction between the craftsman and the painter in book X of the same work).[33]

There are two arguments in the application of the general principles to the specific example of the cosmos to which we need to pay attention. These are 3 (i) and (iii) in the structure outlined above. The logic of the two arguments is similar in two ways: they both start off with an exclusive disjunction, and they both add an additional premiss to the general principles outlined at the outset. But in other ways the arguments are formally dissimilar, for two different kinds of syllogism are involved. Indeed it is interesting to note that they anticipate the two major kinds of syllogism developed in ancient philosophy.[34]

(a) *First argument* (28b4-c2)
    a. The cosmos *either* has always existed *or* has come into being.
    b. It has come into being.
    c. *For* it is corporeal and therefore sense-perceptible.

---

[33]*Rep.* 509d-510b, 596a-597e; cf. Cornford *op. cit.* (n. 17) 27.

[34]To my knowledge this has not hitherto been observed by modern commentators; but see the remarks of Proclus *in Tim.* 1.292.20ff., 328.16ff.

After the disjunction we get what would later become an Aristotelian categorial syllogism in barbara.
Thus

> A is B or C
> A is D
> D is C
> therefore A is C
> (where A is cosmos; B always existent; C come into being; D corporeal/sense-perceptible).

(b) *Second argument* (28c5-29b1)

  a. *Either* the cosmos is fair and its maker good in that he looked to an eternal model *or* the cosmos is not fair in that he looked to a model subject to becoming.
  b. He looked to an eternal model.
  c. *For* the cosmos is the fairest of things that have come into being and its maker is the best of causes.

The disjunction here introduces what would later be called the indemonstrable syllogisms in Stoic propositional logic.[35]
Thus

> if A, then B, or if C, then D
> A
> therefore B
> (where A cosmos fair, demiurge good; B demiurge looked to eternal model; C cosmos not fair, demiurge not good; D demiurge looked to non-eternal model).[36]

As mentioned above, these arguments differ from what was affirmed in the general principles because they each contain an additional premiss, both of which in fact contain problematic elements.

In the first argument Plato affirms that the cosmos is a corporeal and therefore sense-perceptible object. On what is this affirmation based? It would seem to be empirically founded: the cosmos is the kind of thing that we can see and touch. This might suggest that the arguments in the *procemium* are subject to the same strictures of mere plausibility that govern the whole of Timaeus' account from 29e

---

[35]On these cf. A. A. Long, *Hellenistic Philosophy* (London 1974) 143ff.; M. Frede, *Die Stoische Logik* (Göttingen 1974) 127ff.

[36]We note in passing that the alternative argument—if A, then B, or, if C, then D, C, therefore D—is a formal representation of the route taken by later Gnostic thinkers. Since the world was evidently an evil place, it must have been made by an evil demiurge, who took as his model the image of himself reflected in the abyss.

onwards (except, I would argue, at least parts of 48e-52d). I do not believe that the εἰκὼς μῦθος at 29d2 is meant to be given such retrogressive force. Plato must consider that there is a difference between the two propositions 'the cosmos is corporeal and therefore sense-perceptible' and 'this star consists mainly of fire'. Precisely what this difference is is not made clear.[37] In fact the entire procedure of talking of the cosmos as the sum of corporeal reality is problematic, as Kant demonstrated in his celebrated account of the antinomies.[38] There is also a further related problem. Premiss a. of the first argument is based on the general principle set out in 27d6-28a4, where Plato distinguishes between what belongs to the realm of unchanging being and what belongs to the realm of becoming and is *subject to coming into being and passing away* (28a3 γιγνόμενον καὶ ἀπολλύμενον). But it will emerge in the course of Plato's argument that the cosmos (and even some of its parts) will in fact not be destroyed (41aff.). So the substitution of the cosmos as the sum of corporeal reality in the first argument outlined above is also from this point of view not without its difficulties.

We move on now to the second argument outlined above, the argument where the language of excellence makes it debut in the *Timaeus*. The two superlatives do not, however, come right 'out of the blue'. As Proclus observes in his commentary,[39] the ground has been prepared: the two superlatives are preceded by the 'positive' forms of the adjectives, καλός and ἀγαθός, in the major premiss; moreover the dilemma καλός/οὐ καλός already occurs in the more general context of the third principle at 28a6-b2. In the antecedent premiss of the syllogism, evidently, Plato makes a qualitative jump not strictly required by the logic of his argument. The cosmos is not only καλός, it is κάλλιστος; its maker is not only ἀγαθός, he is ἄριστος. For this reason the conclusion obviously follows (29a4 παντὶ σαφές). But what is obvious to Plato may not be so to us. On what grounds, we ask again, does he affirm this premiss?

The most straightforward answer to this question is once again an answer on empirical grounds. It is obvious to everybody because we

---

[37] As Donini has acutely pointed out (*art. cit.* (n. 18) 32-36, Plato has allowed for the fact that a limited amount of empirical data is necessary for the basis of the dialectical exercise by affirming in the famous passage 47a-c that the man's gift of sight is the starting point of all philosophy; see further my forthcoming article cited in n.30.

[38] Cf. A. E. Taylor, *A Commentary on Plato's* Timaeus (Oxford 1928) 70.

[39] *In Tim.* 1.330.21-24.

experience the ordered beauty and rational design of the universe of which we are a part. The argument is then similar to the well-known cosmological argument or argument from design, arguing the existence (and certain properties) of God from the ordered nature of reality, which cannot come into existence spontaneously, but must be the product of rational design on the part of a creating deity.[40]

It is interesting at this point to consult Proclus' Commentary on the *Timaeus*, in which he specifically poses the question why according to Plato the cosmos is not fair but the fairest.[41] The source of its beauty is the model, he argues, and it is fairest because it is modelled on the first and most eternal of eternal beings. A little later he adds that there can be no doubt that Plato was right in his affirmation of the cosmos' excellence, as can be seen from its visible beauty, the order of the heavenly revolutions, the harmony of its souls and so on.[42] Proclus is surely right in presenting this last argument merely as a confirmation *a posteriori* of Plato's premiss and not its actual grounds. For if the move from καλός/οὐ καλός to κάλλιστος is based on *observation* of the cosmos' beauty, this would not only place an even bigger strain on the dialectical basis of Plato's argument than there is already, but also presume to an uncomfortable degree the results of Plato's cosmological exposition rather than laying the foundations for it. But for the same reason the Neoplatonist's argument for the jump is not convincing as it stands. It is the nature of the model that Plato is trying to determine in the argument, so it will not do to invoke an aspect of that model[43] in order to justify the formulation of one of the premisses of that argument.

So how can Plato boldly affirm that the cosmos is the 'fairest of things that come into being'? There must be a *hidden premiss* in the argument that is not made explicit. This is, I submit, the premiss that the cosmos is the fairest of things that come into being *because it contains all other things that come into being*, coming into being

---

[40]Enunciated prior to Plato by Diogenes of Apollonia and Socrates according to Xenophon's Memoirs; cf. A. S. Pease, 'Caeli enarrant', *HThR* 34 (1941) 164ff.

[41]*In Tim.* 1.330.25-331.7.

[42]*In Tim.* 1.332.19-29.

[43]*In Tim.* 1.330.28 πρός τὸ τῶν ἀιδίων ἀιδιώτατον; cf. ἀίδιον] in the conclusion 29a3.

(γένεσις) being the characteristic of that which is corporeal, and the universe containing all that is corporeal.[44]

The question now immediately raises itself: is this another example of *a posteriori* argumentation? Is it not that case that Plato only proves the comprehensiveness of the cosmos later in the dialogue? This is true; Plato only assumes the doctrine at this point, indicating it by the phrases ὁ πᾶς κόσμος (28b2), τοῦδε τοῦ παντός (28c4). But the unicity and comprehensiveness and self-sufficiency of the cosmos is not demonstrated *metaphysically* until 30c-31b and not *physically* until 32c-34a, τελεώτατος thereafter being an epithet of the cosmos which is prominent in the summaries at 68e3 and 92c8.[45] The former of these demonstrations is of particular interest to us, because it is precisely there that the language of excellence is first used of the model contemplated by the demiurge. It therefore completes the triad of excellence outlined of this section of my paper. Let us briefly turn to this argument.

To which of the eternal noetic living beings does the cosmos, as a living being, show resemblance, one of the partial ones or the one that is complete? It must be to the one that is fairest and in every way complete (30d2 καλλίστῳ καὶ κατὰ πάντα τελέῳ), i.e. the one that *embraces* (περιλαβόν) all other noetic living beings within itself, just like the cosmos as corporeal living being contains all other corporeal living beings within itself (30c7-d1). What is the force of the καὶ in the Greek phrase just cited? Is it epexegetic, and so meaning 'and therefore', i.e. the noetic living being is κατὰ πάντα τέλεος because it is κάλλιστος? It seems to me more likely that it is the other way around: the noetic cosmos is κάλλιστος because it is κατὰ πάντα τέλεος.[46]

---

[44]This argument is explicitly given in de Pseudo-Aristotelian *De mundo* 5 397a4-7: ἡ δὲ ὁμόνοια τοῦ πάντων γενετῆρος καὶ περικαλλεστάτου κόσμου. τίς γὰρ ἂν εἴη φύσις τοῦδε κρείττων; ἢν γὰρ ἂν εἴπῃ τις, μέρος ἐστιν αὐτοῦ. Other passages in this work that use the 'language of excellence' are 5 397a14-16 (cosmos), 6 399b20-22. The influence of the *Timaeus* may be mediated via Aristotle, who without doubt also used this language extensively, above all in his exoteric works; cf. *Metaphys.* 7 1072b28-30, *De caelo* 2.5, *De phil.* fr. 12, 14, 16, 19c Ross. Note too that many scholars have discerned a close relation between the *De mundo* and Philo (Pohlenz once suggested that its addressee, Alexander, was Philo's nephew!).

[45]See the inventory of superlatives above *sub* 2.

[46]As noted above Plato, after deriving the perfection of the cosmos from the model, proceeds to describe the former with the superlative τελεώτατος. Why does the model not receive this epithet? Perhaps because there are ideas that are more comprehensive, e.g. the μέγιστα γένη of the *Sophist*. But why then is the model

Because the corporeal cosmos resembles this all-embracing model, Plato feels able to deduce that it also must be unique, just like its model is unique (31a3-b3).

Now this deduction has got him into hot water, so to speak, in the estimation of recent exegetes. The demiurge is crazy, he does not know when to stop. When looking to the model in making the cosmos, he copies attributes proper to the model, e.g. its living-beingness, but goes on to add features that are common to all ideas, e.g. unicity, eternity (to the extent possible), completeness etc.[47] Various lines of defence have been proposed. The one I will support[48] is to insist that unicity and completeness are proper attributes of the model, not just as a form, but as specifically as model for the cosmos. The model is a special form which can only uniquely be instantiated precisely because it embraces all other living beings as its parts. What is preventing the demiurge from making five cosmoi, each of which is complete (cf. 55d where the possibility of that many is tentatively proposed)? Presumably because then these cosmoi would not be the universe, i.e. that particular living being that embraces all other living beings.[49]

The model, therefore, is κάλλιστος because it is κατὰ πάντα τέλεος. What is exactly meant by the last phrase? This points not only to its perfection, i.e. that it has reached its τέλος and is self-sufficient, but also implies that it possesses completeness or wholeness?[50] If so, there must be a relation between this completeness and the fact that it contains all other noetic living beings whether singly or generically as its parts. How are we to imagine this containment in terms of the

---

described as κάλλιστος? Is this term no more than an elative, since there are obviously forms of greater 'containment'? Or is the παντελὲς ζῷον fair to a degree not shared for example by the idea of Being? There are difficulties here, which the concept of the κόσμος νοητός in Neoplatonism tried to overcome.

[47] Cf. D. Keyt, 'The mad craftsman of the Timaeus', PhR 80 (1971) 230-235: Plato commits the fallacy of division in that he fails to distinguish between the proper and the ideal attributes of a form.

[48] Though it would not affect my reconstruction of Plato's reasoning if he happened to make a logical error.

[49] Cf. R. D. Parry, 'The unique world of the Timaeus', JHPh 17 (1979) 1-10, R. Patterson, 'The unique worlds of the Timaeus', Phoenix 35 (1981) 105-119. For a different approach see R. D. Mohr, The Platonic cosmology (Leiden 1985) 9-52, who argues on the basis of the 'standard-establishing properties' of forms. But issues involved are far too large to be dealt with in the confines of this paper.

[50] Contra Mohr op. cit. 33.

theory of ideas? It is to be agreed that we should not imagine the model as a structured *system* or whole entirely analogous to the corporeal cosmos itself. The model embraces all noetic living beings of which the concept ζῷον can be predicated in the way that the English word animal can be said to embrace (referentially, of course) all living beings to which the word can be applied, i.e. noetic animal contains noetic cat and noetic mouse (though not noetic Tom and noetic Jerry). The way, therefore, that the part/whole relation works on the noetic level is different to what happens on the corporeal level, since in the latter physical containment is meant, whereas in the former we can only envisage inter-participation in the manner Plato outlines in the μέγιστα γένη of the *Sophist*. Thus the τελειότης of the model (cf. also τὸ παντελὲς ζῷον 31b1) is not just a matter of self-sufficiency (all other living beings participate in it, it does not participate in them), but also of completeness. Making an image of the model means that the image, if it is to be most similar (ὁμοιότατον, cf. 30c7, 39e1), must contain all those living beings, the forms of which participate in the model. Plato articulates for the first time the *principle of plenitude*, an idea with a long career ahead of it (cf. esp. συμπληρωθείς in the summary at 92a6).[51] At the physical level, too, Plato argues for the cosmos' completeness, which results in its perfection and self-sufficiency. If it were not made out of perfect parts (i.e. parts taking up the entire amount of the four elements) and did not form a unity, it would be susceptible to attack from the outside (e.g. through breathing in such external bodies, as in the case of man) and disease from within (cf. 32c-34a).[52]

So when Plato twice in his summaries describes the cosmos as τελεώτατος (68e3, 92c8), we are clearly meant to think of both the metaphysical and the physical grounds just outlined. They are complementary, the one emphasizing the formal plenitude of the universe, the other its material completeness. Both contribute to its perfection, and so to its excellence.

On both occasions, we further observe, that Plato describes the bequeathal of τελειότης to the cosmos by the demiurge, he stresses that it involves an act of rational calculation (32c8 διανοηθείς, 39e9 διανοήθη, cf. 30b4 διὰ τὸν λογισμόν on the placement of mind in soul and soul in body). A clear distinction is made between knowing, i.e. the

---

[51]Cf. Lovejoy *op. cit.* (n. 14) 52ff.

[52]There is a weakness in the argumentation which Aristotle attempted to shore up in his *De Philosophia*; cf. Runia *op. cit.* (n. 1) 193.

David T. Runia

contemplation of the model, and the application of that knowledge to the task of making the cosmos by means of discursive reasoning. The demiurge has to *calculate* how to achieve the best result, given the situation of pre-cosmic disorder with which he is confronted.

This brings us back to the nature and activity of the demiurge, who in the dialectical argument of 28c5-29a5 was described not just as ἀγαθός, as in the better known passage at 29e1, but in superlative terms as ἄριστος τῶν αἰτίων.

As has often been pointed out,[53] the best understanding of the way Plato conceives the nature of the demiurge's activity is through a reading of the criticism of Anaxagoras's account of the γένεσις of the cosmos as placed in the mouth of Socrates at *Phd.* 97b-99d. Socrates reads that νοῦς is ὁ διακοσμῶν τε καὶ πάντων αἴτιος, and so will be the cause which will organize things for the *best* (97c6 ὅπῃ ἂν βέλτιστα ἔχῃ, cf. 98a8). In order to explain the causes of things, it is not enough to analyze how or out of what things come to be, but one must explain primarily why it is best for them to be as they are. Plato exalts teleological reasoning, which looks to the purpose and functionality of a thing, i.e. its goodness and excellence.

Socrates was cheated of his expectations when he read Anaxagoras' book, but listening to Timaeus' long monologue would have given him intense delight. Timaeus' demiurge is all that the Anaxagorean νοῦς failed to be. But we note that there is no mention in the *Phaedo* that the ordering mind is the best of causes. Only that he should act for the best, as every rational agent who is good, including man, should do. And in the τύποι περὶ θεολογίας in book II of the *Republic*, when Plato argues in favour of the unconditional goodness of the gods, whatever Homer and poets might say, there is also no intrusion of superlatives.[54]

---

[53]E.g. Taylor *op. cit.* (n. 38) 72; S. K. Strange, 'The double explanation in the *Timaeus*', *Ancient Philosophy* 5 (1984) 25-39.

[54]Cf. *Rep.* 379a-e; Plato stresses that god is not πάντων αἴτιος, but ὀλίγων μὲν τοῖς ἀνθρώποις αἴτιος, πολλῶν δὲ ἀναίτιος (e3-4). This is obviously not incompatible with the Timaeus which vigorously denied divine omnipotence, but the emphasis differs. The θεός referred to in general terms here only partially corresponds to the demiurge in the *Timaeus*, for there is a hierarchy of θεοί in that work. At 381b-c, when discussing divine immutability, Plato does use superlatives: b4 ὁ θεός γε καὶ τὰ τοῦ θεοῦ πάντῃ ἄριστα ἔχει; c8-9 κάλλιστος καὶ ἄριστος ὢν εἰς τὸ δυνατὸν ἕκαστος αὐτῶν μένει ἀεὶ ἁπλῶς ἐν τῇ αὑτοῦ μορφῇ. Note that (1) the language in the second citation is reminiscent of *Tim.* 42e, but that (2) the statement is qualified in a way that would be unnecessary for the demiurge at the top of the divine hierarchy (the controversial

So, in order to determine the basis of Plato's assertion that the demiurge is the best of causes, we have once again to postulate a *hidden premiss*, the same one as before. The demiurge is the best of causes because he is the cause of that corporeal living being that embraces all other living beings, i.e. the universe. But this is emphatically not to say that the two passages just cited are irrelevant to Plato's argument. For it could be argued that the maker of the universe could also be the worst of causes and make the worst (since most comprehensive) of things that come into being.[55] Not, however, if he is a god. He is good (29e1 ἀγαθὸς ἦν). This is a principle derived from men of understanding (30a παρ' ἀνδρῶν φρονίμων). And, if he is good, he will also not contrive to make the cosmos incomplete when he contrives to make it resemble the model. It is not legitimate (οὐ θέμις) for the best to do anything that is not the best (30b5). The two phrases of the premiss in 29a thus interlock: the cosmos is fairest because it is made by the demiurge, the demiurge is best because it is he who has made the cosmos. For this reason Plato considers it proven that the demiurge looked to the model which is eternal, and as we are later told, fairest and in every way complete. We may conclude, therefore, that the foundations of the language of excellence have thus been laid in the *procemium* before Plato has even begun to give a description of the rational order that the demiurge and later his helpers impose on the pre-cosmic chaos.[56]

I will not dwell long on the rest of the language of excellence that we outlined at the beginning of the paper, because its basis is now pellucidly clear. The god and his helpers, because they are gods and good, make the cosmos and its parts *as excellent as they can* (i.e. the terminative culminatives we listed above). They cannot just do as they please, for they have to calculate how best they can counteract the irreducibly intractable aspects of the material they are working with. Within these limits they produce the best results possible. Another aspect of the language of excellence which is hardly less important is

---

question of how the activity of the demiurge is compatible with divine immutability is a different issue).

[55]The Gnostic argument noted above in n.36.

[56]Donini *art. cit.* (n. 18) 44-47 regards the affirmation of the demiurge's goodness at 29e-30a as at the highest level of probability in the εἰκὼς λόγος, and makes much of its derivation from ἄνδρες φρόνιμοι. My view is that this affirmation is already prepared in the *prooemium*, i.e. before the εἰκὼς λόγος starts, and that it is based on the results of dialectic (i.e. φρόνησις).

its expression of a hierarchy of value. Just as the cosmos is best and fairest because largest and most comprehensive, so its parts have their relative excellences: the stars, made largely out of fire, are fairest to see (the cosmos as whole cannot be seen); man's structure is organized so that the head has the primacy, containing the most divine part, and so on. Plato's chief method here is analogy, as embodied in the relation between macrocosm and microcosm, at the level of the city as unit of social organization and at the level of man as individual structure of body and soul and their parts.[57] Excellence, in short, is the result of purposeful thinking that works within the limits imposed by both the nature of rational organization and the nature of the materials at one's disposal.

IV

It is time to draw some threads together. Let us return first to Plato's language in the *Timaeus*. It would be wrong to assert, I believe, that the work is wholly devoid of lyricism. One thinks of the description of the dancing motions of the stars (40c3 χορείας), and also of the praise of sight as furnishing man with philosophy (47a-c). But such effusive language is in fact strictly—and, I suspect, deliberately— curtailed. The chief vehicle of Plato's celebratory, or if you wish hymnic, language in the *Timaeus* is the use of superlatives, which I have summarized under the title 'the language of excellence'. Although it is true that some of this usage has little more purpose than to give elevation to the language of the work—e.g. when sight in the passage just mentioned above is called the *greatest* contribution to man's well being (46e8, 47a2, cf. 47b1)—, my argument has been that the chief motivation for the extended use of this language has been not stylistic but philosophical.

The most important statement of the language of excellence— concerning the cosmos and its maker at 29a5-6, emphatically summarized (though only in respect of the cosmos) in the final words of the dialogue at 92c7-8—is presented to the reader in the dialectical section of the *procemium* before Plato has even embarked on his 'probable account'. Because the cosmos or universe is the sum total of what has come into being, it must be the fairest of what has come into

---

[57] It is customary to refer to the monograph of A. Olerud, *L'idée de macrocosmos et de microcosmos dans le 'Timée' de Platon* (Upsala 1951) on this theme; but this seminal idea deserves a better treatment.

being, and its maker, because he has given it its excellence, must be the best of causes. Evidently, *how* the demiurge made the cosmos fairest and best, e.g. by placing mind in soul and soul in body, is to be explained by the probable account, and Plato, though persuaded that his attempt is a true account (i.e. ἀληθὴς δόξα), would accept that it might require modification and improvement. *That* the cosmos has been made κάλλιστον ἄριστόν τε by the demiurge, however, is not subject to the qualifications imposed by the nature of the probable account.   This, Plato argues, is true in accordance with the demonstrability of dialectic.

It is Plato's conviction that there is only one way to make the universe in the best way, and that is the way the god actually made it. Nor could be it otherwise.   This, the hallmark of what we might perhaps anachronistically call a rationalist philosophy, was to have as long a career as the language of excellence that accompanied it. Leibniz wrestled with its consequences, and when he discovered the calculus, he felt he was able to peer right into the actual calculations of the divine mind.[58] Plato is the start of all this, the first to try to apply the rigour of logic to enquiry on the nature of the universe.

It is, I think, particularly the rationalist conviction that what is must be and what must be is that induces Plato to exploit the linguistic device of the superlative to the remarkable degree he does in the *Timaeus*. The superlative, when used strictly in its culminative sense, picks out one instance of the noun it qualifies and raises it above the rest.   No subjective criteria are involved, as in lyrical descriptions of beauty and goodness and so on. One instance has the requisite quality to the highest degree, and it is the task of the philosopher or scientist to explain why that is so. We might feel uncomfortable with the way Plato relates statements of fact and statements of value, but we cannot complain that he is soft-headed about it. In its own way the *Timaeus* is as hard-headed as the *Parmenides*.[59]

---

[58]Cf. N. Rescher, 'Leibniz on Creation and the Evaluation of Possible Worlds,' in *idem*. *Leibniz's Metaphysics of Nature* (Dordrecht 1981) 1-18; note the significant difference that Leibniz spoke of the 'best of all possible worlds', Plato of the 'best of things that have (actually) come into being'.

[59]Cf. G. Vlastos, *Plato's Universe* (Oxford 1975) 29, 65. But his description of the *Timaeus* as a 'metaphysical fairy tale' seems to me unfortunate. Fairy tales may have fanciful premises (presumably the point of the label), but do not present rigorous argumentation.

Finally, I return to the three authors with which I began. Needless to say, an adequate examination of the way in which Plato's 'language of excellence' was picked up and developed in the later philosophical tradition, and particularly in later Platonism, would be too large a subject for the present context. Nor do I wish to suggest that Plato's dialogue was the only or even the determinative influence on the cosmic lyricism of these thinkers.[60] All I shall do now is append some brief comments which focus on the texts cited earlier in the article.

What is immediately striking about the passage in Philo is its emphasis on the role of God as demiurge. As we have amply observed, he invokes the authority of Plato in describing both the demiurge and the cosmos in terms of the language of excellence. But there is no doubt that in the *Timaeus* the weight of emphasis falls on the excellence of the cosmos, and not on that of its maker. Indeed in the final summary the demiurge does not even receive a mention.[61] This is part of Plato's curious reticence concerning the figure of the demiurge. One has a very strong feeling that he is a *deus ex hypothesi*, indispensable in order to explain the nature of the cosmos, but not a divine being to be admired and worshipped in his own right. How different the Philonic approach! The entire point of the παλαιὸς λόγος is to stress the praise, thanksgiving and worship that should be directed towards the Creator. Patently Philo's fervent Jewish monotheism intercedes. For Philo God is not an abstract philosophical principle, but the supreme Being, whom man must worship in fear or in love.[62]

It would be foolish, however, to see Philo's Jewishness exclusively at work here for a similar emphasis is patent in Plutarch's text at *Mor.* 1014A. The Platonism of the period was also remarkably theocentric, a fact that goes much of the way to explaining its attractiveness to Philo.[63] The words in *Tim.* 29a5-6 which Plutarch explicitly cites are a

---

[60]Prof. Brenk points out to me that both Philo and the Middle Platonists may have been influenced by the use of hymn genre for praise of the creator god in archaic Greek texts and also Near Eastern literature. This literature already exerted influence on the *Timaeus* itself, as Hadot *art. cit.* (n. 15) argues.

[61]Reading νοητοῦ and not ποιητοῦ in 92c7; on this text see further Runia *op. cit.* (n.1) 352.

[62]Cf. *Deus* 69. See further the perceptive remarks of E. R. Goodenough, *An Introduction to Philo Judaeus* (Oxford 1962²), 80ff. For M. Harl, *Quis rerum divinarum heres sit*, Les oeuvres de Philon d'Alexandrie 15 (Paris 1966) 153, Philo is 'le premier représentant d'un type nouveau d'homme religieux'.

[63]Cf. Runia *op. cit.* (n. 1) 491ff.

premiss in an argument focussed on the model contemplated by the demiurge. But in Plutarch's own text the model is conspicuous by its absence. In fact, as Cherniss pointed out, the final words, in which an ὁμοίωσις relation is postulated between God and unformed matter (cf. Tim. 29e3), go close to identifying the demiurge with the model.[64] In the other text at *Mor.* 720B, however, Plutarch is in a much more scholastic frame of mind. The three entities which are described by superlatives are, of course, the famous three principles of Middle Platonist scholasticism. Although Plutarch explicitly affirms that these three are derived from the *Timaeus*, only the description of god is textually based. The ἰδέα (note the singular)[65] is called τῶν παραδειγμάτων κάλλιστον because in Middle Platonism it was standard practice to define ideas in terms of their roles as models.[66] In the *Timaeus* it is κάλλιστον, as we saw, but no explicit comparison is made with other ideas.[67] The argument at 28e5-29a6 starts off with the words πρὸς πότερον τῶν παραδειγμάτων; the demiurge has the choice between two paradigms—one in the realm of being, one in the realm of becoming—, so that superlatives are obviously inappropriate. The description of ὕλη as τῶν ὑποκειμένων ἀτακτότατον requires the Middle Platonist identification of the Platonic receptacle with Aristotelian substrate in order to make sense. In the *Timaeus* the τρίτον γένος is a very solitary concept indeed, being the only entity that cannot be accommodated with the diaeresis of being and becoming set out in 27d-28a.[68] Plato does not use the comparatives and superlatives of the language of excellence in order to describe it.[69] But if the pre-cosmic

---

[64]*Op. cit.* (n. 7) 181, cross-referring to *Mor.* 1007C-D: εἰκόνες δε' εἰσὶν ἀμφω τοῦ θεοῦ, τῆς μὲν οὐσίας ὁ κόσμος τῆς δ' ἀιδιότητος <ὁ> χρόνος. H. Dörrie went so far as to question Plutarch's Platonist orthodoxy on this point, but the Chaeronean found a staunch defender in C. J. de Vogel, 'Der sog. Mittelplatonismus, überwiegend eine Philosophie der Diesseitigkeit?', in *Platonismus und Christentum; Festschrift für H. Dörrie*, JbACErg 10 (Münster 1983) 283-287 (with further references).

[65]Cf. Philo, *Opif.* 16, 25 (ἀρχέτυπος ἰδέα τῶν ἰδεῶν); Tim. Locr. 10.

[66]Cf. Alcinous, *Did.* 12. The source is perhaps chiefly the role of the model in the Timaeus, but also texts such as *Rep.* 484c, 500e, 592c, *Parm.* 132d were significant.

[67]Though, as Prof. Baltes points out to me, it is implicit at 30b3 where Plato asks whether the demiurge looked to partial (noetic) ζῷα or to the complete one of which the others are parts.

[68]Cf. Runia *art cit.* (n. 30) p.21

[69]We note only 51b1, where it is δυσαλωτότατον, and in 50e10 a comparison with the making of shapes out of a soft substance which is λειότατον.

disorder is interpreted in terms of a substrate or matter or primary stuff,[70] then it can be compared to the underlying materials of a house or a garment or a statue,[71] and so may deserve the not entirely felicitous description of 'most disordered of substrates'.

Theocentrism is not foreign to Plotinus. The opening words of the impressive *prosopopeia* placed in the mouth of the cosmos in *Enn.* 3.2.3 are ἐμὲ πεποίηκε θεός, words which have appropriately compared to the inscription on the cultic statue of a god.[72] But which god is meant? Surely the demiurge, we would say. But Plotinus' appropriation of this figure is notoriously complex.[73] His contemplative activity belongs to the realm of the νοῦς as second hypostasis, while his actual demiurgic activity is the province of the world-soul (whom he once, arguing significantly against his Gnostic opponents calls τὸν ἡγεμόνα τοῦδε τοῦ παντός, ψυχὴν μακαριωτάτην[74]). The context shows that the god meant by Plotinus must be the κόσμος νοητός.[75] The model has returned to the centre of the stage, but has been transformed into an entire cosmos, as all-embracing at the intelligible level as the visible cosmos is at the sense-perceptible level. Inseparable from the νοῦς as the subject of its intellection, it is the ἄτιος of the cosmos and its ἀρχέτυπον καὶ παράδειγμα, i.e. combines the roles of demiurge and model that are separate in the *Timaeus*. Both these cosmoi are described in terms of the language of excellence derived from the *Timaeus*; the one is πάντων κάλλιστον, the other ἐν αἰσθητῷ κάλλιστον.[76] The relation is not only one of model to image, but also of a *necessary production of* the one by or from the other. It is not proper to speak ill—as the Gnostics do—of the cosmos as if it were not the best of bodily things, nor should one blame the one who is αἴτιος of its existence. For it exists of necessity (ἐξ ἀνάγκης), and is not the result of

---

[70]I.e. οὐσία, originally a Stoic term; cf. *Mor.* 1014B.

[71]The triple comparison is given in *Mor.* 1014B, a few lines below the text cited at the beginning of the article.

[72]*Enn.* 3.2.3.21; cf. V. Cilento, 'Mito e poesia nelle Enneadi di Plotino, in *Les sources de Plotin*, Entretiens Hardt 5 (Vandoeuvres-Geneva 1960) 302.

[73]Cf. Proclus *in Tim.* 1.305.16; Matter; L. Brisson, *Le même et l'autre dans la structure ontologique du* Timée *de Platon* (Paris 1974) 64ff.

[74]*Enn.* 2.9.9.33, combining *Tim.* 34b8, 36e5 (cf. above n. 13) with *Phdr.* 246e4, 250b7-c1.

[75]Cf. P. Boot, *Plotinus, Over voorzienigheid (Enneade III 2-3 [47-48])* (diss. Amsterdam 1984) 87.

[76]See texts above at n.11 and 13.

a process of reasoning (λογισμός), but rather of a superior nature naturally producing a likeness of itself.[77] The fact that Plotinus explicitly denies the role of discursive reasoning in the formation of the cosmos shows the extent of his reinterpretation of the *Timaeus*, for, as we saw, the task of rational calculation is intrinsic to the demiurge's role. But his affirmation of the necessity of the cosmos' production amounts to a reformulation of the dialectical necessity which we saw at work in Plato's *procemium* in ontological terms. The world is as it is because it cannot be in any other way. In spirit, therefore, Plotinus of our three authors stands closest to the deeper motivations of Plato's language of excellence.[78]

---

[77]3.2.3.1-6 (partly cited at no. 12 above.)

[78]The author wishes to thank the Board and the staff of the Fondation Hardt, Vandœuvres-Geneva, where the initial research was done in ideal surroundings. An early version of the paper was read to members of the Departments of Greek and Philosophy at the University of Sydney in October 1987. The author is grateful to Dr. H. Tarrant and other members of the audience for valuable remarks, and also to Professors A. P. Bos and M. Baltes who commented on a later version. The research for this article was carried out with the financial support of the Netherlands Organization for Scientific Research (N.W.O.).

Darkly Beyond the Glass: Middle Platonism and the Vision of the Soul

FREDERICK E. BRENK, S.J.

The formulation, seeing God "face to face," appears to be a masterpiece of simplicity.[1] But for Middle Platonism, the only real philosophy of the time of the New Testament which could espouse a direct intellectual vision of God as man's destiny, the matter was very problematic. The difficulties are inherent in Greek religion, upon which Middle Platonism drew for its success. But there were also imprecisions within Platonism itself, leading to a wavering over the role of the "beatific vision" (*thea makaria*), first in Plato and then in Middle Platonism.

Before treating Middle Platonism explicitly, though, it is necessary to glance at the roots of the problem in archaic Greek religion. The success of Middle Platonism was due partially to its adaptation of a more erudite and impersonal Platonism, which it had inherited, to the contemporary aspirations for immortality and a blessed afterlife as represented in religion. For example, the myth of Eos (the Dawn) and Memnon, her "Ethiopian" son, found in the post-Homeric "Epic Cycle" seems related to a very old Indo-European myth in which the

---

[1] This article has profited greatly from the recent volume, R. Van den Broek, T. Baarda, and J. Mansfield, eds., *Knowledge of God in the Graeco-Roman World* (EPRO 112) (Leiden 1988), in particular the contributions by D. T. Runia, "Naming and Knowing: Themes in Philonic Theology with Special Reference to the *De mutatione nominum*," 69-91, J. Mansfield, "Compatible Alternatives: Middle Platonist Theology and the Xenophanes Reception," 92-117, P. L. Donini, "La connaissance de dieu et la hiérarchie divine chez Albinos," 118-131, and J. M. Dillon, "The Knowledge of God in Origen," 219-228.

Dawn goddess is a symbol of immortality, bringing the Sun back to life each day.[2] Since Dawn and Sun are light *par excellence*, the myth is something of a grandfather of the Middle Platonic doctrine.

Greek religion at times presents the epiphany, or vision, of a god— sometimes in psychedelic grandeur—as the goal of mystical experience. The climax of the *Homeric Hymn to Apollo*, the lightning epiphany of the god, is typical:

ἔνθ' ἐκ νηὸς ὄρουσεν ἄναξ ἑκάεργος Ἀπόλλων ἀστέρι
εἰδόμενος μέσῳ ἤματι· τοῦ δ' ἀπο πολλαὶ σπινθαρίδες πωτῶντο,
σέλας δ' εἰς οὐρανὸν ἷκεν·

...

πᾶσαν δὲ Κρίσην κάτεχεν σέλας· αἱ δ' ὀλόλυξαν Κρισαίων ἄλοχοι
καλλίζωνοί τε θύγατρες ... μέγα γὰρ δέος ἔμβαλ' ἑκάστῳ.

Then he leapt from the ship, the Lord, far-working Apollon, a star in appearance, in midday. And from him many sparks of fire flew, and the flash reached to heaven

. . .

and all Krisa—the radiance lay hold of, and they cried aloud. . . . for great fear he cast upon each.
(440-447).[3]

Archaeology suggests that even in the Ninth Century B.C. Greek cult stooped low to produce a vicarious epiphany, wheeling cult statues into bright light; later architects bathed the cult statue in light through apertures built into temples.[4] In the Hellenistic worship of

---

[2]Proklos, *Aithiopis* in T. W. Allen, *Homeri Opera* V (Oxford 1912, rev. 1946) 106, 6-7; treated by G. Nagy, *The Best of the Achaeans. The Concept of the Hero in Archaic Greek Poetry* (Baltimore 1979) 175. A. Dihle in "Beobachtungen zur Entstehung sakralsprachlicher Besonderheiten," in E. Dassmann and K. Thraede, eds., *Vivarium* (Münster 1984) 107-114, argues for "bright"--which would enhance the vision part-- rather than "sacred" in Empedokles' eschatology at fragment B 47: ἀθρεῖ μὲν γὰρ ἄνακτος ἐναντίον ἀγέα κύκλον   (109).

[3]F. Cassola, *Inni Omerici* (Milano 1975) 142, commentary, 512-513.

[4]See J. N. Coldstream, "A Protogeometric Nature Goddess from Knossos," *Bulletin of the Institute of Classical Studies, London* 31 (1984) 93-104: Knossos T. 107.114--pithos urn with representation of a goddess on a wheeled cart (96, fig. 1 and pls. 8c, d; 98 frig. 2). Professor Robin Hägg believes the cart was for bringing the statue into the light. However, more recently W. Burkert, "*Katagogia-Anagógia* and the Goddess of Knossos," in R. Hägg, N. Marinatos, G. C. Nordquist, ed., *Early Greek Cult Practice* (*Skrifter Utgivna av. Svenska Institutet i Athen* 4o, 38) (Stockholm 1988) 81-88, would see front and back views of the goddess as representing the processional cart on the festivals of arrival and departure of a goddess of vegetation.

Isis a high point of the daily devotion was the solemn revelation of the statue.[5]

Most probably religious practice of the Hellenistic period influenced the importance given the philosophical concept. The Eleusinian mysteries of the Classical period were a model for Plato's depiction of a "beatific vision."[6] But the *epopteia*, the visual culmination of the mysteries, was probably not a vision of the cult statue—potentially symbolic of the ultimate vision of the initiate—but of certain mysterious objects of the cult.[7] Middle Platonists, especially in Alexandria, might have been thinking in terms of the ritual of Isis.[8] A vicarious epiphany is startlingly portrayed in the *Metamorphoses* (or *Asinus Aureus*) of the Second Century A.D. Platonist, Apuleius:

> ac dehinc paulatim toto corpore perlucidum simulacrum
> . . .super frontem plana rutunditas . . . lunae candidum lumen
> emicabat, . . .semenstris luna flammeos spirabat ignes . . . 'En
> adsum tuis commota, Luci precibus, prima caelitum, deorum
> dearumque facies uniformis, . . .

> . . . gradually with the whole body, a radiant image . . . a flat
> disk above her forehead, . . . the moon's clear light, shone . . . a
> half-moon flaming fires breathed . . . "Lo, I am with you,

For the Hellenistic period see P. Hommel, "Giebel und Himmel," *Istanbuler Mitteilungen* 7 (1957) 11-55, esp. 31-33, 41. For special light effects for the statue of Apollo at Bassai and later Hagia Sophia, see W. L. MacDonald, *The Architecture of the Roman Empire* I (New Haven 1965) 121.

[5]For the importance of a vision of the cult image in Egyptian religion and, more particularly, in the cult of Isis, see S. Morenz, *Ägyptische Religion* (2nd ed., Stuttgart 1977) (=*Egyptian Religion* [London 1960]) 94, 98, 112; S. Sauneron, *Les prêtres de l'ancienne Égypte* (Paris 1957) 81-82 (rev. ed., 1988, 86-87); F. Dunand, *Le culte d'Isis dans le bassin oriental de la Méditerranée* III (*EPRO* 26) (Leiden 1973), 200-202; M. Malaise, *Les conditions de pénétration et de diffusion des cultes égyptiens en Italie* (*EPRO* 22) (Leiden 1972) 231. R. Seaford, "1 Corinthians XIII.12," *Journal of Theological Studies* 35 (1984) 117-120, notes the influence of mystery religion on the mirror analogy.

[6]See É. des Places, "Platon et la langue des mystères," *Annales d'Aix* 38 (1964) 9-23) (= M. J. Vermaseren, ed., *Études platoniciennes. 1929-1979* [*EPRO* 90] [Leiden 1981] 83-98); C. Riedweg, *Mysterienterminologie bei Platon, Philon und Klemens von Alexandrien* (Berlin 1987) 5, 7 —on the Derveni papyrus (c. 400 B.C.) col. XVI 1; W. Burkert, *Ancient Mystery Cults* (Harvard 1987) 91-93.

[7]See G. E. Mylonas, *Eleusis and the Eleusinian Mysteries* (Princeton 1961) 274-278.

[8]See É. des Places, "Éléments de sotériologie orientale dans le platonisme à la fin de l'antiquité," in U. Bianchi and M. J. Vermaseren, eds., *La soteriologia dei culti orientali nell'Impero Romano* (*EPRO* 92) (Leiden 1982) 243-252.

Lucius, moved by your prayers . . . the first of heavenly beings,
of gods and goddesses, the universal visage . . ." (11.3-5).[9]

Perhaps even more significant for evolution in religious
mentality, is the hardly modest and somewhat contradictory claim of
Lucius after his initiation, to have had a dream of (Osiris) "the greatest
and highest ruler of the greatest (gods), not disguised as another
person, but in his own essence" (11.30).[10] Lucius's high-sounding
eschatological language, however, later contrasts with the humble
nature of the apparition.

Still, though we often find an epiphany in Greek literature,
frequently with light images or metaphors, a vision of God or gods is
not the normal goal of a blessed afterlife. In myth fortunate mortals
are invited to the banquets of the gods, and even share their bed, but
simply looking at Olympians is not considered a special form of
felicity. In the philosophical eschatology of Plato, God or gods are the
guides or mystagogues, or fellow visionaries, but not worthy as the
object of vision itself. To make matters worse, Greek literature is filled
with suggestions of the impossibility of real communion between men
and gods, and the disastrous consequences which can result: the
unshared meals of Odysseus and Kalypso (*Odyssey* 5.194-200), the
flawed sacrificial banquet of gods and men (Hesiod, *Theogony* 533-560),
the failed romance of Eos, the Dawn, with Tithonos and Orion, and of
Demeter with Iasion (*Odyssey* 5.1-2, 116-128). Frequently, in fact, the
epiphany of a god has devastating consequences. The experience is
frightening in the *Homeric Hymns*, almost terrifying the worshippers
into establishing the cult site. The mother of Dionysos, Semele, is
blasted with lightning when she sees God (Zeus) "in all his glory."
According to myth and Greek tragedy, Dionysiac epiphanies in
particular were rather nasty affairs. In some versions of the myth,
Aphrodite, after seducing the hero Anchises, father of Aeneas, cripples
him forever with lightning.

Platonism was initially steered in a different direction, away from
any vision of God. Where Plato speaks of the vision, it is directed

---

[9]See J. G. Griffiths, *Apuleius of Madauros. The Isis-Book* (*Metamorphoses, Book XI*)
(*EPRO* 39) (Leiden 1975) 74-75 and 143-144. P. G. Walsh, "Apuleius and Plutarch," in H.
J. Blumenthal and R. A. Markus, eds., *Neoplatonism and Early Christian Thought*
(London 1981) 20-32, argues that Apuleius' transformation of the Loukios story into "an
apologia" for the Isiac mysteries was strongly influenced by Plutarch (23-24).

[10]Noted by G. Mussies, "Identification and Self-Identification of Gods in Classical and
Hellenistic Times," in Van den Broek, 1-18.

toward the intelligible Form of the Good/Beautiful rather than to God. Nor are matters at all simple. True, in Plato's "middle period," that of his great eschatological dialogues, the vision of the intelligible form (or "Idea") of the Beautiful or Good (*Kalon-Agathon*) or other transcendent Forms was clearly the destiny (*telos*) of the soul. In the *Phaidon* (*Phaedo*) 80D-81A, Plato is, in fact, close to Middle Platonic formulations. The soul resembles the divine (invisible, immortal, wise, intelligible, eternal) while the body resembles the mortal (79D-80A).[11] The "saints" (*Hosioi*) (113D) rise to a pure habitation on the earth, but some souls ascend to habitations even more beautiful (114C). Still, the *telos* is not really God. The soul departs for "the realm of Hades" (the invisible), "to the good and wise god," "for the place, intelligible like itself, noble and pure" (80D). The concept is reinforced by 108B-C, where the good soul finds gods for companions and guides (not to satisfy his burning desire for the intellectual vision).

The eschatological scenes of the *Phaidros*, dominated as they are by the concept of vision, do not make God the object. Throughout, the reader is bedazzled with many sensible and intelligible "beatific visions" (247A). In fact the language sounds like St. Paul: in this life we only approach these images "through the darkling organs of sense" (250B), but then the souls saw beauty shining in brightness, saw the "blessed vision and sight," were initiated into the mysteries, permitted as initiates to the sight of the complete and simple and blessed apparitions, seen in pure light (250B-C), with beauty shining in brilliance among those visions—now seen in this world only in copies or intimations (250D-251A).[12] Similar ideas appear in other Platonic dialogues, such as the *Symposion*. But in spite of the spectacular description of the ascent to the Beautiful in this life, Plato only implies its culmination in the next.

The conversion in the *Politeia* (*Republic*) of the Form of the Good into a super-Idea with the attributes of a supreme God did not catch the Middle Platonists sleeping. The Good has "an inconceivable beauty" and is "the cause of knowledge and truth," and yet surpasses them in beauty, just as the sun itself is incomparably superior to light and vision (508E-509A):

---

[11]For the soul's relationship in Plato to the Ideas and God see É. des Places, *La religion grecque* (Paris 1969) 250-259, esp. 251-253, and *Syngeneia. La parenté de l'homme avec Dieu. D'Homère à la patristique* (Paris 1964) 63-94.

[12]250B: δι' ἀμυδρῶν ὀργάνων.

. . . the objects of knowledge not only receive from the presence of the Good their being known, but even their existence (*to einai*) and being (*ousia*); for the Good is not being, but is above being in seniority (*presbeia*) and power (509B).[13]

The passage also suggests a difference between the Good in Itself (above being and beyond our reach) and the intellectual vision of the Good-like, closer to ourselves—something like the distinction between God and His radiance.

Having brought us along so far, though, Plato suddenly turns our apparent destination into a cyclic *cul de sac*. In the popular myth of Er, souls descending to earth speak of "delights and visions indescribable in respect to their beauty" (*Politeia* 615A).[14] But with sleight of hand he introduces these not as the expected ultimate *telos*. Rather, in this alternating current eschatology, souls are gloriously rewarded above or miserably punished below for periods of 1000 years, constantly returning in new bodies to the earth (614D-615A).

Disturbing is the absence of the final vision of the soul in what most scholars consider a later dialogue, the *Timaios*. A virtuous soul returns to its home star (42B). Whether forever or temporarily is unclear, but the dynamic of the work hints at the constant reanimation of the universe. The *Timaios*, as a cosmological treatise, was under no compulsion to develop the moral and religious concerns of our destiny. Rather its problem was the animation of the universe through soul. Still, one detects a new eschatology in which souls simply drift, according to their relative merits, to higher or lower parts of our earth or the universe.[15]

One could perhaps reconcile the newer concept here with the more transcendent concept of a vision, such as in the *Phaidros*. But one suspects a much more immanentist, even profoundly immanentist, attitude toward the world. The world is:

a perceptible (*aisthetos*) god made in the image of the intelligible [Intelligible?] (*noetos*), most great and good and beautiful and perfect, even this one heaven, the only-one of its kind (*monogenes*) (92C).

---

[13]See J. Whittaker, "Ἐπέκεινα νοῦ καὶ οὐσίας," *Vigiliae Christianae* 23 (1969) 91-104. In the Cave simile of *Politeia* VII, the Sun as analogous to the Form of the Good receives enormous prominence, esp., 516B, 517B-C, but the Sun is not compared to God.

[14]Τὰς ... εὐπαθείας ... καὶ θέας ἀμηχάνους τὸ κάλλος.

[15]The fundamental study is that of T. J. Saunders, "Penology and Eschatology in Plato's *Timaeus* and *Laws* ," *Classical Quarterly* 23 (1973) 232-244, esp. 237-238.

We are far removed from Plato's middle dialogues, where the soul sits pining away in its dank prisons, the body and the world, waiting for its liberation. Ascent to the divine is now through knowledge and observance of the magnificent harmony and order of the universe, rather than through dim and murky recollection of Forms once contemplated in another life—abandoned, through the soul's pigritude or by sheer necessity, for the present miserable exile.[16] Plato expresses this in a striking new way which appealed to a Middle Platonist like Plutarch. Man's intellect (*nous*) is his *daimon* (perhaps conceived here as his guardian spirit) given to us by God (90A); we must tend the divine part, the *daimon* who dwells within us, for which the congenial motions are the intellections and revolutions of the universe (90C-D), and bring our own thoughts into harmony with the revolutions of the cosmos, thus "attaining finally to that goal of life proposed by the gods as the most good both for the present and time to come" (90D).

No wonder Middle Platonists turned to the *Timaios*. The *Demiourgos* (Craftsman, God) never is said to gaze upon the Form of the Good/Beautiful, but on the *paradeigmata*, blueprints or models for the universe, identified by Middle Platonists as God's own thoughts (28B-29B). Plato's "Maker and Father of this universe" gazes upon the "eternal" (28C-29A). If the "eternal" is transcendent Good and Beautiful—hinted at, since used to create a beautiful universe—then either God gazes upon Himself as in some way linked to the Form of the Beautiful, or on a Form separate from Himself. Support for an Intelligible Being somehow identified with the Form could also be drawn from 28C, where the "Father and Maker of this universe" is described in exalted language typical of the Form elsewhere. At 36E-37A Plato speaks of the *Demiourgos* as the "best of intelligible beings." His *Sophist* 248E-249D grants *nous*, as to "the perfectly existing being" (τὸ παντέλως ὄν, 248E).[17] But "negative theology" surfaces in *Parmenides* 142A-E—where the One, or Monad, presumably is above or beyond being.

---

[16]See, for example, K. Alt, "Diesseits und Jenseits in Platons Mythen von der Seele, I," *Hermes* 110 (1982) 278-299, "Diesseits und Jenseits in Platons Mythen von der Seele, II," *Hermes* 111 (1983) 15-33; esp. II, 27-33. She interprets the *Timaios* as not offering perpetual beatitude on the "home star" (28).

[17]É. des Places, *Platonismo e tradizione cristiana* (Milano 1976) 21-23, notes the paucity of divine attributes given the *Demiourgos*.

The task of the pious Middle Platonist was rendered even more treacherous by the sneaking suspicion that Plato did not believe in God, at least the traditional one. Certainly, the master was obscure. Was the *Demiourgos* the supreme God of popular religion and philosophy, or an allegorical symbol of the intelligent, self-creative and evolutionary process of the universe itself? Was Plato, in fact, a crypto-Einstein? And if "God" exists, is He the Good or Beautiful? Even Plutarch, in his monotheistic, anthropomorphic-leaning commentary on the *Timaios* shied clear of the latter identification.

The negative climate of eschatological Platonism in the mid-First Century B.C. is revealed in Cicero's *Somnium Scipionis* (*The Dream of Scipio*). In the eschatological myth which ends the *De Republica* (6), Cicero significantly describes no real vision other than the contemplation of the heavens. But his Stoicized God is somewhat like the *telos*. As the outermost sphere, the supreme one (*summus*) belongs to heaven (*unus est caelestis*), and His symbol is the sun (*mens mundi et temperatio*, 17), reserved in Plato for the Good. And Cicero leaves the impression that the cycle of reincarnation is broken, once the virtuous life has been successfully lived (16).[18]

The Alexandrian philosopher, Philo (Philon, c. 15 B.C.-50 A.D.) had to face contradictory texts in the Old Testament, denying and affirming the possibility of seeing God.[19] "*Lasciate ogne speranza, voi ch'intrate.*"[20] Is he hopelessly inconsistent, or does he admit knowledge of God's existence but not His essence?[21] Either approach

---

[18]For Cicero's sources see K. Büchner, *Somnium Scipionis. Quellen, Gestalt, Sinn* (Wiesbaden 1976) 70-72.

[19]D. T. Runia, "Themes in Philonic Theology" argues for a "contextual" approach to Philo, that is, understanding of Philo's subservience to the text in hand as an explanation of emphasis and contradictions (70).

[20]Dante, *Inferno* III.9.

[21]B. A. Pearson, "Philo and Gnosticism," in W. Haase and H. Temporini, eds., *Aufstieg und Niedergang der römischen Welt* II.21.1 (Berlin 1984) 295-342, esp. 302-309, sees more "Gnosis" than Gnosticism in Philo (309). See also J. Whittaker, "Ἐπέκεινα νοῦ καὶ οὐσίας," and "Ἄρρητος καὶ ἀκατονόμαστος," in *Platonismus und Christentum*, 303-306; D. Winston, *Philo of Alexandria. The Contemplative Life, The Giants, and Selections* (New York 1981) 21-30; P. L. Donini, *Le scuole, l'anima, l'impero: la filosofia antica da Antioco a Plotino* (Torino 1982), 101-102; A. Louth, *The Origins of the Christian Mystical Tradition. From Plato to Denys* (Oxford 1981) 19, 24, 26; and J. Ménard, *La gnose de Philon d'Alexandrie* (Paris 1987) 153-154. Studies like those of Louth and H. Chadwick, "Philo," in A. H. Armstrong, ed., *The Cambridge History of*

would seem to underestimate the fundamental problems Philo shared with other Middle Platonists.

We face three different types of texts: those apparently denying a vision of God in the next life, those apparently affirming it, and ones suggesting only direct contact with His thoughts (sometimes His ideas as the Forms), or the *logos* (or Logos, as though a kind of Second God). As an example of the Philonic twist on "They have eyes to see but see not," one can cite *On Flight and Finding* (165):

Ἀλλ' ὅμως ἴσχυσε μηδὲν περὶ τῆς τοῦ ὄντος ἐρευνᾶν οὐσίας·
"Τὰ γὰρ ὀπίσω μου" φησίν "ὄψει, τὸ δὲ πρόσωπον οὐ μὴ ἴδῃς"
(Exod. 33,23). ... τὴν δ' ἡγεμονικὴν οὐσίαν ὁ βουλόμενος
καταθεάσασθαι τῷ περιαυγεῖ τῶν ἀκτίνων πρὶν ἰδεῖν πηρὸς ἔσται.

But the prophet did not succeed in finding anything by search respecting the being of That Which Is (*to On*); for he is told "What is behind Me thou shalt see, but My face thou shalt by no means see." (*Exodos* 33.23) . . . but as for the Directive Being (*hegemonike ousia*) he who wishes to behold Him will be deprived of sight before he sees Him, through the splendor of the rays [of light around Him].[22]

Similar are *The Special Laws* 1.44—an imaginary response of God to Moses, denying an apprehension of Himself by any created thing, ending with the admonition to "Know Thyself." *Questions in Genesis* 4.1 suggests that we see the Form of the Good, but not God Himself: God is not only inaccessible and incomprehensible for man, but also to the purest parts of heaven; therefore, He caused a certain radiance to shine forth, called "form" to fill the soul with an incorporeal light, led by which, the intellect is borne "through the mediation of the form to the prototype."[23]

Some texts seem altogether to deny a vision.[24] Among these are *The Creation* (7-8), where God is the intellect of the universe, greater

---

Later Greek and Early Medieval Philosophy (Cambridge 1967) 135-157 (e.g. 148-149) frequently do not distinguish between vision here or hereafter.

[22] A slightly abbreviated form of the Loeb titles for Philo appears here; texts of the Lyon edition, R. Arnaldez, J. Pouilloux, and C. Mondésert, general editors, *Les oeuvres de Philon d'Alexandrie* (Paris 1961-1988).

[23] Dillon, "Knowledge of God in Origen" (221), notes that in later Platonism light was regarded as incorporeal.

[24] Other texts stating or implying impossibility of vision: *Change of Names* 10 (but neither is our own *nous* perceptible!), 12-14, and *Special Laws* 46—similar to *Change of*

than knowledge, and superior to the Form of the Good and Beautiful. In *Rewards and Punishments* (40) God grants to the virtuous only a vision of His existence, not His essence, since God can only be discerned by Himself, superior as He is to the Good, and the One (Monad). In *Questions in Exodos* 2.68, God is senior to the One and the Monad, and the Beginning (or Principle) (*arche*). *The Contemplative Life* 2 states that Being (*to On*), i.e. God, is better than the Good, purer than the One, more primordial than the Monad.

A few texts suggest contact only with the *logos* (*Logos*) of God. But in no place in Philo is it absolutely clear that the *logos* is a kind of mediator or second god, and not God's own thought or mind operating in the world. *Creation* (146) states that man is united by his intelligence to the divine *logos* (*Logos*?), "being an image or particle or a reflection of the Blessed Nature." *The Confusion of Tongues* (95-98) is similar: God's friends want to gaze on Being (*to On*); but if they should be unable, at least they can see "His image, the most holy *logos* (*Logos*?)," and after this, "His most perfect work, the visible universe (*kosmos aisthetos*). In *The Migration of Abraham* 28, Philo is describing the love of religious wisdom, but his words suggest something eschatological: our native land is not here but with "the holy *logos* (*Logos*?), "the land of wisdom (*sophia*)." *The Unchangeableness of God* 151 states that after death, the soul ascends to the celestial sphere where it "lives among divine natures," and is filled with the vision of "noble and incorruptible (things)"—without reference to God.[25]

On the other hand, a number of texts imply a vision of God, either through the obvious meaning of the words or by an inner dynamic leading from this world to the next. Nonetheless, Philo constantly leaves his reader baffled as to whether he is speaking about this world or the next, and about absolute, complete knowledge of God, or just an

---

Names 10 (even the "powers" [*dynameis*] are incomprehensible in their essence). On *Change of Names* see Runia, "Themes in Philonic Theology."

[25]For the distinctions Philo made between God and His *logos*--treated as a second god in some Middle Platonists--see D. T. Runia, *Philo of Alexandria and the* Timaeus *of Plato* (Kampen 1983) 375-376, 421-422. Reluctant to call Philo a Middle Platonist, he notes Philo's divergence from Middle Platonism on several fundamentals (414-422). In the case of Philo as for Paul, he would underscore that seeing God is an experience, not just an intellectual topic.

In *Cherubim* 49 God is the house or "space" (XWRA) of the Ideas. Philo seldom informs the reader whether the vision belongs to this life or the next, but if he really tries he can be helpful; cf. *Moses* 2.288 and *Giants* 61.

intellectual vision of Him.[26] For example we find in *Noah's Work as a Planter* (22):

> The strong yearning to behold Being (*to On*) with all clarity, gives them wings, not only to strive to reach the furthest *aither* but to pass the very bounds of the entire universe, and speed toward the Unbegotten.

The language is clearly suggestive of the ascent toward the vision of the Form(s) in Plato's *Phaidros* or *Symposion*, but the following words "called up to Him" leave no doubt that the "Unbegotten" is God. *Drunkenness* 152—almost a verbatim parallel—adds: ". . . . toward the vision, absolutely beautiful and worthy of song, of the Unbegotten, speeding."

One finds such visionary language not only in symbolic contexts, but even in more straightforward ones. The beginning of *The Change of Names* (7) clearly denies an apprehension or vision of God, while speaking of His rays, which illumine the mind (6); but the very same dialogue later appears to speak in the clearest possible way of the vision (82). Employing the image of the athlete's crown, frequent in Plato and later Platonists, he speaks of the most fitting wreath as the contemplation of "He Who Is" (*ho On*) and of a distinctly clear perception of God, "who alone is worthy of vision."[27] The presence of two apparently simultaneous but contradictory texts in the same work does not necessarily rule out chronological revision, but the seemingly flat contradiction is baffling. Even if the contradiction is somehow explainable through distinctions between God's thoughts—*logos*-Forms and Himself, not alluded to, one is baffled by the contrary spirit of the two texts. An interesting variant suggests an eschatological vision of God (*to On*), but linked with the simultaneous vision of His "chief powers, which exist immediately with Him," (namely) "the creative, which is called God, and the kingly, which is called Lord"

---

[26]Cf. Porphyry, *To Marcella*, 15-16 (284-285), ed., É. des Places, *Porphyre. Vie de Pythagore, Lettre à Marcella* (Paris 1982) 114-115 (=K. O'Brien Wicker, *Porphyry the Philosopher* To Marcella [Atlanta 1987] 60); and Sextus, 416-418: ed., H. Chadwick, *The Sentences of Sextus* (Cambridge 1959) 60. Both Porphyry and Sextos seem to be speaking of "seeing God" in this life. Philo seldom informs the reader whether the vision belongs to this life or the next, but if he really tries he can be helpful; cf. *Moses* 2.288 and *Giants* 61. Professor Runia notes that Philo in general is not interested in the eschatological perspective.

[27]Other texts implying a vision of God: *Cherubim* 86; *Noah* 18-21; *Flight* 58-59; *Abraham* 56-59; *Moses* 1.158.

(*Genesis* 4.2).[28] However, the assertion is not central to the passage. Another text belongs to the same milieu. In *Dreams* (1.164-165) God is the hierophant and mystagogue of "beauties invisible to the uninitiated;" and those "who have tasted divine loves" are exhorted to rise from their sleep, dispel the mist, and "hasten to the vision contemplated from all sides." Now is Philo's God a mystagogue to the vision of the Forms, like the gods of Plato, or is He somehow both guide and the vision itself?

A late text often treated as "negative theology," *The Embassy to Gaius* (4-5), actually presupposes a vision of God in the next life. Philo appears to be speaking of a metaphorical vision in this life, superior to the intuition or knowledge derived from the study of the universe, such as described in the *Timaios*.[29] "Israel" is "he that sees God." The comment leads to a description of the ascent in beauty—as in the *Symposion*—but ends in an expression of God's transcendence.[30] Virtuous souls see:

> τὸ πρῶτον ἀγαθὸν καὶ καλὸν καὶ εὔδαιμον καὶ μακάριον, εἰ <δὲ> δεῖ τἀληθὲς εἰπεῖν, τὸ κρεῖττον μὲν ἀγαθοῦ, κάλλιον δὲ καλοῦ, καὶ μακαριότητος μὲν μακαριώτερον, εὐδαιμονίας δὲ αὐτῆς εὐδαιμονέστερον, καὶ εἰ δή τι τῶν εἰρημένων τελειότερον.
> the uncreated and divine, . . . the first Good, Beautiful, Fortunate (*eudaimon*) and Blessed . . ., which is better than the Good, more beautiful than the Beautiful, more blessed than blessedness, more happy than happiness itself and than any other thing—should it exist—more perfect than the above (5).

Philo is not a "negative theologian" or "Gnostic" in these passages—as convincingly argued recently: with bravado, and apparently polemical brinkmanship he consigns the supreme entities of his predecessors to the rubbish bin; once a presupposition of negative theology is swept aside, many texts appear more positively to

---

[28]Following the Loeb translation of R. Marcus, *Philo. Supplement I* (London 1953) 271.

[29]For Philo and the *Timaios* see especially Runia, *Philo of Alexandria*, esp. 276-278, and T. H. Tobin, *The Creation of Man: Philo and the History of Interpretation* (Washington 1983) 54-55; 59, 74-77, 178. Some scholars consider the *Embassy to Gaius* a late text of Philo, but Professor Runia believes the chronological problems are very great and that possibly much of the Philonic corpus was written after 38 A.D.

[30]For the technical points in Philo's development of his treatises, and the problems in finding an overriding theme, see D. T. Runia, "Further Observations on the Structure of Philo's Allegorical Treatises," *Vigiliae Christianae* 41 (1987) 105-138 (126-129).

assert seeing God "face to face" in the next life."[31] But neither life nor Philo is all that simple. The ghost of *Questions in Genesis* 4.1 and other texts which overtly state the opposite still haunt us. But through his great *opus* a constant undercurrent flows: God is the model and source of all being and beauty, and the *telos* of the soul.[32] In the long run, however, a part of Philo remains intractable, sharing the ambiguity of his fellow Middle Platonists.

Philo has a fellow traveller here in Plutarch (Ploutarchos, c.40-c.120 A.D.).[33] Plutarch continually suggests that God is our *telos*, that He is identifiable with the Being of Plato (*to On*)—as well as with the Beautiful (*to Kalon*)—and our destiny consists in a vision of Him. But conservative in his Platonic formulations, like Philo, he suggests at times a cleft between knowledge of the Forms and a knowledge of God—just where we would expect him to identify the two.

At the end of *The E at Delphi* (391E-394C), for example, God is the *telos* of the intellect and the supreme being, whose image appears in the sun; now He is seen only as in a dream, but we must rise to contemplate "the vision revealed by Him, which in truth is He." God is never totally beyond our intellectual capacities in some distant realm above being. In the sublimely moving speech of Ammonios, which forms the climax of the dialogue, God's transcendence is the

---

[31]Discussed by J. Dillon, "The Transcendence of God in Philo: Some Possible Sources" *Center for Hermeneutical Studies* 16 (Berkeley 1975) 1-9, followed by the excellent response of G. E. Caspary, 9-18. Professor Runia would see Philo as a typical Middle Platonist in attempting to maintain both the *via negativa* and the *via eminentiae*, similar to the mentality of Alkinoos; see J. Mansfeld, "Compatible Alternatives," 110-112, who notes how Alkinoos, like other Middle Platonists, affirmed--in ways astounding to us--both the *via eminentiae* and the *via negationis* .

[32]On the *telos*, besides passages already cited, cf. *Creation* 144, *Cherubim* 86, *Noah as Planter* 93, *Flight* 63.

[33]See L. Rossetti, "I precursori del neoplatonismo e i neoplatonici," *Grande Antologia Filosofica. Aggiornamento bibliografico* 32 (Milano 1985) 243-260 (246-248); C. Froidefond, "Plutarque et la platonisme," *Aufstieg und Niedergang der römischen Welt* II.36.1 (1987) 184-233, esp. 188-189; F. E. Brenk, *In Mist Apparelled. Religious Themes in Plutarch's* Moralia *and* Lives (Leiden 1977) 28; and "An Imperial Heritage: The Religious Spirit of Plutarch of Chaironeia," in W. Haase and H. Temporini, eds., *Aufstieg und Niedergang der römischen Welt (ANRW)* (Berlin 1987), 248-349 (262-275) (Index, *ANRW* II.36.2 [1987] 1300-1322); J. Dillon, "Plutarch and Second Century Platonism," in A. H. Armstrong, ed., *Classical Mediterranean Spirituality. Egyptian, Greek, Roman* (London 1986) 214-229; and J. Whittaker, "Plutarch, Platonism and Christianity," in H. J. Blumenthal and R. A. Markus, eds., *Neoplatonism and Early Christian Thought* (London 1981) 50-63.

52	Frederick E. Brenk, S.J.

very fullness of being, even though the theme is God as (the) One.[34] Some formulations seem to represent Alexandrian Platonism as transmitted by Ammonios, and do not receive the same emphasis elsewhere in Plutarch's writings. But fundamental to his theology elsewhere is the conception of God as the plenitude of Being, even if One.[35] Moreover, Plutarch's striking use of the sun analogy as a symbol of God, rather than the Idea of the Good, appears, for example in *The Face in the Moon* (944E), in a sense in *The Delay of the Divinity to Punish* (566D), and in *Isis and Osiris* (371F-372A). Moreover, both Apollo and Osiris, who lend mythical or religious names to the supreme God in Plutarch, have strong links with the sun.[36] However, Plutarch—with the possible exception of 566D—never implies like Philo that the purified intellect after death is blinded somehow by rays shielding an inapproachable God.

Plutarch's God has in other ways assumed the function of the Platonic Form of the Good. Such is hinted at in *The Delay of the Divinity to Punish* (550D) while treating "assimilation to God" (ὁμοίωσις θεῷ). According to Plutarch's interpretation of Plato, God puts Himself before us as "a model of all good things in respect to human virtue;" we are to imitate God, through a likeness and sharing in the "idea (form) and excellence (virtue) possessed by the divine," to become settled in virtue, through copying and aspiring to the beauty that is His."[37] This moral imitation of God then spills over into cosmological aspects. A vision of God, however, is not mentioned,

---

[34]For the relation of the First God to the Second see J. Dillon, *The Middle Platonists. A Study of Platonism 80 B.C. to A.D. 220* (London 1977) 12-18, 24-29, and J. Mansfeld, "Compatible Alternatives: Middle Platonist Theology and the Xenophanes Reception," in Van den Broek, 92-117, esp. 101-102, 108."

[35]The fundamental study is that by J. Whittaker, "Ammonius on the Delphic E," *Classical Quarterly* 19 (1969) 185-192. See also J. Glucker, *Antiochus and the Late Academy* (Göttingen 1978) 257-280, esp. 270-275; P. L. Donini, "Plutarco, Ammonio e l'Academia," in F. E. Brenk and I. Gallo, eds., *Miscellanea plutarchea* (Ferrara 1986) 97-110; J. Dillon, "The Academy in the Middle Platonic Period," *Dionysius* 3 (1979) 63-77 (66-68).

[36]Cf. Alkinoos, *Didaskalikos* 10.5 [165.17-23].

[37]C. J. De Vogel, "Der sog. Mittelplatonismus, überwiegend eine Philosophie der Diesseitigkeit?," in H.-D. Blume and F. Mann, eds., *Platonismus und Christentum* (Münster 1983) 277-302 (284); and H. Dörrie, "Le platonisme de Plutarque," *Actes du VIIIe Congrès, Association G. Budé, 1968* (Paris 1969) 519-529, and "Die Stellung Plutarchs im Platonismus seiner Zeit," in R. B. Palmer and R. Hamerton-Kelly, eds., *Philomathes* (The Hague 1971) 36-56 (43, 46-47); Brenk, "Imperial Heritage," 258-259.

and, as in the *Timaios*, "imitation of God" consists in "copying the heavenly motions."

In the eschatological myth of this dialogue, Plutarch suggests the transference of Plato's sun analogy for the Form of the Good to God. The oracle and tripod of Apollo—elsewhere a name for the supreme God—is located at a very high part of the heaven, if not the highest, and the brilliance of the light emanating blinds the visionary, Thespesios (566D). If Thespesios had read Philo, he might have been prepared for the jolting experience. However, since Thespesios is neither dead nor holy, he should not have merited the vision, indicated elsewhere as the destiny of the virtuous. In another important text one wonders whether the *telos* of the soul is God or simply the Form of the Good. In *The Face in the Moon* (944E), the human intellect (*nous*) is separated from its soul (*psyche*), source of the emotions, through love of the "desirable, beautiful, divine, and blessed, which shines forth in the image of the sun, for which all nature in one way or another yearns."[38] Is this God—which seems most likely—or has Plutarch wheeled out the old Platonic Form?

Plutarch, who is more radical in his latest dialogues, was possibly inspired by the Isis cult.[39] His Platonic allegory of the love of Isis for Orisis—who is both supreme God and the Form of the Beautiful—contains, in fact, some of his most original and fruitful ideas.[40] The *telos* is already more than just the Form in Plutarch's *Erotikos*

---

[38] Τὸ ἐφετὸν καὶ καλὸν καὶ θεῖον καὶ μακάριον οὗ πᾶσα φύσις, ἄλλη δ' ἄλλως ὀρέγεται. H. Cherniss and W. C. Helmbold, *Plutarch's Moralia* XII (London 1967) 212, comment, 213. P. L. Donini, "Science and Metaphysics: Platonism, Aristotelianism and Stoicism in Plutarch's *On the Face in the Moon*," in J. M. Dillon and A. A. Long, eds., *The Question of "Eclecticism." Studies in Later Greek Philosophy* (Berkeley 1988) 126-146, notes that Plutarch's *telos* is a conflation of the Good of the *Politeia* with the First God of Middle Platonism.

[39] For the importance of Isis see É. des Places," Éléments de sotériologie," 244; and the earlier treatment "Les dernières années de Platon," *L'Antiquité Classique* 7 (1938) 169-200 (186-200).

On *Peri Isidos* consult the long introduction in C. Froidefond, *Plutarque. Oeuvres Morales V. 2. Isis et Osiris* (Paris 1988), in particular 80-92, 110-125, 173-176.

[40] S. M. Chiodi, "Tematica ierogamica nel *De Iside*," *Miscellanea plutarchea* 121-126; and "Demiurgia e ierogamia nel De Iside plutarcheo. Un'esegesi platonica del mito egiziano," *Studi e Materiali di Storia delle Religioni* 52 (1986) 33-51; F. E. Brenk, "An Imperial Heritage," 294-303; and "Plutarch's *Erotikos*: The Drag Down Pulled Up," in M. Marcovich, F. E. Brenk, J. P. Hershbell, P. A. Stadter, eds., *Plutarch. R. Flacelière in Memoriam. Illinois Classical Studies* 13.2 (1989) 457-472.

(*Amatorius*), where he speaks vaguely of inspiration from the Isis myth. The ultimate object of love's quest is not clearly a divine person, i.e. the supreme God; but the terminology and dynamic of the dialogue demand that the object of love be itself capable of returning love. The *telos* is, indeed, described as the old Form of the Beautiful (765D, 765F). But the key which unlocks love's mystery is not the Platonic dialogues but Egyptian myth—presumably the allegorical interpretation of Egyptian myth found in Plutarch's *On Isis and Osiris*. For all practical purposes, this interpretation identifies the Good with the supreme God, a vision of which is our *telos*.

Plutarch's *Isis and Osiris*, then, makes a great leap forward in not only identifying God with the Good, but in explicitly suggesting that God returns love. God is the "first, sovereign, intelligible" (*protos. . . kyrios. . .noetos*, or perhaps, *proton. . .kyrion. . .noeton*, 352A), and later "first lover and desirable and perfect and self-sufficient" (374D).[41] The terms *protos* and *kyrios*—"first" but also "lord" or "lordly"—are decidedly non-Platonic terminology for the Form. However, in *Politeia* 517C, the Form of the Good is *kyria*, while its image, the Sun is the *kyrios* of the other "gods in heaven" (cf. 508A); and in 509D, the Form of the Good "rules" (as king) over the *noeton* (intelligible) just as the Sun rules over the *horeton* (visible).[42] But Philo used both for

---

[41]*On Isis* 374D 1 codd.: ὁ γὰρ Πόρος οὐχ ἕτερός ἐστι τοῦ πρώτως ἐραστοῦ καὶ ἐφετοῦ καὶ τελείου καὶ αὐτάρκους. Professor Baltes--like Teubner, Loeb, and Froidefond, *Isis et Osiris* 229--prefers Markland's very logical conjecture, ἐρατοῦ ("*l'objet suprême de l'amour*), for ἐραστου' ("lover"). J. G. Griffiths, *Plutarch's De Iside et Osiride* (Swansea/Cambridge 1970), however, notes that ἐρατός is only attested in poetry, in contrast to very Platonic ἐραστής (513). Plutarch's language in the *On Isis* passage is totally philosophical. Moreover, in *Symposion* 203B-204A--which he is closely and explicitly following here, Eros is ἐραστής (203C), and follows his father (Poros [Resource], in Plutarch = Form of Good = Osiris) in constantly "scheming for all that is beautiful and good" (203D). J. Whittaker, "Proclus and the Middle Platonists," in J. Pépin and H. D. Saffrey, eds., *Proclus. Lecteur et interprète des Anciens* (Paris, 1987) 276-291, regards this formulation as an excellent example of subtle Middle Platonic modification of Plato; Froidefond, *Isis et Osiris*, 254.

[42] However, at *Symposion* 197C Plato speaks of Eros as first, best, and most beautiful (*protos, aristos, kallistos*); in *Laws* 4.175E.8, God "holds the beginning and end and middle of all things." Attikos, Fr. 3.9, uses "greatest and most beautiful" (*megistos, kallistos*) indirectly of God.

God, and the "First God" is both a striking and characteristic component of Alexandrian Middle Platonism.[43]

Once again, we worry about vainly running up against the impenetrable wall of the Form(s)—perhaps God's ideas—while He Himself remains hopelessly beyond our reach. Plutarch's love story, the "marriage made in heaven" ends on a strange note. Though Isis is "joined in love" directly with the first God, she joins Him "in the love of good and beautiful things that are with him" (374F-375A).[44] The Forms?. This seems to contradict 352A, where Osiris is obviously the *telos*. Has Plutarch unwittingly drawn us back again into the Platonic *Phaidros*?

A similar distance between God and the Forms appears later. At 382F-383A Osiris (God) is uncontaminated, pure, etc.; but in this life, souls, through philosophy, only get a dim conception (*noesis*) of Him, as in a dream. We would now expect: "but once set free, they migrate toward the invisible and unseen, impassible, and pure, and will see Him as He is." Instead we find:

ὅταν δ' ἀπολυθεῖσαι μεταστῶσιν εἰς τὸ ἀειδὲς καὶ ἀόρατον καὶ ἀπαθὲς καὶ ἁγνόν, οὗτος αὐταῖς ἡγεμών ἐστι καὶ βασιλεὺς ὁ θεὸς ἐξηρτημέναις ὡς ἂν ἀπ' αὐτοῦ καὶ θεωμέναις ἀπλήστως καὶ ποθούσαις τὸ μὴ φατὸν μηδὲ ῥητὸν ἀνθρώποις κάλλος.

but once set free, they migrate toward the invisible and unseen, the dispassionate and sacred; then this God becomes their leader and king, since they will depend upon Him for the insatiable contemplation of beauty ineffable and indescribable to men.[45]

Beauty seems to shift guises, becoming once again the Form, not the supreme God. Isis always associates with it, "from it filling everything here with the beautiful and good." One would expect Isis to gaze lovingly at her handsome husband, the First God. Instead the scene is like two enraptured lovers contemplating the setting sun (or, more mundanely, like spouses, long married, watching the "telly" together). Does Isis attain to the essence of Osiris-Form-God, or only to Form(s) which are His ideas—a kind of *logos*? Once again do the

---

[43] J. Whittaker, "Plutarch, Platonism and Christianity," 50-63, notes that Plutarch, in contrast to Noumenios, never speaks of a First and Second God, the First of which would be beyond human reach (51-54).

[44] Froidefond, 306-307.

[45] Froidefond, 319-320

Forms act like an impenetrable barrier against the direct vision of God?

Now for a postscript on two Platonists who clearly identified God with the supreme Form. They are Alkinoos—whose *Didaskalikos* attributed to Albinos (of Syrmna, Second Century A.D.), has lately been returned to him—and Attikos (c. 150-200 A.D.).[46] Nor are they without surprises.

Alkinoos does not speak directly of a vision of God but seems to imply it. He slightly separates God—whom he calls the First Good (27.1 [179.37]), but also God, and First intellect, and most beautiful— from His thoughts, which are the Platonic Forms or Ideas.[47] As God contemplates Himself, He generates the Idea or Form of the Beautiful. This "intelligible" is beautiful because God is beautiful in the highest degree (10.3 [164.24-25]). All other things receive their beauty through participation in Him (27.2 [179.37-180.3]). Moreover, the Idea is for God, His intellection (*noesis*) (9.1), but for us, the "first intelligible" (*proton noeton*).[48] Alkinoos' language would seem, then, like that of Philo and Plutarch in certain passages, to retain a certain distance between God and the Form. The soul aiming at the First God, the First Good and ultimate Beautiful, seems to hit only the second best, the Form of the Beautiful. However, since the Form of the Good is God's intellection of Himself, in an intellectual vision of the Form of the

---

[46] Translation of Albinos, and commentary on G. Invernizzi, *Il Didaskalikos di Albino e il medioplatonismo* (Rome, 1976). J. Whittaker, whose Budé edition is about to appear, among others, attributes the *Didaskalikos* to Alkinoos; see "*Parisinus Graecus* 1962 and the Writings of Albinus," *Phoenix* 28 (1974), 320-354 (=*Studies in Platonism and Patristic Thought* [London, 1984] XX and XXI), 450-456; "Platonic Philosophy in the Early Centuries of the Empire," *ANRW* II.36.1 (1987), 81-123, esp. 83-87; previously, M. Giusta, Ἀλβίνου Ἐπιτομή ὁ Ἀλκινόου Διδασκαλικός?, "*Atti dell'Accademia delle Scienze di Torino* 95 (1960-1961), 167-194, and "Due capitoli sui dossografi di fisica," in G. Cambiano, ed., *Storiografia e dossografia nella filosofia antica* (Torino, 1986), 171-178; Donini, "La connaisance de Dieu," 118, no 1. Whittaker (98-102) is tempted to believe that Alkinoos may be the Alkinoos mentioned by Philostratos, *Lives of the Sophists* I. 24 (p. 40. 29 Kayser) and/or the Alkinoos referred to by Photios, *Bibliotheka* (cod. 48, p. 34 Henry). On Albinos see Dillon, *Middle Platonists*, 266.

[47] First numbering is that of F. Dübner's posthumous edition in Firmin-Didot, *Oeuvres de Platon* III (Paris, 1873), 225-258, retained by P. Louis, *Albinos. Epitomé* (Paris, 1945) and Invernizzi, and indicated in Whittaker's edition; second of C. F. Hermann, *Platonis Dialogi VI* (Leipzig, 1907).

[48] On these points see Mansfield, "Compatible Alternative," 114-115, although some of his conclusions were anticipated by Whittaker in "Ἄρρητος καὶ ἀκατονόμαστος·"

Good, we should have an intellection of God which is the same He has of Himself.

But in other places, the language is more direct. Alkinoos uses the Platonic process of abstraction from sensibles to arrive at the Form of the Beautiful—not for the Form, but for God Himself (10.3 [165.19]). Similarly, the sun is not the symbol or image of the Form of the Good, but of God. Rising from the experience of beauty in physical objects we ascend to a vision of the Good-in-Itself, to which is then joined a vision of God who excels through His merit" (10.4-6 [165.24-30]). Alkinoos makes this clearer toward the end of his discourse on God:

> . . . Plato in speaking of morality regarded the most esteemed and greatest Good difficult to find . . . but clearly made our good the knowledge and contemplation of the first Good, which can be called God and the First Intellect (*Nous*). (27.1 [179.36-37]).

He means contemplation in this life. By analogy, though, the *telos* of the soul, which is clearly God, should also be the contemplation or vision of God (=Beautiful not the Form of the Beautiful) in the next life. The point might be reinforced by his very strong concluding remarks on our *telos* as "assimilation to God as far as possible" (28.1-4 [181.16-182.11]). If God's principal activity is contemplating Himself (28.3 [181.36-37]), then our *telos* should be to contemplate God—something Alkinoos in general keeps unsaid, though it is implied elsewhere:

> . . . the soul contemplating the divine and the intellections of the divine can be designated as in excellent condition (*eupathein*). Such a condition (*pathema*) of the soul is called wisdom (*phronesis*)—in fact, one should think of assimilation to the divine as nothing else (2.2 [153.4-7]).

Moreover, there is a suggestion that assimilation to the Good is identical with assimilation to God (27.2 [180.6-7]).

Our vision or contemplation of God is not, however, that of the Second God, the *Demiourgos*, since the First God is the creator of the world (10.2 [164.18-20]).[49]

---

[49]P. L. Donini, "La connaisance de dieu et la hiérarchie divine chez Albinos," in Van den Broek, 118-131, offers a challenging reinterpretation of Alkinoos. He argues that Alkinoos' thought is contradictory and inconsistent, but through studying "God's" causality in this world, we would only obtain knowledge of the Second God (*Demiourgos*) (123-127). For the First God as Demiourgos, see M. Baltes, "Zur Philosophie des Platonikers Attikos," *Platonismus und Christentum*, 38-57 (41).

Noumenios (Numenius) of Apameia, who was active in the second half of the Second Century A.D., places a clear gap between the First and Second Gods. In Noumenios the "First Intellect is unknown to men," that "what they believe to be the Intellect, is not the First, since the First is older and more divine" (Fr. 17). Only the *Demiourgos* is known to men (Fr. 26).[50] Presumably, though, Noumenios is speaking about knowledge in this life. Still the Second God is only an imitator of the First God, who is identified with the Form of the Good and the Good-in-Itself (Frs. 12, 16, 20). Moreover, the activity of the Second God, who participates in the good of the First Good (Fr. 20), after creating the cosmos, is contemplation (Fr. 16). This contemplation would seem to be of the First God=Good/Beautiful, since the "Idea" of the *Demiourgos* is the Good (Fr. 20). Thus, the activity of the *Demiourgos* would serve as a model for the human *telos*.[51]

Attikos, like Alkinoos, makes the *Demiourgos* the First God, in fact, "the very First God;" but he also calls him the "hightest principle" and the "greater, more perfect and elder" (Fr. 28.7-8; 37.4-5).[52] He is on the level of the *Paradeigma*, (the Model), but not identical with it, since He is older and its cause. This *Demiourgos*-First God is also identified with the Good (Frs. 12-13). In one passage Attikos makes the Ideas, or the *Paradeigma*, the thought(s) (*noemata*) of the *Demiourgos*-God (Fr. 9.35-45). However, he is criticized by Proklos (Proclus) for elsewhere giving the Ideas an independent existence outside the mind of God (Fr. 28).[53] Individual Ideas could not exist within the Idea (Form) of the Good as developed in the *Politeia*. Thus, once Attikos

---

[50]É. des Places, *Numénius. Fragments* (Paris 1973) 58; see also see H. J. Krämer, *Der Ursprung der Geistmetaphysik* (Amsterdam 1964) 101-105. Mansfeld, "La connaisance de Dieu," 114-116, cites Alkinoos 10.3 (164.30-31), where an indiscriminate listing of names and attributes of the First God results in apparent contradiction, though Alkinoos claims that the object of thought denoted by all is identical. M. Baltes, "Noumenios van Apamea und der Platonische Timaios," *Vigiliae Christianae* 29 (1975), 241-270 (258-264), notes that the First Nous (Intellect), which is on the level of the *Paradeigma* (Model), is identified with the Idea of the Good. See also J. Whittaker, "Philological Comments on the Neoplatonic Notion of Infinity," in R. Baine Harris, ed., *The Significance of Neoplatonism* (Norfolk, Virginia 1976) 155-172 (=*Studies* XVIII).

[51]According to des Places the *Demiourgos* contemplates the First *Nous*; see 57, note 4, with references to Hadot and Henry, and to *Chaldean Oracles*, Fr. 8.

[52]É. des Places, *Atticus. Fragments* (Paris 1977).

[53]According to des Places, Proklos, the source of the fragment, misunderstood Attikos (86, note 5).

equated God with the Idea of the Good, supposedly the Ideas could no longer exist in God, that is be His thoughts.

With Attikos we should have a better chance than in the previous philosophers of actually hitting our target, God, and not being sidetracked forever into the eternal contemplation of an independent Form of the Beautiful. But in the extant fragments Attikos never speaks of a vision of God. He claims that "on an understanding of these (Ideas, which are the thoughts of God [9.40]) depends human wisdom and knowledge, which produce the *telos* for men and the blessed life" (9.50-53). Previously he states that the doctrine of the intelligible and eternal being of the Forms is the summit of Plato's philosophy (9.17-19) and essential to Platonism (9.29-33). Nonetheless, in this context, Attikos does not explicitly subsitute God for the Form of the Good or for the Forms.[54]

For the martyr, Justin (Ioustinos, 100-165 A.D.), however, the matter was quite simple—well, almost. Inspired by the Platonic teaching on the intelligibles and Ideas, in a short time he felt he had become a sage, even expecting "immediately to gaze upon God; for this is the *telos* of Platonic philosophy" (*Dialogue with Tryphon* 2 [52r-52v]).[55]

But perhaps we should end with Plotinos, more sublime, but whose illumination for us is not totally cloudless:

οὕτω τοι καὶ ψυχὴ ἀφώτιστος ἄθεος ἐκείνου· φωτισθεῖσα δὲ ἔχει, ὃ ἐζήτει, καὶ τοῦτο τὸ τέλος τἀληθινὸν ψυχῇ, ἐφάψασθαι φωτὸς ἐκείνου καὶ αὐτῷ αὐτὸ θεάσασθαι, οὐκ ἄλλου φωτί, ἀλλ' αὐτό, δι' οὗ καὶ ὁρᾷ. δι' οὗ γὰρ ἐφωτίσθη, τοῦτό ἐστιν, ὃ δεῖ θεάσασθαι· οὐδὲ γὰρ ἥλιον διὰ φωτὸς ἄλλου. πῶς ἂν οὖν τοῦτο γένοιτο; ἄφελε πάντα.

Thus, the soul is without light, when not contemplating the One; and when it is illuminated, it possesses what it searches. This is the veritable *telos* of the soul, to lay hold of that light— to behold it through itself, not through another light, but by itself, through which one sees. For one should behold the

---

[54]See M. Baltes, "Zur Philosophie des Platonikers Attikos," in *Platonismus und Christentum* 38-57 (41-43), and C. Moreschini, "Attico: una figura singolare del medioplatonismo," *ANRW* II.36.1 (1987) 477-491 (487-489).

[55]Text and commentary in J. C. M. van Winden, *An Early Christian Philosopher, Justin Martyrs's Dialogue with Trypho. Chapters One to Nine* (Leiden 1971) 9, 50-51. C. J. De Vogel, "Der sog. Mittelplatonismus," 289, warns against making the Platonic divine too personal.

source of the illumination. Not the sun through another light. How, then, might this happen? Abandon all (else) (*Enneads* V. 3.17.33-38).[56]

In conclusion, none of the Middle Platonic philosophers treated here—if we exclude Justin, who was undoubtedly influenced by faith as much as by philosophy— explicitly and unambiguously spoke of a vision of God as the destiny or *telos* of the soul. On the other hand, a vision of the Good — or Form (Idea) of the Good — is equivalent to a vision of God in Alkinoos and apparently in Attikos. Each Middle Platonist might have particular problems and his own, often tortuous, mode of expression. But there are two principal causes for not explicitly speaking of a vision of God as the *telos*. One is the very real problem of the gap betwen the First and Second God. Another is the necessity of keeping distinct philosophical concepts such as God and the Good, which were originally separate. In the realm of sleep and dreams, the drowsy shade of Plato might overlook, through the subtleties of verbal distinctions, the change in sacrosanct realities — or more hopefully, through total absorption in the beloved Good.[57]

---

[56]P. Henry and H.-R. Schwyzer, *Plotini Opera* II (Oxford 1977) 233. The Neoplatonic period has been treated by A. H. Armstrong, "Gottesschau (Visio beatifica)," in T. Klauser et al, eds., *Reallexikon für Antike und Christentum* 12 (Stuttgart 1983) 1-19.

[57]Maximos of Tyre (125-185 A.D.), however, speakes of a vision of God, whom he would seem to equate with the Form of the Good (*Discourses* 11.11, H. Hobein, *Maximi Tyrii Philosophumena* [Leipzig 1910] 142.13-143.18). Kelsos (Celsus) in his "True Account" (178 A.D.) also seems to equate God with the Form of the Good, using the analogy of the sun and visible phenomenon (Fr. 7.45 -- R. Bader, *Der Ἀληθὴς Λόγος des Kelsos* [Stuttgart/Berlin, 1940] 188-189).

Thanks are due to Professors John Dillon of Trinity College, Dublin, Pierluigi Donini of the Università di Torino, and especially to John Whittaker of Memorial College, St. John's, Newfoundland, and Matthias Baltes of the University of Münster for reading drafts of this article and offering many helpful suggestions and corrections. Professor David Runia, of the Katoleike Universiteit, Nimegen, who kindly looked over the Philo section, spotted many errors and shared his insights on this difficult matter.

Catachresis and Negative Theology: Philo of Alexandria and Basilides

JOHN WHITTAKER

In a recent intriguing paper[1] David T. Runia has drawn attention to Philo of Alexandria's apparent theological exploitation of the grammatical/rhetorical term κατάχρησις as a designation not simply of the exaggerated metaphor or of loose or incorrect usage but more specifically of "the deliberate misuse of a word in order to represent a meaning *for which no correct word is available*"[2]—a technical signification ignored by Cicero[3] (and not unreasonably, as we shall see) but probably familiar to, although not necessarily approved by, Dionysius of Halicarnassus,[4] insisted upon by Quintilian, who is at

---

[1] "Naming and Knowing: Themes in Philonic Theology with special Reference to the *De mutatione nominum*" published in *Knowledge of God in the Graeco-Roman World*, ed. by R. van den Broek, T. Baarda, and J. Mansfeld (Leiden 1988) pp. 69-91. See in particular pp. 82-89.

[2] *Op. cit.* p. 84. On the origin and development of the Stoic theory of tropes, of which the narrow conception of κατάχρησις is an essential ingredient, see K. Barwick, *Probleme der stoischen Sprachlehre und Rhetorik* (Abhandlungen der Sächsischen Akademie der Wissenschaften zu Leipzig, Phil.-Hist. Kl. Bd. 49, Heft 3: Berlin 1957) pp. 88-97.

[3] Cf. Runia, *op. cit.* pp. 83f. For reasons which will become obvious in the course of this paper I share the reservation of J. Cousin, *Quintilien: Institution oratoire*, tome V (Paris 1978) p. 278, regarding the existence of a supposedly Aristotelian-Ciceronian conception of κατάχρησις posited by Barwick and argued for by Runia, *loc. cit.*

[4] À propos of *Odyssey* XVI. 1-16, Dionysius writes (*De comp. verbi* 3, p. 28 Usher) οὔτε γὰρ μεταφοραί τινες ἔνεισιν εὐγενεῖς οὔτε ὑπαλλαγαὶ οὔτε καταχρήσεις οὔτ' ἄλλη τροπικὴ διάλεκτος οὐδεμία, οὐδὲ δὴ γλῶτται πολλαί τινες οὐδὲ ξένα ἢ πεποιημένα ὀνόματα. Although this passage reads like a deliberate reference to the theory of tropes (for ὑπαλλαγή in place of μετωνυμία cf. Cicero, *Orator* 27. 93), Dionysius misses later in the same work a fine opportunity of employing the term κατάχρησις in the narrow sense (*De comp. verbi* 21, p. 166 Ush.): ἐγὼ μέντοι κυρίοις ὀνόμασιν οὐκ ἔχων αὐτὰς [sc. τὰς

pains to distinguish the technical application of the term from its common broader usage which he condemns (*Inst.* VIII. 6. 34-36; cf. *ibid.* VIII. 2. 5), taken for granted by Ps-Plutarch, *V. Homeri* II. 18, and expounded already by the grammarian Tryphon,[5] whose career fell a generation or more before that of Philo.

Not finding unequivocally convincing the seven supposed instances cited by Runia of Philo's theological exploitation of κατάχρησις in this narrower, more technical sense,[6] I shall, in explanation of my objections, consider in turn each of Runia's examples, beginning with *De sacr.* 101: ἐνίας δὲ ἀρετὰς ἡ φύσις οὕτως διακέκρικεν, ὡς μηδὲ ἐξ ἐπιτηδεύσεως εἰς κοινωνίαν αχθῆναι δύνασθαι· τὸ γοῦν σπείρειν καὶ γεννᾶν κατ' ἀρετὴν ἀνδρῶν ἴδιον, οὐκ ἂν εὕροι τοῦτό γε γυνή· καὶ μὴν ἀγαθὸν οὖσαν γυναικῶν εὐτοκίαν ἀνδρὸς οὐ δέχεται φύσις. ὥστε οὐδὲ τὸ "ὡς ἄνθρωπος" (cf. Deut. 1.31) ἐπὶ θεοῦ κυριολογεῖται, κατάχρησις δὲ ὀνομάτων ἐστὶ παρηγοροῦσα τὴν ἡμετέραν ἀσθένειαν. ἀφελεῖς οὖν, ὦ ψυχή, πᾶν γενητὸν θνητὸν μεταβλητὸν βέβηλον ἀπὸ ἐννοίας τῆς περὶ θεοῦ τοῦ ἀγενήτου καὶ ἀφθάρτου καὶ ἀτρέπτου καὶ ἁγίου καὶ μόνου μακαρίου.

Since the terms κυριολογεῖται and κατάχρησις are here explicitly opposed, and the use of the latter figure justified by Philo on the combined grounds of our own mental weakness and of the

---

γενικὰς τῆς συνθέσεως διαφορὰς] προσαγορεῦσαι ὡς ἀκατονομάστους μεταπορικοῖς ὀνόμασι καλῶ τὴν μὲν αὐστηράν, τὴν δὲ γλαφυράν [ἢ ἀνθηράν], τὴν δὲ τρίτην εὔκρατον. One notes with interest the appearance in this latter text of the term ἀκατονόμαστος, which (as Runia, *op. cit.* pp. 84 and 86, has emphasized) occurs in the grammarian Tryphon's definition of κατάχρησις in the narrow sense. See notes 5 and 24 below. See further Lampe, *A Patristic Greek Lexicon,* s.v.

[5]*De tropis* 2 (*Rhetores graeci* VIII. 731. 1 - 732. 9 Walz = III. 192. 20 - 193. 7 Spengel) Κατάχρησις ἐστὶ λέξις μετενηνεγμένη ἀπὸ τοῦ πρώτου κατονομασθέντος κυρίως τε καὶ ἐτύμως ἐφ' ἕτερον ἀκατονόμαστον, κατὰ τὸ οἰκεῖον· οἷον γόνυ καλάμου, καὶ ὀφθαλμὸς ἀμπέλου, ... διαφέρει δὲ μεταφορὰ καὶ κατάχρησις, ὅτι ἡ μὲν μεταφορὰ ἀπὸ κατονομαζομένου ἐπὶ κατονομαζόμενον λέγεται· ἡ δὲ κατάχρησις ἀπὸ κατονομαζομένου ἐπὶ ἀκατονόμαστον, ὅθεν καὶ κατάχρησις λέγεται. See also M. West, "Tryphon De tropis," *Classical Quarterly* N.S. 15 (1965) p. 238. For other similar definitions of κατάχρησις, both with and without mention of the term ἀκατονόμαστος, see J.A. Schuursma, *De poetica vocabulorum abusione apud Aeschylum* (Amsterdam 1932) pp. 3-11. See also J. Cousin, *Etudes sur Quintilien* II (Paris 1936; repr. Amsterdam 1967) pp. 95f. Of little value for the present study is the recent discussion of Catachresis in J.M. Soskice, *Metaphor and Religious Language* (Oxford 1985) pp. 61-64.

[6]*Op. cit.* p. 85, n. 80. It should be noted that Philo refers to κατάχρησις with some frequency also in other contexts. Runia, *op. cit.* p. 85, names a total of fourteen instances in the Philonic corpus, in many of which, as Runia readily admits, the terminology is used with patent looseness.

inapplicability to God of words pertaining to our mortal sphere, it is easy to suppose that Philo intends κατάχρησις to be understood in its narrower or "hard-line" (as Runia calls it)[7] sense. It is also the case that the apparent reminiscence of Deut. 1.31 (the only reminiscence of that verse of which I am aware in the Philonic corpus)[8] "ὡς ἄνθρωπος" which Philo seeks to explain is not an instance of metaphor, whether extreme or not, aimed at providing a name for something hitherto nameless. It is not a metaphor at all but that much less dangerous and daring figure of speech,[9] a simile (and it should be noted that the juxtaposition of ὡς and ἄνθρωπος is Philo's own adaptation of the Septuagint text in obvious conflict with Numbers 23.19 [οὐχ ὡς ἄνθρωπος ὁ θεός] to which Philo has specifically referred in De sacr. 94f. in introducing a critique of anthropomorphism). The grammarians would not, of course, have recognized a simile as an instance of κατάχρησις, whether in the broad or narrower sense. We must conclude that Philo did not have in mind but rather disregarded the narrow "hard-line" interpretation of this frequently loosely used term when at De sacr. 101 he framed his explanation of the anthropomorphism of, it appears, Deut. 1.31 and, by extension, of other Septuagint anthropomorphisms. In spite of the negative theology of the final sentence of De sacr. 101 which, through the medium of the verb ἀφελεῖς, on the one hand recalls Exodus 13.12 (which Philo has discussed in De sacr. 89ff.) and on the other prefigures similar formulations in Maximus of Tyre,[10] in Clement of Alexandria,[11] and in Plotinus,[12] Philo has not on this occasion

---

[7] Op. cit. p. 83.

[8] De sacr. 101 is the only reference listed in Biblia patristica - Supplément: Philon d'Alexandrie (Paris 1982) p. 82.

[9] On the comparative audacity of simile and metaphor, cf. Ps.-Longinus, De subl. XXXII. 3, and Demetrius, De eloc. 80.

[10] Diss. XI. 11, p. 143. 11-18 Hobein Ἐννόει γάρ μοι μήτε μέγεθος, μήτε χρῶμα, μήτε σχῆμα, μήτε ἄλλο τι ὕλης πάθος, ἀλλ᾽ ὥσπερ ἂν εἰ καὶ σῶμα καλὸν ἀπεκρύπτετο πρὸς τὴν θέαν ὑπὸ ἐσθήτων πολλῶν καὶ ποικίλων, ἀπέδυσεν αὐτὸ ἐραστής, ἵνα εἴδῃ σαφῶς· οὕτω καὶ νῦν ἀπόδυσον καὶ ἄφελε τῷ λόγῳ τὴν περιβολὴν ταύτην, καὶ τὴν ἀσχολίαν τῶν ὀφθαλμῶν, καὶ τὸ καταλειπόμενον ὄψει, αὐτὸ ἐκεῖνο οἷον ποθεῖς.

[11] Strom. V. 11. 71. 3 εἰ τοίνυν, ἀφελόντες πάντα ὅσα πρόσεστι τοῖς σώμασιν καὶ τοῖς λεγομένοις ἀσωμάτοις, ἐπιρρίψαιμεν ἑαυτοὺς εἰς τὸ μέγεθος τοῦ Χριστοῦ κἀκεῖθεν εἰς τὸ ἀχανὲς ἁγιότητι προίοιμεν, τῇ νοήσει τοῦ παντοκράτορος ἀμῇ γέ πῃ προσάγοιμεν <ἄν>, οὐχ ὃ ἔστιν, ὃ δὲ μή ἐστι γνωρίσαντες.

introduced the term κατάχρησις for the purpose of pressing language to its limits in the service of negative theology. His goal is the more restricted one of explaining in a manner satisfactory to himself and to others of similar philosophical aspiration the awkwardly unphilosophical anthropomorphisms of the Septuagint. What of the remaining six instances cited by Runia?

The context of Runia's second example is the following (*De post.* 167-168) τὸ δὲ πρὸς ἀλήθειαν ὂν οὐ δι' ὤτων μόνον, ἀλλὰ τοῖς διανοίας ὄμμασιν ἐκ τῶν κατὰ τὸν κόσμον δυνάμεων καὶ ἐκ τῆς συνεχοῦς καὶ ἀπαύστου τῶν ἀμυθήτων ἔργων φορᾶς κατανοεῖσθαί τε καὶ γνωρίζεσθαι συμβέβηκε. διόπερ ἐν ᾠδῇ μείζονι λέγεται ἐκ προσώπου τοῦ θεοῦ· "Ἴδετε ἴδετε, ὅτι ἐγώ εἰμι" (Deut. 32.39), τοῦ ὄντως ὄντος ἐναργείᾳ μᾶλλον [ἀντι]καταλαμβανομένου ἢ λόγων ἀποδείξει συνισταμένου. τὸ δ' ὁρατὸν εἶναι τὸ ὂν οὐ κυριολογεῖται, κατάχρησις δ' ἐστὶν ἐφ' ἑκάστην αὐτοῦ τῶν δυνάμεων ἀναφερομένου. καὶ γὰρ νῦν οὔ φησιν· ἴδετε ἐμέ - - ἀμήχανον γὰρ τὸν κατὰ τὸ εἶναι θεὸν ὑπὸ γενέσεως τὸ παράπαν κατανοηθῆναι - - ἀλλ' ὅτι ἐγώ εἰμι ἴδετε, τουτέστι τὴν ἐμὴν ὕπαρξιν θεάσασθε. ἀνθρώπου γὰρ ἐξαρκεῖ λογισμῷ μέχρι τοῦ καταμαθεῖν ὅτι ἔστι τε καὶ ὑπάρχει τὸ τῶν ὅλων αἴτιον προελθεῖν· περαιτέρω δὲ σπουδάζειν τρέπεσθαι, ὡς περὶ οὐσίας ἢ ποιότητος ζητεῖν, ὠγύγιός τις ἠλιθιότης.

Created being, Philo argues, cannot of course literally "see" God. But with the aid of the eyes of his understanding[13] man can nonetheless grasp the fact of God's existence by observing his powers in action within the world and the continuous never-ending motion of his ineffable works.[14] Such and no more is the force of the scriptural invitation ἴδετε ἴδετε ὅτι ἐγώ εἰμι. Although the fact of God's existence presents itself to our understanding with a clarity of evidence

---

[12]See J.H. Sleeman and G. Pollet, *Lexicon Plotinianum* (Leiden/Leuven 1980) col. 176f. s.v. ἀφαιρεῖν.

[13]For further Philonic instances of the formulation τὰ διανοίας ὄμματα *et sim.*, cf. *De deo* 6 and H. Leisegang, *Indices ad Philonis Alexandrini Opera*, Pars I (Berlin 1926) pp. 181f., s.v. διάνοια, 5. This and similar formulations are, of course, inspired ultimately by Plato, *Symp.* 219 A 2-4 (ἤ τοι τῆς διανοίας ὄψις ἄρχεται ὀξὺ βλέπειν ὅταν ἡ τῶν ὀμμάτων τῆς ἀκμῆς λήγειν ἐπιχειρῇ), *Rep.* 527 D 6 - E 3 and 533 D 2 (τὸ τῆς ψυχῆς ὄμμα), and are of common occurrence in later literature. For an impression of their prevalence see D. Wyrwa, *Die christliche Platonaneignung in den Stromateis des Clemens von Alexandrien* (Berlin 1983) p. 66, and G. Boter, *The Textual Tradition of Plato's Republic* (Leiden 1989) pp. 339 and 341f. See further note 39 below.

[14]That we cannot know *what God is* but only *that he is* is a favourite argument with Philo. See D. T. Runia, *Philo of Alexandria and the Timaeus of Plato* (Leiden 1986) pp. 436f.

superior to that of verbal demonstration, to say that true Being is visible (ὁρατόν) is a misuse (κατάχρησις) of a term which applies properly not to God but to the powers deriving from him. It is important to note that Philo is not suggesting that the expression ὁρατὸν εἶναι τὸ ὄν involves the deliberate misuse of a word in order to represent a meaning for which no correct word is available. On the contrary, as Philo goes on to point out, it is impossible that God who truly is be conceived at all by created beings. Thus, the formulation ὁρατὸν εἶναι τὸ ὄν can only be either mistaken or slipshod. In either case it is an instance of κατάχρησις in the broader sense. It follows that this term cannot in the context of *De post.* 167-168 carry the weighty theological implication that Runia wishes to impose upon it.

De mut. nom. 11-14, the third of the texts adduced by Runia as evidence of his thesis, is too long to quote in its entirety. Suffice it to say that in the opening pages of this treatise Philo has been concerned to show that a number of seeming scriptural contradictions in regard to the seeing and naming of God are more apparent than substantial. Abraham's vision of God in Genesis 17.1 (ὤφθη κύριος τῷ Ἀβραὰμ καὶ εἶπεν αὐτῷ·" Ἐγώ εἰμι ὁ θεός σου") is not to be taken literally, since man has no organ by which God might be seen. For this reason God said to Moses (Exodus 33.23) "You shall see what is behind me, but my face you shall not see," which Philo interprets thus (*De mut. nom.* 9) "...ὡς τῶν ὅσα μετὰ τὸ ὄν σωμάτων τε ὁμοῦ καὶ πραγμάτων εἰς κατάληψιν ἐρχομένων, εἰ καὶ μὴ πάντα καταλαμβάνεται, μόνου δ' ἐκείνου μὴ πεφυκότος ὁρᾶσθαι.[15] It follows, says Philo (*ibid.* 11), that God has no proper name. Contrary to what might be supposed, the designation ὁ ὤν in Exodus 3.14 is not a proper name,[16] it implies rather that it is God's nature not to be spoken of but simply to be (*ibid.* οὐχ ὁρᾷς ὅτι φιλοπευστοῦντι τῷ προφήτῃ, τί τοῖς περὶ τοῦ ὀνόματος αὐτοῦ ζητοῦσιν ἀποκριτέον, φησὶν ὅτι "ἐγώ εἰμι ὁ ὤν," ἴσον τῷ εἶναι πέφυκα, οὐ λέγεσθαι).[17] This interpretation stands in apparent contradiction with

---

[15]For further Philonic instances of similar interpretation of Exodus 33.23 cf. Runia, *loc. cit.* (previous footnote).

[16]Cf. *De deo* 4. In *De Abrah.* 121, on the other hand, Philo asserts of the πατὴρ τῶν ὅλων that ἐν ταῖς ἱεραῖς γραφαῖς κυρίῳ ὀνόματι καλεῖται ὁ ὤν! For an attempt at reconciliation of these apparently conflicting statements see V. Nikiprowetzky, *Le commentaire de l'Ecriture chez Philon d'Alexandrie* (Leiden 1977) pp. 58-62.

[17]For this characteristically Philonic employment of ἴσον, cf. *De mut. nom.* 29 (see p. 66-67 below), *De sacr.* 12 and 112, and *De fuga* 124. J. Mansfeld, "An echo of Middle Platonist theology in Alexander *De fato* ch. 34," *Vigiliae Christianae* 43 (1989) pp. 86-91,

God's own words reported in the subsequent verse (Exodus 3.15), in which God declares his name to be Κύριος ὁ θεός. Philo seeks to remove the contradiction by arguing that this latter name is to be construed as an instance of κατάχρησις for the following reason (ibid. 13): καταχρήσεως γὰρ ὀνόματος θείου δεῖ τοῖς εἰς τὴν θνητὴν γένεσιν ἐλθοῦσιν, ἵν', εἰ καὶ μὴ πράγματι, ὀνόματι γοῦν προερχόμενοι ἀρίστῳ κατ' αὐτὸ κοσμῶνται. Philo's argument now stands in conflict with Exodus 6.3, in which God declares that τὸ ὄνομά μου κύριον οὐκ ἐδήλωσα αὐτοῖς. To deal with this irksome contradiction Philo resorts to a further literary figure, hyperbaton. God's words do not signify, as they would appear to, "My name of Lord I did not reveal to them." The words τὸ ὄνομά μου κύριον should instead be understood to imply, by hyperbaton, ὄνομά μου τὸ κύριον, i.e. "my proper name" (ibid. τοῦ γὰρ ὑπερβατοῦ μετατεθέντος ἑξῆς ἂν τοιοῦτος εἴη λόγος· "ὄνομά μου τὸ κύριον οὐκ ἐδήλωσα αὐτοῖς," ἀλλὰ τὸ ἐν καταχρήσει διὰ τὰς εἰρημένας αἰτίας). It is, apparently, beyond Philo's power of commentary to make Exodus 6.3 say (as he might have preferred) that God does not have a κύριον ὄνομα at all and for that reason can be addressed only by κατάχρησις. It is because God has chosen not to reveal his κύριον ὄνομα that he must be addressed by κατάχρησις. Since Philo specifically asserts that God does have a κύριον ὄνομα, it surely follows that the notion κατάχρησις in its narrower sense is not entirely applicable to De mut. nom. 11-14.

Runia's next example, De mut. nom. 27-28, provides further comment on Genesis 17.1 as follows: 'Αλλὰ γὰρ οὐδ' ἐκεῖνο προσῆκεν ἀγνοεῖν, ὅτι τὸ "ἐγώ εἰμι θεὸς σός" λέγεται καταχρηστικῶς, οὐ κυρίως. τὸ γὰρ ὄν, ᾗ ὄν ἐστιν, οὐχὶ τῶν πρός τι· αὐτὸ γὰρ ἑαυτοῦ πλῆρες καὶ

---

has drawn attention to the same formulation in similar circumstances in Alexander of Aphrodisias, De fato 34, p. 206. 30 - 207. 2 Bruns = p. 67. 9-12 Thillet (τὸ δὲ κατορθοῦν ἐπὶ τῶν θεῶν οὐ κυρίως ἂν λέγοιτο, ἀλλ' ὡς ἴσον τῷ τὰ ἀγαθὰ ποιεῖν, εἴ γε ἐν οἷς μὲν τὸ κατορθοῦν, ἐν τούτοις καὶ τὸ ἁμαρτάνειν, ἀνεπίδεκτον δὲ ἁμαρτημάτων τὸ θεῖον). For the sentiment Mansfeld compares Clement of Alexandria, Strom. V. 12. 82. 1 (quoted on p. 81 below). For a similar expository application of ἴσος, cf. Alexander of Aphrodisias, In Metaph. p. 25. 18-21 Hayduck (à propos of Aristotle, Metaph. A 3, 983 b 32f.) δόξει δὲ ἐπὶ τῇ λέξει ἐν δευτέρῳ σχήματι δύο λαμβάνειν καταφατικὰς προτάσεις, τῷ μὴ εἰπεῖν τὸ τιμιώτατον πρεσβύτατον, ἀλλὰ τιμιώτατον τὸ πρεσβύτατον, ὃ ἴσον φαίνεται τῷ τὸ τιμιώτατον πρεσβύτατον. Cf. Diogenes Laertius VII. 117 = SVF III. 448 φασὶ δὲ καὶ ἀπαθῆ εἶναι τὸν σοφόν, διὰ τὸ ἀνέμπτωτον εἶναι. εἶναι δὲ καὶ ἄλλον ἀπαθῆ τὸν φαῦλον, ἐν ἴσῳ λεγόμενον τῷ σκληρῷ καὶ ἀτέγκτῳ. For ἐν ἴσῳ similarly used, cf. Philo, De gig. 45 τὸ δὲ 'ἐγὼ κύριος' (Levit. 18.6) ἀκουστέον οὐ μόνον ἐν ἴσῳ τῷ 'ἐγὼ τὸ τέλειον καὶ ἄφθαρτον καὶ πρὸς ἀλήθειαν ἀγαθόν,' ... ἀλλὰ καὶ ἀντὶ τοῦ 'ἐγὼ ὁ ἄρχων καὶ [ὁ] βασιλεὺς καὶ δεσπότης.'

αὐτὸ ἑαυτῷ ἱκανόν, καὶ πρὸ τῆς τοῦ κόσμου γενέσεως καὶ μετὰ τὴν γένεσιν τοῦ παντὸς ἐν ὁμοίῳ. ἄτρεπτον γὰρ καὶ ἀμετάβλητον, χρῇζον ἑτέρου τὸ παράπαν οὐδενός, ὥστε αὐτοῦ μὲν εἶναι τὰ πάντα, μηδενὸς δὲ κυρίως αὐτό.

Man is God's possession, Philo has already argued, a κτῆμα θεοῦ (*ibid*. 26 à propos of Deut. 33.1), but the relationship is not (as is, for example, that between father and son) convertible.[18] All things belong to God, but in the strict sense God belongs to none (*ibid*. 28). Consequently, Genesis 17.1 (ἐγώ εἰμι θεὸς σός) is an instance of linguistic licence (*ibid*. 27 λέγεται καταχρηστικῶς) and is therefore not to be understood literally. It means not what it seems to mean, but is rather the equivalent of "I am Maker and Demiurge" (*ibid*. 29 . . . τὸ "ἐγώ εἰμι θεὸς σός" ἴσον ἐστὶ τῷ ἐγώ εἰμι ποιητῆς καὶ δημιουργός). Here again Philo's invocation of κατάχρησις appears to address no other end than that of clarifying and justifying a scriptural claim which, if taken literally, Philo found open to philosophical objection. He does not suggest that the words ἐγώ εἰμι ὁ θεὸς σός involve the deliberate misuse of a word in order to represent a meaning for which no correct word is available.

Runia refers next to *De somn*. I. 229. The reference might well be extended to include at least the discussion *ibid*. I. 227-231 of Genesis 31.13 (ἐγώ εἰμι ὁ θεὸς ὁ ὀφθείς σοι ἐν τόπῳ θεοῦ), in which, according to Philo, the sacred text distinguishes between ὁ θεός with the definite article and θεοῦ without the article (*ibid*. I. 229) ὁ μὲν ἀληθείᾳ θεὸς εἷς ἐστιν, οἱ δ' ἐν καταχρήσει λεγόμενοι πλείους. διὸ καὶ ὁ ἱερὸς λόγος ἐν τῷ παρόντι τὸν μὲν ἀληθείᾳ διὰ τοῦ ἄρθρου μεμήνυκεν εἰπών· "ἐγώ εἰμι ὁ θεός," τὸν δ' ἐν καταχρήσει χωρὶς ἄρθρου φάσκων· "ὁ ὀφθείς σοι ἐν τόπῳ," οὐ τοῦ θεοῦ, ἀλλ' αὐτὸ μόνον "θεοῦ." Thus far, Philo's discussion of Genesis 31.13 contradicts rather than supports Runia's contention. Philo has argued not that God transcends normal language but instead that the term θεός refers *properly* (ἀληθείᾳ) to God and only *by extension* (ἐν καταχρήσει) to gods in the plural—as we might distinguish between "God" capitalized and "gods" with small initial letter. In fact, as Philo goes on to specify (*ibid*. I. 230), the term θεός without the article in Genesis 31.13 refers to God's πρεσβύτατος λόγος.[19] It should not, however, be concluded, warns Philo, that Scripture intends to cultivate a superstitious scrupulosity in the use of

---

[18]Cf. Runia, *op cit*. (note 1 above) pp. 79f.

[19]Cf. Philo's similar exposition of Genesis 18.2 in *De Abrah*. 121-124.

words: Scripture has one aim only, namely to express the facts (*ibid.* οὐ δεισιδαιμονῶν περὶ τὴν θέσιν τῶν ὀνομάτων, ἀλλ' ἕν τέλος προτεθειμένος, πραγματολογῆσαι). There follows what might be considered the closest approach in the Philonic corpus to the theological exploitation of κατάχρησις in the narrower sense: (*ibid.*) καὶ γὰρ ἐν ἑτέροις σκεψάμενος, εἰ ἔστι τι τοῦ ὄντος ὄνομα, σαφῶς ἔγνω ὅτι κύριον μὲν οὐδέν, ὃ δ' ἂν εἴπῃ τις, καταχρώμενος ἐρεῖ· λέγεσθαι γὰρ οὐ πέφυκεν, ἀλλὰ μόνον εἶναι τὸ ὄν. Philo has evidently in mind Exodus 3.14 and 6.3, as expounded by himself in *De mut. nom.* 11-15, to which text we have already given our attention.[20] Since God has himself declared his lack of name, any appellation by which one might choose to address him will, according to Philo, be applicable not strictly but only in virtue of linguistic licence. One might expect that Philo would now conclude (as he did in *De mut. nom.* 15) that God is not only unnameable but also beyond comprehension. Instead Philo launches into a lengthy defence of scriptural anthropomorphisms (*De somn.* I. 231-241). Once again we are left with a sensation of ambiguity. Can it be that Philo, having ignored in *De somn.* I. 229 the "hard-line" sense of κατάχρησις, siezes upon it in *De somn.* I. 230, but then fails to follow it up in the sequel? Although there is no reason to deny that Philo's schooling might have made him aware of κατάχρησις in the narrower sense, it is hard to avoid the conclusion that he has, in this instance also, failed to grasp adequately the theological potential to which Runia has drawn attention.

The case of *De Abrah.* 120, Runia's next example, is different to the extent that Philo is concerned to defend there not the wording of a scriptural passage but that of an allegorical interpretation thereof. The text in question is the account in Genesis 18 of the three Angelic Visitors entertained by Abraham. In *De Abrah.* 107-118 Philo has already dilated upon the literal interpretation of Genesis 18. In *De Abrah.* 119 he turns explicitly away from the literal interpretation and addresses himself to the symbolic (Τὰ μὲν οὖν τῆς ῥητῆς ἀποδόσεως ὧδὶ λελέχθω· τῆς δὲ δι' ὑπονοιῶν ἀρκτέον), since spoken words are symbols of things apprehended by the understanding alone (σύμβολα τὰ ἐν φωναῖς τῶν διανοίᾳ μόνῃ καταλαμβανομένων ἐστίν).[21] When the

---

[20]See pp. 65f. above.

[21]On Philo's allegorical method see J. Pépin, *La tradition de l'allégorie de Philon d'Alexandrie à Dante* (Paris 1987) pp. 7-40 - Chap. I: "La théorie de l'exégèse allégorique chez Philon d'Alexandrie," and J. Mansfeld, "Philosophy in the service of

soul is illuminated by God, as if at noontime—καθάπερ ἐν μεσημβρίᾳ (cf. Genesis 18.1)—and is filled with intelligible light, a single reality can appear to it as three entities, only one of which represents the real whilst the other two are no more than shadows projected by it. Similarly in the sensible world, Philo says, a single object may often cast two shadows.

At this point, anticipating the development which is to follow, Philo warns (*De Abrah.* 120) μὴ μέντοι νομισάτω τις ἐπὶ θεοῦ τὰς σκιὰς κυριολογεῖσθαι· κατάχρησις ὀνόματός ἐστι μόνον πρὸς ἐναργεστέραν ἔμφασιν τοῦ δηλουμένου πράγματος, ἐπεὶ τό γε ἀληθὲς οὐχ ὧδε ἔχει. In fact Philo is going to argue in the sequel (*ibid.* 121) that of the three Visitors the central figure is the Father of the Universe (ὃς ἐν ταῖς ἱεραῖς γραφαῖς κυρίῳ ὀνόματι καλεῖται ὁ ὤν!) whilst the figures to right and left are God's πρεσβύταται δυνάμεις, respectively the Creative and Ruling Powers. There is no suggestion that the term σκία in *De Abrah.* 119-120 reflects a truth beyond the power of words. On the contrary, Philo proceeds, with no lack of detail or precision, to elucidate its significance.

De deo 4, the final text introduced by Runia in support of his contention, can safely be left out of account, since, although it contains an undoubtedly important statement of Philo's negative theological position, there is no indication in the Armenian translation (our sole witness to this text) that he made use in it of the term κατάχρησις or any of its cognates. As it happens, Philo deals also in *De deo* 4 with the matter of Abraham's three Angelic Visitors in Genesis 18, and draws as to their identity the conclusion that we have already seen him reach in *De Abrah.* 121 and which reappears *Quaest. in Gen.* IV. 2.[22] Folker Siegert has recently given us a new German translation of the *De deo* together with a most useful attempt at retroversion into Greek and a learned commentary, to all of which I have nothing to add of relevance to our present discussion.[23]

We must conclude that there is no compelling evidence in the texts mentioned by Runia that Philo made a clear distinction between

---

Scripture: Philo's exegetical strategies" in *The Question of "Eclecticism"*, ed. by J.M. Dillon and A.A. Long (Berkeley and Los Angeles/London 1988) pp. 70-102.

[22]Cf. also *Leg. ad Gaium* 6.

[23] *Philon von Alexandrien: Über die Gottesbezeichnung "wohltätig verzehrendes Feuer" (De Deo). Rückübersetzung des Fragments aus dem Armenischen, deutsche Übersetzung und Kommentar* von F. Siegert (= Wissenschaftliche Untersuchungen zum Neuen Testament 46: Tübingen 1988).

the narrower "hard-line" employment of the term κατάχρησις and its wider, common usage.[24] It should be observed, moreover, that this conclusion accords well with what we may infer from surviving scholia and later commentaries regarding the use of the term in Hellenistic schools and literary/philosophical commentaries. In fact, the distinction of κυρίως· and καταχρηστικῶς λεγόμενα et sim. is a staple ingredient of the scholia with no attempt made to distinguish between the "hard-line", more technical application of the term and its wider non-technical usage. On this score one may study with profit the comments of, and examples cited by, W.G. Rutherford, whose conclusion it is that "The fact would seem to be that the ["hard-line"] definition is a textbook definition for a species of transfer in meaning,

---

[24]Runia goes on to suppose that Philo's interest in the theological potential of "hard-line" κατάχρησις had been sparked by what he considers an important coincidence. "May we not surmise," Runia argues (op. cit. p. 86), "that his [i.e., Philo's] remarkably associative mind was struck by the word ἀκατονόμαστος in his grammar book (we recall Tryphon's statement above [cf. note 5 above]) and that he observed that it was precisely the same term that Platonists were using in their attempts at negative theology." Runia's supposition would be more persuasive had there been any pre-Philonic evidence of negative theological exploitation of the term ἀκατονόμαστος by Platonists or others, and, more importantly, had Philo himself made frequent use of this term in his own negative theological pronouncements. In fact, G. Mayer, Index Philoneus (Berlin 1974) p. 12, registers only two instances of ἀκατονόμαστος in the Philonic corpus, namely De somn. I. 67 and Leg. ad Gaium 353, in neither of which does the term occur in conjunction with any mention of κατάχρησις. In the latter text the term is put in the mouth of the Emperor Gaius and means not so much "nameless" as "not to be named." To these two Philonic instances of ἀκατονόμαστος listed by Mayer must be added De deo 4, in which negative theological context it is likely that the term occurred, but once again with no mention of κατάχρησις; cf. Siegert's Greek retroversion in his op. cit. (note 23 above) pp. 25f. On the use of the term ἀκατονόμαστος in Philo and elsewhere (the earliest attestations are Epicurean), see my paper "ΑΡΡΗΤΟΣ ΚΑΙ ΑΚΑΤΟΝΟΜΑΣΤΟΣ" in Platonismus und Christentum: Festschrift für H. Dörrie, ed. by H.-D. Blume and F. Mann (Jahrbuch für Antike und Christentum, Ergänzungsbd. 10: Münster 1983) pp. 303-306 = Studies in Platonism and Patristic Thought (London 1984) XII. There is a splendid example of the term, but no mention of κατάχρησις, in a fragment of Eusebius of Emesa on Exodus 3.14 published by R. Devreesse, Les anciens commentateurs grecs de l'Octateuque et des Rois (Studi e Testi 201: Vatican City 1959) p. 88: Ἐπειδὴ οὐχ εὑρέθη τις λέξις σημαίνουσα τὸ ἀκατονόμαστον, Ἐιπέ, φησιν, ὁ ὤν. Τὸ γὰρ ὂν πράγματός ἐστι σημαντικόν, οὐχὶ ὄνομα δηλωτικὸν θεοῦ· ἀλλ' ὁ ὤν, ὁ δι' ἑαυτὸν ὤν, ὁ μὴ παρ' ἄλλου ἔχων τὸ εἶναι. Eusebius' interpretation is, of course, inspired ultimately by Philo's developments upon the same theme, for which see pp. 3-9 above. See further E. Starobinski-Safran, "Exode 3,14 dans l'oeuvre de Philon d'Alexandrie" in Dieu et l'être: Exégèses d'Exode 3,14 et de Coran 20, 11-24, ed. by P. Vignaux (Paris 1978) pp. 47-55, and the contributions of M. Harl, P. Nautin, G. Madec and E. zum Brunn in the same volume.

whereas custom sanctioned a more liberal interpertation of the term defined."[25] In other words, the "hard-line" definition of κατάχρησις was an artificial construct which neither reflected nor respected previously established scholarly usage of the term, and as a result exerted negligible influence upon subsequent practice. Both literary and, as we shall see, philosophical commentators continued to employ the term in its broader sense. It should be added that the attempt of grammarians to limit the meaning of the term appears to have been Stoic-inspired and a natural consequence of Stoic theorizing upon the origin and development of language.[26]

This being the case, it is not surprising that in a cursory review of Christian literature up to the time of Origen, Runia has found little indication outside Philo of the theological exploitation of κατάχρησις.[27] It would be interesting to discover to what result a thorough scrutiny of later Patristic literature might lead. I suspect that the haul would be both meagre and ambivalent.[28] In Middle and Neoplatonic pagan literature a general dearth of interest in the theological potential of the

---

[25]*Scholia Aristophanica* III (London 1905; repr. 1987) pp. 209-211.

[26]Cf. Barwick, *loc. cit.* (note 2 above). Many scholars have emphasized that the "hard-line" conception of κατάχρησις, which may be of utility to philosophers in explaining the development of language, breaks down when it is applied to literary analysis. The stock literary examples of κατάχρησις cited by the grammarians are not, in fact, instances of "hard-line" κατάχρησις at all. For this reason, J.A. Schuursma, *op. cit.* (note 5 above) pp. 9f., remarks: "Attamen facere non possum quin confitear eos grammaticos, qui dixerunt abusionem esse modo tum, cum proprium vocabulum deficiat (ut Graeci dicunt ἐπ' ἀκατονόμαστον), struthocamelorum calliditate praeditos mihi videri. Complura enim ex abusionis necessariae exemplis, quae dederunt, minime necessario orta sunt, neque pro eis vocabula desunt." Yet even the philosophers, as we shall see, do not respect the "hard-line" definition, in spite of its potential utility to them.

[27]Cf. Runia, *op. cit.* pp. 86-89.

[28]Runia *op. cit.* p. 86, n. 84, reports that "Prof. G.C. Stead informs me that the subject may be of relevance to the later Arian controversy." Although the Arian controversy was indeed much concerned with the use of language, metaphorical or otherwise, in regard to the relationship between Son and Father, I have not noticed in the disputants any unequivocal awareness of, or recourse to, the "hard-line" notion of κατάχρησις. For example, although in Eusebius, *Contra Marcell.* I. 1. 2-4, pp. 62. 32 - 63. 13 Klostermann-Hansen, a contrast is drawn between κυρίως and καταχρηστικῶς, it is difficult, against the background of general laxity in the use of such terminology, to assert with conviction that Eusebius had in mind precisely the "hard-line" conception. For a further fascinating Patristic utterance on the subject of κατάχρησις see Gregory of Nyssa, *Ad Graecos* pp. 28.9 - 33.5, in particular p. 32. 5-12 Mueller.

term is indisputable.[29] There occurs nonetheless an impressive instance in Porphyry, *Hist. phil.*, fr. 15 Nauck, reported by Cyril of Alexandria, *Contra Jul.* I. 43, p. 190 Burguière-Évieux (*Sources chrétiennes* 322 = PG 76. 549 A-B) as follows:[30]

Πορφύριος δὲ φησιν ἐν βιβλίῳ τετάρτῳ "Φιλοσόφου ἱστορίας" δοξάσαι τε τὸν Πλάτωνα καὶ μὴν καὶ φράσαι πάλιν περὶ ἑνὸς θεοῦ, ὄνομα μὲν αὐτῷ μηδὲν ἐφαρμόττειν μηδὲ γνῶσιν ἀνθρωπίνην αὐτὸν καταλαβεῖν, τὰς δὲ λεγομένας προσηγορίας ἀπὸ τῶν ὑστέρων καταχρηστικῶς αὐτοῦ κατηγορεῖν. Εἰ δὲ ὅλως ἐκ τῶν παρ᾽ ἡμῖν ὀνομάτων χρή τι τολμῆσαι λέγειν περὶ αὐτοῦ, μᾶλλον τὴν τοῦ "ἑνὸς" προσηγορίαν καὶ τὴν "τἀγαθοῦ" τακτέον ἐπ᾽ αὐτοῦ. Κτλ.

It is tempting to suppose that when he wrote the text upon which Cyril has based this report Porphyry had in mind specifically the restrictive "hard-line" definition of κατάχρησις decreed by Stoic grammarians to the exclusion of the wider connotation sanctioned by common scholarly usage, in spite of the fact that Porphyry's references to κατάχρησις in his *Quaestiones Homericae* follow the practice of other literary commentators of ignoring the artificial limitation which

---

[29]Sleeman and Pollet, *op. cit.* (note 12 above) col. 547, register no instance of the terms κατάχρησις and καταχρηστικός in Plotinus, and one instance only, of no relevance to our enquiry, of the verb καταχρῆσθαι with reference to the misapplication of a word (*Enn.* I. 4. 6. 19-21 Henry-Schwyzer). In regard to Plato's formulation θεοῦ διάνοια at *Phaedrus* 247 D 1, Hermeias comments (*In Phdr.* p. 153. 1-3 Couvreur) εἰ δὲ τὸ τοῦ θεοῦ κυρίως ἀκούομεν, τὸ τῆς διανοίας δῆλον ὅτι καταχρηστικῶς ἀκουσόμεθα, ὥσπερ δὴ καὶ ἀλλαχοῦ [i.e., *Timaeus* 34 A 8, and *not*, as Couvreur wrongly indicates, *Tim.* 30 B] λογισμὸν εἶπε θεοῦ. As was Philo in regard to Scripture, so also is Hermeias concerned to justify by the invocation of κατάχρησις an apparently inconsistent formulation in the inspired text of the Master.   Whether the source (direct or indirect) be pagan Neoplatonic or Patristic, there is a splendid twelfth-century instance of the theological utilisation of κατάχρησις in Nicholas of Methone's *Refutation of Proclus' Elements of Theology* (*Corpus Philosophorum Medii Aevi - Philosophi Byzantini I* [Athens/Leiden 1984]) p. 39. 8-15 Angelou: εἰ δὲ καὶ ὁμοιότητας καὶ ἀνομοιότητας δοκοῦμεν προσάπτειν τῷ θεῷ διὰ τοῦ λέγειν ὅμοια τὰ τούτου καὶ ἀνόμοια καὶ τὸ ἴσον δέ πως καὶ τὸ ἄνισον ἐπ᾽ αὐτοῦ παραλαμβάνομεν, ἀλλ᾽ ἰστέον ὅτι καταχρηστικῶς ἐκ τῶν παρ᾽ ἡμῖν κειμένων λαμβάνομεν πάντα καὶ μεταφέρομεν ἐκεῖ τὰ ὀνόματα μὴ ἔχοντες οἰκεῖα λέγειν τοῦ ἀγνώστου καὶ ἀνωνύμου, ὅπου γε καὶ τὸ ἓν αὐτὸ καὶ τὰ τρία καὶ ἡ κατὰ ταῦτα ταυτότης καὶ ἑτερότης οὐχ ὡς οἰκεῖα πάντῃ παραλαμβάνονται ἀλλ᾽ ὡς ἁπλῶς οὐσίας δηλωτικά. The identification of Nicholas' source would be no mean supplement to our knowledge of the subject. See further the *Index verborum* in Angelou, *op. cit.* p. 191, s. vv. καταχρᾶσθαι and καταχρηστικῶς.

[30]The fragments of Porphyry's *Hist. phil.* have been translated and commented by A.-Ph. Segonds in an appendix to *Porphyre: Vie de Pythagore, Lettre à Marcella* ed. by E. des Places (Paris 1982) pp. 163-197. For fr. 15, see *ibid.* pp. 189f.

grammarians had unsuccessfully attempted to impose upon the accepted usage of the term.[31]

There is, moreover, one further passage of Porphyry in which, since the context is obviously influenced by linguistic theory, it is arguable that Porphyry has used the verb καταχρῆσθαι in the narrow technical sense. I refer to the opening exchanges of Porphyry's question-and-answer Commentary on the *Categories*, in particular the following (*In Cat.* p. 55. 10-14 Busse) . . . οἱ δὲ φιλόσοφοι τῶν τοῖς πολλοῖς ἀγνώστων πραγμάτων ἐξηγηταὶ ὄντες καινοτέρων δεηθέντες ὀνομάτων εἰς παράστασιν τῶν ὑπ' αὐτῶν ἐξευρεθέντων πραγμάτων ἢ αὐτοὶ ἐποίησαν λέξεις καινὰς καὶ ἀσυνήθεις ἢ ταῖς κειμέναις κατεχρήσαντο εἰς δήλωσιν τῶν ὑπ' αὐτῶν εὑρεθέντων πραγμάτων.[32] Since Porphyry speaks here of the transfer of familiar names to hitherto unknown and nameless πράγματα, there is a strong presumption that he has in mind or is at least influenced by the Stoic technical term for this linguistic practice.

However, before drawing any far-reaching conclusion on the basis of this latter text one should note that a few pages later Porphyry uses the same verb à propos not of κατάχρησις in the narrow sense but of metaphor (*In Cat.* p. 67. 4-6 B.) Φημὶ τοίνυν κατὰ μεταφοράν ἐστιν, ὅταν μέν τι πρᾶγμα ἔχῃ ἴδιον ὄνομα, ἄλλως δὲ καταχρήσηταί τις ἐπ' αὐτοῦ ἄλλῳ ὀνόματι μεταφέρων καὶ τούτῳ χρώμενος ὡς κειμένῳ ἐπ' αὐτοῦ.[33] One must take likewise into account that Porphyry's opening exchanges regarding Aristotle's choice of the term κατηγορία (*In Cat.* p. 55. 3 - 56. 13 B.) are parallelled by Dexippus who dilates at similar length upon the novel use to which the term κατηγορία was put by Aristotle (*In Cat.* p. 5. 30 - 6. 26 Busse). Yet although Aristotle's use of this familiar legal term to signify something hitherto nameless might well qualify as "hard-line" κατάχρησις, Dexippus employs in this context neither the term κατάχρησις nor any of its cognates. Instead he

---

[31]Cf. *Porphyrii Quaestionum Homericarum liber I*, ed. by A.R. Sodano (Naples 1970) p. 156, s.vv. καταχράομαι, κατάχρησις, καταχρηστικῶς.

[32]Cf. Cicero, *Acad.* I. VII. 25 (*Dialecticorum vero verba nulla sunt publica, suis utuntur; et id quidem commune omnium fere est artium, aut enim nova sunt rerum novarum facienda nomina aut ex aliis transferenda*). For similar Ciceronian expressions see *De orat.* III. 37. 149, *ibid.* III. 38. 154-156 and *De nat. deor.* I. 17. 44 with the commentary of A.S. Pease. For other examples of καταχρῆσθαι in Porphyry's, *In Cat.* see Busse's *Index verborum* p. 158, s.v.

[33]Porphyry's words are quoted *verbatim* by Simplicius, *In Cat.* p. 32. 22-24 Kalbfleisch, in the course of a long, more or less precise quotation from Porphyry.

74   John Whittaker

makes repeated use of the verb μεταφέρειν.³⁴ In particular, with
Porphyry's use of the verb καταχρῆσθαι at *In Cat*. p. 55. 10-14 B. (quoted
above) one may compare the following statement of Dexippus (*In Cat*.
p. 6. 10-13 B.) ἀνάγκη δὴ πᾶσα τοῖς φιλοσόφοις ἢ χρῆσθαι ξέναις λέξεσι
καὶ τῶν συνήθων ὀνομάτων ἀπηλλοτριωμέναις, ἐπειδὴ καὶ τῶν τοῖς
πολλοῖς ἀγνώστων πραγμάτων εἰσὶν ἐξηγηταί, ἢ τῇ προχείρῳ χρῆσθαι
συνηθείᾳ καὶ τὰ ἐπ' ἄλλων κείμενα ὀνόματα μεταφέρειν.

Moreover, Kalbfleisch lists in his *Index verborum* of Simplicius, *In
Cat*. five instances of the adverbial form καταχρηστικῶς and one of the
comparative adverb καταχρηστικώτερον, in none of which does the term
carry the "hard-line" connotation. In only two of these instances is
Simplicius ostensibly commenting in his own words, i.e., at *In Cat*. p.
151. 24-26 K. (λευκὸν γὰρ λευκῷ ἴσον οὐ κυρίως, ἀλλὰ καταχρηστικῶς
λέγεται, κυρίως δὲ ὅμοια τὰ λευκὰ καὶ πάντα τὰ κατὰ ποιότητα
ἀφωρισμένα [cf. Aristotle, *Cat*. 6, 6 a 26-35]), which coincides in its choice
of vocabulary with Porphyry, *In Cat*. p. 110. 31-32 B. (Ἐ. Ὅταν οὖν
λέγῃ τις ἐπὶ λευκοῦ, ὅτι τόδε τῷδε ἴσον, πῶς λέγει; Ἀ. Οὐ κυρίως ἀλλὰ
καταχρώμενος ἀντὶ τοῦ ὅμοιον) as well as with the comment of
Alexander of Aphrodisias which Simplicius goes on to quote (*In Cat*. p.
151. 35 - 152. 4 K.) ὁ μεντοὶ Ἀλέξανδρος ἀκολούθως τῷ Ἀριστοτέλει τὴν
ῥοπὴν οὐκ ἐν ποσῷ τιθέμενος, ἀλλ' ἐν τῷ ποιῷ, καὶ ἐπὶ τῶν βαρέων τὸ
ἴσον καὶ ἄνισον οὐ κυρίως λέγεσθαί φησιν, ἀλλὰ καταχρηστικῶς· τὸ γὰρ
ὅμοιον καὶ ἀνόμοιον καὶ ἐπὶ τούτων ἁρμόσει, ὥσπερ ἐπὶ τῶν ἄλλων
ποιῶν. Secondly, commenting upon Aristotle's formulation ἔχειν
ἀδυναμίαν at *Cat*. 8, 9 a 14-27, Simplicius writes (*In Cat*. p. 248. 13-15 K.)
ἀλλὰ εἰ αἱ ἀδυναμίαι στερήσεις, αἱ δὲ στερήσεις οὐκ ἔχονται, πῶς οὖν
ἔφη ἔχειν ἀδυναμίαν τοῦ πάσχειν; ἢ τὸ ἔχειν ἀδυναμίαν
καταχρηστικώτερον εἴρηται ἀντὶ τοῦ ἐστερῆσθαι δυνάμεως). Since
Simplicius' reservation regarding the appropriateness of the
formulation ἔχειν ἀδυναμίαν does not seem to have been shared by
Porphyry (cf. his *In Cat*. p. 129. 26 - 130. 4 B.), it is unlikely that
Simplicius took it from him, although he may well have found it
elsewhere in the tradition of commentary upon the *Categories*.

In the remaining four instances of the adverb καταχρηστικῶς listed
by Kalbfleisch, Simplicius claims to be quoting or retailing the

---

³⁴In his parallel exposition Simplicius, *In Cat*. p. 17. 28 - 18. 3 K. (... ἔστιν δὲ ὅτε [sc. οἱ
φιλόσοφοι] τοῖς ἐπ' ἄλλων κειμένοις [sc. ὀνόμασι] κατεχρήσαντο οἰκείως μεταφέροντες,
ὥσπερ νῦν τῷ τῆς κατηγορίας) employs both verbs. For the context see pp. 78f. below.
For μεταφέρειν à propos of "hard-line" κατάχρησις, cf. the definition of Tryphon, quoted
in note 5 above.

opinions of others. Thus, in his comment upon *Cat.* 2, 1 a 16-17 (τῶν λεγομένων τὰ μὲν κατὰ συμπλοκὴν λέγεται, τὰ δ' ἄνευ συμπλοκῆς) Simplicius contends that (*In Cat.* p. 41. 4-7 K.) εἰ δὲ καὶ οἱ παλαιοὶ κυρίως μὲν λεγόμενα τὰ διὰ λόγου σημαινόμενα ἔλεγον, καταχρηστικῶς δὲ καὶ τὰ δ' ἁπλῆς λέξεως, ὁ δὲ λόγος κατὰ συμπλοκὴν λέξεων προφέρεται, εἰκότως τὰ λεγόμενα διαιρῶν τῶν κυρίως λεγομένων πρῶτον ἐμνήσθη. Simplicius refers frequently in his *In Cat.* to οἱ παλαιοί. It is not obvious in the present instance whether he has in mind specifically the Stoics[35] and those who agreed with them or is using the designation οἱ παλαιοί in some other sense. In either case the entire context including the loose use of καταχρηστικῶς is likely to have been inherited by Simplicius through the tradition of commentary upon the *Categories*.

The second instance in which Simplicius uses the term καταχρηστικῶς in recounting the opinions of the others, in this case (*In Cat.* p. 151. 35 - 152. 4 K.) the opinion of Alexander of Aphrodisias on the subject of equality and inequality, we have already quoted.[36] Alexander, according to Simplicius, followed Aristotle in placing weight not in the category of quantity but in that of quality and so, says Simplicius, καὶ ἐπὶ τῶν βαρέων τὸ ἄνισον οὐ κυρίως λέγεσθαι φησιν [sc. ὁ Ἀλέξανδρος], ἀλλὰ καταχρηστικῶς. It is probable that Simplicius repeats here the phraseology of Alexander, and that the loose use of καταχρηστικῶς should be ascribed to the latter.

Similarly in the third instance, Simplicius appears to be quoting more or less *verbatim* a comment of Iamblichus à propos of *Cat.* 14, 15 b 1 as follows (*In Cat.* p. 433. 14-15 K.) ἡμερίαν δὲ ἀκουστέον, φησὶν Ἰάμβλιχος, τὴν τῆς κινήσεως στέρησιν, ἣν καταχρηστικῶς ἐναντίον ἐκάλεσε. The reference is clearly to κατάχρησις in the wider sense.

Lastly, at *In Cat.* p. 436. 3-12 K. = SVF II. 500, Simplicius, still commenting *Cat.* 14, 15 b 1, refers to distinctions of meaning maintained by Stoics in verbs implying rest or absence of motion. The final portion of this passage (*ibid.* p. 436. 7-12 K.) gives the impression of being, as Kalbfleisch supposed, a more or less direct quotation from a Stoic source. The pertinent section opens as follows: χρώμεθα δέ, φασι [sc. οἱ Στωικοί], καὶ ἐπὶ τοῦ μὴ κινεῖσθαι τῷ μένειν, ὥστε καταχρηστικῶς εἰπεῖν ἄν τινα καὶ ἐπὶ τῶν ἀσωμάτων τὸ μένειν ἀντὶ τοῦ

---

[35]Cf. Diogenes Laertius VII. 56 = SVF III. Diog. 20; Sextus Empiricus *Adv. math.* I. 132ff. For other pertinent Stoic-influenced texts see Barwick, *op. cit.* (note 2 above) pp. 12f.

[36]See p. 74 above.

μὴ κινεῖσθαι. Here once again the "hard-line" interpretation is excluded.

If nothing else, our above discussion of κατάχρησις as it occurs in commentaries upon the *Categories* has confirmed that the philosophical commentators were as indifferent as their literary counterparts to the technical niceties of κατάχρησις proposed, but hardly maintained, by grammarians. But before we abandon the topic there is a further lesson to be drawn from it.

Hippolytus (*Ref.* VII. 20. 2-4) gives us what purports to be a verbatim quotation of Basilides on the subject of the transcendent ineffability of the first principle, which, according to Basilides, is not merely ἄρρητον but rather οὐδὲ ἄρρητον, and so (as Ephesians 1.21 puts it) beyond every name that is named.[37] Hippolytus continues as follows (*ibid.* VII. 20. 4)[38] Οὐδὲ γὰρ τῷ κόσμῳ, φησίν [sc. ὁ Βασιλείδης], ἐξαρκεῖ τὰ ὀνόματα - οὕτως ἐστὶ πολυσχιδής -, ἀλλ' ἐπιλέλοιπε· καὶ οὐ δέχομαι, φησί, κατὰ πάντων <πραγμάτων> εὑρεῖν κυρίως [κύρια?] ὀνόματα. ἀλλὰ δεῖ τῇ διανοίᾳ, οὐ τοῖς ὀνόμασι, τῶν ὀνομαζομένων τὰς ἰδιότητας ἀρρήτως ἐκλαμβάνειν· ἡ γὰρ ὁμωνυμία ταραχὴν ἐμπεποίηκε καὶ πλάνην <περὶ> τῶν πραγμάτων τοῖς ἀκρωμένοις. So manifold is the world, says Basilides, that there are more things in it than there are names for. Nor does he himself undertake to discover correct designations for all things. Rather, he says, a person must seek in a wordless manner to grasp, not by means of names but with the aid of the mind,[39] the singularities of whatever is in question. As to

---

[37]Cf. my paper "Basilides on the ineffability of God," *Harvard Theological Review* 62 (1969) pp. 367-371 = *Studies in Platonism and Patristic Thought* (London 1984) X.

[38]Except for some (in my opinion unnecessary) additions, I have, here and elsewhere below, adopted the text established by M. Marcovich, *Hippolytus: Refutatio omnium haeresium* (Berlin 1986).

[39]With Basilides' formulation τῇ διανοίᾳ, οὐ τοῖς ὀνόμασι ... ἐκλαμβάνειν compare Philo, *De Abrah.* 119 [see p. 68f above] (σύμβολα τὰ ἐν φωναῖς τῶν διανοίᾳ μόνῃ καταλαμβανομένων ἐστίν) and *De post.* 167 [see p. 64 above] (τοῦ ὄντως ὄντος ἐναργείᾳ μᾶλλον [ἀντι]καταλαμβανομένου ἢ λόγων ἀποδείξει συνισταμένου). For διάνοια in this connection, cf. Clement of Alexandria, *Strom.* V. 12. 82. 1 [See p. 81 below] as well as Porphyry, *Ad Marcellam* 8, p. 110. 5-7 des Places [= *Pyth. Sent.* 74] (ὁ ἀχρώματος καὶ ἀσχημάτιστος, καὶ χερσὶ μὲν οὐδαμῶς ἐπάφητος, διανοίᾳ δὲ μόνῃ κρατητός) where διανοίᾳ replaces Plato's νῷ in Porphyry's free adaptation of *Phaedrus* 247 C 6-8, on which much-quoted Platonic text see p. 79 below and J. Dillon, "Tampering with the *Timaeus*: ideological emendations in Plato, with special reference to the *Timaeus*," *American Journal of Philology* 110 (1989 pp. 53f. See further note 13 above. For other useful references see A.S. Pease's note on Cicero, *De nat. deor.* I. 19. 49 (*non sensu sed mente*).

homonymy, he says, it has proved itself a source of confusion and error for those who give ear to it.

Hippolytus goes on immediately to accuse Basilides and his followers of having stolen this doctrine from Aristotle (*ibid.* VII. 20. 5) τοῦτο <οὖν> πρῶτον σφετέρισμα καὶ κλέμμα <ἀπὸ> τοῦ Περιπάτου λαβόντες ἀπατῶσι τὴν ἄγνοιαν τῶν συναγελαζομένων ἄμ᾽ αὐτοῖς. πολλαῖς γὰρ γενεαῖς ᾽Αριστοτέλης Βασιλείδου γεγενημένος πρότερος, τὸν περὶ τῶν ὁμωνύμων ἐν ταῖς Κατηγορίαις καταβέβληται λόγον.

It may well strike one that although in the opening chapter of the *Categories* Aristotle has distinguished things homonymous from both the synonymous and the paronymous, there is nothing in that chapter or elsewhere in the work (or indeed anywhere in the Aristotelian corpus) comparable to Basilides' assertion of the deficiency of names in the universe.[40] Where then, unless it be a child of Hippolytus' hostile and none too discerning brain, lies Basilides' σφετέρισμα καὶ κλέμμα? For the accusation raised here by Hippolytus against Basilides of theft from the *Categories* is scarcely justified by the latter's brief mention of the pitfalls of ὁμωνυμία, to which, in any case, Aristotle has made no reference in the *Categories*.[41] The answer seems to be that Hippolytus had in mind not so much the *Categories* themselves as the literature of commentary spawned by that treatise.[42] A constant feature of such commentaries was, as we have already had occasion to note,[43] the discussion of Aristotle's choice of the term κατηγορία. The question is discussed by Porphyry, *In Cat.* p. 55. 3 - 56. 13 B.; by Dexippus, *In Cat.* p. 5. 30 - 6. 26 B.; by Ammonius, *In Cat.* p. 13. 12-19 Busse; by Simplicius, *In Cat.* p. 15. 26 - 18. 6 K.; by Philoponus, *In Cat.* p. 12. 17-27 Busse; by Olympiodorus, *In Cat.* p. 22. 13-37 Busse; by Elias, *In Cat.* p. 127. 24-34

---

[40]The problem was not, of course, unfamiliar to Aristotle; cf., e.g., *De caelo* IV. 1, 307 b 31-33, and *De anima* II. 5, 417 b 29 - 418 a 3.

[41]The sole mention of homonymy in the *Categories* is that contained in the opening sentences (*Cat.* 1, 1 a 1-6) Ὁμώνυμα λέγεται ὧν ὄνομα μόνον κοινόν, ὁ δὲ κατὰ τοὔνομα λόγος τῆς οὐσίας ἕτερος, οἷον ζῷον ὅ τε ἄνθρωπος καὶ τὸ γεγραμμένον. Τούτων γὰρ ὄνομα μόνον κοινόν, ὁ δὲ κατὰ τοὔνομα λόγος τῆς οὐσίας ἕτερος· ἂν γάρ τις ἀποδιδῷ τί ἐστιν αὐτῶν ἑκατέρῳ τὸ ζῴῳ εἶναι, ἴδιον ἑκατέρου λόγον ἀποδώσει.

[42]Cf. the list of commentators provided by Simplicius, *In Cat.* p. 1. 3 - 2. 29 K., and P. Moraux, *Der Aristotelismus bei den Griechen von Andronikos bis Alexander von Aphrodisias*, I. *Die Renaissance des Aristotelismus in I. Jh. v. Chr.* (Berlin 1973) pp. 97-113.

[43]See p. 73 above.

Busse. It is likely, then, that the question was raised and answered along similar lines in other commentaries no longer extant.

Porphyry opens his explanation of Aristotle's choice by pointing out that since philosophers deal with objects which are unknown to the commonalty of mankind they need new-fangled names by which to designate their discoveries. To this end they may invent new and unfamiliar terms or re-use in a novel context (κατεχρήσαντο) already existent terms (In Cat. p. 55. 10-14 B.; quoted p. 73 above).

Dexippus, having informed us that many explanations of the term κατηγορία are to be found in the commentary (now lost) of Alexander of Aphrodisias and in that of Porphyry, remarks as follows (In Cat. p. 6. 6-10 B.) ἐγὼ δὲ τὰς μὲν πλείους [sc. ἀπαντήσεις] παρήσειν ἔοικα, τὴν δὲ φαινομένην εἶναί μοι βαθυτέραν ἐκθήσομαι· οὐ γὰρ συνεξισάζει τοῖς πράγμασι τὰ ὀνόματα οὐδὲ τὴν αὐτὴν ἔχει φύσιν καὶ τάξιν τὰ σημαίνοντα τοῖς σημαινομένοις, ἀλλὰ πάμπολυ τῶν πραγμάτων ἐλαττοῦται ἡ τῶν ὀνομάτων σημασία. The continuation of Dexippus' discussion (In Cat. p. 6. 10-13 B.) we have already had occasion to quote on p. 74 above. The same train of thought reappears, differently phrased, in Simplicius, In Cat. p. 17. 28 - 18. 3 K. as follows: εἰ δὲ ξενίζει τὸ ὄνομα [sc. Κατηγορίαι] παρὰ τὴν συνήθειαν κείμενον, οὐδὲν θαυμαστόν· ἐλλειπόντων γὰρ τῶν ὀνομάτων ὡς πρὸς τὰ πράγματα οἱ φιλόσοφοι οὐ μόνον γινώσκειν τὰ πράγματα βουλόμενοι τὰ τοῖς ἄλλοις ἀγνοούμενα, ἀλλὰ καὶ ἐκφαίνειν τοῖς βουλομένοις μαθεῖν, ποτὲ μὲν ὀνοματοποιεῖν ἀναγκάζονται, ὡς αὐτὸς Ἀριστοτέλης τὸ τῆς ἐντελεχείας ὄνομα ποιήσας, ἔστιν δὲ ὅτε τοῖς ἐπ' ἄλλων κειμένοις ἐπ' ἄλλων κατεχρήσαντο οἰκείως μεταφέροντες, ὥσπερ νῦν τῷ τῆς κατηγορίας. The "more profound" explanation which met with Dexippus' approval and which we find repeated by Simplicius is, the reader will observe, none other than the assertion of Basilides, reported by Hippolytus, that there are more things than names in the universe. Dexippus, as he himself indicates, found it in one or more of the commentaries on the Categories to which he had access, and we must suppose not only that Basilides is likely to have had it from the same or similar source but that Hippolytus recognized or had had brought to his attention that such was the case. This conclusion does not support but rather militates against the assumption that either Basilides or Hippolytus had a first-hand acquaintance with the text of the Categories.[44]

---

[44]On the question of Hippolytus' direct familiarity or lack thereof with the text of the Categories I disagree with Catherine Osborne, *Rethinking Early Greek Philosophy: Hippolytus of Rome and the Presocratics* (Cornell UP 1987) pp. 50-67, who on

Basilides has drawn his argument and Hippolytus his accusation of plagiarism not from the opening sentence of Aristotle's treatise but from a commentary thereon or other form of exposition in which Aristotle's choice of the term κατηγορία was discussed.

This conclusion is fortified by a further consideration. The commentators indicate, as we have seen,[45] that when a philosopher stands in need of a new designation there are two options open to him: (a) he may invent a new term, e.g. Aristotle's ἐντελέχεια, or (b) he may re-use an old term in a new context, e.g. Aristotle's κατηγορία. Basilides, according to Hippolytus, explicitly rejected the philosophers' search for new names. On what ground he rejected the use of neologisms we are not told. But Basilides does tell us that his refusal to re-use already existent terms is founded upon the dangers inherent in homonymy. Thus, Basilides embraced the assertion of the commentators on the *Categories* that the number of things in the universe exceeds the number of names, but spurned the remedies applied to this dilemma by Aristotle and approved by his commentators.

At the same time, it must be observed, Basilides' negative theology remains in unison with the intellectual context in which he lived and wrote, and in the light of which his opinions must be judged. His emphasis upon the limitations of language, his programmatic rejection of linguistic means and reliance instead upon the unaided mind are Middle-Platonic sentiments summed up by Alcinous in Platonic formulations, adapted from respectively the *Seventh Letter* 341 C 5 and the *Phaedrus* 247 C 7f., as follows (*Didask.* p. 165. 4f. Hermann) ἄρρητος δ' ἐστὶ καὶ νῷ μόνῳ ληπτός [sc. ὁ πρῶτος θεός]. Not surprisingly since Basilides has by implication rejected the procedure, neither the term κατάχρησις nor any of its cognates occurs in Hippolytus' account of his teaching. But in practice Basilides no more resigned himself than did any other exponent of negative theology to the contemplation of God *a bocca chiusa* but rather adopts in his own use of words a *modus operandi* or δεύτερος πλοῦς, the precise direction of which, although Basilides is at pains to recommend it to

---

inadequate grounds, it seems to me, has argued for Hippolytus' personal acquaintance with a number of Aristotelian treatises, including the *Categories*. For a more detailed rebuttal of Osborne's thesis, see J. Mansfeld's forthcoming study *The Policy of a Heresiologist: Hippolytus' "Elenchos" as a Source for Greek Philosophy*.

[45]Cf. Porphyry, *In Cat.* p. 55. 10-14 B. (quoted on p. 73 above), Dexippus, *In Cat.* p. 6. 10-13 B. (quoted on p. 74 above), Simplicius, *In Cat.* p. 17. 28 - 18.3 K. (quoted on p. 78 above).

his reader's attention, remains something less than crystalline. Hippolytus reports him verbatim on this topic as follows (*Ref.* VII. 20. 2) Ἦν, φησί [sc. ὁ Βασιλείδης], ποτὲ <ὅτε> ἦν οὐδέν· ἀλλ' οὐδὲ τὸ "οὐδὲν" ἦν τι τῶν ὄντων, ἀλλὰ ψιλῶς καὶ ἀνυπονοήτως δίχα παντὸς σοφίσματος ἦν ὅλως οὐδέν. ὅταν δὲ λέγω, φησί, τὸ "ἦν", οὐχ ὅτι ἦν λέγω, ἀλλ' ἵνα σημάνω τοῦτο ὅπερ βούλομαι δεῖξαι [λέγω, φησίν], ὅτι ἦν ὅλως οὐδέν. Cf. similarly *Ref.* VII. 21. 2: τὸ δὲ "ἠθέλησε" λέγω, φησί [sc. ὁ Βασιλείδης], σημασίας χάριν ἀθελήτως καὶ ἀνοήτως καὶ ἀναισθήτως. Basilides' recommended procedure (and it is not obvious from the continuation of Hippolytus' report that Basilides adhered to his own advice) is comparable to that proposed by Plotinus in the following suggestive passage, from which, once again, we may note the absence of any specific reference to κατάχρησις (*Enn.* V. 3. 13. 1-5 Henry-Schwyzer) Διὸ καὶ ἄρρητον τῇ ἀληθείᾳ· ὃ τι γὰρ ἂν εἴπῃς, τὶ ἐρεῖς. Ἀλλὰ τὸ "ἐπέκεινα πάντων καὶ ἐπέκεινα τοῦ σεμνοτάτου νοῦ" ἐν τοῖς πᾶσι μόνον ἀληθὲς οὐκ ὄνομα ὂν αὐτοῦ, ἀλλ' ὅτι οὔτε τι τῶν πάντων οὔτε ὄνομα αὐτοῦ [cf. Plato, *Parmenides* 142 A 3], ὅτι μηδὲν κατ' αὐτοῦ· ἀλλ' ὡς ἐνδέχεται, ἡμῖν αὐτοῖς σημαίνειν ἐπιχειροῦμεν περὶ αὐτοῦ. Although he does not reject as does Basilides the term ἄρρητον, Plotinus is at pains to emphasize that the formula τὸ "ἐπέκεινα πάντων καὶ ἐπέκεινα τοῦ σεμνοτάτου νοῦ"[46] is not to be taken as a proper name. He shares the concern of Basilides that qualifications of negative theological intent not assume the rank of positive title or proper name.[47] Yet, says Plotinus, even if we can in truth say nothing at all concerning that which is ἄρρητον, we do attempt, as best we can, to make signs to ourselves about it.

Plotinus follows here a line of thought that is reminiscent of Philo[48] and well attested in Middle-Platonic literature. Maximus of Tyre, for example, describes how in our inability to grasp the essence of God we seek to help ourselves out by means of words and sensible images of every kind (*Diss.* II. 10, p. 28. 8 - 29. 2 Hobein) Ὁ μὲν γὰρ θεός ... ἀνώνυμος νομοθέτῃ [ὀνοματοθέτῃ?], καὶ ἄρρητος φωνῇ, καὶ ἀόρατος ὀφθαλμοῖς· οὐχ ἔχοντες δὲ αὐτοῦ λαβεῖν τὴν οὐσίαν, ἐπερειδόμεθα [for which verb in this connection see Clement of Alexandria below] φωναῖς καὶ ὀνόμασιν καὶ ζῴοις καὶ τύποις χρυσοῦ καὶ ἐλέφαντος ...

---

[46]For similar formulations see my paper "ΕΠΕΚΕΙΝΑ ΝΟΥ ΚΑΙ ΟΥΣΙΑΣ," *Vigiliae Christianae* 23 (1969) pp. 91-104 = *Studies in Platonism and Patristic Thought* (London 1984) XIII.

[47]See my "Basilides on the ineffability of God" (note 37 above).

[48]See note 39 above.

ἐπιθυμοῦντες μὲν αὐτοῦ τῆς νοήσεως, ὑπὸ δὲ ἀσθενείας τὰ παρ' ἡμῶν καλὰ τῇ ἐκείνου φύσει ἐπονομάζοντες. Clement of Alexandria dwells similarly upon the cumulative effect of words, none of which is used with precision in reference to God, but which, when heaped together, help to give focus to our minds (*Strom.* V. 12. 82. 1) κἂν ὀνομάζομεν αὐτό ποτε, οὐ κυρίως καλοῦντες ἤτοι ἕν ἢ τἀγαθὸν ἢ νοῦν ἢ αὐτὸ τὸ ὂν ἢ πατέρα ἢ θεὸν ἢ δημιουργὸν ἢ κύριον,[49] οὐχ ὡς ὄνομα αὐτοῦ προφερόμενοι λέγομεν, ὑπὸ δὲ ἀπορίας ὀνόμασι καλοῖς προσχρώμεθα [N.B. not καταχρώμεθα!], ἵν' ἔχῃ ἡ διάνοια, μὴ περὶ ἄλλα πλανωμένη, ἐπερείδεσθαι τούτοις· οὐ γὰρ τὸ καθ' ἕκαστον μηνυτικὸν τοῦ θεοῦ, ἀλλὰ ἀθρόως ἅπαντα ἐνδεικτικὰ τῆς τοῦ παντοκράτορος δυνάμεως. Of the same implication is, no doubt, Alcinous' assertion (*Didask.* p. 164. 30f. H.) θειότης, οὐσιότης, ἀλήθεια, συμμετρία, ἀγαθόν [cf. Plato, *Philebus* 65 A 1-5]. Λέγω δὲ οὐχ ὡς χωρίζων ταῦτα, ἀλλ' ὡς κατὰ πάντα ἑνὸς νοουμένου.[50] One notes the absence from these post-Philonic statements of any mention, despite its undeniable negative theological potential, of the vocabulary of κατάχρησις.

We may conclude our discussion as follows. Although the "hard-line" concept of κατάχρησις could have served well the negative theological aims of Philo of Alexandria and of Middle Platonism generally, and have passed thence into the Neoplatonic and Patristic traditions, no such development took place. The reason why these opportunities were lost is not far to seek and was already apparent in our above discussion of Philo. The artificiality of the narrow definition of κατάχρησις was in such unambiguous conflict with common usage that it could not but fail to impose itself outside the school-rooms of the grammarians. And even in that setting the grammarians, as we have seen,[51] had difficulty in adapting their own

---

[49]On this and similar litanies, cf. Justin, *II Apol.* 6. 2f., with the commentary of A. Wartelle, *Saint Justin: Apologies*, Introduction, texte critique, traduction, commentaire et index (Paris 1987) p. 305.

[50]On the interpretation of these Middle Platonic texts see my "Neopythagoreanism and negative theology," *Symbolae Osloenses* 44 (1969) pp. 109-118 = *Studies in Platonism and Patristic Thought* (London 1984) IX; my "Philological comments on the Neoplatonic notion of infinity" in *The Significance of Neoplatonism*, ed. by R. Baine Harris (Albany, N.Y. 1976) pp. 155-172 = *Studies ...* XVIII; my "ΑΡΡΗΤΟΣ ΚΑΙ ΑΚΑΤΟΝΟΜΑΣΤΟΣ" (note 24 above) pp. 303-306; and the important discussion of J. Mansfeld, "Compatible alternatives: Middle Platonist theology and the Xenophanes reception" in *Knowledge of God in the Graeco-Roman World*, ed. by R. van den Broek, T. Baarda, and J. Mansfeld (Leiden 1988) pp. 92-117.

[51]See note 26 above.

practice to their theory. It must moreover be taken into account that the "hard-line" use of κατάχρησις attributed to Philo by Runia does not conform to the grammarians' definition either. For whereas the grammarians meant by κατάχρησις no more than the extension of an already existent name to something which for whatever reason did not previously have one, Runia would have us believe that Philo on occasion used the term to denote the extension of an existing name, not to something that somehow happened to lack one, but instead to something *essentially nameless*. The two procedures are by no means identical. In the former, as soon as the extension of meaning has taken place, that which was previously nameless ceases to be so, since the extended term now applies properly to it. But in the procedure posited by Runia, the essentially nameless would remain as nameless as ever. There is a further consideration. Although the step from the grammarians' concept of κατάχρησις to that posited by Runia might not be, under appropriate circumstances, difficult to achieve, it would still have been incumbent upon Philo, or whoever else one might hold responsible, to make it clear that the term κατάχρησις was itself now being used καταχρηστικῶς, i.e. that he was employing it neither in accordance with common usage, nor in the narrow artificial sense prescribed by grammarians, but in a new third sense. Thus, if Philo or any other exponent of negative theology had conceived the wish (and, for reasons already indicated in the course of this paper, it is in my opinion unnecessary to suppose that any did) of exploiting κατάχρησις in the manner proposed by Runia, he must soon have realized that such exploitation could be achieved only be redefining the term whenever it occurred with any other meaning than the commonly accepted. For if the new definition were not identified at every occurrence, the reader, or listener, would have no reason to suppose that κατάχρησις was intended otherwise than in the broad customary sense, within which capacious category there is, after all, room enough for the improper but potentially helpful terminology applied by theologians to the essentially nameless. In the event, adepts of negative theology were not prepared to make this effort of constant redefinition which, they must have realized, would inevitably banalize their pronouncements by reducing them to school-room level. The consequence was that the theological possibilities of "hard-line" κατάχρησις remained unrealized.[52]

---

[52]For useful suggestions I am much indebted to my colleagues Prof. W.J. Slater, McMaster University, and Prof. M.A. Joyal, Memorial University of Newfoundland.

Iconoclasmo bizantino e filosofia delle immagini divine nel neoplatonismo

UGO CRISCUOLO

La reciproca accusa di ellenismo ricorre frequente fra le due parti opposte nella documentazione superstite relativa alla controversia bizantina sulle immagini. Così, Costantino V nelle *Quaestiones* ritiene propria degli Elleni la εἰδωλατρεία,[1] laddove per Giorgio Monaco l'imperatore stesso fu certamente un Σαρακηνόπιστος, un 'Ιουδαιόφρων, non un Cristiano, ma un Pauliciano e, «per dire proprie il vero, fu un idolatra, un ministro dei demòni e un sacrificatore di uomini ... Nuovo Giuliano, egli venerava l'Afrodite onorata dagli Elleni e Dioniso»;[2] nella *Vita Nicephori* il basileus persecutore assimila senz'altro agli Elleni gli adoratori delle icone.[3] Fra i testi relativi alla sinodo del 754, ma citati dai padri ortodossi del concilio niceno del 787, gli iconoclasti, «imitando Saraceni, Ebrei, Elleni ... volevano che scomparisse il culto delle venerande immagini».[4] Se l'accusa di ellenismo è topica nelle controversie dogmatiche bizantine, prima e dopo l'iconoclasmo, essa assumeva in questa occasione una particolare rilevanza. L'iconoclasmo non fu infatti un fulmine a ciel sereno

---

[1] *PG* c 420a (= *fr.* 173, pp. 55 s. Hennephof [*Textus Byzantinos ad iconomachiam pertinentes*, ed. H. Hennephof, Leiden 1969]).

[2] *PG* CX 933ab (= *fr.* 34, p. 19 Henn.).

[3] *PG* c 101cd (= *fr.* 71, p. 33 Henn.) ὁ βασιλεύς· τί οὖν; τῶν ἑλληνικῶν οὐ κοινωνοῦσι δογμάτων οἱ τῶν ὁσίων, ὡς ἔφης, ἀνθρώπων δημιουργοῦντες εἰκόνας; ... τῶς χριστιανοὶ τὰς τοιαύτας δημιουργοῦσιν εἰκόνας; πῶς γράφουσιν.

[4] Cfr. J.D. Mansi, *Sacrorum conciliorum nova et amplissima collectio*, Florentiae 1759 ss., XIII 157de (= *fr.* 192, pp. 58 s. Henn.).

nell'universo bizantino, ma ebbe radici profonde e remotissime[5] non
solo nella tradizione apologetica e patristica, ma anche nell'antica
filosofia. È possibile che la tendenza aniconica del Cristianesimo
antico fosse in gran parte dovuta non solo alle proibizioni
veterotestamentarie, che ebbero spesso valore relativo per gli Ebrei
stessi, ma anche e particolarmente alla lotta contro le tradizioni
cultuali antiche, l'antropomorfismo della divinità proprio degli Elleni,
nell'àmbito dei quali gli ἀγάλματα, soprattutto nella prassi popolare,
avevano assunto un significato "demonico" via piú pericoloso agli
occhi dei Cristiani. Dal nostro punto di vista interesserà rilevare che è
fuori di dubbio che, soprattutto nel periodo del secondo iconoclasmo
(815-843), vi fu dall'una e dall'altra parte, ma soprattutto dalla parte
iconomaca, un ricorso alla filosofia degli antichi. La vivacità della
polemica ortodossa attorno a Giovanni il Grammatico, accomunato
nelle *damnationes* a Platone e ai filosofi e all'ex iconoclasta Leone il
Filosofo sembra allusione inequivocabile. Leone aveva avuto accenti
di ammirazione per Porfirio;[6] di Platone aveva egli compiuto
un'esegesi alle *Leggi*,[7] testo che già Clemente Alessandrino[8] aveva
utilizzato per affermare la sua tendenza aniconica e che appare anche a
noi fondamentale per l'individuazione del pensiero dell'antico
filosofo sul problema del culto religioso.

Se un uomo acculturato e *pius* della seconda metà del V secolo a.C.
poteva vedere nel simulacro di un dio solo un segno materiale che
ricorda la divinità, di cui non si vede il vero volto ma con cui si riesce
a parlare nell'íntimo della coscienza,[9] altra era la situazione quale si
profilava alla fine del mondo antico. Il "gentile" interrogato da
Agostino sul perché della sua idolatria risponde che non è l'idolo

---

[5]Cfr. H.-G. Beck, *Kirche und theologische Literatur im byzantinischen Reich*, München
1977 (rist.), p. 296.

[6]*Anth. Pal.* IX 214.

[7]Cfr., anche per la bibliografia, U. Criscuolo, "Iconoclasmo e letteratura" = *Atti del
Convegno "Il Concilio Niceno II° e il culto delle immagini,"* Messina 1987, Messina
1990.

[8]Cfr. Clem. Alex., *strom.* VII 5 al.

[9]E quanto si desume da Eur., *Hipp.* 82-86: Ippolito porta una corona di fiori al simulacro
di Artemide, a cui rivolge una fervida preghiera; egli dichiara di essere assieme alla dea
(σοὶ καὶ ξύνειμι) e di conversare con lei (λόγοις ἀμείβομαι), di ascoltare la sua voce, ma
di non vedere il suo vólto (ὄμμα δ'οὐχ ὁρῶν τὸ σόν). Sul passo cfr. A. J. Festugière, *La
révélation d'Hermès Trismégiste*, IV Paris 1954, p. 258: "la véritable Artemis est celle
qui vit dans sa pensée, dans son coeur."

visibile che è fatto oggetto di venerazione, "ma la potenza invisibile
che vi abita:" nel simulacro è possibile vedere "il segno della realtà"
che si adora.[10] Il salto di qualità subíto dai segni materiali della
divinità era stato preparato dal Neoplatonismo, che aveva teorizzato il
principio per cui tutto partecipa, in un *modus* o nell'altro, della natura
divina. E quanto chiariremo piú avanti. Per ora pare opportuno
notare che l'uomo *religiosus* della tarda antichità poteva disporre, per
l'ἄγαλμα, della presenza concreta del dio lontanissimo: non a caso gli
iconoclasti affermeranno, sulla linea della tradizione patristica, che di
una tale presenza il Cristiano non ha bisogno, avendo nell'uomo
l'immagine di Dio e nell'eucarestia la presenza reale del θεάνθρωπος
nella propria esperienza personale e nella storia.[11]

Le ricerche di Chr. Schönborn hanno individuato in Origene molti
degli aspetti a cui si sarebbero poi rifatti gli avversarî dell'iconodulia e
precisato come in buona parte da Origene dipendano gli argomenti che
Eusebio di Cesarea discute nella nota *Epistola a Costanza*.[12] E possibile
cosí confermare le note tesi di G. Florovsky[13] e avere motivi per
ritenere che "i consiglieri teologici di Leone III, il primo imperatore
iconoclastico, fossero pure degli origenisti con opinioni identiche a
quelle di Eusebio."[14] Ma sottolineare il ruolo di Origene significa
stabilire con certezza il *background* "ellenico" della *quaestio de
imaginibus*, poiché il culto delle immagini, quale si svilupperà
soprattutto a partire dall'età di Giustiniano, continuava, *mutatis
mutandis*, una delle forme della religiosità pagana tardoantica
predicata, sia pure con contraddizioni, dal Neoplatonismo di Plotino,
Porfirio, Giamblico, Giuliano imperatore e Proclo.

1. PLOTINO

Il Neoplatonismo, raccogliendo il messaggio di Platone e la
spiritualità dell'Ellenismo e aprendosi agli influssi piu varî

---

[10]Aug., *enarr. in ps. 113, serm.* 2, 3-4=PL XXXVII 1483.

[11]Cfr., p. es., alcune *quaestiones* di Costantino V: PG C 332d. 333b. 337a. 337c (=*ffr.*
164. 165. 167. 168 Henn.), in linea peraltro col pensiero di Clemente Alessandrino (cfr.,
p. es., *protr.* 10, 98; *strom.* VII 5 e *al.*) e Origene (cfr., p. es., *contr. Cels.* VII 17 s.).

[12]Cfr. Chr. Schönborn, *Die Christus—Ikone. Eine theologische Hinführung*,
Schaffhausen 1984, pp. 55-138.

[13]Cfr. G. Florovsky, "Origen, Eusebius and the Iconoclastic Controversy," in *Church
History* XIX (1950): soprattutto pp. 77-96.

[14]Cfr. J. Meyendorff, *La teologia bizantina* trad. it., Brescia 1984, p. 57.

nell'àmbito del sincretismo tardoantico, offriva all'uomo la piú forte e suggestiva alternativa al Cristianesimo. In un mondo che viene a mano a mano visto intieramente come "emanazione"[15] di Dio, in cui tutto procede da lui per *gradus* e tutto a lui ritorna, tutto è sua rivelazione, anche il problema della materia assume una nuova collocazione, e con esso il problema degli ἀγάλματα e delle εἰκόνες, segni materiali della divinità. Ma è solo con Proclo che, dopo l'evoluzione teurgica del pensiero e la definitiva trasformazione della filosofia in teologia, si perverrà ad una teorizzazione sistematica del nostro problema: in Plotino gli ἀγάλματα, le immagini, pur misteriosamente partecipi della vita dell'archetipo, hanno solo una funzione introduttiva alla conoscenza dell'Uno, che è la vera mèta del filosofare. Anzi il linguaggio ispirato e simbolico del filosofo non lascia mai trasparire se egli con ἀγάλματα intenda le statue di pietra o i segni di Dio nel creato come già Platone nelle *Leggi*[16] e nel *Timeo*.[17] In effetti a IV 3, 10, 17 ss. il filosofo sembra porsi direttamente sulle orme di Platone, riferendosi a *leg.* 889acd[18] col dire che la τέχνη è ὑστέρα rispetto alla φύσις e che di conseguenza la sua mimesi è indistinta, oscura (τέχνη γὰρ ὑστέρα αὐτῆς καὶ μιμεῖται ἀμυδρὰ καὶ ἀσθενῆ ποιοῦσα μιμήματα παίγνια ἄττα καὶ οὐ πολλοῦ ἄξια, μηχαναῖς πολλαῖς εἰς εἴδωλον φύσεως προσχρωμένη) e che per essa sono state elevate nel mondo (ibid. 27 ss.) "le statue degli dèi, le case degli uomini e ogni altra cosa." E piú avanti (IV 3, 11, 1 ss.) viene affermato però che "gli

---

[15]Con emanazione ci si riferisce generalmente al'processo'della realtà dall'Uno; cfr. A.H. Armstrong, "Emanation in Plotinus," in *Mind* XLVI (1937), pp. 61-66. H. Dörrie ha poi sostenuto che il termine applicato a Plotina è alquanto improprio e vale piuttosto per la sua metafora che come concetto filosofico; cfr. "Emanation. Ein unphilosophisches Wort im spätantikischen Denken"=*Platonica minora*, München 1976, pp. 70-85. Sul piano generale va tuttavia tenuto presente quanto opportunamente notava E.R. Dodds, in Proclus, *The Elements of Theology*, Oxford 1963,² pp. 213 s.: il concetto di emanazione può applicarsi al Neoplatonismo se si presupponga la teoria, già accennata in Plat., *Tim.* 42e e fatta forse propria dalla media Stoa, che la "causa" resta inalterata producendo l'effetto.

[16]Cfr. Plat., *Leg.* XI 930-931.

[17]Cfr. soprattutto *Tim.* 37c.

[18]Questo passo platonico è utilizzato anche da Clem. Alex., *strom.* VII 5. In Plotino, tuttavia, il concetto di arte appare alquanto modificato rispetto a Platone, soprattutto per l'influsso di Aristotele. Arte è anche "forma," forma che è insita nella mente dell'artefice-produttore e che si trasfonde nella materia sensibile e in modo tanto piú puro quanto piú la materia cede allazione "demiurgica" (cfr. V 8, 1, 32 ss.).

antichi saggi che vollero avere gli dèi presenti fra di loro e costruirono pertanto templi e statue, guardando alla natura del tutto, intuirono nel loro spirito che la natura dell'Anima si lascia facilmente attrarre dappertutto, ma che sarebbe stata la piú facile di tutte le cose trattenerla addirittura, qualora l'uomo avesse costruito qualcosa di affine e di impressionabile, che avesse potuto accogliere in sé una qualche parte di lui. Il prodotto dell'imitazione è cosí impressionabile, come specchio in grado di attrarre un aspetto (dell'imitato)." Plotino sembra intuire un principio che vedremo affermato poi nella teurgia; al contrario che in Platone, non resulterebbe piú possibile distinguere fra ἄψυχα ed ἔμψυχα ἀγάλματα, poiché tutto è ἔμψυχον e la mimesi dell'arte non è piú solo formale, ma attira anche nei suoi παίγνια pur sempre una qualche impronta dell'Anima. L'ἄγαλμα partecipa dunque del dio, non appare piú segno inerte atto a soddisfare un'esigenza volgare, ma è un passo sulla via della conoscenza di Lui. Cosí anche le εἰκόνες τῶν ὄντων e τὰ ὄντα appaiono non piú opposti, ma momenti distinti nella via della θεωρία (cfr. II 9, 6, 4 s. ὅταν οἷον εἰκόνας τῶν ὄντων, ἀλλὰ μὴ αὐτά πω τὰ ὄντα θεωρῇ) pur restando ammesso che gli ἀγάλματα ὄντα, e non i γεγραμμένα, dimorano nell'anima del filosofo (V 8, 5, 20 ss. οἷα ἐφαντάζετό τις ἐν τῇ σοφοῦ ἀνδρὸς ψυχῇ εἶναι, ἀγάλματα οὐ γεγραμμένα, ἀλλὰ ὄντα). La εἰκών, in quanto impronta dell'essere—è altrove affermato—resta anche in assenza dell'archetipo, cosí come quando il fuoco è stato allontanato, il calore che esso ha prodotto resta nell'oggetto riscaldato (VI 4, 10, 2 ss. ἔστι γὰρ καὶ εἰκόνα εἶναι ἀπόντος τοῦ ἀρχετύπου, ἀφ' οὗ ἡ εἰκών, καὶ τοῦ πυρὸς ἀπελθόντος τὴν θερμότητα εἶναι ἐν τῷ θερμανθέντι). Ma quando la nostra conoscenza si sublimerà nell'estasi, lo spirito avrà compiuto la sua "fuga da solo a solo," avrà lasciato tutto. Solo allora egli entrerà nel vero tempio dell'Uno: "Persino le cose belle, egli le ha ormai valicate; anzi, egli corre già al di sopra del bello stesso, al di là del coro delle virtú: somiglia a uno che, penetrato nell'interno dell'invalicabile penetrale, abbia lasciato alle spalle le statue rizzate nel tempio; quelle statue che, quando egli uscirà di nuovo dal penetrale, gli si faranno innanzi per prime, dopo l'íntima visione e dopo la comunione superna non con una statua, non con un'immagine, ma con Lui stesso: quelle statue che sono, per certo, visioni di second'ordine."[19] A quel punto l'uomo

---

[19]VI 9, 11, 16 ss. (trad. V. Cilento). Invero il misticismo plotiniano, nonostante la sua intensa religiosità, ha carattere "razionalistico," come ribadisce ora Margherita Isnardi Parente, *Introduzione a Plotino*, Roma-Bari 1984, p. 172 ("Plotino non cerca mediatori fra il divino e l'umano, né si affida a rivelzaioni extra-razionali o a forze

ha conosciuto la vita vera, che è solo riflessa nell'immagine, nelle cose sensibili: "Come infatti nell'immagine dell'uomo molto manca e soprattutto la cosa principale, la vita, cosí anche nelle cose sensibili l'essere è ombra dell'essere, privato di quello che soprattutto è l'essere, voglio dire ciò che era la vita nell'archetipo" (VI 2, 7, 11 ss.).

2. PORFIRIO

Nella *sent.* 33 Porfirio formula *scholastico more* il pensiero che si desume dalle ardite metafore del suo maestro: "Cosí dunque dirai: se l'essere sensibile è nello spazio e al di fuori de sé stesso perché è passato in una massa, l'essere intelligibile non è nello spazio ed è in sé stesso, perché non è passato in una massa: quindi se il primo è un'immagine e l'altro un archetipo, il primo deriva il suo essere dall'intelligibile, l'altro l'ha in sé stesso, perché ogni immagine fisica è immagine dell'intelletto" e passa poi a precisare che il rapporto del corporeo e dell'incorporeo "si manifesta in scambievoli partecipazioni di sostanze della stessa natura, in qualunque modo esso possa realizzarsi, ma trascende tutto ciò che cade sotto la percezione del senso" (trad. A.R. Sodano). Gli ἀγάλματα, le εἰκόνες, pare di poter dedurre, in quanto sensibili e nello spazio, poiché passati in una massa, partecipano dell'intelligibile da cui derivano, di cui sono appunto le immagini.

In Porfirio è tuttavia molto difficile cogliere un'opinione coerente sull'argomento di nostra ricerca, poiché egli comincia ad avvertire la suggestione della teurgia e del caldaismo,[20] che si accingevano a contaminare il misticismo "razionale" che era stato l'approdo plotiniano. Agostino osservava con acuto senso critico che il saggio di Tiro era come diviso fra la sua professione filosofica, che lo induceva a concepir l'elevazione a Dio come purificazione intellettuale e morale, e una "sacrilega" *curiositas* per la magia, per la γοητεία e la teurgia.[21] In effetti, i termini di codesta contraddizione emergono chiari dall'opera

---

irrazionali alternative"). Sotto questo aspetto è egli il vero continuatore e l'epigono di Platone e degli Stoici.

[20]Con Porfirio gli *Oracula* entrano ufficialmente nella tradizione del pensiero greco. Cfr., in proposito, l'introd. di É. des Places all'edizione degli *Oracula* (Paris 1971 [LBL], pp. 18 ss.).

[21]Cfr. Aug., *civ. dei* X 9=I 415 Domb.-Kalb. Sulla conoscenza di Porfirio, e del Neoplatonismo in genere, da parte di Agostino, cfr. W. Theiler, *Porphyrios und Augustin*, Halle 1933 e le precisazioni di H.I. Marrou, *S. Agostino e la fine della cultura antica* trad. it., Milano 1987, soprattutto pp. 45 ss.

porfiriana: si confrontino da una parte la *Lettera ad Anebo*, puntualmente critica verso le superstizioni del tempo, e la piú tarda *Lettera a Marcella*, il testamento spirituale costruito sul sapere piú vario, a modo quasi di gnomologia, e tutto teso nell'esaltazione del saggio e nella teorizzazione dell'ascesa a Dio per virtú e conoscenza, nell'íntimo della διάνοια, che è il vero tempio di Dio, e dall'altra parte il *De abstinentia*,con le ampie aperture teurgiche e "magiche", che Agostino opportunamente accusava.[22] Eppure, anche in questo opuscolo il filosofo conosce la "via maestra" per la purificazione, per il piú vero culto di Dio: a Lui non possiamo offrire niente che sia sensibile, né "con olocausto né con la parola," poiché non c'è niente di materiale che non sia súbito impuro per l'essere immateriale; nemmeno la parola che si esprime tramite la voce è a Dio appropriata, nemmeno il linguaggio interiore, allorché esso sia contaminato dalle passioni dell'anima; noi onoriamo Dio nel puro silenzio (διὰ δὲ σιγῆς καθαρᾶς), nei puri pensieri attorno a Lui (τῶν περὶ αὐτοῦ καθαρῶν ἐννοιῶν); il vero sacrificio si compie nell'impassibilità dell'anima (ἐν ἀπαθείᾳ . . . τῆς ψυχῆς) e nella contemplazione (*abst.* 34-35).

Nel III libro della *Praeparatio euangelica* Eusebio di Cesarea testimonia l'esistenza di un opuscolo di Porfirio *De cultu simulacrorum*, di cui tramanda alcuni frammenti.[23] È molto probabile che in questa opera il filosofo non seguisse un intento sistematico, ma che fosse mosso dalla *curiositas* accusata da Agostino, anche se non si può escludere che il suo atteggiamento resultasse alla fine oscillante fra teurgia e misticismo plotiniano. Il primo dei frammenti sembra esaminare la *quaestio* dell'origine del culto degli ἀγάλματα: secondo il filosofo esso sarebbe stato il prodotto di una σοφία θεόλογος, per la quale gli uomini hanno designato Dio e le potenze divine attraverso delle immagini "affini" (σύμφυλοι) ai sensi umani, "imitando

---

[22]P. Hadot (cfr. *Entretiens sur l'Antiquité classique*, XII Vandœuvres-Genève 1966, pp. 129 s.) osservava giustamente che la teologia di Porfirio è allo stesso tempo "une métaphysique au sens aristotélicien et une éoptique au sens platonicien" e che essa non si fonda solo sull'esegesi di Platone, ma anche su quella degli *Oracula*, ritenuti rivelazione divina. Tra gli opuscoli 'contraddittori' di Porfirio è anche il *De regressu animae*, che unisce mistica plotiniana e teologia caldaica (cosí J.H. Waszink, in *Entretiens*, cit., p. 45).

[23]Euseb. Caes., *praep.* III 7, 1, 2-4. 9, 1-5. 11, 1, 5, 7, 9-16, 22-44, 45. 13, 2 (ed. É. des Places, *SC* 228). Il titolo dell'opuscolo porfiriano, non dato da Eusebio, viene da Stob., *ecl.* I 1, 25=p. 31 Wach., che tramanda il primo dei frammenti come dal *De simulacris* (Πορφυρίου περὶ ἀγαλμάτων). L'insieme dei frammenti fu edito da J. Bidez, *Vie de Porphyre le philosophe néoplatonicien*, Gand-Leipzig 1913 (rist. anast. 1964).

l'invisibile con dei modelli visibili." Ma le statue—pare di capire-
sarebbero qualcosa di piú che la materia, se súbito dopo si afferma che
non c'è nulla di strano se "i piú ignoranti" ritengano le statue legno o
pietra, "allo stesso modo che quelli che non sanno affatto leggere
vedono solo delle pietre nelle stele, del legno nelle tavolette e nei libri
dei papiri intrecciati."[24] Ma piú avanti, commentando un lungo
frammento poetico orfico su Zeus, il filosofo osserva che il grande dio
è l'insieme del cosmo, il vivente fra i viventi e il dio fra gli dèi. Zeus,
di conseguenza, è l'intelletto, per cui egli produce tutte le cose e le crea
in virtú dei suoi pensieri. E poiché i teologi avevano interpretato in
questo modo la condizione divina, non sarebbe stato possibile creare
un'immagine quale la ragione aveva indicato e, anche se qualcuno lo
avesse immaginato, non avrebbe potuto mostrare quel che Dio ha di
divino, di intellettuale, di provvidente. Cosí "essi hanno
antropomorfizzato" la rappresentazione di Zeus, poiché era l'intelletto
secondo cui egli creava e per le "ragioni seminali" portava tutto a
compimento.[25] Pare indubitabile il tentativo del filosofo di spiegare
storicamente l'origine dell'antropomorfismo come una sorta di
volgarizzazione di verità teologiche. Il pensiero resta comunque nel
suo insieme di difficile interpretazione e forse aveva ragione J. Pépin[26]
ad ipotizzare che Porfirio sarebbe giunto alla legittimazione
dell'antropomorfismo delle rappresentazioni divine sulla base della
convinzione della connaturalità esistente fra la divinità e l'intelletto
umano. Eusebio infatti si preoccupa súbito dopo di chiarire che un
corpo umano non può avere nulla di simile all'intelletto divino, cosí
come l'intelletto umano è diverso da quello divino, che è incorporeo,
ἀσύνθετος e ἀμερής, laddove "l'opera artigianale" imita la natura del
corpo mortale e della carne vivente e per il mezzo di una materia
morta e inanimata traccia un'immagine che è "sorda e muta."[27] Ma,
ciò nonostante, resta legittimo pensare che Porfirio non si sia
allontanato in quest'opera da quello che appare il suo atteggiamento di

---

[24]*fr.* 1 Bid.(=Euseb. Caes., *praep.* III 7, 1=pp. 180-183 des Pl.).

[25]*fr.* 3 Bid. (=Euseb. Caes., *praep.* cit.,=pp. 187 ss. des Pl.). Il frammento orfico è il
168 Kern (cfr. anche Clem. Alex., *strom.* V 128, 3. 122, 2). Cfr. anche Festugière, *La
révélation.* cit., IV 287. Nel *fr.* 2 Bid. (=Euseb. Caes., *praep.* III 7, 2=pp. 182 s.)
Porfirio affermava che gli uomini fecero ricorso alla materia diafana (cristallo,
marmo di Paro, avorio) e preziosa (oro), poiché "il divino è luminoso, soggiorna in una
effusione di fuoco celeste e resta invisibile a dei sensi occupati dalla vita mortale."

[26]Cfr. J. Pépin, *Idées grecques sur l'homme et sur Dieu*, Paris 1971, pp. 16 s.

[27]Euseb. Caes., *praep.* III 10, 15=pp. 204 s. des Pl.

fondo, comportante una distinzione di qualità nella θρησκεία, pur indubbiamente riconoscendo la legittimità ad un culto per immagini fatte di materia, poiché anche la materia può in qualche misura partecipare dell'immateriale. Ciò appare confermato *explicite* dal frammento 77 Harnack del *Contra Christianos*, in cui si parla di "ingenuità" di alcuni Elleni che giungevano a credere che negli idoli vivessero gli dèi.[28] Ma sarà opportuno ritenere quanto affermato nella *Lettera a Marcella* come l'approdo ultimo del suo pensiero: il filosofo non ha affatto bisogno di statue e di templi, poiché è il suo spirito (διάνοια) il vero tempio di Dio; è nello spirito che il filosofo appresta un santuario e l'adorna di "una statua vivente," l'intelletto, dove Dio ha impresso la sua immagine; è empio non chi omette di circondare di circondare di culto e di cure le statue degli dèi, ma chi attribuisce a Dio come sue caratteristiche le opinioni del volgo.[29] E in questo messaggio che appare il vero discepolo di Plotino, il filosofo che aveva risposto ad Amelio, che insisteva perché partecipasse ai riti sacri, con le "oscure" parole: "Spetta agli dèi venire a me, non a me andare da loro."[30]

3. GIAMBLICO

Giamblico supera definitivamente la contraddizione porfiriana segnando la prevalenza della teurgia sulla filosofia. In un mondo in cui "il tutto è un vivente unico" e le sue parti "sono spazialmente distanti, ma per la loro natura unica tendono l'una verso l'altra,"[31] per

---

[28]Nel frammento si osserva anche che piú ingenua è peraltro la fede cristiana nell'incarnazione di Dio e nella sua contaminazione con la materia. A Porfiorio allude Agostino quando, in *civ. dei* X 28=I 446 Domb.-Kalb, critica quei filosofi platonici che, pretesi spiriti puri e vergognosi del loro corpo (allusione a Plotino; cfr. Porphyr., *vit. Plot.*, 1), immemori di genitori e di patria, ostentano verso Cristo, figlio di una donna e morto sulla croce (*propter corpus ex femina acceptum et propter crucis opprobrium*) disdegno e disprezzo.

[29]Porphyr., *Marc.* 11. 17=pp. 111 s. 116 des Pl.

[30]Porphyr., *vit. Plot.* 10, 35 s.=I 15 Henry Schwyzer (ed. OCT di Plotino).

[31]Iamblich., *myst.* IV 12=p. 155 des Pl. Come è noto, la paternità giamblichea del trattato (ammessa da autorevoli studiosi, fra di cui E.R. Dodds e É. des Places) è da molti discussa (cfr. l'introduzione di A.R. Sodano, in Giamblico, *I misteri egiziani* [Abammone, *Lettera a Porfirio*]. Introd., trad., apparati... di A. R. Sodano, Milano 1984), pur non constestandosi l'impronta del giamblichismo. Si osserverà però che molti aspetti di *myst.* rilevano un Giamblico in buona parte diverso da quello noto dal *Protrepticon* e anche da altri testi di sicura attribuzione; è d'altronde non sempre possibile accertare se quanto Giuliano riporta a Giamblico sia da attribuire direttamente al Calcidese o ai suoi discepoli, conosciuti e frequentati dall'imperatore.

il principio della "simpatia cosmica" e "teurgica",[32] riesce molto difficile isolare la presenza di una autonoma problematica delle immagini. In *myst*. II 11 (=p. 96 des Pl.) è affermato che "non l'atto del pensiero unisce agli dèi i teurgi, poiché che cosa in questo caso impedirebbe a coloro i quali praticano la filosofia teoretica di ottenere l'unione teurgica con gli dèi? Ma la verità non è questa: piuttosto, l'adempimento delle azioni ineffabili e compiute in maniera degna degli dèi e al di sopra di ogni intellezione, e la potenza dei simboli senza voce, comprensibili agli dèi soltanto, operano l'unione teurgica ... Infatti, senza che noi interveniamo con il nostro pensiero, i simboli stessi compiono da sé stessi la loro opera propria, e la potenza ineffabile degli dèi, cui questi simboli appartengono, riconosce le sue proprie immagini essa stessa da sé stessa, non con l'incentivo del nostro pensiero: perché ciò che contiene non è per natura posto in movimento da ciò che è contenuto, né il perfetto dall'imperfetto, né l'universale dalle parti."[33] E perciò attraverso la teurgia che la potenza ineffabile degli dèi riconosce da sé le sue proprie immagini: essa non viene risvegliata dal nostro pensiero, che riesce ad essere al piú solo una concausa non necessaria. Ma, come la filosofia cede alla teurgia, cosí "l'arte umana" (ma nox è agevole dire cosa si voglia cosí designare) è giudicata per lo piú negativamente, in quanto "svia altrove" i principî radicati nella natura (*myst*. IV 12 [=p. 156 des Pl.]:

Sul problema, oggetto qui del nostro interesse specifico, sarà opportuno avvertire che esso rientra in quello piú ampio del simbolismo, variamente sviluppato dal giamblichismo (cfr. *myst*. VII) e riconosciuto da Giamblico stesso (cfr. *Vit. Pyth.* 23) proprio degli Egizî "e dei primissimi teologi greci" e "particolarmente importante nella scuola di Pitagora." Giamblico stesso testimonia che il problema del culto iconico fu oggetto di discussione presso i Pitagorici (cfr. *vit. Pyth.* 32, dove Abari pone a Pitagora, ottenendo risposta, questioni essenzialmente religiose intorno alle "immagini sacre," alla provvidenza, ai corpi celesti, ai pianeti) e che Pitagora, emulo di Orfeo da cui aveva derivato la sua teologia, "venerò gli dèi alla maniera di Orfeo: gli dèi raffigurati in statue e nel bronzo, non legati alla nostra figura, ma in forme divine, che tutto in sé abbracciano e a tutto provvedono, affini al tutto per forma e natura" (*vit. Pyth.* 28), il che pare escludere un antropomorfismo e orientare piuttosto verso "segni" divini (da qui certamente anch la *religio philosopha* testimoniata in Platone e nell'*Epinomide*).

[32]Iamblich., *myst*. V 7=p. 162 des Pl., dove l'universo è detto "animale unico e avente dovunque una sola ed identica vita;" 9=pp. 163 s.: la simpatia terugica è nell'íntima relazione, nel rapporto che unisce "chi opera a ciò che è operato, chi genera a ciò che è generato" (cfr. anche II 9=p. 55: non è vero che gli dèi si aggirano soltanto in cielo, perché "tutto è pieno di essi").

[33]Trad. Sodano, *op. cit.*, p. 113.

"Vedendo dunque questi principî cosí radicati nella natura e distribuiti per essa, l'arte, distribuita anch'essa multiforme per la natura, li attira in vario modo e li svia altrove: e cosí trasporta nel disordine ciò che era in sé ordinato, riempie la bellezza e la simmetria delle forme di asimmetria e di bruttezza ... fornisce una materia che è inadatta a generare il bello, o perché non lo riceve del tutto, o perché lo trasforma in altro modo"), e severo è il giudizio contro i fabbricatori per magia e artificio, demiurghi a loro modo, di immagini "che sono in grado di agire," poiché non si dovrebbe scambiare le immagini "con ciò che esiste realmente:" codeste "immagini" sono apparenze illusorie, non sono prodotte da un dio, ma da un uomo e "non da essenze della forma dell'Uno," ma dalla materia che è utilizzata. Di conseguenza, si chiede il filosofo, "quale cosa potrebbe divenire buona se germina dalla materia, dalle cose materiali, dalle potenze materiali e corporee che stanno nei nostri corpi?"[34] Ma piú avanti (ibid. V 23=pp. 177-179 des Pl.) il problema è diversamente affrontato e si afferma la possibilità che la "materia divina" sia adatta a ricevere gli dèi, poiché la "sovrabbondante potenza" delle cause supreme è ognora per natura tale da essere superiore al tutto anche in questo, nell'essere cioè "presente senza ostacolo in tutto in maniera eguale." Cosí "i primi splendono negli ultimi e gli immateriali sono immaterialmente

---

[34]L'argomento è sviluppato a III 28-30=pp. 138-143 des Pl., capitoli di non agevole interpretazione che vanno certamente collegati a II 8=pp. 89 s. 10= pp. 942., dove si definiscono gli errori dell'arte teurgica, che consistono nella produzione di φάσματα e φαντάσματα, che "non sono la verità stessa, ma diversi, somiglianti alla realtà ... essi partecipano della menzogna e dell'inganno, come le forme che si vedono negli specchi ... Saranno essi pure fallaci alterazioni: ché a nessuno dei generi veri e chiaramente esistenti conviene l'imitazione della realtà." Codeste false immagini allontanano i contemplanti "dalla vera conoscenza degli dèi" (trad. Sodano, *op. cit.*, p. 111). È chiaro che il filosofo mette in guardia dai rischî della teurgia, pur non avvertendo la contraddizione con altre affermazioni contenute e esemplificate nell'opera sulla natura pressoché divina del teurgo. A questo proposito può essere ricordato l'episodio raccontato in Eunapio circa Massimo di Efeso, il "maestro" di Giuliano: il filosofo-teurgo avrebbe convocato nell'Ecatesio molti a testimonî di un suo prodigio e a spettatori delle sue superiori "qualità": dopo aver bruciato incenso e cantato "a sé stesso" un inno, egli fece sí che il simulacro della dea iniziasse a sorridere e poi a ridere; allo stupore dei presenti Massimo avrebbe fatto seguire una piú ardita operazione teurgica: le fiaccole di pietra nelle mani della dea si sarebbero illuminate. L'ammirazione con cui gli astanti, e Giuliano stesso, avrebbero seguíto il prodigio (cfr. *vit. soph.* 7, 2, 7 ss.=p. 44 Giangrande) dimostra a quali pericolosi risvolti fosse pervenuto il neoplatonismo. L'autore di *myst.* si dimostra, pur fra le contraddizioni, da essi ancóra alieno.

presenti nei materiali."[35]   La materia può essere pertanto pura e
divina, poiché è anch'essa nata dal "padre e demiurgo del tutto," e
acquista di conseguenza anche la perfezione adatta a ricevere gli dèi,
poiché infatti era necessario che anche il terrestre non fosse per nulla
impartecipe della comunione con gli dèi, anche la terra ne ricevette
una parte divina, capace di accogliere gli dèi." Bisogna pertanto che
l'arte teurgica ricerchi di fra quegli elementi, di fra quegli oggetti sacri
perfetti e deiformi e che crei da questi "un ricettacolo perfetto e puro."
Giamblico richiama i "precetti arcani" (=la sapienza oracolare), a cui
bisogna prestar fede e questi precetti affermano che una certa materia è
consegnata dagli dèi attraverso le "beate visioni," ed essa è perciò di
natura affine a quegli stessi enti che la dànno, cosicché "il sacrificio di
tale materia spinge gli dèi a manifestarsi, li invita immediatamente a
lasciarsi prendere, li contiene quando sopraggiungono e li mostra
perfettamente."   Gli ἀγάλματα quindi possono contenere il dio;
l'ingenuità che Porfirio rinfacciava ad alcuni degli "Elleni" è ora fatta
propria dai suoi continuatori. Ma a codesta conclusione si perviene
dopo varî passaggi che appaiono, come visto, con essa in
contraddizione. In effetti il discorso della teurgia verte su tutta la
problematica dei simboli divini e poiché codesti simboli coprono in
pratica tutto il reale, anche gli ἀγάλματα sono solo uno dei modi per cui
il divino mostra in atto la sua presenza.

4. GIULIANO IMPERATORE

Giuliano—è noto—considerava Giamblico il momento piú alto
della rivelazione divina al mondo tramite la filosofia e la παιδεία, il
testo sacro del nuovo Ellenismo; ma allorché egli tenta di individuare
il cammino per un ecumenismo religioso, il distacco dal
giamblichismo in direzione di Platone, Plotino e Porfirio diviene
piuttosto evidente. Se nell'*Inno ad Elios re* in preda all'esaltazione
mistica, l'imperatore teologo si confessa sotto l'influenza prevalente di
Giamblico (cfr. 150d παρ' οὗ καὶ τἆλλα πάντα, ἐκ πολλῶν μικρὰ
ἐλάβομεν), il *Contra Galilaeos* mostra in atto un superamento della
teurgia: è ora il *Timeo* di Platone ad essere posto alternativo alla
narrazione cosmogonica dell'Antico Testamento; è l'allegoria
porfiriana, sul tipo di quella del *De antro nympharum*, che spiega i
"miti" piú assurdi degli Elleni. Porfirio—osserva J. Rist—aveva
manifestato "more sympathetic attitude to popular cult ... Is it

---

[35]Questo principio avrà poi sviluppo sistematico nell'àmbito del triadicismo procliano.

possible that Julian might similarly have regarded Porphyry as at least
a major inspiration, perhaps even for harnessing popular religion in
the service of both Neoplatonism and of the State?"[36] Sta di fatto che,
se i trattati dogmatici rilevano un Giuliano piuttosto giamblicheo,
nell'opera di divulgazione dell'Ellenismo e di costituzione della
"Chiesa degli Elleni," o di polemica diretta contro i Cristiani, l'apparato
teurgico giamblicheo è quasi del tutto assente. Affermiamo tuttavia
ciò con una certa prudenza, non essendo ancóra in grado di
distinguere il puro giamblichismo dagli sviluppi impressi dai piú tardi
discepoli, ma resta tuttavia significativo l'atteggiamento giulianeo nei
testi non direttamente destinati agli "iniziati." Sul problema delle
immagini, elemento "quotidiano" della prassi religiosa, il pensiero
dell'imperatore emerge con sufficiente chiarezza e si riconosce solo
parzialmente nel giamblichismo.

Documento fondamentale è in primis l'ep. 89b Bidez, in cui si
afferma che quando noi volgiamo lo sguardo alle statue degli dèi, che
vanno fatte oggetto di προσκύνησις allo stesso modo che i templi, i
recinti e gli altari, "non dobbiamo credere che esse sieno soltanto pietra
o legno, ma nemmeno che sieno gli dèi stessi." Ed infatti, nemmeno
in rapporto alle icone imperiali bisogna sostenere che esse sieno
soltanto pietra, legno o bronzo e tantomeno che esse sieno gli
imperatori, ma solo immagini dell'imperatore. E come chi è fedele al
sovrano ama vederne l'icona, e il congiunto ama l'icona del
congiunto, cosí anche chi è amante del divino rivolge volentieri il suo
sguardo alle statue e alle icone, nella venerazione e nell'insieme nel
timore degli dèi che dall'invisibile guardano verso di lui. Le
immagini, fatte di materia, possono anche essere periture, poiché non
vengono dagli dèi, ma dagli uomini "e ciò che è fatto da un uomo
saggio può essere distrutto da un uomo malvagio e ignorante." Se
codesta precisazione allude alla distruzione dei simulacri pagani in
atto ormai da anni da parte dei Cristiani, è di fondamentale
importanza quanto l'imperatore passa poi a dire circa le "statue
viventi degli dèi," che restano invece eterne e che sono "gli dèi che si
volgono in giro attorno al cielo," cioè gli stessi segni del divino nel
mondo, già individuai dai Pitagorici, da Platone, dall'autore
dell'Epinomide[37] ed entrati quali ipostasi nel Neoplatonismo. Ma su

---

[36]Cfr. De Jamblique à Proclus=Entretiens sur l'Antiquité Classique XXI, Vandœuvres-
Genève 1974, p. 67.

[37]Iulian., ep. 89b, 294bcd-295a=P. 162 Bid.; cfr. anche, ibid. 293a=pp. 160 s.: "sempre
bisogna avere pensieri pii circa gli dèi e guardare con rispetto e devozione i loro templi

tutto prevale il rispetto per il sacerdote sacrificante, che va guardato
come τὸ τιμιώτατον τῶν θεῶν κτῆμα, poiché "sarebbe strano se noi
venerassimo le pietre di cui son fatti gli altari, per l'essere stati essi
consacrati agli dèi, perché hanno forma ed immagine conveniente al
servizio liturgico per cui sono stati allestiti, ma sosterremmo al
contempo che non bisogna onorare l'uomo che si è consacrato agli
dèi."[38] Di fronte all'attacco cristiano all'idolatria pagana, ma anche in
riguardo all'incipiente culto cristiano delle immagini, Giuliano si fa
sostenitore di una sorta di culto relativo di ἀγάλματα ed εἰκόνες, in
quanto riportano ad una realtà divina che non va però con essa
confusa, e índica quali sono le vere immagini divine, gli dèi visibili,
che vanno rese oggetto di culto, e addita nell'uomo che si è reso simile
a Dio l'immagine, per cosí dire, tangibile di Dio stesso fra gli uomini.

5. PROCLO

Il concetto giamblicheo della superiorità della teurgia sulla filosofia
e sulla conoscenza razionale è ribadito anche da Proclo, poiché "tutto

---

e loro statue, venerandoli come se si vedessero in essi presenti gli dèi. Infatti i nostri
padri posero statue ed altari e la custodia del fuoco inestinguibile, ed insomma tutti i
siffatti simboli, come segno della presenza degli dèi, non perché noi li ritenessimo dèi,
ma per venerare per il loro mezzo gli dèi. E poiché noi viviamo in un corpo ed era perciò
necessario che rendessimo agli dèi un culto corporale, laddove essi sono incorporei, i
nostri padri ci mostrarono come primi simulacri la seconda generazione degli dèi,
quella che viene dopo la prima e che si volge in giro attorno a tutto l'orbe del cielo." Di
notevole rilievo, anche se piú marcatamente orientate in senso teurgico, alcune
affermazioni nel *Discorso alla madre degli dèi* (=*or.* 8): cfr. 160a: "E la dea, come se
volesse dimostrare al popolo romano che non conducevano dalla Frigia un simulacro
inanimato (ξόανον .. ἄψυχον), ma che quello che portavano, avendolo ricevuto dai Frigî,
aveva indubbiamente una qualche potenza piú grande e divina;" 160d-161a: "il carico
che portavano dalla Frigia non era di lieve valore, ma sommamente degno; non era
opera umana, ma veramente divina; non era materia senz'anima, ma entità dotata di
vita e di forza demonica" (οὐδὲ ὡς ἀνθρώπινον τοῦτον, ἀλλὰ ὄντως θεῖον, οὐδὲ ἄψυχον
γῆν, ἀλλὰ ἔμπνουν τιχρῆμα καὶ δαιμόνιον).

[38]Ibid. 296b-297a=pp. 163 s. Bid.: "Conviene adorare non soltanto le statue degli dèi, ma
anche i templi, i recinti e gli altari. E peraltro molto saggio che rispettiamo i sacerdoti
come liturghi e ministri degli dèi, in quanto compiono per noi i doveri verso gli dèi
... Sarebbe infatti strano se noi circondassimo di onori le pietre, di cui son fatti gli altari,
per il fatto che sono consacrate agli dèi, poiché hanno aspetto e figura conveniente alla
liturgia per cui sono stati allestiti, ma non ritenessimo che bisogna onorare l'uomo
consacrato agli dèi." In *myst.* VI 6=pp. 186s. des Pl., erano state sottolineate le
particolari qualità del teurgo e la potenza che a lui viene per "l'unione con gli dèi, che
gli ha data la conoscenza dei simboli arcani." Cfr. U. Criscuolo, "A proposito di Gregorio
di Nazianzo, *or.* 4, 96," in Κοινωνία XI (1987), pp. 43-52.

in virtú di ciò è conservato e si unisce alle cause primordiali, alcune cose attraverso la follia amorosa, altre attraverso la filosofia divina, altre infine attraverso la potenza teurgica, che è piú forte di ogni umana saggezza e scienza, raccogliendo i beni tutti della mantica e le potenze purificatrici che derivano dal compimento dei riti, insomma gli effetti tutti dell'ispirazione che rende posseduti dal dio"[39] e con la teurgia è accettato tutto il complesso sistema di simboli e di segni del divino. Ma tutto è inserito un una realtà animato concepita triadicamente ed in perpetuo movimento di ritorno, di *conversio* (ἐπιστροφή) al termine primo della triade, l'Assoluto e il non mosso. Nel processo triadico acquista realtà la vita tutta dell'universo: le fasi della permanenza, della progressione e della conversione sono rese possibili poiché l'essere producente produce restando quale è, indiminuito ed immutato, moltiplicando sé stesso per la potenza fecondatrice e da sé stesso fornendo le ipostasi successive (*inst. theol.* 27); esso fa sussistere gli esseri simili a sé prima che i dissimili (ibid. 28) e come ogni progressione si compie per via di somiglianza delle cose seconde rispetto alle prime (ibid. 29) e il prodotto è all'insieme identico e diverso, cosí ogni conversione si compie per la somiglianza di chi ritorna a ciò a cui ritorna (ibid. 32).

La ricerca di una autonoma teologia delle immagini in codesta grandiosa struttura metafisica non avrebbe senso, poiché tutto ciò che procede è in certo modo immagine, e perciò partecipante, dell'essere da cui procede ed è attraverso le somiglianze fra gli enti che è possibile risalire sino al mondo divino. "E possibile infatti—viene affermato nel *Commentario al Timeo*[40]—partendo da questi principî come da immagini risalire al tutto. I Pitagorici, ricercando dalle analogie le somiglianze degli esseri risalirono dalle immagini ai paradigmi . . . Occorre dunque che anche noi riportiamo al tutto quelle che ora sono dette immagini." La risalita, la ἀναφορά ai παραδείγματα, viene a prospettarsi come necessità metafisica, ma si invera anche come processo gnoseologico. Di conseguenza, nell'àmbito del discorso

---

[39]Procl., *theol. Plat.* I 25=I 113, 4 ss. Saffr.-West. (e commento a p. 161). Va preliminarmente osservato che il termine stesso εἰκών (e termini correlati) implica di norma in Proclo il concetto della "partecipazione" al παράδειγμα; cfr., p.es., *theol. Plat.* III 6=III 24, 6 Saffr.-West. πᾶς λόγος ψυχῆς εἰκών, μα soprattutto *inst. theol.* 65, *def.*=p. 62 Dodds πᾶν τὸ ὁποσοῦν ὑφεστὸς ἢ κατ' αἰτίαν ἐστιν ἀρχοειδῶς ἢ καθ' ὕπαρξιν ἢ κατὰ μέθεξιν εἰκονικῶς. 195, *def.*=p. 170 πᾶσα ψυχὴ πάντα ἐστι τὰ πράγματα, παραδειγματικῶς μὲν τὰ αἰσθητά, εἰκονικῶς δὲ τὰ νοητά.

[40]Procl., *in Plat. Tim.* 11b=I 33, 6 ss. Diehl.

teologica, gli ἀγάλματα, le εἰκόνες non sono dei puri segni materiali, ma assumono in quanto momenti conoscitivi lo stesso rilievo degli ὀνόματα divini. Tutto il *Commentario al Cratilo* fa perno attorno a questo concetto. Se l'ὄνομα è un ὄργανον che insegna e rivela la essenza delle cose (διδασκαλικὸν καὶ ἐκφαντορικόν),[41] esso in quanto ὄργανον ha bisogno di chi ne fa uso, cosí come l'immagine necessita della risalita al modello e allo stesso modo dell'ὄνομα non è soltanto un σύμβολον, o l'opera di una ἕσις τυχοῦσα, ma condivide col modello la natura (συγγενής).[42] Ed ancóra si afferma che l'immagine è l'ὄνομα, il modello la νόησις[43] e che gli ἀγάλματα degli dèi, prodotti dalla scienza iniziatica (τελεστική) sono creazioni dell'Anima e sono fatti idonei a ricevere le illuminazioni da parte degli dei: bisogna di conseguenza venerarli per la loro συγγένεια con gli dèi.[44]

Il pensiero di Proclo emerge perspicuo da un lungo passo della *Theologia Platonica* relativo ai nomi divini: "Orbene, par dirla in breve, dei nomi quelli che sono i primi e piú appropriati e veramente divini, devono essere considerati come stabiliti al livello degli dèi stessi; quelli invece che sono di secondo rango e che sono similitudini diquesti, esistenti al livello dell'intelletto, bisogna dire che hanno una sorte demonica, quelli che infine sono al terzo rango rispetto alla verità e che sono formati in virtú di ragionamento poiché ricevono a quest'ultimo livello un'apparenza degli esseri divini, affermeremo che essi sono rivelati dagli esperti che agiscono ora sotto un'ispirazione divina, ora al modo intellettivo, mettendo alla luce delle immagini mobili delle loro visioni interiori. Come infatti l'Intelletto demiurgico fa venire all'esistenza apparenze materiali delle forme primissime che

---

[41]Cfr. Plat., *Crat.* 388 bc ὄνομα ἄρα διδασκαλικόν τί ἐστιν ὄργανον καὶ διακριτικὸν τῆς οὐσίας ὥσπερ κερκὶς ὑφάσματος. Il problema dei "nomi divini" aveva avuto peraltro ampio spazio nel neoplatonismo, in Porfirio, secondo la testimonianza di Eusebio di Cesarea, e in Giamblico (cfr. *myst.* VII 4-5), con una differenza di posizioni notevole (cfr. Sodano, *op. cit.*, pp. 354-356, nota 114), anche se si conveniva che i "nomi divini" sono ricevuti per rivelazione e sono adatti alla natura degli esseri. Tale dottrina fu presente anche fra i Padri cristiani, soprattutto in Clemente Alessandrino (cfr. *strom.* I 21) e in Origene (cfr. *contra Cels.* I 24, 16-29) e, piú tardi, per l'influsso di Proclo, in Ps.- Dionigi Areopagita. Sulla particolare posizione procliana, cfr. W. Beierwaltes, *Proklos. Grundzüge seiner Metaphysik*, Frankfurt 1979² = *Proclo. I fondamenti della sua metafisica* trad. it., Milano 1988, pp. 84-86.

[42]Procl., *in Plat. Crat.* 16=p. 7, 12 ss. Pasq.

[43]Ibid. 71=p. 33, 11 s.

[44]Ibid. 51=p. 18, 27-19, 24.

sono in lui e produce dagli esseri eterni immagini temporali, e dagli esseri indivisibili delle immagini divisibili e dagli esseri che veramente sono delle immagini che hanno la consistenza dell'ombra, al medesimo modo, io penso, la nostra scienza, prendendo a modello l'attività produttrice intellettiva, fabbrica attraverso i discorsi delle similitudini di tutte le altre realtà ed in particolare degli dèi stessi: in esse, ciò che è senza complessità essa lo rappresenta per il complesso, ciò che è semplice per il diverso, ciò che è unico per il molteplice. E così producendo i nomi essa li manifesta alla fine come icone del divino: infatti genera ciascun nome come un simulacro degli dèi, e come la teurgia, attraverso certi segni simbolici, invoca la bontà generosa degli dèi in vista dell'illuminazione di statue confezionate artificialmente, allo stesso modo la conoscenza intellettiva relativa agli esseri divini, rivela l'essere nascosto degli dèi attraverso delle composizioni e delle divisioni di suotti articolati."[45] Ἀγάλματα, εἰκόνες, sono così prodotti dell'anima e se la loro somiglianza con la natura divina è un dato di fatto che è implicito nella concezione cosmico-teologica procliana, è còmpito peraltro della teurgia, dell'iniziato, risvegliare in essi la presenza divina, richiamarvi l'illuminazione che permette la risalita, che ha a sua mèta la conoscenza suprema.[46]

---

[45]Procl., *theol. Plat.* I 29=I 114 s. Saffr.-West.

[46]Cfr. Procl., *in Plat. Tim.* 83f=I 273, 10 s. Diehl; la "gnosi" è così soprattutto un atto di fede (cfr. ibid. 65d=I 212, 19ss.), che presuppone una "speranza" ἄτρεπτος, il rendersi ricettacolo della luce divina dopo l'essersi reso estraneo da tutte le varie necessità, ἵνα μόνος τις τῷ θεῷ μόνῳ συνῇ καὶ μὴ μετὰ πλήθους τῷ ἑνὶ συνάπτειν ἑαυτὸν ἐγχειρῇ. Il "processo" è mirabilmente descritto sulla linea plotiniana, ibid. 288f-289a=III 160, 7 ss.: la "gnosi" del divino è "entusiastica;" la nostra mente si unisce a Dio quando è priva di ogni altra conoscenza, quando ha superato il momento dimostrativo; in tale *status* avviene l'ἔλλαμψυις, "poiché come il sole ci si manifesta attraverso ciò che è fulgido come il sole, così anche la divinità ci si rivela tramite l'illuminazione." E quello della preghiera e dell'illuminazione un punto qualificante della dialettica ascensiva di Proclo, poiché l'atto del trascendere assume in lui un carattere esclusivamente religioso. Infatti "la preghiera sgorga da una necessità del pensiero stesso, poiché esso è condotto e determinato da quello che è il suo fondamento e la sua mèta, l'Uno in quanto realtà divina" (Beierwaltes, *op. cit.*, p. 347). Sempre nel commentario al *Timeo* la preghiera è la premessa della illuminazione, poiché essa abitua gradualmente l'anima alla luce divina (I 213, 5 s. κατὰ μικρὸν συνεθίζουσα τὴν ψυχὴν πρὸς τὸ θεῖον φῶς). E chiaro che a fondamento v'è la teoria della πίστις come atto dello spirito che supera i limiti del pensiero discorsivo, attinge il non-pensiero, che rende possibile l'unità con l'Uno. Cfr. anche *theol. Plat.* IV 9=IV 31, 6-16 Saffr.-West., dove Proclo, sviluppando punti dal *Fedro* platonico, e per l'influsso degli *oracula*, stabilisce i tre gradi dell'ascesa: "Quanto a me, io ritengo che Platone riveli chiaramente a quelli che prestano attento ascolto alle sue

Porfirio, tracciando l'ascesa di Plotino alla conoscenza, aveva affermato che il filosofo, dall'anima pura e sempre anelante al divino, per la pura "luce demonica" risaliva al Dio, che è primo e al di sopra di ogni cosa, lo conosceva nel suo pensiero, seguendo la strada indicata da Platone nel *Simposio*.[47] Dio non ha forma né aspetto, è al di là dell'intelligenza, al di là dell'intelligibile.[48] Il molteplice, il diviso, porta solo una sua impronta; è l'ἔλλαμψις che concede di superare il momento speculativo e teologico, di tradurlo nella gnosi mistica, poiché il pensiero intravede la realtà, ma non riuscirà mai a possederla. La γνῶσις è l'approdo supremo del platonismo. Infatti fu Platone stesso a scoprire il primissimo principio dell'universo in virtú di una ispirazione divina,[49] esso che è nascosto "nel luogo inaccessibile;"[50] infatti anche la scienza che tratta degli dèi attinge ancóra a forme intelligibili e che l'anima può conoscere in virtú di uno slancio intuitivo (δ' ἐπιβολῆς); ma è la funzione propriamente intellettiva dell'anima che è in grado di cogliere le forme dell'intelletto e le loro differenze: è essa il punto punto piú alto dell'intelletto, "il suo fiore."[51] Vi sono infatti in noi molte possibilità di conoscenza, ma è esso solo che ci permette di entrare naturalmente in relazione con il divino, di parteciparvi. In effetti, la "classe degli dèi" non si apprende né per la sensazione, dal momento che essa è al di là di tutto ciò che è corporeo, né per l'opinione o il ragionamento, che sono operazioni divisibili in parti e adattate alle realtà multiformi, e nemmeno per l'attività dell'intelligenza assistita dalla ragione, poiché questo genere di conoscenza è relativo agli esseri che sono realmente, laddove la pura esistenza del divino è al di là del dominio dell'essere . . . "Ed è per

---

parole le tre cause operative dell'ascesa: l'amore, la verità, la fede. Cosa è che in effetti unisce al Bello se non l'amore? Dove si trova la pianura della verità" (Plat., *Phaedr.* 248b 6) se non in questo luogo? Quale è la causa di questa indicibile iniziazione se non la fede? Infatti l'iniziazione non si ha attraverso l'intellezione né attraverso l'atto del giudizio, ma attraverso un silenzio unitario e piú forte di ogni operazione di conoscenza, silenzio che è la fede a donarcelo, essa che colloca nella classe ineffabile e inconoscibile degli dèi le anime universali ed anche le nostre." Su tutta questa problematica e i suoi precedenti cfr. ancóra Beierwaltes, *op. cit.*, pp. 354 ss.

[47]Cfr. Plat., *symp.* 210-211.

[48]Porphyr., *vit. Plot.* 23=I 31, 7-12 Henry-Schwyzer.

[49]Procl., *theol. Plat.* * 3=I 14, 5 s. Saffr.-West.

[50]Ibid. = p. 14, 6 ἐν ἀβάτοις ἀποκεκρυμμένην.

[51]Ibid. = p. 15, 3 s. (l'espressione richiama direttamente agli *Oracula*; cfr. la nota degli editori *ad 1*.).

questo motivo che Socrate ha ragione quando dice nell'*Alcibiade Primo* (133bc) che è rientrando in sé stessa che l'anima ottiene la visione non solo di tutto ciò che resta, ma anche di Dio."[52] Il μύστης, che riscopre in sé l'unità dell'essere, riceve in maniera assolutamente pura l'illuminazione divina e diviene cosí veracemente partecipe del divino.[53] Gli ἀγάλματα, le εἰκόνες, in quanto molteplici, costituiscono momenti inferiori della conoscenza, sono la prassi di una religiosità inferiore, ma è l'anima, "nella calma delle nostre δυνάμεις," che tende direttamente al divino, raduna in quella unità tutta la molteplicità "e lasciandosi indietro tutto ciò che viene dopo l'Uno" si congiunge all'Indicibile, a ciò che è al di sopra du tutto l'essere.[54] Anche il contemplante di Plotino al momento supremo dell'ingresso nel tempio aveva lasciato alle sue spalle ogni altro segno sensibile del divino. Il platonismo era pervenuto alla piú alta forma di religiosità acristiana nel mondo antico.

CONCLUSIONE

Fenomeno molto complesso, la questione delle immagini presso i Bizantini risentiva degli influssi piú varî, della situazione storica dell'VIII secolo con l'affermarsi di un nuovo Oriente, di una ecúmene araba che metteva in crisi molte certezze. Ma tutto il lungo dibattito del mondo antico sul culto religioso, di cui simulacri ed immagini costituivano il referente concreto, fece sí che l'iconoclasmo bizantino fosse qualcosa di molto diverso da quello arabo od ebraico. Sarebbe peraltro errato riportare iconoduli o iconoclasti al pensiero neoplatonico quale noi abbiamo cercato di delineare, ma è innegabile che molti aspetti di questo ricorrono nelle argomentazioni degli uni e degli altri. Resta tuttavia certo che il culto bizantino delle immagini, quale cominciò ad affermarsi in modo preoccupante nell'età di Giustiniano, ereditava per buona parte la teurgia neoplatonica, tendendo a scoprire nell'"idolo", fatto di materia, qualcosa di ἔμψυχον, una δύναμις taumaturgica. Ma dal Neoplatonismo stesso veniva la

---

[52]Ibid. = p. 15, 21-23.

[53]Ibid. = p. 16, 2-6.

[54]Ibid. = p. 16, 9-17.

teorizzazione di un culto *spiritualis*, l'indicazione di una strada per l'elevazione a Dio da scoprire tramite il ritorno dell'anima in sé stessa, tramite il superamento del molteplice, in una dimensione in cui il richiamo materiale della presenza del divino non fosse piú necessario. Sarà questa la strada che percorrerà la teologia mistica bizantina. Ἀγάλματα, εἰκόνες, pur ἔμψυχα avevano acquistato nei tardi eredi di Platone un valore puramente relativo, e relativo doveva essere il culto a loro riservato. Su questo principio si riconosceranno piú tardi, *mutatis mutandis*, i difensori della iconodulia, un giovanni Damasceno e un Teodoro Studita. Ma vo notata tuttavia che la situazione cristiana era intimamente nuova ed originale: non si trattava piú di tradurre in immagini materiali un Dio inaccessibile e inconoscibile, ma di raffigurare nella materia il Dio che si era fatto materia, che avevo preso in tutta la sua pienezza la forma umana, che della materia aveva condiviso la precarietà e l'infermità. Sotto questo profilo una questione iconoclastica non avrebbe dovuto aver luogo in ambiente cristiano, se vi fu e segno nell'Oriente con tanta intensità un secolo di vita cristiana, gli è forse perché essa non aveva mai cessato di essere al centro del dibattito religioso degli "Elleni" fin dai Pitagorici e da Platone.

Il *De facie* di Plutarco e la teologia medioplatonica

PIERLUIGI DONINI

Non molti anni sono trascorsi da quando studiosi eminenti del platonismo antico discutevano la concezione del divino in Plutarco come se il problema fosse quello di decidere una volta per tutte fra i poli opposti dell'immanentismo e della trascendenza[1]; oggi le cose sono forse sensibilmente cambiate non tanto perché si sia affermata una posizione intermedia, ma perché il consenso di massima che la tesi trascendentistica sembra meritare è di solito temperato da considerazioni di vario modo che servono comunque a distinguere la teologia plutarchea da quella di un Apuleio o di un Numenio.[2] Questa posizione appare indubbiamente la più solida allo stato attuale delle ricerche; ma è fuor di dubbio che tutto sarebbe stato fin da principio più chiaro (e che sarebbe stato molto più difficile parlare di immanentismo) se si fosse osservato per tempo che Plutarco conosce e

---

[1]Esponenti tipici di questa impostazione e delle due tesi opposte furono H. Dörrie e C.J. De Vogel. Del primo si vedano p.es. lo studio *Die Stellung Plutarchs im Platonismus seiner Zeit*, in *Philomathes*. Studies in memory of Ph. Merlan, The Hague 1971, 36-56 (inoltre, i numerosi articoli ricordati da F.E. Brenk nella nota 34, 267 del lavoro citato qui sotto, in nota 2); della seconda, il saggio *Der sog. Mittelplatonismus, überwiegend eine Philosophie der Diesseitigkeit?* in *Platonismus und Christentum*, Festschr. für H. Dörrie, Münster 1983, 277-302.

[2]Esemplare in questo senso mi pare la ricca e documentata rassegna di studi plutarchei curata da F.E. Brenk, *An Imperial Heritage: the Religious Spirit of Plutarch of Chaironeia*, in "Aufstieg und Niedergang d. Römisch. Welt" II 36.1, 1987, 248-349. All'inizio del suo esame Brenk trova una formula felice quando parla di "Plutarch's timid but creeping transcendentalism and theism" (249).

riproduce qua e là nei suoi scritti la tipica gerarchia delle figure divine[3] che è comune nel mondo medioplatonico e che, distinguendo una divinità suprema assolutamente intelligibile da una o più figure inferiori poste a contatto con il mondo della generazione e con quello umano, esalta e allontana il dio supremo a un punto tale, che sarebbe del tutto privo di senso domandarsi ancora, a proposito di questa divinità, se sia immanente o trascendente (fatti salvi i caratteri peculiari a ciascun autore, si può pensare alle serie gerarchiche di Numenio, di Apuleio o del *Didaskalikos*). C'è naturalmente una giustificazione molto forte per questo ritardo: Plutarco non presenta mai direttamente (intendo dire: non presenta nella forma di una lezione dogmatica di teologia) le sue gerarchie divine. Queste ricorrono nelle sue pagine sempre in modo allusivo e per lo più in contesti di carattere mitico; c'è sempre bisogno di un notevole e delicato impegno esegetico per risalire dal mito alla teologia filosofica.

E'mia intenzione segnalare qui alcuni testi dal mito conclusivo del trattato *De facie in orbe lunae*[4] nei quali è possibile ritrovare i lineamenti tipici della teologia medioplatonica con le sue gerarchie divine e, in particolare, con la distinzione di una suprema figura intelligibile, lontanissima dal mondo fisico e da quello umano e sovraordinata ad altra figura, o ad altre figure poste invece a contatto con questo mondo inferiore.

A 944E il narratore del mito, Silla, si decide finalmente a spiegare come avvenga quella "seconda morte" cui aveva accennato alcune pagine prima (942F-943A), soltanto dicendo in quella occasione (943B), che essa consiste nella separazione dell'intelletto dall'anima e che questa separazione avviene sulla luna. Ora, a 944E apunto, Silla aggiunge che l'intelletto è separato dall'anima "per amore dell'immagine che è nel sole, attraverso la quale sfolgora quell'oggetto di desiderio bello, divino e beato a cui tutta quanta la natura aspira, in un modo o nell'altro."

---

[3]Credo che i lineamenti generali della teologia medioplatonica siano oggi abbastanza largamente noti; per indicarne una esposizione concisa e intelligente, credo che il riferimento alle pagine di A.H. Armstrong sia sempre valido (*An Introduction to Ancient Philosophy*, London, 1947, poi più volte ristampato, cap. XIII: *Philosophy of the earlier Roman Empire. The revival of Platonism*).

[4]Giustamente Brenk (nel lavoro citato sopra, in n. 2, 270) adduce il mito nel *De facie* insieme con quello di Timarco nel *De genio Socratis* come il testo da cui si indurrebbe per Plutarco la nozione di "a strong transcendental God."

Dunque, la separazione dell'intelletto dall'anima (e la sua successiva ascesa al sole, adombrata in 945C) avvengono *immediatamente* "per amore dell'immagine che è nel sole," ma *in realtà* e in ultima analisi per amore dell'oggetto estremo del desiderio, bello, divino e beato, che nel sole traspare e sfolgora come in una sua immagine: tutta quanta la natura, infatti, aspira in realtà a quell'oggetto ultimo senza accontentarsi della immagine di lui che appare nel sole. Già di qui si intuisce benissimo che Silla sta descrivendo una gradazione di oggetti desiderati dal *nous* e dunque, probabilmente, allude a una gerarchia di entità (verisimilmente divine) che rappresentano i fini successivi del desiderio e dell'ascesa dell'intelligenza. Ma c'è un punto importante ancora da chiarire: è forse il sole *come sole* (corpo celeste divino) il termine immediato dell'amore e dell'ascesa dell'intelligenza? Bisogna certo por mente al fatto che Silla parla di "amore *dell'immagine* che è nel sole;" ma forse questo linguaggio non è ancora per sé decisivo, perché si potrebbe sempre intendere[5] che si tratti dell'immagine *visibile* del Bene che si scorge nel sole. Tuttavia c'è un'altra considerazione che può risolvere ogni dubbio: il soggetto portatore dell'aspirazione verso "l'immagine che è nel sole" è infatti nel mito del *De facie* non l'anima con ogni sua facoltà e ancor meno, ovviamente, la persona in cui l'anima si era incarnata, con tutti gli organi dei sensi ancora integri; ma è l'intelletto, il solo e puro *nous*: è impensabile, dunque, perché è autocontraddittorio, che l'aspirazione del *nous* si volga in primo luogo a un'immagine che sarebbe visibile nel sole: deve trattarsi invece, necessariamente, dell'immagine *intelligibile* di un oggetto più elevato e anch'esso puramente intelligibile. Letto con un poco di attenzione, il testo di Plutarco permette dunque di concludere all'esistenza di una gerarchia di oggetti intelligibili, con ogni verisimiglianza anche divini, il secondo dei quali appare in qualche modo, inoltre, collegate al sole.

Ma questi oggetti intelligibili dovrebbero anche essere, a loro volta, intelligenze. La cosa, anzi, si può assumere come sicura per il secondo, dato che esso appare collegato al sole la cui funzione eminente è proprio quella (945C) di "riseminare" l'intelligenza nella luna in modo che questa produca nuove anime; non si può dimostrare invece, a quanto mi è dato di vedere, per il primo intelligibile in qualche maniera conclusiva; ma le probabilità che Plutarco pensasse a un

---

[5]Come appunto mostra di intendere H. Cherniss nella sua nota (213, g) al testo dell'edizione Loeb dello scritto di Plutarco; era probabilmente influenzato, in questa interpretazione, dal passo del *De E* 393D, su cui si veda qui sotto.

principio supremo che fosse al di là dell'intelligenza non sembrano
certo molto forti. La concezione che sembra di poter intuire dietro il
mito della "seconda morte" si apparenta dunque evidentemente a
tematiche comuni nelle teologie medioplatoniche: la gerarchia degli
intelletti divini ricorda Numenio e Alcinoo (il supposto "Albino,"
autore del *Didaskalikos*), il collegamento del secondo intelletto con il
sole fa pensare ancora a Numenio e a Galeno, al funzione assegnata
all'intelletto solare—di trasmettere a livelli inferiori del cosmo
l'intelligenza—ha un sorprendente parallelo (in un'opera di scienza
naturale!) in Galeno e ancora in Numenio.[6] Temi che potevano
sembrare tipici del platonismo del pieno secondo secolo sarebbero così
stati anticipati da Plutarco all'inizio del secolo o persino alla fine del
primo (perché sulla datazione dello scritto *De facie in orbe lunae* non
sappiamo realmente nulla di preciso).

E'interessante notare che la gerarchia delle figure divine così
allusivamente adombrata nel passo del *De facie* rappresenta
comunque un approfondimento e forse una precisazione ben calcolata
e voluta della concezione attribuita da Plutarco al suo maestro
Ammonio nel *De E* a proposito del rapporto fra il sole e Apollo. Qui
infatti Ammonio dice:

> invitiamo (*scil.* coloro che identificano senza esitazioni il
> sole e il dio) a procedere più in alto e a contemplare la realtà
> effettiva e la natura di lui (*scil.* il dio), pur onorando anche
> questa sua *immagine* e venerando la fecondità[7] che le è propria:
> per quanto è possibile compiere a un oggetto *sensibile*
> immagine dell'*intelligibile* e a un oggetto in movimento
> immagine di uno stabile, essa (*scil.* l'immagine) fa trasparire,[8]
> come una sorta di riflessione in uno specchio, bagliori della
> benevolenza e della beatitudine di lui (*De E* 393D).

Per quanto grande sia la somiglianza delle immagini e del
vocabolario, oltre che della tematica, fra questo passo e quelli del mito
nel *De facie*, non si può trascurare il fatto che nel discorso di Ammonio
è esplicitamente detto quel che nel *De facie* è omesso, che cioè il sole è

---

[6]Mi riferisco qui ai frammenti 12 (specialmente) e 17 Des Places di Numenio; al
capitolo X del *Didaskalikos* e a Galeno, *De usu partium* II 446, 3-447, 21 Helm. Per
un'interpretazione di questi testi sono costretto a rinviare al mio precedente studio
Motivi filosofici in Galeno, "La parola del passato" 194, 1980, specialmente 335-42.

[7]Anche per questo particolare ci sono paralleli nel mito del *De facie*: 944E, alla fine, la
luna aspira a"essere fecondata" dal sole.

[8]διαλάμπουσαν: cfr. *De facie* 944E ἐπιλάμπει.

considerato un'immagine visibile del dio; il che è pienamente logico nel *De E* poiché i soggetti ai quali il sole si propone come immagine da contemplare non sono in questo testo pure intelligenze disincarnate, ma uomini vivi che contemplano il sole innanzitutto con i loro occhi. La funzione del sole è dunque la stessa, ma su piani radicalmente diversi, nei due dialoghi:

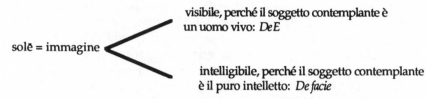

sole = immagine

visibile, perché il soggetto contemplante è un uomo vivo: *De E*

intelligibile, perché il soggetto contemplante è il puro intelletto: *De facie*

Al di là del sole e nel regno dell'intelligibile sembra che Ammonio ponga un solo dio; è forse pericoloso, però, trarre illazioni che porterebbero a escludere l'ammissione di una gerarchia. Forse nel *De E* non c'era semplicemente la ragione, o l'opportunità, per alludere al problema come avviene invece nel mito del *De facie*.

Il secondo caso che merita la nostra attenzione nel mito del *De facie* è molto chiaro nelle sue linee generali, ma piuttosto difficile da capire nei particolari anche a causa di alcuni considerevoli guasti nel testo manoscritto. Più di una volta il narratore del mito, Silla, accenna a una gerarchia di personaggi divini in cui compare costantemente al secondo posto la figura di Crono, mentre il rango superiore è occupato ora da Eracle (941C), ora da Zeus (941F-942A). Probabilmente non ha alcuna importanza, almeno quanto al significato filosofico implicito, questa oscillazione nel nome del personaggio divino sovraordinato a Crono; a 941C la presenza di Eracle è infatti collegata strettamente all vicenda (supposta come storica) delle migrazioni dei Greci, mentre ha molto maggior sviluppo, nel seguito del testo, la descrizione del più ovvio e atteso rapporto fra Crono e Zeus: e qui si annida appunto un intero campionario di luoghi comuni della teologia medioplatonica.

L'inferiorità di Crono[9] rispetto a Zeus è segnalata in maniera tipica: non solo egli è "vincolato" (*desmos* 941F) a uno stato di sonno (941F, 942A) dal volere del suo divino figliuolo, ma si limita a "sognare" quel che prima Zeus ha pensato (942A). Troviamo dunque qui due figure divine la prima delle quali pensa oggetti intelligibili che l'altra non possiede come propri, ma soltanto in maniera riflessa e, si direbbe,

---

[9]Che è il punto che distingue nettamente la presentazione di Plutarco dalle interpretazioni neoplatoniche ricordate da Cherniss nel suo commento, 188 n.a.

indebolita; inoltre, lo stato di inferiorità ontologica di questo dio sembra sottolineato dalla condizione del sonno a cui egli è costretto. Come non ricordare immediatamente, allora, i testi di Alcinoo ("Albino") in cui il primo dio pensa le idee[10] e desta da un sonno profondo l'intelletto cosmico, il secondo dio,[11] che a lui poi si rivolge per riceverne l'intelligibile?[12] Materiali concettuali e simbolici sono evidentemente gli stessi nei due testi: dunque a Plutarco erano perfettamente note dottrine tipiche del platonismo medio come quella della gerarchia divina, le idee come pensieri di dio, l'immagine del sonno del dio inferiore. Tuttavia anche dal breve riassunto che ho fatto risulta non meno evidente che questi materiali sono organizzati almeno in un punto in modo molto diverso dai due autori: mentre secondo Alcinoo il dio supremo desta dal sonno l'inferiore, per Plutarco l'azione di Zeus su Crono è precisamente quella contraria: Zeus tiene Crono sprofondato nel sonno. Come si può spiegare questa singolare discrepanza?

È a questo punto che lo stato del testo nell'ultima parte di 942A costituisce un serio ostacolo alla comprensione. Se ci si affida alle ricostruzioni dei due ultimi editori, del resto largamente divergenti nei particolari,[13] ciò che lascia più perplessi—a parte la pesantezza e il numero degli interventi sul testo tramandato, specialmente sospetti nella restituzione di Cherniss, costretto dalla sua prima congettura[14] a

---

[10]P. 164, 26 sg. H. Per il problema dell'autore del *Didaskalikos* cfr. da ultimo la messa a punto di J. Whittaker, *Platonic Philosophy in the Early Centuries of the Empire*, "Aufstieg und Niedergang d. Röm. Welt" II 36.1, 1987, 83 sgg.

[11]165, 2 ἐπεγείρας 169, 31-33 ἐγείρων . . ὥσπερ ἐκ κάρου.

[12]169, 33-35; cfr. 164, 22 e 167, 7 e, per la spiegazione di tutti questi passi e del rapporto fra primo e secondo dio in Alcinoo, il mio saggio *La connaissance de Dieu et la hiérarchie divine chez Albinos*, nel volume *Knowledge of God in the Graeco-Roman World*, ed. by R. van den Broek, T. Baarda and J. Mansfeld, Leiden, 1988, specialmente pp. 124 sg.

[13]Il testo dei mss. per 942A è questo: εἶναι δ' ἀνάστασιν τὰ τιτανικὰ πάθη καὶ κινήματα τῆς ψυχῆς ἐν αὐτῷ παντάπασιν ὁ ὕπνος ***** καὶ γένηται τὸ βασιλικὸν κτλ. Pohlenz (nell'ed. Teubner) scrisse ἐπειδὰν στασιάσαντα τὰ τιτανικὰ πάθη καὶ κινήματα τῆς ψυχῆς ἐν αὐτῷ παντάπασιν ὁ ὕπνος [κατακοιμήσῃ] καὶ γένηται κτλ. E questo è il testo di Cherniss: εἶναι δ' ἀνάτασιν τὰ τιτανικὰ πάθη καὶ κινήματα τῆς ψυχῆς [ἕως] ἂν αὐτῷ πάλιν ἀνάπαυσιν ὁ ὕπνος [καταστήσῃ] καὶ γένηται κτλ.

[14]Per quanto attraente si presenti, a prima vista, la congettura di Cherniss (ἀνάτασιν) all'inizio del passo, non si può non notare che proprio in essa è l'origine di tutte le complicazioni, di ordine testuale e concettuale, cui va incontro la ricostruzione da lui proposta. Le difficoltà del secondo tipo cerco di illustrarle qui sopra nel testo; quanto

riscrivere anche quel che potrebbe dare un senso eccellente—è il fatto che entrambi implichino con le loro ipotesi, con maggiore o minor grado di chiarezza, un alternarsi di periodi di sonno e di veglia per il secondo dio: un'alternanza di cui, però, non si trova alcuna traccia nelle altre parti della narrazione, dove lo stato di sonno a cui è costretto Crono appare come qualchecosa di persistente e di difinitivo,[15] nessun particolare del racconto lasciando anche minimamente sospettare che quel sonno sia periodicamente interrotto o che a intervalli Zeus ritorni a "vincolare" con il sonno Crono perché, a intervalli, questi si sarebbe ridestato dal suo sopore. Non solo: la stessa situazione del *De facie* si presenta anche nel passo del *De defectu oraculorum*[16] che, accennando brevemente, ma in termini assai simili a quelli del *De facie*, al sonno di Crono nell'isola sorvegliata dai demoni, o riassume la sostanza del mito del *De facie* (se questo dialogo è presupposto), o in qualche modo ne annuncia la prossima composizione (se il *De facie* è posteriore al *De defectu*); niente, nemeno nel *De defectu*, lascia pensare che il sonno di Crono non debba essere continuo.

Due argomenti supplementari contro l'ipotesi di un'alternanza di sonno e di veglia in Crono meritano di essere brevemente ricordati.

---

alle prime, mi sembra evidente che proprio perché vuole conservare all'inizio del passo quanto più possibile della lezione manoscritta Cherniss è costretto poi a intervenire pesantemente sul seguito del testo, se non per altra ragione perché deve introdurre qui una congiunzione che giustifichi il congiuntivo γένηται; poiché inoltre la sua congettura ἀνάτασιν implica che si introduca nel testo anche la nozione di un periodo di veglia, Cherniss è ulteriormente costretto a far cessare questa veglia cambiando e riscrivendo un gruppo di parole che ha tutta l'aria di andare benissimo così come è (ἐν αὐτῷ παντάπασιν) e che infatti Pohlenz può conservare integre. Non c'è dubbio dunque che, da un punto di vista puramente formale e esteriore, la soluzione di Pohlenz appare più economica (il che non significa ancora che sia adeguata alla difficoltà). Quanto alla congettura ἀνάτασιν (di cui Cherniss era molto compiaciuto: si vedano le sue *Notes on Plutarch's De facie in orbe lunae*, "Class. Philol." 46, 1951, 150) aggiungerei che non è certo un modello di linearità del metodo indurla da riferimenti a testi neoplatonici molto posteriori a Plutarco e che la sua impossibilità è comunque manifesta dalla stessa versione di Cherniss: "the motions ... *make him rigidly tense*" (il corsivo è mio): un greco come εἶναι ἀνάτασιν τὰ κινήματα non può infatti significare questo. Si direbbe che in realtà Cherniss non osava *tradurre* ἀνάτασιν direttamente come *intendeva* il vocabolo (= veglia) sulla base dei testi neoplatonici che citava (ἔγερσις = ἀνάτασις ὑπὸ τῆς ψυχῆς, Procl. *In Rem publ.* I 181, 23 Kroll) e cercava perciò di tradurre il termine nel solo modo attestato e possibile per Plutarco.

[15] 941F αὐτὸν μὲν γάρ τὸν Κρόνον ἐν ἄντρῳ βαθεῖ περιέχεσθαι πέτρας χρυσοειδοῦς καθεύδοντα.

[16] 419F-420A.

Cherniss sembra essere stato indotto a quella ricostruzione del testo anche dalla considerazione[17] che difficilmente i servitori di Crono potrebbero conoscere i sogni del dio, su cui essi fondano i loro vaticini (942A, inizio) quando la mente di lui è interamente concentrata in se stessa, il che avviene appunto durante il sonno; c'è dunque bisogno di un periodo di veglia durante il quale—sembra inevitabile concludere in questo modo il ragionamento di Cherniss—il dio racconterebbe i propri sogni ai demoni servitori. Al che si può facilmente obiettare che la logica del senso comune non è probabilmente quella del mito e che, anzi, se la supposta veglia di Crono coincidesse in lui con il ridestarsi dei movimenti "titanici" dell'anima irrazionale ai quali il testo allude[18] e che Cherniss con la sua ricostruzione richiama effettivamente in attività, questa veglia agitata e scomposta forse sarebbe una condizione ancora meno favorevole di quella del sonno pacificato per chi dovesse conoscere la mente del dio. In realtà, mi pare evidente che è un eccesso di razionalismo assolutamente contrario all'atmosfera del mito porsi il problema del modo in cui i demoni servitori conoscerebbero i sogni di Crono; Plutarco ha semplicemente ignorato il problema e questa ignoranza non è affatto, nella situazione del racconto mitico, una colpa imperdonabile.

Inoltre, nessuna utilità avrebbe richiamarsi all'unico altro testo[19] in cui Plutarco allude al motivo dell'anima cosmica che sprofonda nel sonno. Nel passo del *De animae procreatione in Timaeo* (1026E) si allude effettivamente a un periodico ritorno dell'anima allo stato del sonno, ma in un quadro completamente diverso da quello del mito nel *De facie:* qui, infatti, la condizione del sonno è certamente quella che consente alla mente di Crono[20] di fruire di uno stato di assoluta intergrità e purezza—un'idea, d'altra parte, che non deve stupire incontrare in Plutarco, poiché può essere confermata almeno da un frammento dello scritto *Sull'anima*[21]—mentre nello scritto esegetico il sonno che invade la parte razionale dell'anima coincide con il

---

[17]P. 150 dell'articolo citato sopra, nella nota 14.

[18]Cfr. *De Is. et Os.* 371B.

[19]L'unico in assoluto anzi, secondo W. Deuse, *Untersuchungen zur mittelplatonischen und neuplatonischen Seelenlehre*, Akad. d. Wiss. Mainz/Wiesbaden 1983, 84, che non prende in considerazione il *De facie*.

[20]E'logico pensare che dietro le ultime parole di 942A (γένηται ἀκήρατον) si nasconda l'interpretazione platonica di *Crat.* 396B, τὸ καθαρὸν αὐτοῦ καὶ ἀκήρατον τοῦ νοῦ.

[21]Fr. 178, 108, 32 sgg. Sandbach.

momentaneo prevalere delle parti più legate alla sensazione e alla corporeità (il che sembra più conforme, anche se non identico, alla funzione negativa che il sonno assume anche nella costruzione di Alcinoo).

È molto difficile dire che cosa si può concludere sensatamente da tutte queste considerazioni, almeno quanto alla costituzione del testo in 942A: forse è chiaro soltanto che bisogna rinunciare a qualsiasi congettura che comporti l'ammissione di un'alternanza di sonno e veglia per il secondo dio.[22] Quanto alla filosofia che si nasconde dietro il mito, sembra di dover riconoscere che Plutarco ha nel *De facie* utilizzato in modo molto personale e del tutto nuovo il motivo medioplatonico del sonno dell'anima cosmica: contrariamente ad Alcinoo e persino alla sua stessa presentazione del tema nel *De animae procreatione* Plutarco ha dato al sonno del secondo dio nel mito del *De facie* il significato positivo dell'imposizione dell'ordine e del trionfo della razionalità per opera del dio supremo. Forse non è casuale, allora, che sia nel *De facie*, sia nella più breve allusione del *De defectu*, il sonno sia sempre definito allo stesso modo e con le stesse parole, come un "vincolo" (*desmos*) che è stato "escogitato" (*memechanesthai*) dal primo dio e da lui imposto al secondo: sono due termini che Platone usa nel *Timeo* per descrivere la generazione dell'anima per opera del demiurgo.[23] Plutarco ha forse voluto così alludere precisamente all'imposizione dell'ordine razionale nell'anima precosmica e alla sua personale interpretazione della generazione dell'anima nel *Timeo*.

---

[22]Con un minimo di interventi sul testo tradito si potrebbe ottenere un senso eccellente accettando da Cherniss l'idea che l'infinito εἶναι si giustifichi dal discorso indiretto e supponendo inoltre (qui, del tutto diversamente da Cherniss) che nell'impossibile ἀνάστασιν si nascondano un aggettivo (o un participio) che si riferisce allo stato in cui è tenuto Crono e la congiunzione (non temporale!) di cui si ha bisogno per spiegare poi sia il cogiuntivo γένηται, sia l'altro verbo che non si può fare a meno di integrare nella lacuna dopo ὕπνος come reggenza degli accusativi τὰ κινήματα. Cioè: ...εἶναι δ' † αναστασ † ἵνα τὰ τιτανικὰ πάθη καὶ κινήματα τῆς ψυχῆς ἐν αὐτῷ παντάπασιν ὁ ὕπος [κατασβεννύῃ] καὶ γένηται κτλ. Il participio (o l'aggettivo) potrebbe essere, per il senso, anche soltanto καθεύδοντα (o δεσμώτην), ma un filologo vorrebbe probabilmente qualcosa di meglio dal punto di vista paleografico. Κατασβεννύῃ era venuto in mente a Cherniss; κατακοιμήσῃ, che andrebbe anche bene per il senso, a Pohlenz. Traduzione del testo qui proposto: "e (Crono) è tenuto addormentato (?) affinché il sonno spenga in lui completamente le passioni e gli impulsi titanici dell'anima e l'elemento divino si mantenga per sé solo puro e incontaminato."

[23]*Tim.* 34C ἐμηχανήσατο, 36A δεσμῶν.

In conclusione, credo che sarebbe impossibile, letti i due passi del *De facie*, sostenere che a Plutarco sia estranea la nozione di un dio lontano e distaccato dal mondo—insomma, di un dio assolutamente trascendente; talmente lontano dal mondo fisico e da quello umano da comunicare con questi soltanto attraverso figure intermediarie e innanzi tutto per mezzo del secondo dio: proprio come in Numenio e in Alcinoo il demiurgo è effettivamente il dio inferiore. Nel mito di Plutarco, infatti, i demoni trasmettono all'uomo, come oracoli riguardanti le cose più importanti, non direttamente i pensieri di Zeus, ma i sogni di Crono: 942A. E chi semina l'intelligenza sulla luna non è il principio supremo la cui immagine sfolgora, intelligibile, nel sole, ma appunto il sole, o meglio l'intelletto solare: 945C.

Rimane tuttavia il fatto innegabile che questa nozione, in sé perfettamente chiara e ottimamente collegata ad altre che riproducono le strutture concettuali constantemente ricorrenti nelle teologie medioplatoniche, non è mai presentata in modo diretto o come una verità acquisita dalla filosofia che Plutarco professa, ma è soltanto fatta intuire mediante il linguaggio allusivo e immaginoso del racconto mitico; Plutarco non dice mai esplicitamente che c'è una gerarchia divina al cui vertice sta un dio trascendente: preferisce raccontare fiabe, dalle quali l'interpretazione filosoficamente impostata può dedurre le sue conclusioni, se riesce a capire. Questo atteggiamento è certamente singolare e deve essere ricordato per evitare l'errore di attribuire a Plutarco una dottrina scolastica irrigidita in formule e in dogmi; anche se è vero che i suoi miti appaiono quasi sempre come eleganti ricami inseriti sul tessuto delle dottrine scolastiche, lo sforzo di Plutarco sembra essere sempre quello di occultare con il ricamo la dottrina tramandata e consacrata nelle scuole.

È inevitabile domandarsi perché mai questo avvenga.[24] Forse le ragioni sono più di una; ma una potrebbe in ogni caso essere questa, che l'area della teologia è certamente una di quelle in cui Plutarco, proprio in quanto si considerava un filosofo platonico e academico, il che per lui implicava l'adesione a una tradizione filosofica sentita come una e capace di contenere in sé tanto Senocrate quanto Carneade,[25] riteneva di dover esercitare una particolare cautela del

---

[24]Muovendo da una posizione del problema del tutto diversa anche Brenk (nel lavoro citato sopra, n. 2) arriva alla conclusione che il mito nel *De facie* rinvia a una qualche struttura trascendente e divina posta al di là dell'universo visibile (275).

[25]Cfr. a questo proposito J. Glucker, *Antiochus and the late Academy*, Göttingen 1978, 268 e il mio studio *Lo scetticismo academico, Aristotele e l'unità della tradizione*

giudizio, poiché la natura e le operazioni del divino non sono cose che gli uomini possano mai pretendere di conoscere a fondo. Affermazioni dottrinarie circa l'esistenza e i modi di strutturazione di una gerarchia divina sarebbero state comunque arrischiate e inopportune, non degne di un vero platonico, di un erede degli Academici. La stessa fedeltà alla tradizione della propria scuola, così come egli la intendeva, imponeva dunque a Plutarco di non essere mai troppo scolastico.

---

platonica secondo Plutarco, in *Storiografia e dossografia nella filosofia antica*, a cura di G. Cambiano, Torino 1986, 203-27.

Plotinus and Christianity

A. HILARY ARMSTRONG

I

This essay is not intended as an attempt to discover allusions to Christianity in the *Enneads* or to the distinctive Platonism of Plotinus in Christian authors. It is, rather, a speculative meditation designed to help our understanding of the relations of Platonism and Christianity from the 2nd to the 4th centuries C.E. by trying to bring out some important points of convergence and divergence between the thought of Plotinus and that of his Christian contemporaries. It is the thought of Plotinus, not "Platonism" or "Neoplatonism" in general, which I shall be considering: as my study of the *Enneads* has continued over the years I have become more and more convinced of the highly distinctive and individual character of the Platonism of Plotinus as compared with that of his Middle Platonist predecessors and Neoplatonist successors.[1] This is not, of course, intended as a denial that they have a great deal in common, or that "Platonism" and "Neoplatonism" remain useful general terms in many contexts. On the Christian side I shall confine my attention to mainstream, that is to say non-Gnostic Christians: the subject of Plotinus and the Gnostics has been, and continues to be, sufficiently discussed, and I shall try to keep clear of it, though I realize, of course that many Christian groups which would usually be described as Gnostic shared some of the views attributed in what follows to mainstream Christians, and that the boundaries between them, and in general between Christian heresy

---

[1] I have tried to say something about this distinctive character in a paper, *Platonic Mirrors*, to be published in the *Eranos Jahrbuch* for 1986.

115

and orthodoxy at this period, cannot be too precisely drawn.[2] And among mainstream Christians I shall concentrate on those with whom Plotinus might have thought that he had enough in common to make some sort of dialogue possible, those, that is, who had received a reasonably good Hellenic education and whose thought had been influenced to some extent by some kind of Platonism.

There is no solid evidence whatever that any such dialogue actually took place. It seems to me to be firmly established that Origen the Christian and Origen the Platonist mentioned in Porphyry's *Life of Plotinus* were two different persons.[3] And Schwyzer's recent very careful and critical re-examination of the evidence about Ammonius Sakkas[4] makes it very unlikely that, if Origen the Christian had any contact at all with Ammonius and his circle, it was more than minimal and superficial: nor is there any other identifiable serious Christian thinker who might have been at Alexandria at the appropriate time who there has ever seemed any reason to suppose might have met Plotinus. Nor is there evidence for any such contact at Rome: though here we should bear in mind what was said above about the undesirability of attempting to define or delimit "Gnostics" too precisely. But of course the fact that we have no evidence of something does not rule out the possibility that it did in fact occur: and this is particularly true when we are dealing with a period of religious and philosophical thought about which our information is decidedly scrappy and with a person about whose intellectual and spiritual development during the greater part of his life we really have no hard information whatever. We should not exclude the possibility that Plotinus did at some point in his life have a serious and fairly non-polemical conversation with intelligent mainstream Christians any more than we should exclude the possibility that at some time in Alexandria he talked to an Indian well read in his scriptures, though in neither case should we assume that any such encounter actually

---

[2]There are some very helpful remarks on the use of "gnosticism" as a category in the *Appendix* to Patricia Cox-Miller's "In Praise of Nonsense" in *Classical Mediterranean Spirituality* (Vol. 15 of *World Spirituality*), ed. A.H. Armstrong, New York, Crossroad 1986, pp. 501-2.

[3]The evidence on Origen the Platonist is collected and discussed in K.-O. Weber, *Origenes der Neuplatoniker* (Zetemata 27) Munich, Beck 1972.

[4]H.R. Schwyzer, *Ammonios Sakkas, Der Lehrer Plotins* (Opladen, West Deutscher Verlag, 1983).

took place and attempt to build any sort of hypothesis on the assumption.

II

The area in which there seems to be the strongest convergence between the thought of Plotinus and that of the Christians we are considering here is the one which both sides would have considered most important, that of the doctrine of the nature of the Divine. Most Christians of this sort would have agreed with Plotinus that God was spiritual, that is, immaterial or incorporeal, with all that this implies: and also that he was transcendent, in a sense which by no means excludes immanence and implies mystery, a transcendence of our speech and thought. If we express the convergence in these general terms, it is easy to see both that the Christians agreed with Plotinus and that the agreement is in no way surprising, since their formulated theology owed at least as much to contemporary Platonism as to Christian scripture and tradition.[5] But there are some implications of this generalization which need to be rather more carefully examined before we can be sure that we are encountering here an area of genuine convergence. The first concerns spirituality or incorporeality. To say that God is incorporeal meant to Plotinus that he was *apathes*, without feelings, passions or affections. Now, surely, the unfeeling, uncaring God of Plotinus is very different from the loving Father of even the most Platonically influenced Christians. If, however, we consider what was actually held by both sides rather more precisely, we shall find that the difference in doctrine is by no means as great as has sometimes been suggested, and that there are good reasons for seeing a strong convergence here. There are, certainly, important differences of tone and emphasis between Plotinus and the Christians: but these seem to be due primarily to the different character of the sources

---

[5]This has of course been vigorously contested, notably in recent times by that fine scholar the late Heinrich Dörrie. But the spirited discussion stimulated by Dörrie's views has solidly confirmed for me my own belief that "Christian Platonists" from the beginning really have been Platonists. I have been particularly influenced here by the work of E.P. Meijering, from his *Orthodoxy and Platonism in Athanasius* (Leiden, Brill 1968) to his *Die Hellenisierung des Christentums Im Urteil Adolf von Harnacks* (Amsterdam/Oxford/New York, North-Holland Publishing Co. 1985): and by the demonstrations of the depth, strength and persistence of Platonism in Christian thought in the works of Werner Beierwaltes, above all *Denken des Einen* (Frankfurt, Klostermann 1985).

which they are expounding: on both sides we are concerned with exegetes, who regard it as their main business to bring out the true and deepest meaning of the texts which they regard as authoritative.[6]

We must at this point consider the ancient meaning and implications of "apathy" or "impassibility". What is being asserted by those who maintain the *apatheia* of God is, as the word itself clearly shows, that he is free from all *pathos*, and *pathos*, which we rather misleadingly translate "passion", always denotes passivity: to be subject to *pathos* is to be negative, weak, defective, liable to attack from and requiring to have one's needs supplied from outside. This is why Plotinus insists so strongly that the Good does not need any of the things which he brings into being and would be in no way affected if they did not exist: and on this point the Christians strongly agree with him. Indeed, they explicitly and vigorously assert the *apatheia* of God, whatever difficulties this may at times raise in the exegesis of their Scriptures:[7] and, at least from the time of the Christological controversies of the 4th and 5th centuries, explicitly apply this to the divine nature of Christ.[8] This has remained the traditional faith of the Church. And if we add to this the consideration that the passionless Good of Plotinus is supremely communicative, the eternal and unchanging giver of all goods (a Good which does not communicate good would be inconceivable and meaningless to him, as to any Platonist): and if we remember that this communication of good by the Good, though leaving the Good unchanged and unaffected, must be thought of as having an inconceivable intensity far exceeding any human kindness or generosity (which in ordinary human experience is often more helpful in trouble or distress if it is comparatively passionless): we shall still be inclined to maintain a strong convergence of doctrine here.

The second question which needs further examination before we can confidently assert a real convergence between the thought of Plotinus and that of his Christian contemporaries concerns

---

[6]Cp. A.H. Armstrong "Philosophy, Theology and Interpretation" in *Eriugena: Studien Zu Seinen Quellen* ed. W. Beierwaltes (Heidelberg, Winter 1980) pp. 7-14: "Pagan and Christian Traditionalism" in *Studia Patristica* XV ed. E.A. Livingstone (Berlin, Akademie-Verlag 1984) pp. 414-431.

[7]E.g. Athenagoras, *Legatio* 8.3, 10.1: cp. 21.1. Clement of Alexandria *Stromateis* II.16.

[8]E.g. Theodoret. *Eranistes* 3. τοῦ παθητοῦ σώματος τὸ πάθος εἶναι φάμεν, τὴν ἀπαθῆ δὲ φύσιν ἐλευθέραν μεμενηκέναι τοῦ παθοῦς ὁμολογοῦμεν (4.190).

transcendence and mystery. There is a widespread and still very influential view that, in spite of apparent similarities and some Neoplatonic influence (generally regarded as unfortunate) on later patristic and some mediaeval thought, assertions of the transcendent mystery of the Divine do not mean at all the same in even the most Hellenized and Platonized Christian thinkers of the age of the Fathers and in Plotinus.   In the Christians, however transcendent their language, God always remains the Supreme (or Absolute) Being and Supreme Intelligence.   In Plotinus he is the One or Good beyond and utterly transcending the Divine Being which is also Divine Intellect, the *hen on* or *Nous*.   It is maintained that on this point Christian theology, even after the point at which some distinctively Neoplatonic influence on it can be discerned, remains essentially Middle Platonist or Aristotelian rather than Neoplatonist.   But again, as with *apatheia*, if we consider more carefully what was actually meant by those on the one side who maintained that God was Being and Intellect and those on the other, like Plotinus, who insisted that the ultimate divinity transcended Being and Intellect, we shall find that the contrast becomes considerably less sharp and that it is reasonable to speak here of convergence. The Middle Platonists generally thought of their first divine principle as a *Nous*, an Intellect.   But it was a very superior sort of intellect indeed, for transcending human or even lower divine minds, with a thinking very different indeed from anything we normally think of as thinking here below (in this they are perhaps not far from the real theology of Aristotle).   This supreme mind and thinking which is also supreme being almost escapes our awareness and totally escapes our comprehension.[9] And on the other side any careful reading of the *Enneads* will soon disclose that Plotinus's denials that we can stop in our ascent to the Divine with *Nous*, or that the One thinks, are not designed to lead us to some great void unconsciousness but to propel us towards an ultimate awareness and waking life far beyond anything that we can even begin to think about as thinking.   Christians, with their strong Biblical sense of the mystery of God, found the aspect of Middle Platonist thinking about God in which it draws closest to Plotinus quite acceptable when applied to the Father and were not likely, if and in so far as they understood what Plotinus was really saying about the One's transcendence of Intellect, to find it incongruous with their own theology.

---

[9]Numenius Fr. 2 Des Places (11 Leemans).

When we turn to consider the doctrine of God as Being and Plotinus's insistence that the Good transcends being, we shall again find that the incompatibility of the two positions which has been asserted by controversial metaphysicians is by no means clearly evident. It should hardly be necessary to say nowadays that there is no "metaphysic of Exodus" either in the Bible or in the teaching of the early Church. Thanks to the work of Pierre Hadot we can be reasonably certain where our Western Christian metaphysic of Absolute Being originates. It originates with Porphyry: or, on the most skeptical and critical view which it seems to me possible to take of the evidence and of Hadot's treatment of it, with some fourth-century Neoplatonist whose position is very close to what is likely to have been Porphyry's. Porphyry was of course the devoted disciple of Plotinus, and is most unlikely to have thought that he was doing anything more than developing certain aspects of the thought of his revered master. And it is quite possible that Plotinus might have agreed with him. A good deal of intense study is now proceeding on the relationship of the thought of the fragmentary anonymous commentary on the Parmenides which is the basis of Hadot's reconstruction of Porphyry's metaphysics[10] to that of the *Enneads*, especially, though not exclusively, the two great treatises VI 7 (38) and VI 8 (39), which stand next to each other in both the chronological and the Ennead order, and which it is therefore not unreasonable to suppose that both Plotinus and Porphyry would have thought should be read together. A recent article by Dr. Kevin Corrigan, to appear in 1988,[11] gives a very good idea both of the essential unity of this whole Plotinian-Porphyrian metaphysic and of the extremely complex and subtle relationship within it of the One beyond Being and the One-Being, which makes it possible to use more than one form of expression, once one has fully accepted the fundamental assumption of all Neoplatonic theology that all our forms of expression are totally inadequate at this level. Once one has understood how close Plotinus and Porphyry really are here one can begin to see how Christians might find even Plotinus's most radical assertions of Divine transcendence acceptable if they penetrated deeply enough into his

---

[10]P. Hadot, *Porphyre et Victorinus*, Paris, Etudes Augustiniennes 1968, 2 vols. (Text in Vol. II).

[11]K. Corrigan "Amelius, Plotinus and Porphyry on Being, Intellect and the One", to appear in *Aufstieg U. Niedergang D. Romischen Welt*.

thought and grasped that his theology of the One beyond Being has a very positive content and is not only a theology of negation and abstraction. The profound and intelligent use made by Marius Victorinus of this metaphysic in the exposition and defence of the Nicene doctrine of the Trinity[12] provides good evidence (once one has stopped setting the positions of Porphyry and Plotinus in diametrical opposition) that one Christian thinker at least did do so. In studying Plotinus, and all authentic Neoplatonic thought, one needs to remember continually that the two great negations of Being and Thought (which, as the later Neoplatonists make clear; must themselves be negated) are not designed to project the mind into void and unconsciousness but to liberate it, in the end, from its own theology (a liberation which must sometimes be sought by violent and paradoxical means) and wake it to the presence of God. Once this has been understood, then Being for a Neoplatonist can take its place as an iconic name, a signpost on the way, alongside One, and Good, and Nothing, and the Unsayable, or that variant of the last to which Patricia Cox-Miller has rightly drawn our attention, the Sayable-only-in-Gibberish.[13]

There are two points of alleged disagreement between Plotinus (or "Platonic" or "Hellenic" thought about the Divine in general), and Christianity, which have sometimes been made much of, and which do not seem to me substantial or sufficient to prevent the recognition of a real convergence between the thought of Plotinus and that of his Christian contemporaries about the Divine. They concern the freedom and the personality of God. I have written on the first elsewhere, and would still stand by the views I then expressed.[14] Briefly, I suggested that the profound and magnificent doctrine of the freedom of the One expounded by Plotinus in VI 8 would indeed have been objected to (and perhaps was actually objected to) by those Christians for whom the essential thing about God's freedom (and

---

[12]Marius Victorinus *Traités Théologiques De La Trinité*, ed. Paul Henry and Pierre Hadot, Paris, Editions Du Cerf, 1960, 2 Vols.

[13]P. Cox-Miller "In Praise of Nonsense" in *Classical Mediterranean Spirituality* (Vol. 15 of *World Spirituality*: New York, Crossroad 1986) pp. 481-505. Her commendation of nonsense names for God is liable to give a shock to respectable theologians, but I have found myself that the shock is a salutary one.

[14]A.H. Armstrong "Two Views of Freedom: a Christian Objection in Plotinus VI 8 (39) 7, 11-15?" in *Studia Patristica* XVIII ed. E. Livingstone (Oxford and New York, Pergamon Press 1982) pp. 397-406.

perhaps freedom in general) is absolute indeterminacy, unbridled freedom of choice, the taking of decisions by a bare act of will: and there were certainly some of those in his time, and a great many later: the idea of divine arbitrariness seems to have a curious attraction for the pious. But there were, and have continued to be, other Christians (including Origen) who had a different understanding, much closer to the Platonic tradition, of the essence of freedom and the nature of God: and I do not think they should have found much to quarrel with in the great treatise *On Free Will and the Will of the One*. Nor do I think that either side (given an amount of good will and willingness to understand each other which is admittedly rather unlikely) should have, or would have been likely to have, made divine personality into a major point of dispute and divergence. The Christians certainly, since they were devoted to the study and exposition of their Scriptures, were bound to use a more vividly and picturesquely personal language about God than a Hellenic philosopher whose main concern was with the exegesis of Plato: but I do not think that in the time of Plotinus, or even later, there is to be found among Christians that passionate concentration on the idea of personality, that putting it in the center of the whole debate about God, which is characteristic of modern personalist Christian thinkers and writers. And the thought and language of Plotinus about the Divine, especially the One or Good, and human encounter with God, certainly cannot simply be dismissed (or commended) as "impersonal".[15]

III

The area of deepest divergence between Plotinus and even those Christians who were closest to him in their teaching about the Divine and in their general outlook and temper of mind lies elsewhere. It is in fact the area so accurately identified by St. Augustine in the famous chapter on his reading of the "books of the Platonists" (*Confessions* VII.9): though it will be discussed here on the basis of a passage from the *Enneads* and from a Plotinian, or more generally Hellenic, rather than a Christian point of view: the Christian view of the matter has been frequently and admirably presented from St. Augustine onwards. The passage is one in the treatise *Against the Gnostics* (II.9 (33)), which

---

[15]Cp. A.H. Armstrong "Form, Individual and Person in Plotinus" in *Dionysius* I (1977) pp. 49-68 = *Plotinian and Christian Studies* (London, Variorum 1979) XX.

it is easy to recognize as having a wider application than to whatever small groups his Gnostic friends and acquaintances may have belonged to, and in which, though he is speaking in his own voice and in terms of his own philosophy, he is speaking for the whole Hellenic tradition. It occurs in the ninth chapter, at the conclusion of a vigorous attack on the pessimistic Gnostic view of the badness of the material universe:

> But one ought to try to become as good as possible oneself, but not to think that only oneself can become perfectly good - for if one thinks this one is not yet perfectly good. One must rather think that there are other perfectly good men, and good spirits as well, and still more, the gods, who are in this world and look to the other, and, most of all, the ruler of this universe, the most blessed Soul. Then at this point one should go on to praise the intelligible gods, and then, above all, the great king of that other world, *most especially by displaying his greatness in the multitude of the gods. For it is not contracting the Divine into one but showing it in that multiplicity in which God himself has shown it, which is proper to those who know the power of God, inasmuch as, abiding who he is, he makes many gods all depending upon himself and existing through him and from him.* And this universe exists through him and looks to him, the whole of it and each and every one of the gods in it, and it reveals what is his to men, and it and the gods in it declare in their oracles what is pleasing to the intelligible gods. But if they are not what that supreme God is, this in itself is according to the nature of things. But if you want to despise them, and exalt yourself, alleging that you are no worse than they are, then, first of all, in proportion to a man's excellence, he is graciously disposed to all, to men too. Then the man of real dignity must ascend in due measure, with an absence of boorish arrogance, going only so far as our nature is able to go, and consider that there is room for the others at God's side and not set himself alone next after God; this is like flying in our dreams and will deprive him of becoming a god, even as far as the human soul can. It can as far as intellect leads it; but to set oneself above intellect is immediately to fall outside it. But stupid men believe this sort of talk as soon as they hear "you shall be better than all, not only men but gods" — for there is a great deal of arrogance among men — and the man who was once meek and modest, an ordinary private

person, if he hears "you are the son of God, and the others whom you used to admire are not, nor the beings they venerate according to the tradition received from their fathers; but you are better even than the heaven without having taken any trouble to become so" — then are other people really going to join in the chorus? (II 9, 9, 26-60 tr. A.H.A.).

The discussion will concentrate on the lines italicized, which present the main point of divergence and opposition clearly. But it is necessary to quote at least that portion of the chapter given here to appreciate that Plotinus is speaking for the whole Hellenic tradition, and how substantial and vigorous the reaction of that tradition was to the challenge of an alien kind of monotheism. For this is how the issue should properly be presented. Cilento qualifies the sentence beginning "For it is not contracting the Divine into one...." as "concetto antiebraico, anticristiano, antimonoteistico".[16] His first two epithets are obviously correct, but the third is not. The passage seems to me obviously monotheistic, once one is prepared to admit that there can be more than one kind of monotheism. Once one has observed this, the consequences can be seen to be very far-reaching indeed, and late antiquity, with its conflicts and interactions between the Hellenic and the Judaeo-Christian religious traditions, is a very good place to observe it. That the Hellenic tradition of piety and religious reflection had issued in its own kind of monotheism, very different from what we are accustomed to call "classical theism", is now widely recognized.[17] Its character has been excellently explained in a recent article by John Kenney:

Hellenic monotheism was a theology of divine ultimacy. As a spiritual tradition rooted in ancient polytheism, its understanding of the divine began with the multiple divine powers and then focused on a primordial divine unity and a final principle of order and value for the sacred cosmos. Throughout this tradition the gods were not rejected, although they were superseded as theological interest was concentrated upon that absolute and transcendent principle into whose

---

[16]V. Cilento *Paideia Antignostica* (Firenze, Le Monnier 1971) p. 247.

[17]J.P. Kenney "Monotheistic and Polytheistic Elements in Classical Mediterranean Spirituality" in *Classical Mediterranean Spirituality* (see n. 13) pp. 269-292: cp. Peter Brown *The World of Late Antiquity* (London, Thames and Hudson 1971) Chapter VI: R.A. Markus *Christianity in the Roman World* (London: Thames and Hudson 1974) Chapter 2.

fecund unity all gods and divine powers could be resolved – for they were its manifestations at derivative levels of reality. Yet this theology was always an inclusive monotheism, for it seems to be endemically modalistic — ever willing to consider whatever divine powers it could recognize as modes of this ultimate divine One. Hence, it was a religion of theophanies. Throughout its long history we find repeatedly the notion that primordial divinity may show itself in very many ways through its numerous powers, although a cohesive, if not always apparent, unity lies behind them all.[18]

As against this, Plotinus and other Hellenic thinkers of his time had become conscious of the emergence into their world of a very different kind of monotheism, which in its Jewish form had attracted comparatively little attention, hostile or favourable, but in its Christian form was increasingly perceived as a challenge to their whole tradition of belief, piety and reflection, and so to the whole culture intimately bound up with it. This was the intransigently exclusive monotheism of the One God, true belief in and worship of whom involves the rejection of all other gods, who is not present in them and is not to be normally apprehended in all the theophanies of the cosmos and in the minds and souls of wise and good men everywhere and at all times, but, either exclusively or overwhelmingly predominantly, in the single theophany or series of theophanies in which he reveals himself to those whom he chooses. The single theophany or unique and exclusively true self-revelation of God seems to be intrinsic to this kind of monotheism: it might be logically possible to maintain the one without the other, but in fact the two seem always to go together, and I do not think that the exclusive monotheism of God without and against the gods has ever been asserted except in the context of what is usually referred to as a "revealed" religion (all genuine religions have some kind of belief in divine revelation, but not necessarily in one unique exclusive revelation). And it was certainly the Christian insistence on the exclusive self-revelation of God, which necessarily for them took a very strong form, since the substance of their revelation was God himself made man in Jesus Christ, which made the divergence from and the challenge to their traditions of worship and reflection clearly apparent to Plotinus and other Hellenes in a way in which it had not

---

[18]J.P. Kenney art. cit. (n. 17) p. 289.

been when exclusive monotheism was only presented in its Jewish form. The point of deepest divergence was in fact, as Augustine saw, the historic Incarnation.

In the necessarily brief attempt which follows to indicate the meaning and implications of this divergence I shall be trying to go deeper than the polemic of both sides and shall inevitably be concerned with what this divergence looks like from our contemporary point of view. If we do not at least try to do this (while remaining conscious that in trying we shall be unlikely altogether to escape the dangers of anachronism) we shall not understand the depth and persistent significance of the divergence or the intensity of feeling which it aroused on both sides. We have seen from the passage quoted above from the *Enneads* with what force the accusation of spiritual pride made by Augustine against the pagan philosophers could be made by those philosophers from the point of view of Hellenic monotheism against the Christians (as Augustine himself of course knew very well) and how very different what the Jews and Christians call "idolatry" looked from the other side: but we need to explore the reasons for this a little further. I do not think that charges made by the Hellenes against the Christian doctrine of the historic Incarnation on the grounds that it involved some descent, demeaning, or defilement of the Divinity can be regarded as anything but superficial and polemical. Christian language here, down to and including the Nicene Creed, would of course have caused great difficulty to Hellenes: and there would be plenty of Christians then and now, who would insist that it was in this more Scriptural language, taken more or less literally, "was made flesh", "come down from heaven", that the authentic Christian message was to be found. But let us suppose that that improbable but not impossible conversation between Plotinus and Christians of a sort with whom some mutual understanding might have been attainable had taken place: and that it had been carried on with a mutual good will and readiness on both sides to try to understand each other's thought in depth which probably was impossible in the third century. The Christians would have strongly stressed their agreement with the Platonists on divine *apatheia* (see above p. 118) and insisted that the God-head of Christ remained *apathes* in the Incarnation, and was in no way changed or affected by his assumption of humanity: and they would have been indignant at the suggestion that they really believed that he had "come down". The Logos, with the Father and the Spirit, they would have said, had been most intimately and immediately present in his creation from the beginning. Nor was his divine transcendence in any way diminished by the Incarnation. He still reigned in heaven when he died on the Cross or lay in the tomb. And on his side Plotinus would have had to agree that of all Platonists he most stressed the intimate and immediate omnipresence in the cosmos and in all humanity of all divinity, of Soul and of Nous (which he might not have much minded calling Logos for the purposes of the discussion) and above all the One or Good: of course always without change or affection or any impairment of transcendence. I have often thought that Plotinus's doctrine of universal divine presence can be excellently described by the four great adverbs of Chalcedon, *Asunchutós, Atreptós, Adiairetós, Achoristós.* "Without confusion, without change, without division, without separation".

But this very suggestion brings out clearly where the divergence lies. The Christians did indeed strongly assert the presence of the eternal Logos through whom all things were made in the world of his creation. But since they held this belief in the context of intransigent and exclusive monotheism, such "natural" knowledge of and contact with God as came from this presence was insignificant in comparison even with the One God's preliminary self-revelation of himself to one particular and peculiar people in the Old Testament, and the union of God and man in Christ differed in kind, not merely in degree, from all other modes of divine presence in the world, and reduced them, once it had occurred, to religious irrelevance: and of course all the pagan cults and pieties were for them not even good natural religion but the consequence of sin and diabolical delusion. This was as true of the most Hellenized and Platonized Christians as of the simplest and least educated of the faithful. And it was precisely this which seemed to Plotinus and the Hellenes for whom he spoke sacrilegious arrogance. For them it was in the vast living complex of multifarious theophanies in the cosmos and the divine illuminations which had shone out in the thought of wise and good men everywhere from remotest antiquity that the One God was rightly to be worshipped. One could properly have one's personal and traditional preferences among the sages, and external and material cults and pious observances might mean much or little to one (they meant little to Plotinus). But the sacredness of the whole in all its rich diversity had to be maintained. Plotinus might, just conceivably, have accepted Christ as a theophany, and a great one, if he had been preached to him differently. But he could never have accepted him as the one and only theophany, excluding or devaluing all others. Nor could he have accepted a supernatural authority of Scripture and Church sharply distinct from and transcending (even if not contradicting) the natural self-revelation of the Good in the spiritual and material universes with their multitude of gods and godlike men: at the most improbable degree of acceptance he could not have gone beyond accepting the Christian fact as what, as a matter of historical fact, it always has been, a part of the great whole, offering one way to God among others.

Two points of difference which were made much of by Christians at the time, and sometimes since, in so far as they were not based on misunderstanding, seem to me to derive their separative force from the felt congruity or incongruity of the positions adopted with the belief in historic Incarnation and exclusive revelation. These are the doctrines of the everlastingness of the cosmos and the natural immortality and co-eternity with God of the soul, involving the possibility of a succession of embodied lives. Given that willingness to try to understand opposed positions in depth which we can assume in our imaginary dialogue because it is imaginary, and which is certainly required from ourselves, the Christians should have been able to see that the unbounded duration of the material universe, and of matter, and the eternal existence of even human souls did not in the thought of Plotinus mean that souls, cosmos and matter are uncaused or independent. They are as totally and continually dependent on their creative source, and as unnecessary to that source, as the created universe of the Christians. And Plotinus's account of the creative outgoing which eternally produces them is compatible, as I have already suggested, with a high doctrine of God's freedom. But even if they had recognized this, as they generally did not, they would probably have still felt that their own beliefs about world and soul were not only more in accord with their Scriptures than those of Plotinus but more congruous with that view of history as a linear future-directed pattern of events, with a beginning, a middle and an end, which springs naturally from belief in the One God's single self-revelation in a particular history and one supreme divine event in that history.[19]

It would falsify our history, and leave little hope for the future of religion in our world, to assert that the distinction and frequent

---

[19]On the Hellenic understanding of the meaning of history, as contrasted with the Christian, cp. A.H. Armstrong "The Hidden and the Open in Hellenic Thought" in *Eranos* 54 (1985) pp. 106-117.

opposition of the two kinds of monotheism which I have been trying to show in this consideration of Plotinus and the Christians means an incompatibility so absolute that no attempt at reconciliation is worth while, even if complete reconciliation may never be possible. So I shall try to conclude constructively by indicating those elements in the developing Christian thought of the time of Plotinus which, at least if he could have been aware of some of their later developments, might have seemed to him to go some way towards bridging the gulf. The recognition of the light given by the Logos in the teachings of the great Hellenic philosophers by some Christians, above all Clement of Alexandria (and later, as regards Plotinus himself, by Augustine), was already by the third century sometimes free and generous, perhaps deplorably so by the standards of strict and exclusive Biblical monotheism. And in more recent centuries of the Christian era this recognition of the light of the Logos outside the Church has become much freer and more generous, especially in my own lifetime (which has included most of the twentieth century), so that some Christians (of course against vigorous opposition from others) will admit the teachings of other great religions, along with free philosophical speculation and scholarly and historical research as of practically equal value in our thinking about God with the Bible and Church teaching, which are often interpreted by these other lights (as of course they often have been in the past, even when this was unconscious or unadmitted).

On the side of cult and piety, the Jewish and Christian belief in the power and dignity of the angels somewhat modified from the beginning the intransigence of their monotheism: though, as the influence of this on Christian cult and piety does not seem to have been very great, it should not be overstressed. And the cult of the saints, which was already beginning in the time of Plotinus, developed, especially after it had been overwhelmingly reinforced a century or so later by the cult of the Mother of God, to give Christians something like the Hellenic self-revelation of the One in and through the Many, a sense of the great divine company manifested in innumerable local theophanies. This sort of *rapprochement* was by no means the intention of the orthodox and authoritarian Church leaders who vigorously promoted these cults,[20] and Christian theologians who approve and defend them have generally been reluctant to admit it,

---

[20]Cp. Peter Brown, *The Cult of the Saints*, London SCM Press 1981.

though those who oppose them insist on it frequently and vigorously. But when all due notice has been taken of differences, it seems right to say that in popular Catholic and Orthodox piety, more than in doctrine or theology, there has been a real narrowing of the gap between the two monotheisms. And within my own lifetime the increasing strength of a kind of tolerant, in a sense skeptical, often Platonically influenced Christian thinking—the beginning of which goes back at least to the Renaissance[21]—has led some Christians to move a good deal further towards bridging that gap. They may disregard the ecclesiastical limitations imposed in the spirit of exclusive monotheism on the membership and veneration of that great company, and be prepared to see in the gods of the heathen not devils or delusions, but unfamiliar faces of the Logos, and in their saints and sages spiritual guides as worthy of veneration as any proposed by the Church.

It will be clear from what has just been said that I do not think that the Hellenic monotheism of Plotinus is by any means a thing of the past. The tense co-existence of the two monotheisms has, I believe, persisted throughout our history, and the presence of both is very evident in the religious life and thought of our own time, partly, though not entirely, because of the greater contact of Christians with other religious ways of the Hellenic rather than of the exclusive or Biblical kind, and our need to come to terms with them. The tension, and sometimes the dialogue between the two is now apparent, more clearly than ever before, within the Christian Church. One can still of course hear from Christian pulpits the accents of an Athanasius or an Ambrose. But one can also hear voices which sound much more like those of the tolerant pluralist pagans of late antiquity, of Symmachus or Themistius: and even, sometimes, something like the great voice of Plotinus.

---

[21]On the earlier stages of this movement, especially in England, I have found two books by Margaret L. Wiley, *The Subtle Knot* (London, Unwin, 1952: reprinted New York, Greenwood Press 1968) and *Creative Sceptics* (Allen and Unwin, London 1966: reprinted Calcutta, Scientific Book Agency 1969) particularly enlightening.

Plotinus and the Chaldaean Oracles

JOHN DILLON

This is a topic on which, one would think, there was really very little to be said.[1] Plotinus never alludes explicitly to the *Oracles*, Porphyry gives no indication in his *Life* that his master knew of them, and it seems safe to say that they were not the sort of material to which Plotinus would accord much credence.

However, that will not quite do as a conclusion of the question. We know, after all, that Porphyry, at least, had a profound interest in the *Oracles*, dating back to before his time with Plotinus, and it is hard to believe that Plotinus was allowed to remain quite ignorant of them, even if he was profoundly out of sympathy with their theurgical tone. What I would like to do in this paper, which I have pleasure in dedicating to a great master in this field, is to assemble and consider all the evidence in favour of Plotinus' having at least read through the *Oracles*, and deriving in consequence, if not intellectual stimulation, at least some striking turns of phrase. There is in fact a certain number of interesting words and phrases in Plotinus' vocabulary whose presence is most plausibly explained, I think, as deriving from this source.

One must begin, however, with a caution. In the case of most, if not all, of the words to be considered, since they are predominantly poetical, there is the possibility of Plotinus' having derived them from some earlier poetic source (either immediately, or through the mediation of a later prose author of stylistic pretensions, such as Numenius), from which the author of the *Oracles* may also have

---

[1] In fact, a number of possible Chaldaeanisms have been noted by Willy Theiler, in 'Ammonios der Lehrer des Origenes', in *Forschungen zum Neuplatonismus* (Berlin, 1966), p. 41, n. 75, and noted by Édouard des Places in his collection of the Fragments. Even these have been disputed by Pierre Hadot, in H. Lewy, *The Chaldaean Oracles and Theurgy* (repr., Paris, 1978), pp. 709-11.

derived them. While recognizing this possibility in all cases, I would still regard it as the less plausible alternative, though it cannot be disregarded. That said, let us turn to the evidence.

We should begin, perhaps, with the one phrase which outside evidence alleges to be Chaldaean in inspiration, and that is the beginning of *Ennead* I 9, the 'fragment on Suicide' (Περὶ ἐξαγωγῆς): Οὐκ ἐξάξεις, ἵνα μὴ ἐξίῃ, "Thou shalt not take it out (sc. your soul), that it may not go (sc. taking something with it)." Psellus, as we know[2], quotes a metrical[3] form of this utterance: Μὴ 'ξάξῃς, ἵνα μή τι ἔχουσα/ἐξίῃ . . . explicitly ranking it as an Oracle, and saying that Plotinus includes it in his treatise Περὶ εὐλόγου (or ἀλόγου!) ἐξαγωγῆς.

What are we to make of this? Henry and Schwyzer, in their big edition, are so uncomfortable about it that they make the rather desperate suggestion that perhaps this 'oracle' actually derives from Plotinus rather than the other way about[4], but I think that we may dismiss that possibility. Plotinus, I should say, is plainly quoting something. The format is otherwise too elliptical even for him. Admittedly, he goes on to explain it immediately afterward (ἐξελεύσεται γὰρ ἔχουσά τι, ἵνα καὶ ἐξέλθῃ, τό τε ἐξελθεῖν ἐστι μεταβῆναι εἰς ἄλλον τόπον), but this simply reinforces the impression that the original phrase is an elliptical allusion to something.

Why, then, would Plotinus on this occasion deviate from his otherwise (apparently) universal disregard for these theosophical productions? We cannot even suggest, after all, that he picked up this tag from Porphyry—at least if Porphyry's chronological listing is honest—since this tractate, no. 16 in Porphyry's list, was composed before Porphyry joined him. What I would like to suggest here is that this impression of Plotinus' total ignorance of, or disregard for, the *Chaldaean_Oracles* is a misleading one, and that thus there need be no great fuss made about this unparalleled quotation, even if we cannot explain exactly why he chooses to quote the *Oracles verbatim* (or almost *verbatim*) only here.

A full tally of possible Chaldaeanisms, alphabetically ordered, might comprise, I think, the following:

(1) Ἀγλαΐα (ἀγλαΐζω, ἀγλάϊσμα, ἀγλαός) 'splendour'.

---

[2] *Exegesis* 1125d = p.164 in des Places' Budé ed. of the *Oracles*.

[3] Metrical, at least, when slightly emended by des Places.

[4] In this they are followed by Armstrong, in his Loeb edition, *ad loc*.

This is not a very compelling example, but it should be mentioned for the sake of completeness. Only the adjective *aglaos* is actually to be found in the extant fragments of the *Oracles* (Fr. 214, 1 des Places)[5]: πάντα γὰρ ἀνθρώποισι θεοῦ πέλει ἀγλαὰ δῶρα.[6] but, though the word-family (at least *aglaos*, *aglaia*, and the middle/passive of *aglaizō*) is Homeric[7], and Plotinus is quite capable of borrowing it directly from Homer (as he does many other phrases), the *Oracles* remain a possibility. For Plotinus, *aglaia* is most characteristically used of the glory of the noetic realm, e.g. III 8, 11, 30, τοῦ νοῦ ... ἐν πάσῃ ἀγλαΐᾳ κειμένου; IV 3, 17, 21; V 3, 8, 31 (where Soul is made to find satisfaction in τὴν ἐν αὐτῷ (sc. τῷ νῷ) ἀγλαΐαν; VI 9, 4, 18. Out of ten uses of the word, eight have this reference. *Aglaisma* (in the plural) is used, similarly (all the usages occurring in one chapter (9) of *Enn.* III 5), of the *logoi* of *Nous* projecting themselves onto Soul, which is called *aglaos* in the previous chapter (in the guise of Aphrodite) in virtue of this. One of the two uses of the verb also occurs in III 5, 9 (the other one comes from VI 9, 9, 57, in a similar context). Primarily, then, for Plotinus, this word expresses the brilliance of the intelligible realm, and of its projection of itself upon its inferiors. It is almost a technical term. He could, of course, have borrowed it directly from Homer, or even from Pindar (who likes the word), but I think it is a reasonable conjecture that his use of it is an echo of some source nearer at hand, where it had already acquired the restricted sphere of reference which he gives it. The single surviving Chaldaean use of *aglaos*, Homeric cliché though it is, would seem to bear this out. The gifts of God come to mortals from the noetic world, after all.

(2) Ἀίσσω, 'dart, swoop'.

The Chaldaean pedigree of this verb is unfortunately doubtful. It is actually a conjecture of Kroll's, although a probable one (ἦξεν for ἤξεν of the mss. of Proclus, *In Remp.*), in a quotation which is probably, but not certainly, from a Chaldaean oracle (it is identified by Proclus as an *oracular* response, at least, at II 126, 19). The passage runs (Fr. 217, 4-6):

---

[5]All references are to des Places' Budé edition, Paris, 1971.

[6]Listed by des Places as a dubious fragment, though he is confident that it is Chaldaean. It is quoted by Didymus the Blind, *De Trinitate* III 28, only as emanating from *hoi exô*, by which he means 'the pagans', but the *Oracles* seem the obvious source. *Aglaa dôra* is, of course, a common Homeric formula, often with *dosan*.

[7]*Aglaizō* in the active is poetical (Aristophanes), but also found in late prose; *aglaisma* may actually have been coined by Aeschylus (*Ag.* 1312), but is also to be found in late prose.

Οὐχ ὅστις σπλάγχνοισιν ἐπίφρονα θήκατο βουλὴν
ἤδη καὶ πρὸς Ὄλυμπον ἀποσκεδάσας τόδε σῶμα
ᾖξεν ἀειρόμενος ψυχῆς κούφαις πτερύγεσσιν ...

"It is not because one has put one's confident trust in
entrails (sc. one who relies on sacrifices) that, having shaken off
this body, one has already leapt[8] towards Olympus, raised on
the light wings of the soul . . .."

Once again, we have to do with an Homeric word, used also by the
tragedians, but very rarely in prose (and only in high-flown passages),
but in this Chaldaean context the word has the connotation of darting
upwards, to union with divinity. Let us see how Plotinus uses it.

There are four usages (V 3, 17, 17; V5, 4, 8; VI 7, 16, 2; VI 8, 19, 8),
and in all the context is that of a leap towards the One, or at least
'upwards' (*pros to anô*, VI 7, 16, 2, which in the context means 'towards
the One'). Plainly for Plotinus this poetic verb has just that technical
connotation which we find in the *Oracles* passage. The use at the end
of the late tractate V 3 is in a particularly hieratic, indeed ecstatic,
passage, which ends with the famous injunction, '*Aphele panta*'.

(3) Ἀμφίστομος, '*having two fronts*'.

This is a more persuasive example, already picked out as
Chaldaean by Theiler (see n. 1 above). Proclus employs the term at *In
Tim.* II 246, 19, and again *ibid.* 293, 23, in either case in conjunction
with *amphiprosopos* (in combination with which it forms the latter
part of an hexameter), to describe the dual role of the soul, both
contemplating the noetic realm and directing itself towards the
physical world. In Chaldaean terms, this would refer to Hecate, who
fills this role in Chaldaean theology. Des Places, strangely, allows
amphiprosopos the status of a fragment (Fr. 189), but not the closely
associated *amphistomos* (though he mentions it in the apparatus).
There can hardly be any doubt, though, that they go together.

Plotinus uses the term only once, at III 8, 9, 31, but most
significantly. He employs it as an epithet of Intellect, with reference to
its dual role of proceeding forth to what is below it, and yet reverting
upon the One:

ἦ δεῖ τὸν νοῦν οἷον εἰς τοὐπίσω ἀναχωρεῖν καὶ οἷον ἑαυτὸν
ἀφέντα τοῖς εἰς ὄπισθεν αὐτοῦ ἀμφίστομον ὄντα, κἀκεῖ, εἰ ἐθέλοι
ἐκεῖνα ὁρᾶν, μὴ πάντα νοῦν εἶναι.

---

[8]Proclus, in commenting on this (*In Remp.* II 126, 26), speaks of a *hormê* of the soul
towards the upward ascent, which virtually assures the correctness of Kroll's
emendation.

"Rather, the Intellect must return, so to speak, backwards, and give itself up, in a way, to what lies behind it (for it faces in both directions); and there, if it wishes to see that First Principle, it must not be altogether Intellect." (trans. Armstrong)

Here we have to do with not an Homeric term, not even a poetic one (so far as we know), but one chiefly attested in technical prose contexts, whether zoological, military or geological. However, it was also (as we may gather from Plutarch, *Life of Numa*, XIX 5) used as a translation of the Latin epithet of Janus, *bifrons*, and Plotinus was probably aware of that. But the case is good, I think, for seeing his use of it as a verbal echo of its use in the *Oracles*.

(4) Ἄνθος, 'bloom.'

Here is a term very characteristic of the *Oracles* (though perfectly common in the rest of Greek also). In the metaphorical meaning, 'bloom' or 'flower' (e.g. of youth or beauty), it goes back to Homer, and once again is available to Plotinus from that source, or indeed from many others, such as Aeschylus or Pindar, not to mention Plato himself (*Symp.* 183C, *Rep.* X 601B). The *Oracles* propound the doctrine of the *anthos nou*, 'the flower of the intellect', that highest, almost supranoetic aspect of the intellect by virtue of which the One may be apprehended Fr. 1, 1): Ἔστιν γάρ τι νοητὸν, ὃ χρή σε νοεῖν νόου ἄνθει. (Cf. also Fr. 49, 2)[9]

Plotinus uses the word twice, the first usage (interestingly, in view of the Chaldaean usage mentioned in n. 9) in connexion with the light of the sun (II 1, 7, 29), but the second (VI 7, 32, 31) in a context nearer to, though not identical with, the technical Chaldaean one (Plotinus' term for that level of intellect is actually 'intellect drunk'—*nous methustheis tou nektaros*, VI 7, 35, 25). In this second passage, speaking of the One, he says: δύναμις οὖν παντὸς καλοῦ ἄνθος ἐστί, κάλλος καλλοποιόν, which I take to mean, "being the potency of all that is beautiful, it is the flower (thereof), beauty (*qua*) productive of beauty." His argument has been that the One can only be termed 'beautiful' or 'Beauty' in so far as it is the *source* of beauty. *Anthos* here has, it seems to me, a rather curious meaning, not really 'the quintessence of beauty', but rather that aspect of beauty which is beyond beauty, which comes close to the meaning of *anthos* in the phrase *noou anthei*. I am afraid that *anthos* is too common a term for

---

[9] Apart from these instances, the term occurs four times (Frs. 34, 2; 35, 3; 37, 14; 42, 3), in the phrase *puros anthos*.

any Chaldaean connexion to be convincingly made here, but it seems to me that a consideration of the Chaldaean use of the word does help to throw light on Plotinus' employment of it in VI 7, 32.

(5) Ἄπλετος, 'immense'.

Here again we have a word sufficiently widely used to be available to Plotinus from the literary tradition in general[10], but which yet exhibits an intriguing coincidence of use between him and the *Oracles*. Both he and the *Oracles* use it twice (*Enn.* IV 8, 6, 14; V 5, 6, 14; *Or. Chald*. Fr. 54; Fr. 61a1). Plotinus uses it in either case with reference to the One, at IV 8, 6, 14 to describe its power (*dynamis*), which he has just above characterized as *aphatos*—another rather high-flown word—and at V 5, 6, 14 to characterize the One itself, or rather its 'nature': γελοῖον γὰρ ζητεῖν ἐκείνην τὴν ἄπλετον φύσιν περιλαμβάνειν, "for it is absurd to seek to comprehend that boundless nature".

This last phrase has an interesting similarity to Fr. 54 of the *Oracles*:

Νώτοις δ' ἀμφὶ θεᾶς φύσις ἄπλετος ἠώρηται
"Upon the back of the goddess a nature immense is lifted"

Any echo there may be is only verbal, however, since the 'nature' here referred to is that of the Moon, as a manifestation of Hecate, ruling over the realm of (sublunary) Nature. But then verbal echoes are all that we are looking for, after all.

(6) Ἁρπάζω, συναρπάζω, 'snatch.'

Most of Plotinus' uses of this word are literal, and so of no interest in the present context, but there is one use of the simple verb (VI 9, 11, 12) and one of its compound *synarpazo* (V 3, 4, 12), that seem to involve a 'technical' meaning known from the *Oracles*. In VI 9, 11, 12 it is used in the course of a description of one who has been initiated into the 'mysteries' of the One: ἀλλ' ὥσπερ ἁρπασθεὶς ἢ ἐνθουσιάσας ἡσυχῇ ἐν ἐρήμῳ καὶ καταστάσει γεγένηται ἀτρεπεῖ, "but, as it were, snatched up, or filled with divinity, he has come to be still, in solitude and unwavering stability."

The meaning here is very much that of the English 'rapt', though that word gains its meaning, not from Platonism, not yet from the

---

[10]Not Homeric, but used by Empedocles, Pindar and Sophocles, among poets, and Herodotus, Xenophon, Plato and Aristotle,. among Classical prose writers. Plato, however, uses it only three times, once in the *Sophist* (246c2), with considerable pseudo-poetic irony (ἐν μέσῳ δὲ περὶ ταῦτα ἄπλετος ἀμφοτέρων μαχή τις, ὦ Θεαίτητε, ἀεὶ συνέστηκεν), and twice in Book III of the *Laws* (676b7, 683a7), where his language is generally high-flown, to describe immense stretches of time (ἄπλετόν τι καὶ ἀμήχανον (sc. χρόνου πλῆθος); ἐν χρόνου τινὸς μήκεσιν ἀπλέτοις).

Oracles, but rather from the Bible, in its Latin version, with reference to such figures as Elijah or St. Paul. Plotinus here, with the use of *hôsper*, does seem to be using the term somewhat self-consciously (he then glosses it with *enthousiasas*), as if he were quoting. However, there is precious little antecedent in the Greek literary tradition for such a usage. One could adduce the use of the verb by Plutarch, in the *Life of Antony*, ch. 28, to describe Cleopatra's effect on Antony, but even that is not very close.

The second usage, with the compound verb, refers to the effort of the human intellect to cognise Intellect, and in that context Plotinus states the view that one must really step outside oneself, and become 'other':

> κἀκείνῳ ἑαυτὸν νοεῖν αὖ οὐχ ὡς ἄνθρωπον ἔτι, ἀλλὰ
> παντελῶς ἄλλον γενόμενον καὶ συναρπάσαντα ἑαυτὸν εἰς τὸ ἄνω
> μόνον ἐφέλκοντα τὸ τῆς ψυχῆς ἄμεινον·

> "and by that (sc. Intellect) he thinks himself again, not any longer as man, but having become altogether other and snatching himself up into the higher world, drawing up only the better part of soul, . . ."

(trans. Armstrong)

The connotation, in both these uses, is of cutting oneself off from what is below in one's striving for what is above. This is certainly the connotation also in the single use of the verb in the *Oracles* (Fr. 3, 1):

> ὁ πατὴρ ἥρπασσεν ἑαυτόν,
> οὐδ᾿ ἐν ἑῇ δυνάμει νοερᾷ κλείσας ἴδιον πῦρ.

> "The Father snatched himself (up),
> not even in his intellectual Power enclosing his own fire."

Psellus, who quotes this verse (*Exeg.* 1144a 8-9), says that it describes the Father's making himself unknowable to all that is below him, even his own Power. Proclus, in his many references to this verse (e.g. *In Crat.* 58, 8 Pasq.; *In Parm.* 628, 11; 1033, 27; 1067, 3 Cousin) bears this out. Porphyry similarly (if it is he!), in the Turin *Parmenides Commentary*, IX 1-2, refers to the verse with reference to the One.

Plotinus, on the other hand, uses the verb only with reference to the individual 'snatching himself up' from contact with the physical world and the concerns of the lower soul. Such language in connexion with the One itself would probably seem too 'mythological' for his taste (the One should not be doing anything so active as snatching itself up, or away, from what is below it), though he would have no quarrel with the doctrine implied in the verse. If we have, then, to do here with a Chaldaean reminiscence, it is once again largely verbal, adapted by Plotinus to the acceptable situation of the self-snatching up of the individual soul or mind.

(7) Ἐκθρῴσκω, 'leap forth'.

This Homeric verb is found fully four times in the surviving fragments of the *Oracles* (Frs. 34, 1; 35, 1; 37, 3; 42, 1)[11], always of a lower principle 'leaping forth' from a higher. Matter 'leaps forth' from the Fount of Founts (i.e. the Paternal Intellect) in Fr. 34, as do the 'implacable thunderbolts' of the Forms in Frs. 35 and 37; and Eros 'leapt forth' (*ekthore*) first from Intellect in Fr. 42. So there is a definite Chaldaean usage of the term, as is recognized by later Neoplatonists.

Plotinus' single use of the word conforms to this. At VI 4, 16, 29, he speaks of the All-Soul as 'leaping out, as it were' (*hoion exethoren*) into particularity, to inhabit an individual body. To achieve a complete analogy, we would have to have the individual souls leaping forth from the All-Soul, but Plotinus' very subtle view of the relation between the All-Soul and the individual souls (cf. the first *aporia* of *Enn.* IV 3, chs. 1-8) causes him to express himself in this way. We do in fact, however, have to do with an inferior entity proceeding from a superior, or at least a superior entity proceeding into inferiority. The rather self-conscious *hoion* before *exethoren* seems to me a sign that Plotinus is 'quoting', even if he is none too willing to acknowledge the source.

(8) Ὀπισθοβαρής, 'weighed down behind'.

This remarkable word, employed only once by Plotinus (VI 9, 4, 22), and found once in the surviving fragments of the *Oracles* (Fr. 155), is virtually unknown in earlier Greek[12]. In the *Oracles*, if we are to believe Proclus, who quotes the passage at *In Remp.* II 77, 9-10 Kroll, it refers to 'the nature of the passions' (*hê tôn pathôn physis*):

δύσκαμπτος καὶ ὀπισθοβαρὴς καὶ φωτὸς ἄμοιρος

"intractable and weighted down behind and without share of light".

The Chaldaean connotation of the word is that of something which drags one down from higher concerns, or levels of consciousness, to lower. Proclus employs the word in two other places in the *Republic Commentary* (I 119, 17, and II 190, 10), as well as once

---

[11]The other occurrence in the *Oracles* (Fr. 61a 1) refers to the *apletos hormê* of the moon.

[12]Its frequency, and that of other compounds of *thrôiskô*, is noted by Willy Theiler. 'Die chaldäischen Orakel und die Hymnen des Synesios', in *Forschungen zum Neuplatonismus*, p. 269.

in the *Cratylus Commentary* (61, 10 Pasq.), and in all cases in such a connexion. At both *In Remp.* passages the reference is to the 'vehicle' (*ochêma*) of the soul when not properly purified, and in the *Cratylus* commentary he is speaking of those who have chosen an anagogic and intellectual life, and are not *embritheis* and *opisthobareis*.

Plotinus' use of the word fits this meaning very well. It occurs in a context of *Enn*. VI 9 where he is discussing the difficulties in the way of apprehension of the One. He has just said that some souls may never have attained vision of the splendour (*aglaia*) there, while another may have received the true light (*phôs alêthinon*), and have filled itself with light, but is frustrated of unimpeded ascent through being weighted down from behind with elements which impede its vision (ἀναβεβηκέναι δέ, ἔτι ὀπισθοβαρὴς ὑπάρχων, ἃ ἐμπόδια ἦν τῇ θέᾳ).

Apart from postulating a lost common poetic source (such as perhaps the Orphic poems) of both *Oracles* and Plotinus, I do not see how one can reasonably deny that Plotinus, here at least, is making use of a Chaldaean turn of phrase. The close proximity of *phôs* and *aglaia* (cf. *phôtos amoiros* of the Chaldaean fragment) would seem to point in the same direction. One can only conclude that the word, and the imagery implicit in it, tickled Plotinus' fancy.

(9) Πικρός, *'bitter'*.

The Chaldaean associations of this word relate to one particular use of it, in connexion with Matter (Fr. 129), where the body is referred to as

τὸ πικρᾶς ὕλης περίβλημα βρότειον,

"the mortal envelope of bitter matter".

The image is presumably that of Matter as the bitter dregs of the universe, though that is not made explicit, and since the epithet is not actually applied to Matter elsewhere in Greek literature, we are left to guess its precise significance. However, if that *is* the image, then Plotinus is presenting it more explicitly in his employment of the phrase at *Enn*. II 3, 17, 24, where he speaks of Matter as οἷον ὑποστάθμη τῶν προηγουμένων πικρὰ καὶ πικρὰ ποιοῦσα, "a sort of dregs of the things above it, bitter and productive of bitterness." The notion of Matter as a *hypostathmê* is derived ultimately from *Phaedo* 109B, where water, mist and air are described as the *hypostathmê* of aether, which flow together into the hollows of the earth in which we live, but it requires a further step to transfer this to an actual description of Matter.

Who first took this step we cannot be sure, but I would suggest that it is implicit in the Chaldaean characterization of Matter as *pikra*, and so not a development due to Plotinus. *Hypostathmê* becomes an accepted epithet of Matter in later Neoplatonism, as represented by Proclus and Damascius[13]. They may be dependent on Plotinus, but they may also be drawing on a now lost line of the *Oracles*. At any rate, in the absence of a more obvious source, I suggest that we may take Plotinus' reference to Matter as 'bitter dregs' to be a Chaldaean reminiscence.

What, then, has this investigation achieved? Ten items, after all, are a fairly thin harvest from the whole corpus of the *Enneads*, and by no means all of these are entirely plausible. I would stand firm (as would many others, including Édouard des Places) on ἀμφίστομος, ἁρπάζω, ἐκθρῴσκω, ὀπισθοβαρής and πικρά (ὕλη), as well as on the phrase with which we began, but one must be less confident about such words as ἀγλαΐα, ἀΐσσω, ἄνθος or ἄπλετος.[14]

What seems to me to explain the situation best is the assumption that Plotinus had actually perused the *Chaldaean Oracles* at some stage of his career, and, as we have seen, probably not just at Porphyry's prompting (since I 9 and VI 9, at least, were composed before the latter's arrival on the scene), but that he derived from them no more than the memory of certain striking turns of phrase, which he employed occasionally (and often with a self-conscious *hoion* or *hôsper*) when they seemed appropriate. Such use implies no approval of Chaldaean doctrine (though there was much in the *Oracles* to which Plotinus would have, at least, no objection), and an admission that Plotinus had read them hardly, I think, need alter our views on his philosophical influences. But such an admission does clear up a small mystery that has bothered students of his, and adds something, I think, to our appreciation of his 'literary' influences.

---

[13]The only known use of it is actually a remarkable one, τῆς ἀσεβείας ὀπισθοβαρεῖς ἀναγκαί, in the Nemrud Dagh inscription of Antiochus I of Commagene, composed shortly before 31 B.C. (Dittenberger, *OGI* 383, 1. 120), but we may assume that it is not original there. Antiochus' language throughout the whole inscription is distinctly orotund. A similar compound, *opisthobrithês*, is found in a fragment of Aeschylus (Fr. 338 Nauck), and I would not be surprised if this word were in fact Aeschylean or Pindaric.

[14]On the other hand, there may be other words, too general in their ancestry to be identified, such as *augê* or *menos* or *phôs*, which might in fact constitute Chaldaean echoes, but that we can never know.

Porphyry's Commentary on the "Harmonics" of Ptolemy and Neoplatonic Musical Theory[1]

STEPHEN GERSH

It is not surprising that the Neoplatonists, the most influential philosophers of late antiquity, should reveal a considerable interest in musical theory. As primary legatees of the Pythagorean tradition, they were attracted by the notion of a numerical basis of reality demonstrated by the dependence of aural consonances upon ratios in the lengths of sound-producing strings or pipes. In general, what Neoplatonic writers have to say about harmonics is contained in their commentaries upon works of Plato where issues related to music are raised. For example, the discussion of the world soul's harmonic structure in the *Timaeus* and the astronomical interpretation of the Sirens in the final pages of the *Republic* produced elaborate responses in the commentaries on those texts by Porphyry and Proclus. Other musical ideas occurring in the *Phaedo*—the comparison of the human soul with harmony—and the *Philebus*—the association of limit and infinity with musical pitch—lead to discussions in the corresponding commentaries of Damascius and Olympiodorus. However, a more interesting and in some respects unique example of Neoplatonic musical theory occurs in the form of Porphyry's commentary on the *Harmonics* of Ptolemy.

---

[1] Since this paper was written, the following items relevant to my discussion have appeared: Barker, A. (transl.) 'Ptolemy, *Harmonics*', *Greek Musical Writings* II, *Harmonic and Acoustic Theory*, Cambridge 1989, pp. 270-391. Solomon, J. 'A Preliminary Analysis of the Organization of Ptolemy's *Harmonics*', *Music Theory and its Sources, Antiquity and the Middle Ages*, ed. A. Barbera, Notre Dame, Indiana 1990, pp. 68-84.

This commentary is one of a small class of extant works: that of Neoplatonic commentaries on mathematical or scientific texts, and shares certain features with Proclus' later commentary on the *Elements* of Euclid, to cite the most well-known example. But despite its unusual status, it has received almost no attention from scholars. A modern edition of the text was published by Ingemar Düring in 1932[2] together with some critical notes, yet his interest in the work was restricted entirely to its preservation of fragments from earlier Greek musical theorists. For these reasons, it may be useful to examine the commentary for once on its own terms.

In his review of musical theory in the *Harmonics*, Ptolemy discusses the following topics. Two introductory chapters consider the purpose and methods of harmonic science in general. This is followed by a treatment of the production of sound in the physical medium. After a further chapter on the division of sounds into those of equal and unequal pitch, of the unequal into continuous and discrete, of the discrete into unmelodic and melodic, and of the melodic into dissonant and consonant, the main subject of book I begins: the discussion of intervals interpreted, in general according to Pythagorean theory, as numerical ratios. In chapter 12 and chapter 1 of book II, Ptolemy turns to the smaller intervals within the consonance of the fourth by discussing the three genera of diatonic, chromatic, and enharmonic. After another chapter in which is advocated the use of a new instrument, the 'helicon', for demonstrating the truths of harmonics, the main topics of book II are broached: the theories of octave species and of the Greater and Lesser Perfect Systems. This book concludes with an account of the traditional instrument for studying harmonics, the monochord, and with a set of tables giving precise numerical values for the three genera. The two introductory chapters of book III are concerned with the tuning methods of the fifteen-stringed canon. This account is followed by a radical shift in subject-matter from the details of harmonic science to an evocation of its power. Ptolemy develops this in terms of a series of comparisons between the elements of harmonics outlined in books I and II and features of the most perfect natures i. e. human souls and heavenly bodies. The three consonances are associated with parts of the soul in chapter 5, the three genera with the parts of the theoretical and practical sciences in chapter 6, and modulations among the octave

---

[2]*Porphyrios Kommentar zur Harmonielehre des Ptolemaios*, herausgegeben von Ingemar Düring, Göteborg 1932.

species with modifications of conduct in chapter 7. Then he turns from psychology to astronomy where, as explained in the next chapter, the parallelism is mainly between the recurrence of notes in successive octaves and the circularity of celestial motions. In this way, the three consonances are linked with angular divisions of the zodiac in chapter 9, and the differences between the genera and modulations according to octave species with motions of the planets in the remaining chapters of book III.

Porphyry's commentary on the *Harmonics* extends only as far as book II, chapter 7. More than three quarters of this text is devoted to Ptolemy's first book with roughly half of the total concerned with the first four chapters of that book. This means that the Porphyrian discussion is an elaboration upon certain issues raised by the *Harmonics* rather than a systematic treatment of the whole work.

Perhaps the central problem identified by Porphyry is that of evaluating the relative importance of the two psychic faculties of 'reason' (λόγος) and 'sensation' (αἴσθησις) in the judgment of sounds. Here, the Neoplatonist takes up a position in relation to the traditional debates between Pythagoreans stressing the priority of reason and Aristoxenians emphasizing that of sense. Ptolemy reports the disagreement between the two schools on many pages of the *Harmonics*, himself inclining towards the Pythagorean viewpoint on most questions. Porphyry similarly lines up on the Pythagorean side but sharpens the emphasis upon reason with a more explicitly Platonic epistemology. As a result, the commentary devotes much attention to the notion of numerical ratios as the true basis for the study of musical consonance.

In chapter 1 of Ptolemy's text, the notion that hearing and reason which relate to matter and form respectively are the criteria of harmonics[3] leads Porphyry into elaborate developments of his own. He takes up the contrasts between the two psychic faculties of sensation and reason[4], and between the two metaphysical principles of matter and form.[5] This in turn leads to important notes on the epistemological process of abstracting form from physical objects and on the ontological distinction between various types of 'reasons'

---

[3]Ptolemy: *Harm.* 3. 3-5. References to Ptolemy's *Harmonics* will hereafter be given in a shortened form: Ptolemy + number. The text is that in *Die Harmonielehre des Klaudios Ptolemaios*, herausgegeben von Ingemar Düring, Göteborg 1930.

[4]Porphyry: *In Harm.* 11. 7-9, 12. 2-3, 13. 24 ff., 15. 23-8, and 16. 30-32.

[5]*Ibid.* 12. 2-3, 12. 14-20, 13. 17-19, 13. 21-4, and 14. 22-5.

(λόγοι) which can be physical, mathematical—including the kind relevant to music—and demiurgic.[6] Ptolemy's comparison of the distinction between a purely sensory awareness of sound and the mathematicians' judgment of ratios with that between the visual observance of a circle and the geometricians' knowledge of the corresponding perfect figure[7] also attracts Porphyry's attention.[8]

Chapter 2 of the *Harmonics* explains that the student of this science will reveal how the works of nature are 'according to reason and an ordered cause' (μετὰ λόγου ... καὶ τεταγμένης αἰτίας)[9]. Porphyry evidently detected a reference to the cosmology of the Platonic tradition which he expands in terms of the Plotinian exegesis. On this view, the nature to which Ptolemy alludes is a principle subordinate to universal soul, while his ordered cause is the universal soul itself or one of its phases.[10]

Ptolemy's third chapter deals with the physics of sounds especially in terms of the Aristotelian categories of quantity and quality. His conclusion that the distinction between high and low pitches is related to quantity[11] is developed by Porphyry into a discussion of the numerical ratios underlying sounds.[12] The commentator notes Ptolemy's agreement with the Pythagoreans in emphasizing the role of the quantitative and appends an idea not in the original text: that rhythms are based on ratios and therefore have 'the same nature' (τῆς αὐτῆς φύσεως) as melodies.[13]

Chapter 4 of *Harmonics* book I sets out the classification of sounds into equal and unequal, continuous and discrete, and so on. Ptolemy's point that a sound is 'irrational' (ἄλογος) since a 'ratio' (λόγος) requires two terms and sound as opposed to interval involves only one[14] leads the commentator to reflect on the term *logos*. According to Porphyry, the characterization of a sound as irrational depends upon a specific

---

[6]*Ibid.* 12. 5 ff., 12. 14-20, 13. 12-14, and 13. 21-4.

[7]Ptolemy 3. 20-4. 9.

[8]Porphyry: *In Harm.* 19. 16-19.

[9]Ptolemy 5. 13-24.

[10]Porphyry: *In Harm.* 24. 22-4.

[11]Ptolemy 6. 14 ff.

[12]Porphyry: *In Harm.* 37. 11-14.

[13]*Ibid.* 37. 21-4.

[14]Ptolemy 10. 19-23.

notion of *logos* as 'the relation between two magnitudes of the same kind' (δύο μεγεθῶν ὁμογενῶν σχέσις)[15] Further, the question whether equal sounds can be said to have *logos* but not 'interval' (διάστημα) is left open until more detailed discussion of consonances has been completed[16]. Although Porphyry does not strictly speaking add any fresh ideas to the original text, his insistence that the sense of *logos* is limited here points to his own wider and more metaphysical interpretation of the term in the comments on chapter 1.

Ptolemy's fifth chapter begins the lengthy and important discussion of intervals in terms of Pythagorean ratio theory. His use of the term 'excess' (ὑπεροχή)[17] in the arithmetical context gives Porphyry the opportunity of distinguishing between this notion and that of ratio by quoting the opinion of Thrasyllus[18]. According to this author, the ratios between 6 and 3 and between 2 and 1 are the same although the excesses are different: 3 in the former case and 1 in the latter. Porphyry's concern to clarify the difference between excess and ratio fits into a wider context in which he considers the relation of both notions to that of interval by quoting Eratosthenes, Aelian the Platonist, and Philolaus[19].

In the commentary on the remaining chapters of *Harmonics* book I and the early chapters of book II, Porphyry repeats much of the terminological clarification made previously. For example, in commenting on chapter 7 of book I he reiterates the point about the irrationality of the sound[20]; in discussing chapter 9 he develops the contrast between the spatial intervals envisaged by the Aristoxenians and the ratio intervals of Pythagorean tradition[21]; in commenting on chapter 7 of book II he develops the analogy between musical sound and interval and geometrical point and line[22]. In most of these interpretations, the metaphysical standpoint of a Neoplatonist lurks in

---

[15]Porphyry: *In Harm.* 87. 21 ff.

[16]*Ibid.* 88. 11-18.

[17]Ptolemy 11. 1 ff.

[18]Porphyry: *In Harm.* 91. 13-92. 9.

[19]*Ibid.* 91. 3 ff.

[20]*Ibid.* 113. 1 ff.

[21]*Ibid.* 125. 19-21.

[22]*Ibid.* 173. 18-21.

the background even if it does not lead to extensive shifts from the viewpoint of the original text.

Porphyry's commentary on the *Harmonics* of Ptolemy displays at least two general features typical of a Greek philosophical school text of the post-Plotinian period: the integration of quotations from certain established authorities in the prior tradition, and the treatment of classic Neoplatonic philosophical ideas as a kind of backdrop to the musical discussion. Taking the question of sources first, we naturally find Plato's name invoked at crucial junctures in the argument. For a thinker trained in the school of Plotinus, the primary authority of the dialogues and especially of the *Timaeus* is a matter beyond controversy. Accordingly, Porphyry quotes 'the universal soul-production' (ἡ ψυχογονία τοῦ παντός) described in this text as an illustration of the possibility of extending the musical gamut beyond two to four octaves,[23] and as evidence for the equation of ratio and 'interval' (διάστημα) in the theory of scales.[24] The *Timaeus* is also utilized for its description of the physical circumstances of sound and hearing at three or four points in the commentary.[25] Other Platonic texts are cited from time to time. The *Philebus* supplies ideas concerning the interrelation of limit and infinity in the transformation of physical qualities[26]—an appropriate parallel since these notions in Plato's text are inherently Pythagorean and musical in character. The *Symposium* furnishes one minor detail in quoting Socrates' habitual practice of saying the same things on the same topics.[27]

Porphyry is historically important within the Neoplatonic tradition for establishing the systematic study of Aristotle as part of the philosophical curriculum. So it is not surprising to find Aristotelian quotations side by side with Platonic ones in the commentary on Ptolemy. Among the works of Aristotle, the *Categories* are employed to elucidate the notion of 'quality' (ποιότης) which is significant in Ptolemy's account of the physical production of sound.[28] In the same general context, the second book of *De Anima* provides a number of

---

[23] *Ibid.* 115. 28 ff. Cf. Plato : *Tim.* 35 b.

[24] *Ibid.* 92. 12-18. Cf. Plato: *Tim.* 36 a-b.

[25] *Ibid.* 46. 3 ff. and 48. 32-49. 1. Cf. Plato: *Tim.* 67 b.

[26] *Ibid.* 78. 4 ff. Cf. Plato: *Phil.* 24 a.

[27] *Ibid.* 5. 4-6. Cf. Plato: *Symp.* 221 e.

[28] *Ibid.* 41. 14 ff. and 42. 29 ff. Cf. Aristotle: *Categ.* 8. 9ª-10ª.

details regarding the propagation of sounds through the physical medium of air.[29] Other Aristotelian texts are also included in the exegetical repertoire. The *Metaphysics* are quoted in connection with the definition of harmony according to form, matter, or the composite at the beginning of Ptolemy's text.[30] *De Sensu et Sensibili* is the source for an interesting analogy between consonance and colour.[31]

Besides Plato and Aristotle, the presence of other authorities in Porphyry's commentary is indicative of its style and methods. The tendency to resort to Pythagorean ideas is normally quite pronounced in Neoplatonic writers of late antiquity, and this naturally gains reinforcement in the context of a treatise on harmonics. In fact, this commentary is a veritable repository of Pythagorean fragments including extensive materials from pseudo-Archytas[32], from Ptolemais of Cyrene[33], and Thrasyllus[34] in particular. Another characteristic of Neoplatonists from the time of Porphyry onwards is their interest in the exegesis of occultist literature like the *Chaldaean Oracles*. There seems to be one allusion to such an oracle in a passage comparing the intellect's approach to being to the leaping of a spark although this reference is admittedly fleeting[35].

Use of sources is not the only feature marking out this commentary as typically Neoplatonic, since there is also the question of the ontological backdrop of the text itself. This consists of references to the doctrine of the school of Plotinus that the first principles are various levels of being or consciousness: the One, Intellect, Soul, and Nature. Although the scope for elaborating such ideas is not great in a technical treatise on harmonics, there are at least enough allusions to establish the Neoplatonic pedigree of the commentary.

In the philosophy of Porphyry, the second principle or hypostasis is 'Intellect' (νοῦς) containing a unified plurality of intellects together with its correlative object 'Being' (ὄν) embracing a unified plurality of intelligibles or Forms. In an interesting passage of the commentary on

---

[29]*Ibid.* 39. 10 ff., 47. 13 ff., 49. 16-26, and 52. 15-17. Cf. Aristotle: *De Anim.* II. 8. 419^b-420^a.

[30]*Ibid.* 11. 21-3. Cf. Aristotle: *Metaph.* 1042^a·

[31]*Ibid.* 152. 1-6. Cf. Aristotle: *De Sens.* 439^b.

[32]*Ibid.* 31. 27-33. 4, 56. 4-57. 23, 92. 29, and 93. 5-17.

[33]*Ibid.* 22. 23-4, etc.

[34]*Ibid.* 12. 21 ff. and 91. 13-15.

[35]*Ibid.* 14. 3-6.

the *Harmonics*, these intelligibles, associated with being, incorporeal, transcending the sensible, accessible to intellect only are contrasted as primary intelligibles with a kind of secondary intelligible: the sensible object when accessible to an attention or comprehension of intellect. The starting point for this comparison is Ptolemy's reference to certain 'intelligibles through sensation' (δι' αἰσθήσεως νοητά) in explaining the relation of sense and reason in harmonic theory, and Porphyry comments that this rational element in the perception of sounds is intelligible only in his secondary sense.[36] The second principle or Intellect itself is described several times in the earlier part of the comments on chapter 1. In one passage it appears as 'the external or transcendent intellect (ὁ θύραθεν καὶ ἐπαναβεβηκὼς νοῦς) to which another principle the 'materiate intellect' (ὁ ὑλικὸς νοῦς) becomes subject in the cognitive process.[37] Here, the allusion is to the relation of active and passive intellects in Aristotle reinterpreted Neoplatonically as that of universal and particular intellects. Elsewhere, the second hypostasis is compared to a fire from which a spark leaps forth when projected cognitively towards 'that which is really being' (τὸ ὄντως ὄν).[38] In this passage the imagery of fire is reminiscent of those *Chaldaean Oracles* which Porphyry was the first professional philosopher to use systematically.

According to Neoplatonic doctrine, the next principle or hypostasis is 'Soul' (ψυχή). Its structure is more complex since it implies a further unfolding into multiplicity, and Porphyry's own teaching vacillates from one text to another. However, he seems to envisage as distinct unfoldings of this principle the following: a highest phase of universal soul in which it is intellective corresponding to the 'Craftsman' (δημιουργός) of Plato's *Timaeus*; the first of the individual souls equivalent to the world soul of the same text; various other individual souls of heavenly bodies, demons, and men; and a lower phase of universal soul which infuses sensible forms into bodies described as 'Nature' (φύσις). All these manifestations of soul occur in the commentary on the *Harmonics* at least in allusive form. The Craftsman is mentioned in commenting upon Ptolemy's references to reason as a criterion of harmonics and to the inherent regularity of

---

[36]*Ibid.* 17. 13 ff.

[37]*Ibid.* 13. 17-19.

[38]*Ibid.* 14. 13 ff.

natural phenomena[39]; the world soul is introduced as an instance of a harmonic structure formed by a series of ratios extending to four octaves[40]; individual souls enter into the theoretical discussions of Ptolemy's views on the interrelation of reason and hearing in harmonic perception[41]; and Nature is mentioned as an additional factor in the passages discussing the activity of the Craftsman.[42]

The Porphyrian commentary on the *Harmonics* of Ptolemy is clearly not intended as a metaphysical treatise, and so the epistemological or ontological ideas which it contains are expressed in an allusive manner, perhaps functioning as signposts towards more detailed analyses elsewhere. Since Neoplatonic writers invariably hold that all terminology in the texts upon which they comment is technical in character and fixed in its range of meanings, even passing allusions evoke complex structures of thought extending considerably beyond the basic sphere of discussion. There are several good illustrations of this feature in the present commentary where key notions of harmonic theory or at least of Ptolemy's version are invested with profound significance in relation to Porphyrian thought as a whole.

The first technical term which functions in this way is 'power' (δύναμις). This is a concept of notorious complexity in the Greek philosophical tradition, and Ptolemy uses it in at least two senses in the *Harmonics*. The first sense occurs in the definition of the science itself which begins the treatise: 'harmonics is a power comprehending the differences of high and low pitches' (ἁρμονική ἐστι δύναμις καταληπτικὴ τῶν ἐν τοῖς ψόφοις περὶ τὸ ὀξὺ καὶ τὸ βαρὺ διαφορῶν).[43] In this context, the notion seems to be that of an ability or faculty of the soul. The second sense is stated most clearly in the section of book II discussing the Greater Perfect System where any one of the fifteen notes can be named either 'according to position' (παρ' αὐτὴν τὴν θέσιν) or 'according to power' (παρὰ τὴν δύναμιν αὐτήν).[44] The idea here is that a given pitch name such as *mese* can be applied both to a fixed pitch within the basic system or to another pitch performing the

---

[39]*Ibid*. 12. 14-20 and 24. 22-4.

[40]*Ibid*. 115. 28 ff.

[41]*Ibid*. 11. 7-9, 12. 10, 13. 21-4, and 14. 22-5.

[42]*Ibid*. 24. 22-4 and 114. 13.

[43]Ptolemy 3. 1-2.

[44]Ptolemy 52. 10-11.

analogous harmonic function as the first within a transposed system. Porphyry clearly understands both these senses of power which he employs with technical precision in different parts of the commentary.[45] Yet he makes the issue more complicated by treating them as two meanings within a wider range of possibilities.

Additional senses of power are revealed in the commentary on the *Harmonics* itself where implications of Ptolemy's first type are being drawn out. In one passage, he further defines harmonics as something having an existence primal in rank, an elemental power, and a theoretical status in respect of primaries.[46] This formulation characterizes the science in terms of three aspects of metaphysical principles in general according to the Porphyrian system. In the continuation of these comments, he explains that the power which harmonics represents does not correspond to 'what is potential and imperfect' (δυνάμει ... ἀτελής). It is rather equivalent to 'what is powerful and acts perfectly' (τὸ δύνασθαι ... ἐνεργεῖν ἤδη τελείως)[47]. These comments situate Ptolemy's notion neatly within the framework of the different Aristotelian senses of power also used in Neoplatonism.

Other works by Porphyry significantly extend the notion of power in directions which can only be briefly sketched here. A basic feature of his theory is that in the hierarchy of being, power proceeds from higher principles towards lower and then returns from lower principles to higher in a quasi-circular motion. This is illustrated in his interpretation of Plato's *Symposium* myth where the inclining of an incorporeal soul towards matter corresponds to an 'emptying' (κένωσις) of its power, and its elevation towards Intellect to a 'fulness' (τὸ πλῆρες) of that power, these two states of soul being symbolized by the figures of Poros and Penia respectively.[48] Elsewhere Porphyry notes that the quasi-circular transformation of power is between poles

[45]Porphyry: *In Harm.* 6. 8-9, 11. 7-9, and 13. 24 ff. (power as psychic faculty). Cf. *ibid.* 104. 5-8, 166. 4, and 166. 16 (power as harmonic function).

[46]*Ibid.* 5. 24-7 and 128. 8-10.

[47]*Ibid.* 6. 33-7. 5.

[48]Porphyry: *Sent. ad Intell.* 40. 51. 3ff. Cf. *ibid.*

of perfection and imperfection[49], unity and multiplicity[50], and power and bulk[51]: these being varied aspects of a single ontological process.

This more comprehensive notion of power underlies Porphyry's comments on the concept which occurs in the *Harmonics* and even explains the two features noted earlier: subjectivity and relativity. Ptolemy had first described as power the ability to distinguish high and low pitches. This subjective element fits easily into the Porphyrian framework since the Neoplatonist, in commenting on this idea, has already noted that the power involved is perfect and active rather than imperfect and passive. Furthermore, perfect power is associated by Porphyry with the motion of a principle's return to its prior and this in turn with the intellective actualization of the principle[52]. Ptolemy had also described as according to power the analogous functions of pitches in different transpositions. This relativistic element also fits naturally into the Neoplatonic elaboration since it is a peculiar feature of Porphyry's doctrine that a given level of power on the continuum between perfection and imperfection can be understood from different viewpoints as a degree of fullness or of emptiness. Thus, any principle can possess fullness of perfect power in relation to intelligibles and emptiness of perfect power in respect of sensibles at the same time as emptiness of imperfect power in relation to intelligibles and fullness of imperfect power in respect of sensibles.[53]

Another technical term in harmonic theory which is invested with deeper philosophical significance by Porphyry is *logos* meaning 'ratio', 'reason', or 'cause' according to context. The commentator repeats much of Ptolemy's own discussion of this concept, noting the requirement that *logos*—here meaning 'ratio'—should involve two terms[54] or that it must be contrasted with the notion of excess.[55] He also describes the application of *logoi* to musical sounds, where the concept refers strictly not to the sound itself but to the length of string which produces it[56]. Yet of greater interest are passages where Porphyry veers

---

[49] *Ibid.* 11. 5. 4 and 32. 29. 7.

[50] *Ibid.* 11. 5. 1-4 and 33. 36. 5 ff.

[51] *Ibid.* 34. 39. 4-12 and 35. 39. 13 ff.

[52] *Ibid.* 37. 45. 5-9.

[53] Porphyry: *De Abstin.* I. 30. 6 ff.

[54] Porphyry: *In Harm.* 87. 21 ff. and 113. 1 ff.

[55] *Ibid.* 85. 27-30 and 91. 19 ff.

wildly from the technical discussion of harmonics onto metaphysical terrain.

A striking example of this can be found within the commentator's extended response to Ptolemy's statement that hearing and *logos*—now meaning 'reason'—are the twin criteria of harmonic theory.[57] Since this is one of the most metaphysical paragraphs in the entire commentary, it is perhaps worth translating in full.

'The term *logos* is employed in numerous senses. It can equally mean the physical *logos*: that of the seminal power which brings together the activities of nature itself. The mathematicians also speak of a *logos* of numbers, as used in banking, which implies the relation of similar units to one another through proportions. Because of this, the most important and pre-eminent *logos* is that which simultaneously holds the relation and summation of the natural coming together of things, and which the reasoning (λογισμός) of the soul imitates after a fashion. This is what confers form on matter, since matter is informed as if through a reckoning and summation. The affections and dispositions which arise in it are brought together according to their relation and concordance with one another. In an analogous mode of harmonization, all things are controlled both according to their individual mode of causality and the ambient of the universe. The god who is leader of wholes employs this kind of *logos* or reasoning (λογισμός) as if having a divine knowledge and thinking, and according to his design nature produces each of the things in the world'[58].

This passage is the most extensive discussion of the term *logos* in Porphyry and is remarkable not only for the careful classification of meanings, in which it invites comparison with a similar text in Theo of Smyrna, but also for the application of quasi-numerical terminology to the highest *logos*.

Passages in other Porphyrian works echo these differing senses of *logos*. The physical type is introduced into a discussion of myth where he speaks of the 'seminal' (σπερματικός) *logos* which pervades all things under the control of Zeus and whose descent into the materiate substratum is symbolized by Priapus.[59] The mathematical *logos* occurs elsewhere in Porphyry in connection with soul, since Plato in the

---

56*Ibid*. 66. 20 ff. and j67. 7-8.

57Ptolemy 3. 3-4.

58Porphyry: *In Harm*. 12. 6-20.

Timaeus had explained the fashioning of the world soul by the Craftsman in terms of proportionality.[60] Finally, the highest type also occurs in the discussion of myth where he mentions a 'demiurgic' (δημιουργικός) *logos* which represents the activity of the Craftsman or Hermes in creation, capable of producing things without matter.[61]

Another technical term undergoing transformation in Porphyrian philosophy is 'harmony' (ἁρμονία) itself. This is also a concept of wide application in the Greek tradition, and Ptolemy reflects this spectrum of meanings in the *Harmonics*. One sense is illustrated near the beginning of the treatise where he notes that 'the criteria of harmony are hearing and reason' (κριτήρια μὲν ἁρμονίας ἀκοὴ καὶ λόγος)[62]. Since the definition of harmonics occurs immediately before this in the text, ἁρμονία seems to relate to ἁρμονική as object to subject, or as the arrangement of sounds to the faculty of judging that arrangement. However, the predominant sense of harmony is that occurring repeatedly in book III when the discussion is shifted from the analysis of sounds to broader questions of metaphysics. It is implied in passages where Ptolemy attempts to situate harmony in relation to concepts like nature, God, and reason[63], or to treat it as a power present in more perfect things like human souls and the motions of heavenly bodies[64]. Porphyry's usage reflects a similar range of meanings, although predictably with a greater emphasis upon metaphysical applications.

One example of such a usage occurs in the commentary on the *Harmonics* where Ptolemy's idea that there are different limits of high and low pitches in relation to sound and hearing respectively is developed.[65] Porphyry cites the Pythagorean notion of the 'harmony of the universe' (ἡ τοῦ παντὸς ἁρμονία) in which the rotation of the heavenly bodies produces a sound unheard by men because its magnitude overwhelms their hearing as confirmation of the point

---

[59]Porphyry: *Ad Gaur.* 14. 1. 53. 28-31, *De Simul.* 3. 6* 9-10, 7. 10* 20-11* 1, and 8. 17* 16-18.

[60]Porphyry: *In Tim.* fr. 69 (= Proclus: *In Tim.* II. 214. 4-215. 5).

[61]Porphyry: *De Simul.* 8. 17* 15-18, 10. 18* 12-14, and *In Tim.* fr. 51 (=Proclus: *In Tim.* I. 391. 4-396. 26).

[62]Ptolemy 3. 3-4.

[63]Ptolemy 92. 19-27.

[64]Ptolemy 92. 21 ff.

about limits.[66] It is interesting that he explicitly interprets this 'magnitude' (μέγεθος) as involving extremely high and low pitches beyond the aural capacity of the human ear rather than an excessive loudness as in some other ancient reports of the music of the spheres.

Another example of the metaphysical application of harmony occurs in passages of the same commentary where a distinction suggested but not elaborated by Ptolemy between 'harmony' (ἁρμονία) and 'the harmonized' (τὸ ἡρμοσμένον)[67] becomes an important dogma. On Porphyry's view, harmony can be distinguished from the harmonized in the same way that 'number' (ἀριθμός) is contrasted with 'the numbered' (τὸ ἀριθμητόν): that is as form is distinguished from the composite of form and matter[68]. Furthermore, this metaphysical dualism within the harmonized explains why it is necessary to judge the latter not with sense alone but with a combination of reason and sense.[69] It is not difficult to see that Porphyry is here developing a basically Aristotelian analysis into a more Platonic dichotomy of intelligible and sensible being.

Passages in other Porphyrian works provide further illustrations of these ideas. His interpretation of the cosmogony in Plato's *Timaeus* of which significant extracts are preserved in Macrobius explores the harmony of the universe. According to this theory, the intervals of fourth, fifth, octave, twelfth, and double octave occur in the actual sounds produced by the heavenly bodies as they pass through the atmosphere. The different pitches arising from the planetary rotations are signified mythically by the Sirens and Muses described by writers like Plato and Hesiod, while the combination of all these pitches is symbolized by the ninth Muse.[70] Elsewhere, Porphyry elaborates the famous image of the psychic harmony in Plato's *Phaedo* in terms of the distinction between harmony and the harmonized. Here, an analogy is established between a musician passively responding to his instrument's strings as the external manifestation of a 'separate harmony' (ἁρμονία χωριστή)   which impassively causes the resonance, and the ensouled being passively responding to sense objects as the exterior manifestation of the separable soul impassively

---

[65]Ptolemy 9. 19-21.

[66]Porphyry: *In Harm.* 80. 28-81. 4.

[67]Ptolemy 94. 21 cf. 94. 24.

[68]Porphyry: *In Harm.* 12. 2-3.

[69]*Ibid.* 19. 15-19.

causing the sensation. This complicated psychological doctrine derived from Plotinus gives rise to various problems, even if the basic distinction between transcendent harmony and physical objects is reasonably clear.[71]

The handling of notions like power, *logos* and harmony in Porphyry's commentary on the *Harmonics* clearly illustrates the manner in which, in the hands of a Neoplatonic writer, technical terms in the science of music can be invested with elaborate metaphysical meanings. That musical concepts could be employed in this way by Neoplatonists is a fact which has not entirely escaped the attention of modern scholars. However, the peculiar significance of the Porphyrian commentary on Ptolemy within this tradition seems to have passed largely unnoticed.

---

[70]Porphyry: *In Tim.* fr. 66 (=Macrobius: *In Somn. Scip.* II. 1. 14-25).

[71]Porphyry: *Sent. ad Intell.* 10. 9. 1-13.

Relecture de Jamblique,
De mysteriis, VIII, chap. 1-5

HERVÉ D. SAFFREY

Le Père des Places avait apprécié l'analyse que j'ai faite naguère des livres I et II du *De mysteriis*.[1] Dans le prolongement de cette recherche, je voudrais lui offrir maintenant une relecture des cinq premiers chapitres du livre VIII. Ils forment en effet une unité qui a été reconnue par Th. Hopfner dans la division générale qu'il a proposée de ce traité en neuf parties. Dans cette division, c'est la septième partie qu'il a intitulée: "Sur les premiers principes de l'univers et du divin selon la doctrine des Égyptiens."[2]

Ces chapitres présentent une autre caractéristique qui rend leur lecture spécialement instructive. En effet, on sait que le titre vrai de cet écrit de Jamblique n'est pas celui tout artificiel que lui a donné Marsile Ficin, quand il l'a traduit au XVe siècle: *De mysteriis Aegyptiorum Chaldaeorum Assyriorum*. Il faut revenir à l'intitulé des manuscrits, le seul authentique, que l'on peut traduire: "Réponse de Maître Abamon à la Lettre de Porphyre à Anébon, et solutions des difficultés qu'elle contient." On sait d'ailleurs par une citation du commentaire de Proclus sur les *Ennéades* de Plotin que, dans l'archétype des manuscrits conservés, cette lettre de Porphyre à Anébon précédait la réponse, et que Maître Abamon n'est rien d'autre

---

[1]Cf. E. des Places, *La religion de Jamblique*, dans *De Jamblique à Proclus* (Entretiens sur l'Antiquité classique, t. 21), Vandoeuvres-Genève 197583: allusion à mon article *Plan des livres I et II du De mysteriis de Jamblique*, dans *Zetesis*, Bijdragen . . . aangeboden aan E. de Strijcker, Anvers-Utrecht 1973, 281-295.

[2]Cf. Th. Hopfner, *Ueber die Geheimlehren von Jamblichus*, Leipzig 1922, XXII: Ueber die Ur—und Grundprinzipien des Weltalls und des Göttlichen nach der Geheimlehre des Aegypter = VIII 1-5.

qu'un pseudonyme de Jamblique.[3] Cet écrit de Jamblique doit donc être examiné comme un traité en forme de lettre dans un échange de correspondance entre Porphyre et lui. Malheureusement la lettre de Porphyre est perdue. Mais il est évident que, pour interpréter correctement les réponses de Jamblique aux difficultés de Porphyre, il faut s'efforcer de retrouver chaque fois les questions posées par ce dernier. Or il n'est pas toujours facile de remonter à la formulation même des problèmes de Porphyre; pourtant s'il y a une partie du traité où ces interrogations sont clairement conservées, c'est justement le début du livre VIII, où Jamblique lui-même a reproduit pour commencer la liste des questions posées par son correspondant. C'est par là que nous devons commencer nous aussi.

Je vais donc relire les chapitres 1 à 5 du livre VIII du *De mysteriis*. Je traduis le grec en suivant le texte établi par le P. des Places et, dans quelques cas où je m'en écarte j'indique entre parenthèses la leçon ou la conjecture que je préfère. J'imprime en italiques les phrases qui sont, à mon avis, des citations soit littérales soit *ad mentem* de Porphyre. Je divise le texte en péricopes selon les articulations que je crois y reconnaître et je commente au fur et à mesure.

De myst. VIII 1, p. 260. 3-9: Liste des questions de Porphyre.

Abandonnant le précédent sujet, comme tu dis, *tu souhaites que soient clarifiées pour toi les questions suivantes:*

I.   1)   *Que pensent les Égyptiens de la cause première?*

2)   *Pensent-ils qu'elle soit un intellect ou au-dessus de l'intellect*

3)   *Pensent-ils qu'elle soit la seule cause ou qu'elle soit accompagnée d'une autre ou de plusieurs autres?*

4)   *Pensent-ils qu'elle soit incorporelle ou corporelle?*

5)   *Pensent-ils qu'elle soit identique au démiurge ou supérieure à lui?*

II.   *Les Égyptiens pensent-ils que c'est de l'unité ou de la multiplicité que vient tout ce qui existe?*

III. 1)   *Les Égyptiens connaissent-ils la matière ou des corps premiers qualifiés?*

2)   *La matière est-elle pour eux inengendrée ou engendrée?*

Voilà une série de huit questions que l'on peut regrouper sous trois problèmes: le premier concerne la cause première, le deuxième le

---

[3]Cf. M. Sicherl, *Die Handschriften, Ausgaben und Uebersetzungen von Iamblichos De mysteriis* (Texte und Untersuchungen, 62. Bd.), Berlin (1957): 20-21 et 166.

problème de l'un et du multiple, le troisième celui de la matière. On reconnait les problèmes fondamentaux de la philosophie grecque depuis Plotin. Sur ces questions, Porphyre demande des informations sur la doctrine des Égyptiens. Nous verrons pourquoi plus loin. En effet, Porphyre pense que, pour les Égyptiens, toutes les causes se ramènent à celles de l'ordre de la nature (*infra*, 268. 4-5). Jamblique va dire qu'il n'en est rien. Mais avant de répondre à ces questions, il présente un *status quaestionis* sous la forme d'un excursus ou exposé préliminaire.

DE MYST. VIII 1, 260. 10-261. 7: EXPOSÉ PRÉLIMINAIRE

Quant à moi, je veux te dire d'abord la raison pour laquelle, dans les écrits des anciens scribes sacrés sont rapportées sur ces questions des opinions nombreuses et variées, et pourquoi chez les savants qui sont encore en vie, l'enseignement relatif à ces sujets importants est loin d'être simple.   Je veux dire en réalité ceci: parce qu'il existe une quantité d'êtres et qu'ils diffèrent du tout au tout, leurs principes aussi ont été enseignés en grand nombre et présentés dans des classifications qui varient selon tel ou tel des anciens prêtres.   Ainsi les principes universels, Hermès les a parfaitement bien exposés dans ses 20.000 livres (chiffre enregistré par Séleucos) ou dans ses 36.525 livres (renseignement donné par Manéthon), tandis que les principes des êtres particuliers, les Anciens les expliquent de multiples manières pour avoir assumé (διαλαβόντες Gale), qui tel principe, qui tel autre. Sur tous ces principes, il faut découvrir la vérité et te l'expliquer dans la mesure de nos forces d'une manière brève.

Avant de répondre aux questions posées par Porphyre, Jamblique veut avertir son correspondant de la complexité des problèmes. Puisqu'il y a une multiplicité d'êtres qui ont des statuts variés, il y aura aussi une pluralité de principes. Il y a au moins la grande distinction entre les êtres universels et les êtres particuliers, mais il est suggéré qu'il y a encore, à l'intérieur de cette division, des quantités de distinctions. Ces distinctions sont exposées dans des écrits composés par les Anciens, et continuent à être élaborées dans les écoles parmi les maîtres actuellement en vie. Jamblique a déjà fait allusion au livre I (1, p. 3. 4) à ces maîtres actuellement vivants. Il semble qu'il puisse s'agir de l'enseignement donné au sein même de l'école de Jamblique à Apamée par des Égyptiens, comme était précisément Anébon. Les livres des anciens scribes sacrés sont attribués à Hermés,[4] ils sont 20.000 selon Séleucos, 36.525 selon Manéthon, chiffres peut-être symboliques.[5] Jamblique fait ici preuve d'érudition, les Grecs aimaient bien cela. En tout cas, l'exposé des principes universels qui suivra sera tiré d'Hermès dont le nom revient constamment, *infra*, p. 262. 9, 262. 14 (sujet sous-entendu de προτάττει), 263.4 (sujet sous-entendu de ἐπονομάζει). En revanche, l'étude des principes des êtres particuliers sera attribuée aux Égyptiens en général, p. 264. 4 (αὐτοῖς), 264. 8 (sujet sous-entendu de διδόασι et des verbes au pluriel), p. 265. 1; peut-être s'agit-il alors pour une part des discussions contemporaines dans l'école. Ayant formulé ces avertissements, Jamblique aborde les questions de Porphyre pour y répondre dans l'ordre.

DE MYST. VIII 2, P. 261. 7-262. 13: RÉPONSE À I 1)

Écoute en premier lieu ma réponse à ta première question. Au-dessus des êtres réellement êtres et des principes universels, il y a un dieu Un, supérieur (πρῶτος = πρότερος) même au premier dieu et roi, demeurant immobile dans la solitude de son unicité. En effet, ni aucun intelligible ni quoi que ce soit d'autre, ne lui est attaché, et il est dressé comme un modèle du dieu qui, engendré par lui-même, est père de lui-même et son seul père, le Bien réellement bien; il est en effet meilleur, supérieur, source de tout et fondement des premiers intelligés que sont les Idées.

A partir de cet Un-là, s'est mis de lui-même à briller le dieu qui se suffit à lui-même, c'est pourquoi il est non seulement père de lui-même mais aussi principe de lui-même; car celui-là est principe et dieu des dieux, monade issue de l'Un, supérieur à l'être et principe de l'être. A partir de lui, en effet, dérive l'essence et l'être c'est pourquoi il est appelé "père de l'être;" car il est l'être supérieur aux êtres, principe des intelligibles, c'est pourquoi il est dénommé "chef des intelligibles."

Voilà donc les principes les plus vénérables[6] de tout ce qui existe, qu'Hermès a classés au-dessus des dieux de l'éther et de l'empyrée, et au-dessus des dieux du ciel, lui qui a donné à la tradition 100 traités sur

---

[4]Sur ces anciens scribes sacrés et leur science, cf. F. Cumont, *L'Egypte des astrologues*, Bruxelles (1937): 121-122 et 151-154.

[5]Pour ces références à Manéthon et à Séleucos, cf. F Gr H III c, 609 F 26 et 634 F 3. On sait que pour ces auteurs, F. Jacoby n'a pas composé son commentaire.

[6]Autres traduction possible: les principes les plus importants, c'est-à-dire les plus élevés, donc les tout premiers principes.

l'étude des dieux de l'empyrée, autant sur ceux de l'éther, et 1000 sur ceux du ciel.

Dans ce passage, Jamblique répond à la première question de Porphyre sur ce que les Égyptiens pensent de la cause première, et il montre que, au-dessus des principes universels, qui sont ceux des êtres réellement êtres, c'est-à-dire des intelligibles, il faut classer deux principes. Le premier est le dieu Un (εἷς), dans la solitude (μονότητι) de son unicité. Il est un modèle suprême pour le dieu qui le suit dans la hiérarchie. Le deuxième principe émane spontanément de l'Un, c'est un dieu qui se suffit à lui-même, il est engendré par lui-même et donc père de lui-même. Il est aussi le Bien réellement bien. C'est seulement de ce deuxième principe que dérive dérivent l'être et les êtres réellement êtres que sont les intelligibles, d'où ses deux noms: "Père de l'être," et "Chef des intelligibles." Procédant de ce deuxième principe, viendront les intelligibles et ensuite les dieux cosmiques, de l'empyrée, de l'éther et du ciel.

C'est alors que Jamblique nous dit que cette classification remonte à Hermès. Je ne crois pas que l'on puisse retrouver dans les écrits hermétiques conservés cette classification des principes telle qu'elle est ici formulée par Jamblique. Mais il est vrai que l'on peut reconnaître dans le *Corpus hermeticum* des approches de cette théorie jamblichéenne dont notre philosophe a pu s'emparer pour élaborer sa propre doctrine. Par exemple, c'est fréquemment qu'Hermès dit que dieu est εἷς καὶ μόνος,[7] une fois même il parle d'un principe dont dépend le principe de l'univers, qu'il dit être "un et seul."[8] Il semble donc s'agir d'un principe transcendant. Une fois, ce dieu est dit αὐτοπάτωρ,[9] et le dieu créateur est aussi dit αὐτάρκης.[10] Plus étroit encore est le parallèle que l'on peut instaurer entre notre texte et le traité hermétique retrouvé dans les *Papyri* de Nag Hammadi, où J.-P. Mahé[11] a pu dégager la triade hermétique: Inengendré, Engendré-par-soi, Engendré. L'Inengendré peut être assimilé au dieu Un, l'Engendré-par-soi est évidemment le deuxième principe que

---

[7]Cf. CH. IV 1, p. 49. 4; IV 5, p. 51. 6; IV 8, p. 52. 11; XI 5, p. 149. 9; Stob. Exc. II A 15, p. 7. 16.

[8]Cf. CH. X 14, p. 120. 1.

[9]Fragm. divers 13.

[10]Cf. CH XI 6, p. 149. 19.

[11]Cf. J.-P. Mahé, *Hermès en Haute-Égypte* I (Bibliothèque copte de Nag Hammadi, textes -3-), Québec 1978, p. 48-52.

Jamblique dit "engendré par lui-même," les autres principes pouvant rentrer dans la catégorie de l'Engendré.

Élaborée dans les catégories hermétiques, la doctrine des principes exposée dans ce passage est celle propre à Jamblique. Témoin Damascius, dans son traité *Des principes*,[12] lorsqu'il se demande combien il y a de principes supérieurs à la première triade intelligible, il répond que, selon Jamblique et lui seul, il y en a deux. C'est d'ailleurs la théorie qu'il reprend à son compte en l'exposant en des termes voisins de ceux de notre traité. Autre témoin, Proclus. Lorsqu'il a reconstitué l'histoire des exégèses des hypothèses du *Parménide*, exposant celle de Jamblique, il nous apprend que, d'après cet auteur, la première hypothèse concerne "dieu et les dieux." L.G. Westerink et moi[13] avons établi que cette formule signifie en réalité: "le premier dieu et les dieux intelligibles," ce qui, transposé dans les termes du *De mysteriis* donnerait: le deuxième principe, chef des intelligibles, et les intelligibles.

Ainsi ce passage nous fournit la théorie jamblichéenne des premiers principes, exprimée en termes hermétiques. Ailleurs, nous trouverions cette même théorie exprimée en termes chaldaïques. Les néoplatoniciens recherchaient ces accords entre les diverses traditions théologiques. Mais ce qui prouve mieux que tout le reste que cette classification des principes n'est pas formellement hermétique, c'est ce qui vient aussitôt après, au moment où Jamblique annonce une autre classification des principes selon Hermès.

DE MYST. VIII 3, P. 262. 14-263. 6: RÉPONSE À I 2)

En suivant une autre classification, (Hermès) classe au-dessus le dieu KNEPH comme commandant les dieux célestes, qu'il dit être un intellect qui s'intellige lui-même et qui convertit ses intellections vers lui-même; encore au-dessus de ce dieu, il classe l'Un indivis et ce qu'il dit être un premier mis au monde par accouchement, qu'il nomme "EIKTŌN"; dans le premier mis au monde il y a le premier intelligeant et le premier intelligible, quant à l'Un in-divis on l'honore par le culte du seul silence.

Jamblique donne ici une autre classification hermétique des premiers principes. Il part du dieu KNEPH qui est un intellect, et il va

---

[12]Cf. Damascius, *Traité des premiers principes* II, p. 1. 1-6. 15 Westerink-Combès.

[13]Cf. H.D. Saffrey et L. G. Westerink, *Proclus, Théologie platonicienne* III, Introduction, p. XVII-XL.

montrer que, dans cette classification, Hermès pose deux autres dieux au-dessus de l'intellect. Ce faisant, il répond à la question de Porphyre numérotée I 2): "Les Égyptiens pensent-ils que la cause première soit un intellect ou au-dessus de l'intellect?" La réponse est donc: Hermès classe deux principes au-dessus de l'intellect KNEPH. Ces principes sont maintenant décrits comme l'un indivis d'une part, et d'autre part un autre principe qu'Hermès appelle en grec μαίευμα et en égyptien EIKTŌN. Or, ni μαίευμα ni EIKTŌN ne se retrouvent dans les nomenclatures connues de principes ou de dieux soit grecs soit égyptiens. Le mot grec μαίευμα signifie "mis au monde par accouchement," il est employé une fois par Platon dans le *Théétète*, 160 E 3, lorsque Socrate dit à Théétète: "Voilà ton petit nouveau-né, et voilà le résultat de mon office d'accoucheur." Chez Jamblique, peut-être pouvons-nous comprendre de quoi il s'agit par les mots qui suivent aussitôt, lorsqu'il dit que ce principe contient "le premier intelligeant et le premier intelligible," ce que je comprends comme signifiant le premier intelligible conçu par le premier qui intellige. Il s'agit donc d'un accouchement intellectuel. L'un indivis est évidemment celui qui est honoré par le culte du seul silence.[14] Ainsi nous retrouvons une classification de trois principes, un indivis, premier intelligible, intellect, dont deux sont au-dessus de l'intellect.

N'étant pas égyptologue, je ne puis m'aventurer dans le domaine des noms égyptiens qui apparaissent ici. KNEPH qui dans la littérature gréco-égyptienne tardive semble pouvoir être identifié à KMEPH,[15] est l'intellect démiurgique chez Porphyre.[16] Jamblique le présente comme exerçant le commandement sur les dieux célestes (cosmiques). EIKTŌN est plus mystérieux. Hopfner,[17] se recommandant des savants plus anciens Jablonski et Röth, proposait d'y reconnaître les mots égyptiens *jachto* ou *heka-to*, signifiant respectivement *mens mundi* et *imperator*

---

[14]Cette doctrine est parfaitement hermétique, cf. CH, Fragments divers, fr. 3a: "Dieu est un, et l'un n'a pas besoin d'un nom, car Celui-qui-est est sans nom," avec les parallèles à l'Asclépius.

[15]Voir A. Delatte et Ph. Derchain, *Les intailles magiques gréco-égyptiennes*, Paris, 1964, p. 57. Voir aussi la note 115 de A.R. Sodano, *Giamblico, I misteri egiziani*, Milano 1984, p. 357-377 (sur tout ce passage).

[16]Cf. Porphyre, *De cultu simulacrorum*, fr. 10 = Eusèbe, *Praep. Ev.*, III, 11, 45, p. 143. 1 Mras: τόν δημιουργόν, ὃν Κνὴφ οἱ Αἰγύπτιοι προσαγορεύουσιν ... Plutarque, *De Iside et Osiride* 21, p. 150. 15 Cwyn Griffiths, connaît Kneph comme un dieu des Égyptiens, "inengendré et immortel," et voir la note, ibid., p. 374.

[17]Cf. Th. Hopfner, op. cit., p. 257-258, n. 131.

mundi. Plus prosaïquement, J. Yoyote[18] suggère de lire *ei-kto*, participe du verbe signifiant "venir," suivi du statif de *qd* "se retourner." Le sens reste énigmatique, et ne semble pas pouvoir se comprendre comme le mot dont μαίευμα serait l'équivalent grec, puisque, en égyptien, "né par accouchement" serait normalement *ms*. Je laisse donc cette question à plus savants que moi.

Jamblique continue de répondre aux questions de Porphyre en abordant le démiurge.

DE MYST. VIII 3, P. 263. 6-264. 3: RÉPONSE À I 5)

Après ces dieux-là, d'autres chefs président à la démiurgie des choses visibles. En effet, l'intellect démiurgique, protecteur de la vérité et de la sagesse, parce qu'il se porte vers le monde créé et met au jour la puissance invisible des raisons (séminales) cachées, est dit "AMOUN" dans la langue des Égyptiens; parce qu'il mène à la perfection tout ce qu'il fait sans se tromper et avec un art véritable, il est dit "PHTAH" (les Grecs assimilent PHTAH à Héphaistos, appliquant seulement ce nom à sa qualité d'artisan): et parce qu'il est créateur de biens, il est appelé "OSIRIS," sans compter d'autres dénominations à raison de ses autres puissances et opérations.

Porphyre avait demandé si la cause première, chez les Égyptiens, est "identique au démiurge ou supérieure à lui." En introduisant maintenant, à la suite des dieux précédents, les dieux qui sont les artisans du monde, il répond à cette question. L'intellect démiurgique, pouvant être considéré de plusieurs points de vue, reçoit de ce fait plusieurs noms. Tous ces noms sont bien connus de la théologie égyptienne diffusée chez les auteurs grecs. Ainsi le nom AMOUN et son explication ("met au jour la puissance des raisons [séminales] cachées") étaient connus par Manéthon, rapporté par Plutarque.[19] AMOUN était assimilé à Zeus, et Zeus est le démiurge pour les néoplatoniciens. D'autre part, selon Chérémon,[20] rapporté par Porphyre, les Égyptiens disent que le dieu KNEPH fait sortir de sa bouche un oeuf duquel naît un dieu qu'eux-mêmes dénomment PHTHAH, et les Grecs Héphaistos, et l'oeuf signifie le monde." Selon

---

[18]Par lettre du 16. 12; 89.

[19]Cf. Plutarguq, *De Iside* 9, p. 130. 11-20 Gwyn Griffiths, avec la note, p. 285.

[20]Cf. Chaeremon, fr. 17 D Van der Horst = Eusèbe, *Praep. Ev.*, III 11, 46, p. 143. 5-8 Mras. Ce fragment est extrait du *De culta simulacrorum* de Porphyre, fr. 10.

une autre tradition, c'est PHTHAH lui-même qui produit l'oeuf du monde. De même, Chérémon[21] enseigne qu'OSIRIS est la puissance fertilisatrice, qualité que Plutarque[22] traduit en interprétant le nom OSIRIS comme signifiant ἀγαθοποιός.

Ainsi s'achève cette deuxième classification selon Hermès, qui comprend: (1) l'un indivis, (2) le premier mis au monde, intelligeant-intelligible, (3) l'intellect qui s'intellige lui-même, (4) l'intellect démiurgique. Du même coup, les autres questions de Porphyre trouvent leur réponse. Dans les deux classifications, la cause première est évidemment l'Un, qui est unique et seul, ce qui répond à la question I 3). La question I 4) est implicitement traitée: il est évident que la cause première est incorporelle.

Cela dit, Jamblique peut passer à un autre problème, celui de l'un et du multiple.

DE MYST. VIII 3, P. 264. 4-265. 5: RÉPONSE À II

Maintenant, il y a encore, chez les Égyptiens, un autre commandement sur la totalité les éléments du monde du devenir et des puissances qu'ils contiennent, quatre masculins et quatre féminins, qu'ils attribuent au Soleil, et un autre principe de la totalité de la nature soumise au devenir qu'ils donnent à la Lune. Ensuite, distinguant le ciel partie par partie, en deux ou en quatre ou en douze ou en trente-six ou en deux fois ces trente-six, ou divisant en un autre nombre de parties quel qu'il soit, ils classent au-dessus d'elles des commandements aussi en plus ou moins grand nombre, et de nouveau ils placent au-dessus l'unité qui leur est supérieure.

De cette façon donc, depuis le sommet jusqu'aux plus bas degrés, le traité des principes chez les Égyptiens prend son départ à partir d'une unité, procède vers la pluralité, les multiples étant à leur tour gouvernés par une unité, et à tous les degrés la nature sans détermination étant maîtrisée par une mesure déterminée et par la cause la plus élevée unificatrice de tout ce qui existe.

En rappelant la doctrine égyptienne de l'organisation des éléments du monde créé, Jamblique se trouve sur un terrain plus solide et mieux connu. Il résume d'abord le système théologique hermopolitain, qui est celui de l'ogdoade qui produit le Soleil. Nous connaissons les noms de ces dieux et de ces déesses: Noun et Naunet =

---

[21]Cf. Chaeremon, Ibid. = Eusèbe, *Praep. Ev.*, III 11, 50, p. 144. 2-3 Mras.

[22]Cf. Plutarque, *De Iside* 42, p. 184. 22-24 Gwyn Griffiths.

océan primordial, Houh et Hauhet = eau courante, Kouk et Kauket = les ténèbres, Amon et Amaunet = l'espace vide. C'est d'eux qu'émerge le premier tertre où peut naître le soleil dans un lotus.[23] Les divisions du ciel en parties sont également connues: deux hémisphères, quatre points cardinaux, douze signes du zodiaque, trente-six décans, soixante-douze demi-décans. Jamblique affirme que chacune de ces pluralités dérive d'une unité, si bien qu'il peut conclure que c'est de l'unité et non pas de la multiplicité que vient tout ce qui existe. De cette façon il répond à la question de Porphyre. Et Jamblique peut passer à la question suivante, qui est en même temps la dernière, relative à la matière.

DE MYST. VIII 3, P. 265. 5-10: RÉPONSE À III

Quant à la matière, le dieu l'a fait sortir de l'essence de l'être, la matérialité ayant été retranchée par en-dessous. Recevant cette matière, le démiurge, parce qu'elle est pleine de vie, a fabriqué à partir d'elle les sphères simples et incorruptibles, et il a mis en ordre ce qui en restait en vue (de la fabrication) des corps engendrés et corruptibles.

Le Père Festugière avait reconnu que ce texte est cité par Proclus dans son *Commentaire sur le Timée* et formellement attribué à Jamblique.[24] Proclus précise que cette doctrine égyptienne est d'Hermès. De fait, elle éclaire des points difficiles de la cosmogonie du Poimandrès. De cette matière le démiurge fabrique les corps célestes et les corps mortels.

Mais si Porphyre avait soulevé toutes ces questions auxquelles Jamblique vient de répondre, c'est parce que la lecture des livres qu'il avait rencontrés, lui faisait se demander si même elles avaient été posées par les Égyptiens. Jamblique est donc amené à reprendre l'examen des sources d'information de Porphyre.

DE MYST. VIII 4, P. 265. 11-266.10: SUR LES LIVRES ÉGYPTIENS

Une fois ces questions bien analysées de la façon que voilà, évidente est la solution *des difficultés contenues dans les livres que tu dis avoir trouvés par hasard.*

---

[23]Sur cette théologie, cf. J. Vandier, *La religion égyptienne*, Paris 1944, p. 33-34 et 61-62.

[24]Cf. Proclus, *In Tim.* I, p. 386. 10-11: "Le Divin Jamblique a rapporté que, selon Hermès, la matérialité est dérivée de la substantialité," et A.J. Festugière, *La révélation d'Hermès Trismégiste* IV, Paris 1954, p. 39-43.

En effet, les uns donnés comme ayant Hermès pour auteur, contiennent des doctrines hermétiques, même si souvent ils font usage du langage des philosophes, car ils ont été traduits de la langue égyptienne par des gens qui n'étaient pas sans expérience de la philosophie. Quant à Chérémon et ses pareils quels qu'ils soient, qui se sont mis à l'étude des causes premières de l'univers, ils ont expliqué les principes qui sont les derniers; et ceux qui enseignent les planètes, le zodiaque, les décans, les horoscopes, les (astres) que l'on appelle "puissants" et "chefs," mettent en lumière des distributions particulières des principes. Les autres, qui font partie des *Salmeschiniaca*, ne contiennent qu'une toute petite partie des doctrines hermétiques; et ce qui concerne les astres, les phases, éclipses, croissances et décroissances de la lune, sont au plus bas degré dans la théorie des causes chez les Égyptiens.

Comme on le voit, Jamblique donne de nouveau la parole à Porphyre qui parle des difficultés qu'il a trouvées dans des livres égyptiens qu'il a rencontrés par hasard. Aussitôt, notre Jamblique se lance dans un petit morceau d'érudition pour caractériser chacun de ces livres. Les premiers sont les livres hermétiques, traduits de l'égyptien dans le vocabulaire de la philosophie grecque. Aux yeux de Jamblique, ce sont les plus sérieux, ceux auxquels il vient de faire appel dans les réponses qu'il a déjà données à Porphyre. Les deuxièmes sont ceux de Chérémon;[25] en fait de causes premières, ils ne font que traiter des causes dernières de l'univers physique; ce n'est donc pas dans ces livres qu'il faut chercher la théorie des causes chez les Égyptiens. Encore moins dans les troisièmes qui sont les *Salmeschiniaca*[26] (nos almanachs), livres populaires, sans valeur scientifique.

Il est probable que les livres recontrés par hasard, que Porphyre a lus, devaient appartenir à ces deux dernières catégories. Nous avons la chance d'avoir encore le texte même de la *Lettre à Anébon*, conservé

---

[25]Cf. H.-R. Schwyzer, *Chairemon* (Klassich-Philologische Studien, Heft 4) Leipzig 1932, et P. W. Van der Horst, *Chaeremon, Egyptian Priest and Stoic Philosopher* (Études préliminaires aux religions orientales dans l'Empire romain, tome 101), Leiden 1984, où l'on voit que la plupart des fragments de Chérémon viennent de Porphyre et de Jamblique.

[26]Cf. Fr. Boll, *Sphaera*, Leipzig 1903, p. 376-378, Id., *Aus der Offenbarung Johannis*, Leipzig 1914, p. 51-52. W. Kroll, dans P.W. Suppl. V (1931) col. 843-846, W. Gundel, *Dekane und Dekansternbilder*, Hamburg 1936, p. 342, W. Gundel u. H.G. Gundel, *Astrologumena*, Wiesbaden 1966, p. 15-16 et 155, G. Fowden, *The Egyptian Hermes*, Cambridge 1986, p. 139, 140.

par Eusèbe de Césarée.[27] Porphyre s'exprime ainsi: "Chérémon et ses pareils pensent qu'il n'y a rien d'autre au-dessus des mondes visibles, sous le nom de principes, ils mettent ceux des Égyptiens et n'admettent pas d'autres dieux que les astres appelés planètes, les étoiles qui remplissent le zodiaque, et celles qui se lèvent à côté d'elles, les divisions en décans, les horoscopes, les astres qu'on appelle 'puissants' et 'chefs', dont les noms se trouvent dans les *Salmeschiniaca,* avec les maladies qu'ils guérissent, les levers et les couchers, et les prévisions de l'avenir." Dès lors, la difficulté éprouvée par Porphyre saute aux yeux: les Égyptiens ne disent-ils pas que tout ce qui existe est du domaine de la nature? Jamblique n'aura pas de peine à lui montrer qu'il n'en est rien.

DE MYST. VIII 4, P. 266. 10-267. 13: LES CAUSES SUR-NATURELLES

Les Égyptiens ne disent pas que *tout ce qui existe est du domaine de la nature,* mais ils distinguent de la nature non seulement la vie de l'âme mais aussi la vie de l'intellect, non seulement dans le cas de l'univers mais aussi dans notre cas à nous; plaçant au-dessus comme des êtres en soi l'intellect et la raison, ils disent que les êtres en devenir sont fabriqués de la façon suivante: ils classent le démiurge au-dessus des êtres en devenir comme un tout premier père,[28] et ils connaissent une puissance vivifiante, l'une supérieure au ciel, l'autre dans le ciel; ils placent au-dessus du monde un intellect pur, et un intellect indivis dans le monde entier, et un autre intellect divisé selon chacune des sphères. Et ils ne considèrent pas du tout cette classification d'une manière purement théorique, au contraire ils recommandent de s'élever par le moyen de la théurgie hiératique dans les régions plus élevées, plus universelles et supérieures à la Fatalité vers le dieu et démiurge, sans s'attacher à la matière et ne s'adjoignant rien d'autre que la seule attention au moment favorable.

A la difficulté de Porphyre, Jamblique répond que les Égyptiens ne disent pas ce que Porphyre leur fait dire, à savoir que "tout ce qui existe est du domaine de la nature." Au contraire, eux aussi admettent une hiérarchie d'hypostases supérieures à la nature: l'âme et l'intellect, tant pour l'univers que pour l'homme. Chaque sphère céleste a son

---

[27]Cf. *Praep. Ev.* III 4, 1, p. 116-12-18 Mras.

[28]Pour cette traduction qui rejoint le sens de προπάτωρ dans le *Corpus hermeticum* et les papyrus magiques, j'ai suivi la proposition de Festugière dans *Hermès Trismégiste* III, p. XVI et Stob. fr. II A § 13. 3.

intellect, et il y a un intellect du monde entier, et encore au-dessus un intellect pur, qui est le démiurge, le père suprême. Les Égyptiens tiennent aussi la même doctrine à propos de l'âme, mais Jamblique n'en dit rien à cet endroit, il en parlera plus loin (VIII 6, p. 269. 1-5). La doctrine de cette échelle des degrés n'a pas seulement une valeur spéculative, elle est le moyen de s'élever jusqu'à dieu par la théurgie et d'échapper à la Fatalité qui règne sur le monde cosmique. Notons que c'est en effet en vue de la pratique de la théurgie que, dans les chapitres précédents, Jamblique avait donné les noms barbares des divinités. La théurgie exigeait que l'on invoquât les dieux par ces noms dont les sons articulés sont porteurs de l'énergie divine. Jamblique l'avait expliqué plus haut (V 5). Évidemment cette conclusion ne pouvait qu'augmenter l'inquiétude de Porphyre qui n'était pas un adepte de la théurgie. Et puisque Porphyre est insuffisamment informé, Jamblique va lui indiquer les meilleures sources de la théologie égyptienne.

DE MYST. VIII 5, P. 267. 14-268. 8: CONCLUSION

De fait, Hermès a tracé cette voie, et le prophète Bitys l'a expliquée au roi Ammon, l'ayant trouvée gravée en caractères hiéroglyphiques dans le sanctuaire de Saïs en Égypte; et il a transmis le nom du dieu (Hermès) qui est répandu dans le monde entier. Il y a encore beaucoup d'autres classifications sur les mêmes sujets, de telle sorte que ce n'est pas à bon droit que tu me sembles *rapporter toutes les causes connues des Égyptiens aux causes de l'ordre de la nature.* En effet, il y a chez eux des principes nombreux et portant sur des êtres nombreux, et des puissances hypercosmiques dont ils célèbrent le culte au moyen du rituel hiératique.[29]

Jamblique tire la conclusion de son dialogue avec Porphyre: il n'est pas bien documenté. Lire Chérémon ne suffit pas. La "voie du bonheur" (*infra,* p. 291. 11) qui conduit à la connaissance des dieux, a été tracée par Hermès,[30] et le prophète Bitys l'a expliquée au roi

---

[29]La phrase suivante n'est pas la dernière de ce chapitre, mais la première du chapitre suivant (p. 268. 8-13): "Eh bien, il me semble que cela fournit des points de départ généraux pour la solution de toutes les questions posées après celles-là. Mais puisqu'il ne faut pas en laisser aucune sans l'examiner, abordons, ces problèmes-là aussi, et sondons-les de tous côtés pour voir s'ils comportent quelque chose de fêlé."

[30]Sur la métaphore de la voie, cf. B. Couroyer, *Le chemin de vie en Egypte et en Israël,* dans Rev. Biblique 56, 1949, 412-432, en particulier 412-428.

Ammon dans un traité.[31] C'est dans cet écrit hermétique, perdu pour
nous, mais encore connu de Jamblique, que l'on peut trouver les
classifications des principes premiers rappelées dans les chapitres
précédents, et bien d'autres encore. C'est pourquoi, Porphyre n'a pas
raison de "rapporter toutes les causes connues des Égyptiens aux causes
de l'ordre de la nature." La conclusion finale est donc qu'il y a une
théologie au sens néoplatonicien du terme dans les écrits hermétiques
(au moins dans quelques-uns d'entre eux), écrits dont Jamblique s'est
inspiré pour sa propre théologie. Cette théologie est le fondement de
la théurgie, rite qui ouvre la porte vers le divin (p. 291. 14) et qui sauve
la vraie vie en l'élevant vers son Père (p. 291. 8-9).

* * * * *

Nous pouvons maintenant récapituler l'argument qui organise ces
cinq chapitres du livre VIII. Dans ses lectures des traités égyptiens,
Porphyre avait trouvé que tout ce qui existe est du domaine de la
nature et que toutes les causes se ramènent aux causes de l'ordre de la
nature. Il a lu ces thèses dans Chérémon et les *Salmeschiniaca*. Peut-
être même les a-t-il rencontrées dans quelques traités hermétiques,
puisque deux fois au moins dans le *Corpus Hermeticum*,[32] l'auteur se
demande s'il y a quelque chose au-dessus du ciel, dans le sentiment
qu'il n'y a rien. C'est pourquoi il s'est tourné vers Anébon, et il lui
énumère les questions que lui suggère cette théologie qui ne
dépasserait pas la physique. Elles concernent naturellement la cause
première, l'un et le multiple, la matière.

A ces questions, la réponse de Jamblique arrive en deux temps:
D'abord il répond une par une aux questions soulevées: oui, il y a une
cause première chez Hermès; oui, elle est supérieure à l'intellect; oui,
elle est supérieure au démiurge; oui, tout procède de l'un vers le
multiple; oui, les Égyptiens connaissent la matière, elle vient aussi de
l'être. Ensuite, il explique à Porphyre pourquoi il n'a pas trouvé lui-
même ces réponses. C'est parce qu'il ne connaît pas complètement la
littérature hermétique, et en particulier parce qu'il ignore le traité
traduit par le prophète Bitys. S'il le connaissait, il aurait appris deux
choses: la métaphysique égyptienne remonte jusqu'à la cause
première qui est l'Un, et elle admet l'échelle des hypostases

---

[31] Tout ce que l'on sait sur ce prophète Bitys a été rassemblé par G. Fowden, *The
Egyptian Hermes*, p. 150-153.

[32] Cf. CH IV 5, p. 51. et XI 19, p. 155. 16.

inférieures, l'intellect, l'âme, le monde. Cette échelle des degrés s'offre alors comme un support à la théurgie qui supplante ainsi la philosophie.

Cet argument était une flèche visant particulièrement Porphyre. Toute sa vie, Porphyre avait cherché une *via universalis animae liberandae*,[33] et il croyait l'avoir trouvée dans la philosophie, et singulièrement dans la philosophie de Plotin. Or, dans le *De mysteriis*, tout l'effort de Jamblique est de montrer, sur tous les sujets, la supériorité de la théurgie sur la philosophie. C'est encore ce qu'il prouve sur ce sujet particulier qui traite de la connaissance des premiers principes et de la remontée de l'âme jusqu'aux premiers dieux. Jamblique avait fait sienne l'attitude des prêtres égyptiens qui "ne considéraient pas du tout la classification des dieux d'une manière purement théorique, et qui au contraire recommandaient de s'élever par le moyen de la théurgie hiératique dans les régions plus élevées, plus universelles et supérieures à la Fatalité vers le dieu et démiurge." En lisant la réponse de Jamblique à sa *Lettre à Anébon*, Porphyre a dû être bien inquiet!

---

[33]Tous les auteurs qui se sont occupés de Porphyre ont relevé le thème du salut de l'âme comme l'un des thèmes majeurs de cet auteur, voir E. Zeller, *Die Philosophie der Griechen*,5 Leipzig 1923, p. 7-2, n. 2; P. Hadot, *Porphyre et Victorinus* I, Paris 1968, p. 89, n. 2; W. Pötscher, *Porphyrios* ΠΡΟΣ ΜΑΡΚΕΛΛΑΝ; Leiden 1969, p. 70; A. Smith, *Porphyry's Place in the Neoplatonic Tradition*, The Hague 1974, p. 128-139. C. Zintzen, *Bemerkungen zum Aufstiegsweg in Jamblichs De mysteriis*, dans Platonismus und Christentum, Festschrift für H. Dörrie, Münster 1983, p. 312-328, en particulier p. 317-318.

Soul Vehicles in Simplicius

H. J. BLUMENTHAL

There has been a not inconsiderable amount of discussion of the nature and function of the ὄχημα — or ὀχήματα — the body or bodies made of not quite bodily substance which served as an intermediary between body and soul in various Neoplatonisms from Porphyry, or even arguably Plotinus, down to and including Proclus. Rather less attention, and, in Simplicius' case virtually none,[1] has been paid to the nature and role of such intermediary vehicles in the Neoplatonist commentators on Aristotle.

The purpose of the following pages will be to examine the use of the concept in Simplicius. In particular it will seek to establish
1) how many such vehicles there were
2) what they were made of
3) what was their function, and, related to 3)
4) what was their life-expectancy
5) were they simply such as one would expect to find in the work of a Neoplatonist at this time, or are they in some way modified by the commentary context.

In considering these matters special attention will be paid to the vocabulary used to discuss them. It should not, however, come as a surprise to discover that it is not significantly, if at all, different from that of those Neoplatonists who did not concentrate their endeavours on the exposition of Aristotle.

References to the Aristotelian commentators are by page and line of the Berlin Academy edition, *Commentaria in Aristotelem Graeca (CAG)*.

[1]But see I. Hadot, *Le problème du néoplatonisme alexandrin: Hiéroclès et Simplicius* (Paris 1978) 181-83.

* * *

The answer to the first question might seem to be obvious, namely two. But let us pause before simply accepting it.

In the texts from the *Timaeus* which were normally regarded as authority for giving vehicles to souls, each soul had one.[2] And that was the form the doctrine took in its earlier versions.[3] It seems to have been Proclus who introduced a second, so that the upper and lower souls could have one each. That gave them both an intermediary between immaterial soul and substantially different body, and *inter alia*, meant that it was easier for soul to operate with a body in the physical world without undergoing substantial (κατ' οὐσίαν) change, a matter on which Proclus appears to have differed from his predecessor Iamblichus, and Damascius from Proclus.[4] Simplicius' own position is not clear. Recent discussions have arrived at different answers.[5] In any case we should neither assume that his partnership with Damascius at Athens need imply that they shared the same view, nor that his training in Alexandria points in the opposite direction.

Since we know that he certainly believed in two ὀχήματα, even though he may not have been the first to do so, let us look briefly at Proclus. At first sight it might appear that he believed not only in two, but even in three such vehicles, for in the *Timaeus* commentary we find that he apparently refers to that number. There, at III 298.27-29 he writes, τὸ μὲν οὖν συμφυὲς ὄχημα ποιεῖ αὐτὴν ἐγκόσμιον, τὸ δὲ δεύτερον γενέσεως πολῖτιν, τὸ δὲ ὀστρεῶδες χθονίαν: the vehicle which

---

[2]41D-E; 44E; 69C.

[3]For the history of this doctrine cf. R. C. Kissling, "The ΟΧΗΜΑ-ΠΝΕΥΜΑ of the Neoplatonists and the *De Insomniis* of Synesius of Cyrene", *AJP* 43 (1922) 318-330; E.R. Dodds, *Proclus. The Elements of Theology* (Oxford 1963) Appendix 2, 313-21 and 347f.; A. Smith, *Porphyry's Place in the Neoplatonic Tradition* (The Hague 1974) Appendix 2, 152-58; J.F. Finamore, *Iamblichus and the Theory of the Vehicle of the Soul*. American Classical Studies 14 (Chico 1985).

[4]Cf. C. Steel, *The Changing Self. A Study on the Soul in later Neoplatonism: Iamblichus, Damascius and Priscianus*. Verh. van de Kon. Academie voor Wetenschappen, Letteren en Schone Kunsten van België, Kl. Lett. 40, 1978, 85 (Brussels 1978) 52-73.

[5]Steel, ibid.; I. Hadot (op. cit. (n. 1) 170-74 and "La doctrine de Simplicius sur l'âme raisonnable humaine dans le commentaire sur le Manuel d'Epictète", in H.J. Blumenthal and A.C. Lloyd ed., *Soul and the Structure of Being in Late Neoplatonism* (Liverpool 1982) 47-70; Blumenthal, ibid., 91f. and 71f.

is natural to it puts it inside the cosmos, the second makes it (i.e. the soul) a citizen of the world of becoming, the one that is like a shell makes it an inhabitant of the earth. Their relations, he goes on, are analogous to that of the earth to becoming and of that to the cosmos: that also applies to their accompaniments (περιθέσεις). The one always exists because the soul is always in the cosmos, the one exists before this body and after it, being in the sphere of becoming both before and after it, the third only exists when the soul is moving from one partial life to the other (ibid. 298.29-299.4). This passage might suggest that there is one vehicle for the soul outside the cycles of existence—one thinks here of the *Phaedrus*—one for the soul when it is involved in a series of incarnations, and a third, which one would associate with the vegetative or nutrivite soul, which is only needed when a soul is not merely in a condition for embodiment, but actually embodied. The question then arises whether this third vehicle is an intermediary between soul and body, or simply a colourful way of talking about the ordinary earthly body with a view to showing its relationship to soul in direct comparison and contrast with that of the higher "bodies" which are clearly of a different substance. In other words, is ὀστρεῶδες a special kind of body, and thus parallel to terms like αὐγοειδές, light-like, or merely a description of body in its normal sense? Normally Proclus talks in terms of two, one attached to the upper and rational, the other to the lower and irrational soul, and in the sequel to the text we have just looked at he talks of an irrational life which is different both from that of the first vehicle and of the last body: παρά τε τὴν τοῦ πρώτου ὀχήματος καὶ τὴν τοῦ ἐσχάτου σώματος ζωήν (ibid. 300.5-7). Here too a question presents itself: does σῶμα mean body in the normal sense, or body of the kind in question, for the intermediate bodies are often, of course, described as such and such a σῶμα? In any case this third intermediary, if it did exist, had no function distinct from that of the ordinary body, so that its role would have been merely that of completing a triad of additional bodies.[6] That this was indeed its role is further suggested by a text in the *Platonic Theology* (III 5, 125P = 18.24-19.3 Saffrey-Westerink) where we read that of participated souls the first and most divine are in control of simple and eternal bodies, the next of both simple bodies and those tied to matter,

---

[6]The habit of referring to the real body as something analogous to the quasi-material ones goes back to Porphyry, cf. *De abstinentia* I 31 = 109.10-19 Nauck and J. Pépin, "Saint Augustin et le symbolisme néoplatonicien de la vêture", in *Augustinus Magister*. Congrès International Augustinien. Paris 1954. I (Études augustiniennes n.d.) 295f.

simultaneously, while a further set rule, at the same time, over bodies of both these kinds and composite ones. The sequel shows that the first two kinds of body are the light-like vehicle, a "tunic" which is material but made of simple components: by means of these tunics they are associated with composite and multiform (σύνθετοις... καὶ πολυμορφοῖς) bodies (ibid. 19.11-15).[7]

Simplicius too may be found referring to a dependent body which is ὀστρεῶδες in the *Physics* commentary (966.5), but there the point is to contrast the sort of body a soul inhabits in the terrestrial sphere with the ones it associates with in the heavens:[8] that is referred to as πνευματικόν. Discussing an interpretation of Theophrastus he has argued that the soul does not need anything interposed between it and body: its distance is assured by body's unsuitability to receive the soul's irradiation: ἀρκεῖ γὰρ ἡ τοῦ σώματος ἀνεπιτηδειότης πρὸς τὸ μὴ δέχεσθαι τὴν ἔλλαμψιν τῆς ψυχῆς (cf. 965.26-30). It does, however, have ὀχήματα appropriate to its location: the dependent (ἐξημμένον) bodies are his explanation of these ὀχήματα (966.3-9).

Nevertheless, if the lower of the two can be identical with the ordinary body, the pneumatic one cannot, and Simplicius specifically argues that the inability of one body to penetrate another is not sufficient ground for saying that souls which have the lower cannot have the higher too: they are different kinds of body, and therefore any objection to two bodies of the same kind interpenetrating are inapplicable. It is not absurd, he says, for higher and finer bodies which are of a different nature to penetrate grosser and more material ones (ibid. 5-13).

Now if it is the case that Simplicius believed only in one vehicle above the one that is identical or nearly so with the body, then he has returned to the pre-Proclus version of the soul-vehicle doctrine. *Prima facie* that seems unlikely, and, in fact, when we proceed to look at the constituents of the vehicles, we shall see that there is a distinction between two groups of descriptions, of which one appears to apply to a higher, the other to a lower vehicle. What is less clear is just what the several descriptions in these two groups mean, and to that question we must now turn.

* * *

---

[7]On this passage cf. Dodds, loc. cit. (n. 3) 320f. and the *Notes Complémentaires* in Saffrey and Westerink's edition, pp. 113f.

[8]Cf. ὀστρέϊνον σῶμα at *In De an.* 287.16-22 which is again body in the usual sense.

Disregarding for the moment the possible limitation of certain kinds of vehicle-material to certain spheres of existence, let us collect the terms used by Simplicius to describe these materials.

Some we have already encountered above. These are αὐγοειδές— the neuter forms are appropriate because these terms all modify σῶμα — πνευματικόν and, ambiguae status, ὀστρεῶδες (and ὀστρέϊνον). Two of these, we may note straight away, are those we met in our preliminary look at Proclus' views on these matters. Three others are found, namely αἰθερῶδες, ἀρχοειδές, and αὐτοειδές, of which at least one must rest under suspicion of being a textual error.

A further -ειδής word, namely θνητοειδές, is also found with σῶμα, but not with ὄχημα, and so is even more likely than ὀστρεῶδες to be simply descriptive of the ordinary material body rather than of one made of something else which provides an intermediary for the soul: at In De an. 74.1-4 he talks of an ὄχημα συγκατατεινόμενον τῇ ψυχῇ εἰς τὸ θνητοειδὲς σῶμα, a vehicle extended to the mortal kind of body along with the soul. When shortly thereafter Simplicius is discussing Aristotle's definition of the soul, he uses the same word to describe the lowest form of life, below the higher and more perfect one which involves movement: it is the θνητοειδὴς ζωή to which, in furtherance of his Neoplatonizing exposition of the definition, he ascribes ὀργανικόν which, of course, he understands to mean in the position of, or having the status of, a tool (87.25-27). Before leaving this area of the soul's life we should, however, note that Iamblichus had used the word σωματοειδές to describe the soul vehicle of δαίμονες, which would have to be of a different material from that of our ordinary bodies (cf. De mysteriis 12 = 167 des Places).[9] Further, when Proclus cites οἱ περὶ... Ἰάμβλιχον as authority for the view that individual souls have vehicles made of the same pneuma as those of the heavenly bodies, that would indicate that the pneuma in question is of the most refined kind (cf. In Tim. III 266.25-31).

Αὐγοειδές, perhaps the commonest term for the upper vehicle in those systems where there are two, clearly relates the substance it describes to light, and at the same time distinguishes it from it. What exactly it is is probably impossible to ascertain, since the whole point of this non-material quasi-material substance is that it should be other than other substances. At the same time the history of the Neoplatonists' view of light shows that they regarded it as the closest

---

[9]Cf. G. Verbeke, L'évolution de la doctrine du pneuma du stoïcisme à S. Augustin (Paris and Louvain 1945) 378.

possible approach to the immaterial, and of the very highest status below purely intelligible entities.[10] All this is well-known: the reason for recalling it here is to stress that the term in question is a thoroughly appropriate description of the kind of entity we are discussing. We may note in passing that the word does not occur in Simplicius' *De anima* commentary, which may, or may not—because of the low incidence of all these words—throw some light on the question of that work's authenticity.[11]

The *De anima* commentary, is, of course, concerned with the individual human soul: the study of ψυχὴ λογική is given as its σκοπός (cf. e.g. 172.4-8). Elsewhere we may find an αὐγοειδές ὄχημα attached to the soul of the heavens, or the world-soul. So at *In Phys.* 615.31-35 we find the world-soul's light-like vehicle mentioned as a candidate for the identity of the shaft of light described in the Myth of Er (*Republic* 616B). This is as far as I know, the only certain occurrence in Simplicius, but, though the interpretation is ascribed to Porphyry, the language appears to be that of Simplicius himself.

There is, however, a further possible instance in the *De caelo* commentary (469.7-11). There the received text reads αὐγοειδές, but Heiberg has changed it to αὐτοειδές on the basis of the word *autoideale* in Moerbeke's translation. In a majuscule MS the difference is of course minimal, and it seems likely that a scribe unfamiliar with the more abstruse Neoplatonist terminology would have changed a word that looked strange to one superficially more comprehensible. What exactly αὐτοειδές might mean in the present context is far from clear. The text, as printed by Heiberg, reads: εἰ δέ τις τοῦτο τὸ σῶμα τὸ ἐπικήριον ἐξηρτημένος τὸ αὐτοειδὲς αὐτοῦ καὶ οὐράνιον ὄχημα καὶ τὰς ἐν αὐτῷ αἰσθήσεις κεκαθαρμένας σχοίη...: if someone being attached to this perishable body had the heavenly vehicle which was of the same kind, then he would have the pure senses (which would enable him to hear and see things invisible and inaudible to others, and in particular Pythagoras' music of the spheres). As I have translated it

---

[10]For two different views of the significance of light cf. W. Beierwaltes, "Die Metaphysik des Lichtes in der Philosophie Plotins", *Ztschr. für Philosophische Forschung* 15 (1961) 334-62; R. Ferwerda, *La signification des images et des métaphores dans la pensée de Plotin* (Groningen 1965) 46-65.

[11]On this matter cf. the differing views of F. Bossier and C. Steel, "Priscianus Lydus en de "In de anima" van pseudo(?) Simplicius", *Tijdschrift voor Filosofie* 34 (1972) 761-821; I. Hadot, *Le Néoplatonisme* (see n. 1) 193-202 and "La doctrine de Simplicius" (see n. 5) 94; Blumenthal, "The psychology of (?) Simplicius' commentary on the *De anima*", ibid. 73-93.

αὐτοειδές makes no sense, since the whole point is that we should have to be possessed of something other than the body to have these superior perceptions. If, moreover, one were to translate Moerbeke's calque translation of a presumed αὐτοειδές, it is difficult to see what that should mean: "ideal itself"? That would neither be a sensible description of something that had even the smallest component of corporeality, however refined, nor would it be a likely meaning for a compound in -ειδής. Most of these are relatively late, Plato's ἀγαθοειδής (*Republic* 509A) being an early example.[12]   Elsewhere the word αὐτοειδής is rare. It appears much earlier in Marcus Aurelius, at 11.12, where it is almost certainly a wrong reading.[13]

On the other hand there is one text, in the *De Primis Principiis* of Simplicius' contemporary Damascius, where αὐτοειδές does give good sense while bearing the meaning one would expect. There, discussing the Forms and their representations, Damascius explains that the Forms themselves exist at the greatest degree of unification in the Demiurge: subsequently αὗτα ἃ ἐστιν τὰ ἐφεξῆς πάντα αὐτοειδῆ ἐστιν ἀρχόμενα ἀπὸ τῶν θεῶν τούτων: the next set of things that are all of the same kind, having their origin in these divine beings (340=II 201.15-16 Ruelle).[14]   This passage makes it the more likely that the MS reading should be maintained, and αὐτοειδές abandoned at the one point where it occurs as an adjective for soul vehicles in the *CAG* editions of Simplicius.   In fact there is only one other occurrence of the word there, used in a nominal sense.   At *In De an.* 29.15-20 τὰ αὐτοειδῆ figure in a list of the contents of the Ideal Living Being of the *Timaeus*, which Simplicius interprets in the normal way as the noetic *diakosmos*.   Here we are told what it means, namely the first things [that are] and their principles: τὰ πρώτιστα καὶ αἱ τούτων ἀρχαί, which are then listed: ἡ τοῦ αὐτοενὸς ἰδέα ἥ τε τοῦ πρώτου μήκους and so on. In this context αὐτοειδής has a perfectly clear sense of the kind that one would expect, namely the Forms themselves.   Putting this together with the case in Damascius makes it the more likely that this

---

[12]See C.D. Buck and W. Petersen, *A Reverse Index of Greek Nouns and Adjectives* (Chicago 1949) 703-707: apart from a few cases in Herodotus these are virtually none earlier than Plato, with the arguable exception of some in the Hippocratic corpus.

[13]ψυχῆς σφαῖρα αὐτοειδής makes no sense here, and almost all recent editors have abandoned it; for another view cf. A.S.L. Farquharson (Oxford 1944), who retains it, ad. loc.

[14]For the normal use of -ειδής compounds cf. also ταυτοειδής and ἐτεροειδής in the same section, 201.12 R.

is not the word Simplicius used in the *De caelo* commentary to describe a soul-vehicle.

Next αἰθερῶδες: unlike the other terms we have been looking at this is not an -ειδής compound, so that its meaning is not so much aether-like as actually made of aether.[15] Again, it is not common in Simplicius, but is found as a description of a soul vehicle in the *De anima* commentary, where perception and imagination are attributed to τὸ αἰθερῶδες τῆς ἡμετέρας ψυχῆς ὄχημα (17.16-17). On the other occasion on which Simplicius uses the word it describes a possible candidate for the material in the spaces between stars (*In De caelo* 461.18-20): the question is not Aristotle's but the commentator's, and the word is not Aristotelian.[16] These two passages together do, however, confirm that the vehicle is made of some substance other than the ordinary corporeal elements.

The last -ειδής word we have to consider is ἀρχοειδής. At first sight it appears that it may already have appeared as an ὄχημα epithet in the *Phaedrus* commentary of Ammonius' father and academic predecessor Hermias, where the word occurs at 69.18 Couvreur. In fact it is a conjecture of Couvreur's, who replaced the generally accepted αὐγοειδές by ἀρχοειδές on the basis of its appearance a few lines earlier, where, in a different context, it makes perfectly good sense. At 14-18, however, the point at issue is that the human soul by means of the power of perception in the ἀρχοειδές (*sic*) ὄχημα can perceive activity of a divine, or semi-divine vehicle with which its own is contrasted, but with which it thus communicates: κοινωνία...γίνεται τοῦ δαιμονίου ὀχήματος καὶ τοῦ τῆς ψυχῆς. For two reasons the word is suspect in this context. In the first place ἀρχοειδές does not give the expected contrast with a higher kind of entity, which the δαιμόνιον ὄχημα clearly is: it is a word of good Aristotelian ancestry and means superior, or like, having the status of, an ἀρχή. Secondly one would expect, if not a reference to the vehicle's status, then one to its material, which the word does not provide either. Elsewhere in Hermias αὐγοειδές is used, but describes not the soul but the upper heavens to which the divinely led procession of the *Phaedrus* myth aspires (144.26-28): here αὐγοειδές has a clearly comprehensible sense, for the upper heavens might reasonably be described as being like light. So, returning to the

---

[15]For a list of -ῶδης words cf. Buck-Petersen, op. cit. (n. 12) 708-15. It should, however, be said that the suffix is sometimes used with the same sense as -ειδής. On -ῶδης see P. Chantraine, *La formation des noms en grec ancien* (Paris 1933) 429-32.

[16]The commentary is on *De caelo* 290 a29-b11.

ἀρχοειδές ὄχημα, it looks as if once again, as in the case of αὐτοειδές which we have already considered, a word of more obvious meaning, or in this case one better known, has been substituted for the rarer and less perspicuous αὐγοειδές.

We have not yet considered the word most commonly associated with the soul-vehicle, namely πνευματικός. In fact, in the authors we have been discussing it is less common than one might expect: Philoponus shows a different pattern.[17] In Simplicius the πνευματικὸν ὄχημα is the one the soul acquires for embodiment at a higher level than that of the ordinary body here on earth. Its acquisition is a result of soul being inside the cosmos (cf. *In Phys.* 965.31-966.3). That applies to any kind of soul. Thus the specifically human soul also has a vehicle made of *pneuma*: it is not, however, normally described as πνευματικόν: in fact, outside the passage we have just cited, the word occurs only twice in Simplicius, both times in the same section of the *Categories* commentary, where it comes in Stoic contexts and relates to their concept of quality.

This brings us to the second of our initial questions, namely what the soul-vehicles were made of. We have not, however, explicitly answered the first. Let us for the moment say that, contrary to expectations, the texts we have seen suggest that Simplicius, unlike some of his predecessors and contemporaries, operated with one soul vehicle for the individual human soul. A further look at the constituents of these vehicles may help to produce a less tentative answer.

* * *

The terms we have looked at so far suggest various candidates for the material of soul-vehicles: light, *aether, pneuma*. The two first would seem to go together, referring as they do to materials present in the higher reaches of the physical world. *Pneuma*, in spite of its associations with *aether*, is less clearly associated with a particular area of the cosmos.

We have already seen that αὐγοειδές in the places where it occurs in the *Physics*, and possibly also the *De caelo*, commentary is specifically used of the heavenly regions or the world-soul.[18] That this

---

[17]Some 15 examples of πνευματικός, and about 300 of πνεῦμα and its other cognates: Simplicius has about 50.

[18]See above 177-178.

should have a vehicle made of light, or something like it, is appropriate to both its location and function. Is the same material to be found in the human soul vehicle, or, if there is more than one such vehicle, in one of them?

Possibly the three words in question do not indicate distinct materials. Let us go back for a moment to Iamblichus. We find that he uses αὐγοειδές and αἰθερῶδες as descriptions of one and the same thing. Thus in the De mysteriis he talks of prophetic power illuminating the ethereal and light-like vehicle attached to the soul: τὸ περικείμενον τῇ ψυχῇ αἰθερῶδες καὶ αὐγοειδὲς ὄχημα ἐπιλάμπει (III 14 = 117 des Places). Earlier in the same book Iamblichus describes the pneuma in us as light-like, αὐγοειδές (III 11 = 113), and in a later chapter, talking of the purification of the soul and the removal of elements of becoming, as both light-like and ethereal: ἀπορρίπτει τοῦ αἰθερώδους καὶ αὐγοειδοῦς πνεύματος…(V 26 = 182). So here, in the work of the man whom Simplicius at the start of his De anima commentary proclaims as his guide to the understanding of Aristotle (1.14-20), we have one soul vehicle, made of a single substance which is describable by all three of our terms αἰθερῶδες, αὐγοειδές and, being made of pneuma, πνευματικός.

We have already seen indications that the same situation obtains in Simplicius—which would provide an interesting example of the commentator agreeing with Iamblichus against Proclus, who, as we have seen, firmly subscribes to the view that there is more than one soul-vehicle, and whose views one might have expected to be transmitted to Simplicius by way of his pupil and Simplicius' teacher Ammonius.[19] Given the question about the identity of the author of the De anima commentary and the others, it might be as well to say that there is no clear evidence that the doctrine of the De anima commentary differs from that of either the other commentaries on Aristotle or that on Epictetus.[20]

Given the above descriptions of pneuma one might ask whether Simplicius entertained the notion of different qualities of that substance, in so far as the type that is described as αὐγοειδές might not

---

[19]For Proclus as teacher of Ammonius cf. Damascius, Vita Isidori fr. 127 Zintzen = Suda s.v. Aidesia; for Simplicius cf. e.g. In De caelo 271.19.

[20]See the treatments by I. Hadot and Blumenthal referred to in n.11 above; for another view the article of Bossier and Steel cited there. I should add that both authors have since told me that they are more than ever convinced that Simplicius cannot have written the De anima commentary.

be the most appropriate for some of the functions that *pneuma*, or the body constituted by it, are required to perform. In one section of the *De anima* commentary there is a hint that this is indeed what Simplicius has in mind. Discussing why fire does not become alive through the presence of soul, he remarks that it is not a suitable vehicle, ὄχημα, for it: what is is something higher, which is, at least secondarily, of the same sort of composition as things in the heavens, τῆς οὐρανίας ὂν καὶ αὐτὸ συστάσεως δευτέρως (73.33-74.1). He then goes on, in a sentence we have already looked at while considering the use of θνητοειδές, to say that even in our own case a superior vehicle is extended with the soul towards the body.[21] Αὐγοειδές in the one, or two, places where it occurs in Simplicius is used of the *pneuma* in the world's upper regions. Yet its use in other writers indicates that it was by no means confined to that area, but rather may be used of any kind of *pneuma*. Indeed, as early as Galen we find it as a description of a special kind of body when he offers as alternatives that the soul is either made of αἰθερῶδές τε καὶ αὐγοειδές σῶμα, or has an ὄχημα consisting of that substance.[22]

On the other hand, σωματοειδές, which, as we have already seen, may be used to describe something that is other than body, could be taken to denote a kind of vehicle for the individual soul that is of an inferior kind to that described as αὐγοειδές or αἰθερῶδες. Does Simplicius so use it?

In so far as it describes materials, it is used in the *De caelo* commentary to refer to the substance of the heavens, that is to something which, while material, is not, or may not be, made of the same materials as things in the terrestrial world (cf. e.g. 360.29-361.7). When, however, he is commenting on the opening chapter of Book 2 a few pages later, Simplicius uses the term in the same way as Plato, who may have invented it, used it in the passage of the *Timaeus* which Simplicius is discussing there, namely to mean what is in the category of the corporeal.[23] There is, however, a passage in the *Categories* commentary where it is quite clear that σωματοειδές is not just a synonym for σῶμα, for in it the two are explicitly contrasted. Discussing "Archytas" Simplicius writes: δυνατὸν δὲ οἶμαι λέγειν ὅτι

---

[21]See above 177.

[22]Cf. *De Hipp. et Plat. Plac.* V.643 Kuhn = II 474.23-27 de Lacy (*CMG* V 4,1,2). See further R.B. Todd, "Philosophy and Medicine in John Philoponus' commentary on Aristotle's *De anima*", *Dumbarton Oaks Papers* 38 (1984) 108.

[23]36D, quoted at 80.2-6; cf. too *In Phys.* 359.32-35.

ἐπικτητὸν μὲν εἶναι δεῖ καὶ κεχωρισμένον τῆς οὐσίας τὸ ἐχόμενον, οὐ πάντως δὲ σῶμα, ἀλλὰ σωματοειδές (376.33-35).²⁴ Simplicius' further comments, on ζωὴ σωματοειδής, show that he means by σωματοειδές something that is involved with, but not identical with, body (376.37-377.8).²⁵ It appears in this sense too in the *De anima* commentary, where it is used to describe forms of cognition which intellect does not use because they involve both body and soul, namely sense-perception and imagination: οὐδὲ χρῆται σωματοειδεῖ γνώσει αἰσθήσει ἢ φαντασίᾳ (45.26-29). In general the soul, in so far as it is involved with a living being may be involved in the movements, σωματοειδεῖς κινήσεις, pertaining to that form of life (cf. 36.30-31).²⁶ There is some fluctuation in the area of activity to which the word applies: sometimes it is the whole range from *phantasia* downwards, sometimes the sub-sensitive level only.²⁷

The upshot of this examination of the uses of σωματοειδές is that it gives no indication of a special kind of *pneuma* or vehicle for the lower soul. So, in spite of our original assumption of the likelihood that Simplicius believed in more than one such vehicle, it now appears that he did not. Rather, there was only one, made of a substance variously described as αἰθερῶδες, αὐγοειδές and πνευματικόν.

* * *

We now come to the question of its function. To it there is more than one answer. The first, and almost obvious one, is that the vehicle mediates in a way which none of the adherents of this view ever satisfactorily defined, between the immaterial soul and the material body. In this respect it simply provides an answer, on the usual basis of multiplying entities if no other solution is possible, to a question which had quite properly concerned Neoplatonists since those early days when Plotinus, according to Porphyry had spent three

---

²⁴The word Simplicius attributes to Archytas himself is σωματῶδες.

²⁵Cf. too the analogous but different use quoted from Eudemus at *In Phys.* 201.23-27, where Simplicius refers to the elements which are not bodies but produce them.

²⁶For the basis of motion being σωματοειδής cf. also *In De an.* 303.8-10.

²⁷Cf. e.g. 40.30-32 with 57.12-16.

days discussing πῶς ἡ ψυχὴ σύνεστι τῷ σώματι, how the soul is associated with the body (Porphyry, *Vita Plotini* 13).[28]

The second is that the vehicle, rather than either soul or body themselves, is seen as the basis of some of the soul's activities. Here Simplicius with his one vehicle attributes to it the function that Proclus with two attributed to the lower of them, that is to be the basis of sensation and imagination. This view is clearly related to the older notion that *pneuma*, not yet formalized into the material of a soul-vehicle, was the substance in which the images of *phantasia* were realised: Porphyry talks of the image somehow being smeared into the *pneuma* (cf. *Sententiae* 29 = 18.10-12 Lamberz). When we come to Proclus we find that he talks about higher αἴσθησις being ἐν τῷ ὀχήματι. This is the kind of αἴσθησις that is actual cognition, and also imagination, which is essentially the same (cf. *In Tim.* III 286.20-29). It takes place in the πνευματικόν ὄχημα and is opposed to the mere sensation which takes place in the ὀστρεῶδες σῶμα (cf. ibid. 237.24-27).[29] Even more clearly Hermias—and if it is correct to see his work as merely a report of Syrianus' lectures, this may precede Proclus[30]—had made the vehicle of the disembodied soul the subject in perception: τό ὄχημα λαμπρὸν ὂν καὶ καθαρὸν ὅλον δι' ὅλου ἐστὶν αἰσθητικὸν καὶ κατὰ πᾶν ὁρᾷ καὶ κατὰ πᾶν ἀκούει (cf. 68.21-23).

For Simplicius himself the tie between perception and the soul vehicle is such that it is applied even to the heavenly bodies. In the *De anima* commentary their vehicles are described as θεῖα, and it is in them that perception of sensible objects takes place (cf. 215.17-25).[31] In the individual human soul imagination is distinguished from reason, *inter alia*, by being σωματοειδής and therefore unable to deal with simple objects (285.25-28). That statement does not, of course, on its own, associate imagination with the soul-vehicle, the same applies to the description of appetition as σωματοειδής, as opposed to the mind's

---

[28] According to H. Dörrie this discussion was the basis of Plotinus' treatise *On the Problems of the Soul, Enn.* IV 3-5, c.f. *Porphyrios' "Symmikta Zetemata". Zetemata* 20 (Munich 1959) 18 n.1; *contra* Blumenthal, *Plotinus' Phychology* (The Hague 1971) 16 n.20.

[29] Cf. Blumenthal, "Proclus on Perception", *Bulletin of the Institute of Classical Studies* 29 (1982) 3.

[30] The possibility arises because Proclus wrote his *Timaeus* commentary when he was still a young man and Syrianus was still alive, cf. Marinus, *Vita Procli* 13. For αὐγοειδὲς ὄχημα in Syrianus cf. *In Metaph.* 86.3.

[31] Cf. also *In De caelo* 469. 7-11 and p. 178 above.

cognition or βούλησις, at 295.13.15 (cf. 296.19-21). It is only when these
are taken in conjunction with the explicit attribution of the sensitive
soul's cognition to a vehicle that we can infer that the σωματοειδής
nature of such forms of cognition consists not only in association with
the body as such, in which the sense organs reside, but also with the
vehicle which mediates between the different spheres of existence to
which body and soul belong. It is, we may now see, remarkable how
little Simplicius actually says about soul-vehicles as such, the more so
if we compare their incidence in Proclus or, to a lesser extent,
Philoponus.[32]

What does it amount to? Firstly, that the vehicle is seen as a
necessary bridge entity between immaterial soul and material body and
therefore, almost needless to say, found in the philosophy of Plato and
Aristotle. Secondly, that it is involved with those activities which
require the co-operation, in the strict sense, of body and soul, and most
particularly those where the contribution of each might be regarded as
more or less equivalent, that is those which are performed by the
sensitive faculty or faculties of the soul through the organs of the body.
Similar co-operation is, as we have seen, to be found on a lower level
too.

On the other hand there does not, in Simplicius, seem to be any
notion that the higher activities of the soul, those which are a result of
its embodiment but which do not require a direct input from the body,
though they may work with material obtained through its use, require
a separate vehicle. In respect of these, the function of the one vehicle
that Simplicius does have is apparently no more than to provide
conditions for embodiment. Does it, in consequence, disappear when
embodiment ceases?

* * *

Here we come to our fourth question, the length of a vehicle's life.
More precisely, we must ask whether Simplicius' vehicles are added to
the soul at each incarnation and removed thereafter, and in the latter
case, how long thereafter? *Prima facie* this issue relates to the
question, about which there was no consensus, about how much of the
soul might survive death. To illustrate the situation we may refer to
the well known passage in Damascius' *Phaedo* commentary which
tells us that Iamblichus and Plutarch held the view that the soul down

---

[32]For Proclus see above; for Philoponus cf. esp. the preface to *In De an.*, 17ff.

to the irrational part was immortal, while Proclus and Porphyry confined immortality to the rational soul.[33] That indicates that two vehicles and immortality for irrational as well as rational soul do not necessarily go together, for Proclus, as we have seen, believed in two while Iamblichus still had only one. Nor, as that might suggest, was it the case that those who held that there was one vehicle thought that the whole soul must be treated in the same way: if they did, we should not find Proclus and Porphyry in the same slot. To complicate matters further, Proclus himself seems to have believed that the lower vehicle perishes at death, but may have been inconsistent on the fate of the upper: according to the *Elements of Theology* (Prop. 209) and the *Timaeus* commentary (III 267.25-268.3) the αὐγοειδὲς ὄχημα, the higher vehicle, survived, but according to a passage in Damascius' *Phaedo* commentary which may be derived from Proclus, that does not apply to the outstandingly virtuous souls translated to a pure abode in *Phaedo* 114B-C.[34]

All these matters require further investigation. As far as Simplicius is concerned we can only say that there is no view that he might clearly be expected to have held. As it is, the *De anima* commentary does not greatly concern itself with immortality. The same is true of the other text where we might seek evidence, namely the *Encheiridion* commentary. Thus it may well be that the question we have raised here cannot be given more than a speculative answer.

* * *

This brings us to our final question. One might ask whether the absence of prolonged discussions of immortality, and thus of some treatment of the destiny of our soul's vehicles, has anything to do with the fact that there is so little about immortality in the *De anima* itself. To anyone familiar with the methods and procedures of Neoplatonist commentary such questions are hardly worth asking, since these writers notoriously brought in any subject they thought fit. The extent to which their actual interpretations of Plato or Aristotle were influenced by the text they were discussing was another matter, and

---

[33]Damascius, *In Phaed*. I 177.3-5 Westerink = Olympiodorus, *In. Phaed*. 123.13-20 Norvin. On this passage see Blumenthal, "Plutarch's Exposition of the *De Anima* and the Psychology of Proclus", in *De Jamblique à Proclus*. Entretiens Hardt 21 (Vandoeuvres-Geneva 1975) 130f.

[34]Cf. Westerink ad I 551.

might vary. In Simplicius' case that extent, as I have argued elsewhere, was not great.[35] As far as the question of soul vehicles is concerned, they are necessarily independent of the text of Aristotle. In so far as that text allowed the commentators in general, and Simplicius in particular, to find the Neoplatonist division into a rational and an irrational soul, there was scope for Simplicius, once vehicles were admitted, to have either one or two. Hence his views on their number cannot be said to have been influenced by the context provided by the Aristotelian works he was expounding. And in so far as more than one answer was current among Neoplatonists, Simplicius' own, if perhaps no longer the most widely adopted, must be seen against that background, as a product of Neoplatonism rather than of the mind and preoccupations of the Aristotelian commentator.

---

[35]Most recently in "Simplicius (?) on the first book of Aristotle's De Anima", in *I. Hadot*, ed. *Simplicius, sa vie, son oeuvre, sa survie*. Actes du Colloque international de Paris 28.9-1.10. 1985 (Berlin and New York 1987) 91-102. Philoponus may have had a somewhat different approach, cf. "John Philoponus: Alexandrian Platonist?" *Hermes* 114 (1986) 332f.

Platonism and Church Fathers: Three Notes

MIROSLAV MARCOVICH

1. ATHENAGORAS, *LEGATIO* 23 (END)[1]

Καὶ τὸ εἰρημένον αὐτῷ (sc. Πλάτων)· "Ὁ δὴ μέγας ἡγεμὼν
ἐν οὐρανῷ Ζεύς, ἐλαύνων πτηνὸν ἅρμα, πρῶτος πορεύεται,
διακοσμῶν πάντα καὶ ἐπιμελούμενος· τῷ δὲ ἔπεται στρατιὰ θεῶν
τε καὶ δαιμόνων" (*Phaedrus* 246 e 4-6)[2] οὐκ ἐπὶ τοῦ ἀπὸ
5 Κρόνου λεγομένου ἔχει Διός· ἔστι γὰρ ἐν τούτῳ ὄνομα τῷ
ποιητῇ τῶν ὅλων. Δηλοῖ δὲ καὶ αὐτὸς ὁ Πλάτων· ‹ὃς› ἑτέρῳ
σημαντικῷ προσειπεῖν αὐτὸν οὐκ ἔχων, τῷ δημώδει ὀνόματι, |
(A f.339ᵛ) οὐχ ὡς ἰδίῳ τοῦ θεοῦ, ἀλλ' εἰς σαφήνειαν (ὅτι
μὴ δυνατὸν εἰς πάντας φέρειν τὸν θεόν[3]), κατὰ δύναμιν
10 προσεχρήσατο, ἐπικατηγορήσας τὸ "μέγας", ἵνα διαστείλῃ
τὸν οὐράνιον ἀπὸ τοῦ χαμᾶθεν, τὸν ἀγένητον ἀπὸ τοῦ γενητοῦ,
τοῦ νεωτέρου μὲν οὐρανοῦ καὶ γῆς, νεωτέρου δὲ Κρητῶν, οἳ
ἐξέκλεψαν αὐτὸν μὴ ἀναιρεθῆναι ὑπὸ τοῦ πατρός.

---

[1]The text is taken from my edition of Athenagoras, "Patristische Texte und Studien," Band 31, Walter de Gruyter, Berlin, 1990.

[2]A Platonic passage very popular in antiquity: Pseudo-Justin *Cohortatio* 31; Tertullian *Apolog.* 24.3; Arnob. *Adv. nat.* 3.30; Hippolyt. *Refut.* 1.19.8; Origen *Contra Celsum* 8.4 s.f.; Euseb. *De Theophania* p. 96.14 Gressmann. -- Lucian *Piscator* 22; *Bis accusatus* 33; *Rhetorum praecepta* 26; Maxim. Tyr. 4.4 c; 26.7 b; Philostratus *Apoll. Tyan.* 2.22 (p. 64.25 Kayser); Plutarch *Non posse suav. vivi sec. Epicurum* 1102 E, et alibi.

[3]Cf. Plat. *Tim.* 28 c 3: Τὸν μὲν οὖν ποιητὴν καὶ πατέρα τοῦδε τοῦ παντὸς εὑρεῖν τε ἔργον καὶ εὑρόντα εἰς πάντας ἀδύνατον λέγειν, quoted by Athenagoras in *Legat.* 6.2.

1 ὁ δὴ   A (etiam Stobaeus) : ὁ μὲν δὴ Plato Ι 3 στρατιᾶ   A Ι 6 ὅς
addi suad. Maran : ὅτι addi suad. Wilamowitz, agn. Schwartz : post
ἑτέρῳ addi suad. γὰρ Gesner Ι 8 ἰδίωι   Arethas : ἰδίω A Ι 9 κατὰ
δύναμιν τὸν θεὸν A, transp. Schwartz Ι 11 ἀγέννητον et γεννητοῦ A,
corr. cod. Argentoratensis Ι 12 κρητῶν A : Κ‹ου›ρήτων Io. Meursius
(Creta, Amstelodami 1675, p. 72)

Athenagoras already told us that Plato, much like the Christians,
had recognized in the Creator of the universe "the one, uncreated and
eternal God" (Leg. 6.2). He now adds that Plato actually refers to this
"heavenly and uncreated Maker of the universe," when he calls him
"the mighty Leader in heaven Zeus" — ἔστι γὰρ ἐν τούτῳ ὄνομα τῷ
ποιητῇ τῶν ὅλων. It is to distinguish this supreme God from the
earthly and created Zeus, suggests Athenagoras, that Plato adds the
epithet μέγας, "mighty" or "great."

In his classical Commentary to Legatio, J. Geffcken pointed out the
Stoic reinterpretation of the traditional Zeus as a possible source for
Athenagoras,[4] while referring to Seneca Nat. Quaest. 2.45: Ne hoc
quidem crediderunt, Iovem, qualem in Capitolio et in ceteris aedibus
colimus, mittere manu fulmina, sed eundem, quem nos, Iovem
intellegunt, rectorem custodemque universi, animum ac spiritum
mundi, operis huius dominum et artificem, cui nomen omne
convenit.[5]

Leaving apart here the old hymnodic motif of "Zeus of many
names,"[6] Athenagoras' expression, τὸ δημῶδες ὄνομα (i.e., Ζεύς),
reminds us at once of Heraclitus' saying, ἕν, τὸ σοφὸν μοῦνον, λέγεσθαι
οὐκ ἐθέλει καὶ ἐθέλει Ζηνὸς ὄνομα (Fr. 84 Marcovich; B 32 Diels-Kranz),
"One (being), the only (truly) wise, is both unwilling and willing to be
called by the name of Zeus." The saying is preserved only in Clement
(Strom. 5.115.1), who adds: Οἶδα ἐγὼ καὶ Πλάτωνα προσμαρτυροῦντα
Ἡρακλείτῳ γράφοντι …[7]

---

[4]Zwei griechische Apologeten, Leipzig, 1907, 213.

[5]Cf. also Sen. De benefic. 4.7.1; Ps.-Aristotle De Mundo 7; Dio Orat. 12.75 ff. (referred to
by Geffcken).

[6]Cf. Aeschyl. Agam. 160-162 (and Ed. Fraenkel ad loc.); Plato Crat. 400 e 1; K. Keyssner,
Gottesvorstellung und Lebensauffassung im griechischen Hymnus (Würzburger
Studien zur Altertumswiss., 2), Stuttgart, 1932, 46 ff.

[7]We do not know what exact passage of Plato Clement had in mind -- Crat. 396 a-b,
according to H. Jackson and Stählin; or rather Phaedr. 278 d 3, according to A. Le

However, in our passage the contrast between "the heavenly and uncreated Zeus" and "the earthly and created Zeus" is so explicit that it makes the Stoic topic of "Zeus of many names" (such as expressed, e.g., by Pseudo-Aristotle *De Mundo* 7, 401 a 12: Εἷς δὲ ὢν πολυώνυμός ἐστι, κατονομαζόμενος τοῖς πάθεσι πᾶσιν, ἅπερ αὐτὸς νεοχμοῖ) a less likely source of Athenagoras.

Turning to Plato himself, *Cratylus* 396 b 3 (Τοῦτον [sc. τὸν Δία] δὲ Κρόνου υἱὸν ὑβριστικὸν μὲν ἄν τις δόξειεν εἶναι ἀκούσαντι ἐξαίφνης, εὔλογον δὲ μεγάλης τινὸς διανοίας ἔκγονον εἶναι τὸν Δία) could not serve as such a source either, for it is only a prelude to the ensuing etymology of Cronus, not Zeus.

Xenocrates (396-314 B.C.), of the Old Academy, however, made a clear distinction between the heavenly and topmost Zeus, presiding over the intelligible realm, and the nethermost Zeus, ruling this sublunary region of the universe in which we live. Xenocrates' Fr.18 Heinze (apud Plutarch *Quaest. Plat.* 9, 1007 F) reads: Τὸ γὰρ ἄνω καὶ πρῶτον ὕπατον οἱ παλαιοὶ προσηγόρευσαν· ᾗ καὶ Ξενοκράτης Δία τὸν ἐν μὲν τοῖς κατὰ ταὐτὰ καὶ ὡσαύτως ἔχουσιν ὕπατον καλεῖ, νέατον δὲ τὸν ὑπὸ σελήνην.[8] This heavenly and topmost Zeus is called by Xenocrates ὁ πρῶτος θεός (Fr.15 apud Aëtius 1.7.30).

Clement too (*Strom.* 5.116.3) mentions Xenocrates' distinction while advancing an interpretation of his own: Xenocrates meant to say (ἔμφασις = meaning, implication) that the topmost Zeus is God Father, and the nethermost God Son: Ξενοκράτης δὲ ὁ Καλχηδόνιος, τὸν μὲν ὕπατον Δία, τὸν δὲ νέατον καλῶν, ἔμφασιν πατρὸς ἀπολείπει καὶ υἱοῦ.[9]

In conclusion, I think Athenagoras' οὐράνιος καὶ ἀγένητος Ζεύς has its source in Xenocrates' ὕπατος Ζεύς, and his γενητὸς Ζεύς, ὁ χαμᾶθεν,

---

Boulluec, in his Commentary to Clem. *Strom.* Book 5 (Sources Chrétiennes, 279; Paris, 1981, 339).

[8]The text is as edited by H. Cherniss (Plutarch, *Moralia*, Vol. XIII, Loeb, 1976). See Cherniss's Note on p. 92 f. and compare R. Heinze, *Xenokrates*. . ., Leipzig, 1892, 165 f.; M. Isnardi Parente, *Senocrate, Ermodoro, Frammenti*, Naples (Bibliopolis), 1982, Frr. 216-217 and p. 407 f.; H. J. Krämer, *Der Ursprung der Geistmetaphysik*, Amsterdam, 1964, passim (p. 466); J. Dillon, *The Middle Platonism*, Cornell U.P., 1977, 27; H. Schwabl, in *PW RE*, Supplementband XV (1978), 1344 f. (s.v. *Zeus*). -- Xenocrates may well have been influenced by the two aspects of the traditional Zeus -- Ζεὺς ὕψιστος and Ζεὺς χθόνιος (cf. Pausanias 2.2.8), -- but this is besides my point here.

[9]Cf. Le Boulluec, o.c. (supra, note 7), 341. The fact that Xenocrates called his supreme Monad or Zeus also "Father" (Fr. 15 Heinze = Fr. 213 Isnardi Parente) did not influence Clement's explanation.

in Xenocrates' νέατος Ζεύς, ὁ ὑπο σελήνην. Needless to say, μέγας is a standing epithet of the traditional Zeus,[10] and Athenagoras is not convincing when making it a distinctive characteristic of the supreme God.

2. HIPPOLYTUS, *REFUTATIO* 10.33.1-2

The Theology of St. Hippolytus, as extant in *Refutatio* 10.32-34, is highly elaborate, learned and peculiar enough.[11] On this occasion, I shall limit myself to this passage alone; it reads:[12]

Οὗτος οὖν ‹ὁ› μόνος καὶ κατὰ πάντων θεὸς Λόγον πρῶτον
ἐννοηθεὶς ἀπογεννᾷ· οὐ ‹δὲ› Λόγον ὡς φωνήν, ἀλλ᾽ ἐνδιάθετον
τοῦ παντὸς λογισμόν. Τοῦτον ‹οὖν› μόνον ἐξ ὄντων ἐγέννα·
τὸ γὰρ ὂν αὐτὸς ὁ πατὴρ ἦν, ἐξ οὗ τὸ γεννηθέν. ‹Κ›αὶ αἴτιον
5 τοῖς γινομένοις Λόγος ἦν, ἐν ‹ἑ›αυτῷ φέρων τὸ θέλειν τοῦ
γεγεν‹ν›ηκότος, οὐκ ἄπειρός ‹τε ὢν› τῆς τοῦ πατρὸς ἐννοίας.
Ἅμα γὰρ τῷ ἐκ τοῦ γεννήσαντος προελθεῖν, πρωτότοκος τούτου
γενόμενος, ‹ὡς› φωνὴν εἶχεν ἐν ἑαυτῷ τὰς ἐν τῷ πατρικῷ ‹νῷ›
ἐννοηθείσας ἰδέας. Ὅθεν κελεύοντος πατρὸς γίνεσθαι ‹τὸν›
10 κόσμον, | (P f.133ᵛ) τὸ κατὰ ἓν Λόγος ἀπετέλει τὸ ἀρέσκον θεῷ.

---

1 ὁ addidi | 2 δὲ addidi | 3 οὖν addidi | 4 γεννηθέν. ‹Κ›αὶ
Wendland : γεννηθῆναι P | 5 αὐτῷ P, corr. Gottingenses (cf. v.8) | 6
γεγενηκότος P, corr. Miller | τε ὢν addidi | 7 τῷ Miller : τὸ P | 8
ὡς addidi | εἶχεν Wordsworth : ἔχειν P | νῷ supplevi | 9 τὸν
addidi | 10 ἀπετέλει τὸ ἀρέσκον Wordsworth : ἀπετελεῖτο ἀρέσκων P

In this passage, rich in content, two things draw our immediate attention. First, prior to the Creation, God first conceives in his mind the *ideas* or forms of the future things and beings (τὰς ἐν τῷ πατρικῷ ‹νῷ› ἐννοηθείσας ἰδέας, 8-9). This act Hippolytus calls "the Father's

---

[10]Cf. e.g., C.F.H. Bruchmann, *Epitheta deorum* etc., Leipzig, 1893, 133 f.; H. Schwabl, *PW RE*, X A, 334 f. (s.v. *Zeus*).

[11]Cf. L. Bertsch, *Die Botschaft vom Christus und unserer Erlösung bei Hippolyt von Rom*, Trier, 1966; M. Richard, in *Dictionnaire de Spiritualité*, 44-45 (Paris, 1968), s.v. *Hippolyte de Rome*, 545-571; M. Marcovich, in *Theologische Realenzyklopädie*, XV (1986), 385 f., s.v. *Hippolyt von Rom*; Idem, "Plato and Stoa in Hippolytus' Theology, *Illinois Class. Studies* 11 (1986) 265-269.

[12]The text is taken from my edition of Hippolytus' *Refutatio*, "Patristische Texte und Studien," Band 25, Berlin, 1986, p. 410.

mental conception" (ἡ τοῦ πατρὸς ἔννοια, 6). And second, Logos, "the first-born" Son (*Col.* 1;15; Theophil. *Ad Autol.* 2.22), who serves as the only *agent of Creation*, bears in himself the Father's *ideas* as a *voice* (φωνή).

Now, his Demiurgical function consists in transforming the Father's immanent *ideas* into uttered *words*, and, by implication, into physical *things* and *beings* — Καὶ αἴτιον τοῖς γινομένοις Λόγος ἦν (10.33.2); ... ἵνα Λόγος ὑπουργῇ (33.4); "Οσα γοῦν ἠθέλησεν ποιεῖν ὁ θεός, ταῦτα Λόγῳ ἐδημιούργει (33.6); Τα‹ῦτα› δὲ πάντα διῴκει ὁ Λόγος ὁ θεοῦ, ὁ πρωτόγονος πατρὸς παῖς (33.11; again *Col.* 1:15).

(1) Hippolytus' account of the *ideas* of things as existing in the mind of the Father, I would suggest, has its source in the Middle Platonic doctrine of *the ideas as the thoughts of God*. This suggestion may be supported by the following facts.

(a) Hippolytus knew this Platonic teaching, since he quotes it in his exposition of Plato's philosophy (*Refut.* 1.19.2): Τὸ δὲ παράδειγμα[13] τὴν διάνοιαν τοῦ θεοῦ εἶναι· ὃ καὶ ἰδέαν καλεῖ (sc. Πλάτων), οἷον εἰκόνισμα τι, ‹ᾧ› προσέχων ἐν τῇ ψυχῇ ὁ θεὸς τὰ πάντα ἐδημιούργει. "The Paradigm (Archetype) is the thought of God; Plato calls it also *idea*, as being a kind of image on which God concentrates in his soul when constructing this universe."[14] Incidentally, compare the similarity of expression between ἐν τῇ ψυχῇ ὁ θεός and ἐν τῷ πατρικῷ ‹νῷ› (at 10.33.2).

(b) The doctrine was extremely popular in contemporary Middle Platonism and Doxography: Varro apud August. *Civ. Dei* 7.28 (the *ideas* spring from the mind of God just as Minerva did from the head of Jupiter); Seneca *Epist. ad Lucil.* 65.7; Aëtius 1.3.21; 1.10.3; Atticus Fr. 9 40 des Places; Albinus *Didaskalikos* 9.1 Louis (Plato, ed. Hermann, Vol. VI, p. 163.12): Ἔστι δὲ ἡ ἰδέα ὡς μὲν πρὸς θεὸν νόησις αὐτοῦ..., ὡς δὲ πρὸς τὸν αἰσθητὸν κόσμον παράδειγμα...; 9.2 (p. 163.27): εἶναι γὰρ τὰς ἰδέας νοήσεις θεοῦ...; 10.3 (p. 164.26): ἑαυτὸν ἂν οὖν καὶ τὰ ἑαυτοῦ νοήματα ἀεὶ νοοίη, καὶ αὕτη ἡ ἐνέργεια αὐτοῦ ἰδέα ὑπάρχει; Numenius Fr. 16.11 des Places; Ps.-Justin *Cohortatio* 7; Clement *Strom.* 5.16.3: ἡ δὲ ἰδέα ἐννόημα τοῦ θεοῦ; 4.155.2: νοῦς δὲ χώρα ἰδεῶν, νοῦς δὲ ὁ θεός;

---

[13]Cf. Plato *Tim.* 28 a 6: "Ότου μὲν οὖν ἂν ὁ δημιουργὸς πρὸς τὸ κατὰ ταὐτὰ ἔχον βλέπων ἀεί, τοιούτῳ τινὶ προσχρώμενος παραδείγματι, τὴν ἰδέαν καὶ δύναμιν αὐτοῦ ἀπεργάζηται, καλὸν ἐξ ἀνάγκης οὕτως ἀποτελεῖσθαι πᾶν...; Albinus *Didaskalikos* 9.1-2; 12.1 Louis; Apuleius *De Platone* 1.6 (p. 87.20 Thomas).

[14]On *Refut.* 1.19 (Plato) compare C. Moreschini, "La *doxa* di Platone nella *Refutatio* di Ippolito (I 19)," *Studi classici e orientali* (Pisa) 21 (1972) 254-260; J. Dillon, *The Middle Platonists* 410-414.

5.73.3; *Oracula Chald.* Fr. 37.1 f. des Places: Νοῦς πατρὸς ἐρροίζησε νοήσας ἀκμάδι βουλῇ | παμμόρφους ἰδέας..., et alibi.

The formulation of the doctrine in Philo (*De opificio mundi* 19) seems to be close enough to the passage of Hippolytus: Τὰ παραπλήσια δὴ καὶ περὶ θεοῦ δοξαστέον, ὡς ἄρα τὴν μεγαλόπολιν κτίζειν διανοηθεὶς ἐνενόησε πρότερον τοὺς τύπους αὐτῆς, ἐξ ὧν κόσμον νοητὸν συστησάμενος ἀπετέλει καὶ τὸν αἰσθητὸν παραδείγματι χρώμενος ἐκείνῳ.[15]

(c) This is not the only case of borrowing from Platonism in Hippolytus' Theology. Here are a few more examples. God's process of combination of the four elements is called "binding a living organism together" (σύνδεσμος, 10.32.2). The idea is Platonic: *Timaeus* 73 b 3 (ἡ ψυχὴ τῷ σώματι συνδουμένη); *Sympos.* 202 e 6 (ὥστε τὸ πᾶν αὐτὸ αὑτῷ συνδεδέσθαι). Consequently, death is the "undoing" of the elements: θάνατος γὰρ τοῦτο κέκληται, ἡ τῶν δεδεμένων λύσις (32.3). The idea is again Platonic: *Tim.* 41 a 7 (τὸ μὲν οὖν δὴ δεθὲν πᾶν λυτόν). God creates Man out of all four elements (10.33.7: ἐκ πασῶν σύνθετον οὐσιῶν ἐσκεύασεν). This comes from *Tim.* 42e ~ 43a, and Albinus explicitly states (*Didask.* 17.1 = p. 172 Hermann): Οἱ δὴ θεοὶ ἔπλασαν μὲν προηγουμένως τὸν ἄνθρωπον ἐκ γῆς καὶ πυρὸς καὶ ἀέρος καὶ ὕδατος... Hippolytus' explanation of the Delphic injunction, Γνῶθι σεαυτόν, in the sense, "Man, recognize that thou art *god-like*" (10.34.4: ‹Καὶ› τοῦτ' ἔστι τὸ Ἵνῶθι σεαυτόν", ἐπιγνοὺς ‹ἐν σεαυτῷ› τὸν πεποιηκότα θεόν), has its source in the *First Alcibiades* 133 c 4: Τῷ θεῷ ἄρα τοῦτ' ἔοικεν αὐτῆς, καί τις εἰς τοῦτο βλέπων καὶ πᾶν τὸ θεῖον γένος ... οὕτω καὶ ἑαυτὸν ἂν γνοίη μάλιστα.

In conclusion, Hippolytus' teaching of the ideas of things being present in the mind of the Father prior to the act of Creation finds its source in Middle Platonism (the ideas as the thoughts of God). Other philosophical elements contained in the passage under discussion deserve separate study. They are: the well established Stoic ἐνδιάθετος λόγος (lines 2-3);[16] the Father's *Conception* (ἔννοια, 6) and *Will* (ἐν

---

[15]On the origin of this doctrine compare R. M. Jones, "The Ideas as the Thoughts of God," *Class. Philol.* 21 (1926) 317-326; W. Theiler, *Die Vorbereitung des Neuplatonismus*, Berlin, 1930 (1964²), 15 ff.;' 37 ff.; R. E. Witt, *Albinus and the History of Middle Platonism*, Cambridge, 1937 (Reprint, Amsterdam, 1971), 70-75; A. N. M. Rich, "The Platonic Ideas as the Thoughts of God," *Mnemosyne* 1954, 123-133; H.J. Krämer, *Der Ursprung der Geistmetaphysik* 110 ff.; J. Dillon, *The Middle Platonism* 95; É. des Places, *Atticus* (Paris, 1977), 86; D. Wyrwa, *Die christliche Platonaneignung in den Stromateis des Clemens von Alexandrien*, Berlin, 1983, 262.

[16]Compare Sext. Emp. *Pyrrh. hypotyp.* 1.65; 72; 76; *Adv. math.* 8.275; 287; Galen *Protrept.* 1.1; *In Hippocr. de medici officina* XVIII B, p. 649 f. Kühn; *De plac. Hippocr. et Plat.* 2.5

‹ἑ›αυτῷ φέρων τὸ θέλειν τοῦ γεγεν‹ν›ηκότος, 5-6). The Will recurs in 10.33.7, with an allusion to *Psalm* 134:6 (πάντα ὅσα ἠθέλησεν ὁ κύριος ἐποίησεν), while in Hippol. *Contra Noetum* 10 Nautin we read this summary: Θεὸς ... κόσμον ἐννοηθεὶς θελήσας τε καὶ φθεγξάμενος ἐποίησεν. The two dispositions or powers of the Father Bythos — *Conception* and *Will*, — according to Ptolemy (*Refut.* 6.38.5), come to mind: Ἔννοιαν καὶ Θέλησιν· πρῶτον γὰρ ἐνενοήθη τι προβαλεῖν, ὥς φασιν, ἔπειτα ἠθέλησε.

(2) The other problem in our passage is the exact role of Logos as the Father's agent of Creation. Where in Greek philosophy can we find the doctrine of a personified Stoic Προφορικὸς Λόγος transforming the Platonic *ideas* into phenomenal things solely by using his voice — ‹ὡς› φωνὴν εἶχεν ἐν ἑαυτῷ τὰς ἐν τῷ πατρικῷ ‹νῷ› ἐννοηθείσας ἰδέας? As far as I know, nowhere.

To be sure, Logos is not bringing beings into existence simply by naming them, by giving them a name (in the sense of Basilides' ὀνόματι μορφοῦν, *Refut.* 7.18.1). For in the same chapter 33, Hippolytus tells us that the naming of beings did not coincide with the act of their very creation (10.33.7): Ὅτε δὲ ‹ὅσα› ἠθέλησεν› ὡς ἠθέλησε καὶ ἐποίησεν (sc. ὁ θεός) ὀνόμασιν ‹αὐτὰ› καλέσας ἐσήμηνεν.

I would therefore suggest that Logos as the Demiurge serves here only as an *instrument* of his Father, concretely, as the *Voice of God*, and that Hippolytus' main source of inspiration is OT (*Genesis; Psalms*). Consider the following evidence.

(a) Compare Basilides' interpretation of *Gen.* 1:3 (Καὶ εἶπεν ὁ θεός· Γενηθήτω φῶς. Καὶ ἐγένετο φῶς) at *Refut.* 7.22.3 — Οὐ γὰρ γέγραπται, φησί, πόθεν (sc. γέγονε τὸ φῶς), ἀλλ' αὐτὸ μόνον ‹τὸ γενόμενον› ἐκ τῆς φωνῆς τοῦ λέγοντος — with Hippolytus *Contra Noetum* 10: Θεὸς ... κόσμον ἐννοηθεὶς θελήσας τε καὶ φθεγξάμενος ἐποίησεν.

(V, p. 241 K.); Plut. *Maxime cum principibus* 777 C; Heraclit. *Alleg. Homer.* 72.15-16; Porphyry *De abstin.* 3.2; Jamblich. *Vita Pythag.* 218; Hesychius, s.v. ἐνδιάθετος; *S.V.F.* I, Nr. 148; II, Nrr. 135; 223; 840. -- Philo *De vita Mosis* 2.127 and 129; *De spec. legg.* 4.69; *De migrat. Abrahami* 71; *De Abrahamo* 83; *De fuga* 92, et alibi. -- Tatian *Orat.* 5.1; Justin *Dial.* 61.1; Athenagoras *Legat.* 10.2; Theophil. *Ad Autol.* 2.10 and 22; Iren. *Adv. haer.* 2.12.5; Tertullian *Apologet.* 17.1; 21.11; *Adv. Praxean* 5; Clement *Strom.* 5.6.3; 7.53.6; 55.4; Origen *Contra Celsum* 6.65; Basil. Caes. *Hom.* 16.3 (*P.G.* 31, 477 A); Nemes. *De nat. hom.* 14, et alibi. -- M. Mühl, in *Archiv für Begriffsgeschichte*, Bonn (Bouvier), 7 (1962), 7-56; Max Pohlenz, *Die Stoa*[2] I (Göttingen, 1959), 39; 185; 373 ff.; 412; 435; 451; II (Göttingen, 1955), Erläuterungen. -- For possible antecedents cf. Plato *Sophist* 263 e; Aristotle *Anal. Post.* A 10, 76 b 25.

(b)   The influence of the Psalms (and the Jewish Wisdom speculation) is present in the *Logoslehre* of both Hippolytus and Theophilus of Antioch. Compare the link between Reason, Wisdom, Light and Voice or Word:

Hippol. *Refut.* 10.33. 11:

Τα‹ῦτα› δὲ πάντα διώκει ὁ
Λόγος ὁ θεοῦ, ὁ πρωτόγονος
πατρὸς παῖς (cf. *Col.* 1:15), ἡ πρὸ
ἑωσφόρου   (cf. *Ps.* 109:3)[17]
φωσφόρος φωνή.

Theophil. *Ad Autol.* 2.10:

Ἔχων οὖν ὁ θεὸς τὸν ἑαυτοῦ
λόγον ἐνδιάθετον ἐν τοῖς ἰδίοις
σπλάγχνοις (cf. *Ps.* 109:3),
ἐγέννησεν αὐτὸν μετὰ τῆς
ἑαυτοῦ σοφίας ἐξερευξάμενος (Cf.
Ps. 44:2) πρὸ τῶν ὅλων. Τοῦτον
τὸν λόγον ἔσχεν ὑπουργὸν τῶν
ὑπ' αὐτοῦ γεγενημένων, καὶ δι'
αὐτοῦ τὰ πάντα πεποίηκεν (cf.
John 1:3).

Hippol. *C. Noetum* 10:

... φωνὴν φθεγγόμενος (sc. ὁ
θεὸς) καὶ φῶς ἐκ φωτὸς γεννῶν,
προῆκεν τῇ κτίσει κύριον τὸν
ἴδιον νοῦν.

Theophil. *Ad Autol.* 2.22:

Ὁ δὲ Λόγος αὐτοῦ (sc. τοῦ
θεοῦ), δι' οὗ τὰ πάντα
πεποίηκεν, δύναμις ὢν καὶ
σοφία αὐτοῦ (1 *Cor.* 1:24), ...
Ὁπότε δὲ ἠθέλησεν ὁ θεὸς
ποιῆσαι ὅσα ἐβουλεύσατο,
τοῦτον τὸν λόγον ἐγέννησεν
προφορικόν, πρωτότοκον πάσης
κτίσεως (*Col.* 1:15),...

(c)   Finally, Logos in his role of "Voice of God" serves as the transmitter of God's instruction to Man (Adam, the prophets, the Christians):

---

[17] ἐκ γαστρὸς πρὸ ἑωσφόρου ἐξεγέννησά σε. Quoted by Hippol. *Contra Noetum* 16 s.f.

Hippol. *Refut.* 10.33.13:

Καὶ ταῦτα ‹δὲ› θεὸς ἐκέλευε Λόγῳ, ὁ δὲ Λόγος ἐφθέγγετο λέγων ‹τοῖς προφήταις›, δι' αὐτῶν ἐπιστρέφων τὸν ἄνθρωπον ἐκ παρακοῆς.

Theophil. *Ad Autol.* 2.22:

Ὁ δὲ λόγος αὐτοῦ ... οὗτος παρεγένετο εἰς τὸν παράδεισον ἐν προσώπῳ τοῦ θεοῦ καὶ ὡμίλει τῷ Ἀδαμ. Καὶ γὰρ αὐτὴ ἡ θεία γραφὴ διδάσκει ἡμᾶς τὸν Ἀδαμ λέγοντα τῆς φωνῆς ἀκηκοέναι (*Gen.* 1:8). Φωνὴ δὲ τί ἄλλο ἐστὶν ἀλλ' ἢ ὁ λόγος ὁ τοῦ θεοῦ, ὅς ἐστιν καὶ υἱὸς αὐτοῦ;

The *illumination* of Man coming from the *voice* of Logos is clear enough in Hippolytus. Compare *Refut.* 10.34.2 Ταρτάρου ζοφεροῦ ὄμμα ἀφώτιστον, ὑπὸ Λόγου φωνῆς μὴ καταλαμφθέν (cf. 2 *Petri* 1:19); 10.33.11: ἡ ... φωσφόρος φωνή; C. *Noetum* 10 (quoted on p. 196).

In conclusion, in the passage just discussed Hippolytus displays an eclectic combination of the elements deriving from Middle Platonism, Stoa, OT and NT, and the Christian and Gnostic writers of the second century

3. HIPPOLYTUS, *DE UNIVERSO*

In his lost work *De Universo*, Hippolytus doubtless engaged in polemics with Plato. For Photius (*Bibl.* cod. 48) opens his summary of this treatise as follows: Ἔστι δὲ ἐν δυσὶ λογιδίοις. Δείκνυσι δὲ ἐν αὐτοῖς πρὸς ἑαυτὸν στασιάζοντα Πλάτωνα ... (11 b 16 Bekker; I, p. 34 Henry). This fact squares with the title of the work inscribed on the Vatican statue: Πρὸς Ἕλληνας καὶ πρὸς Πλάτωνα, ἢ καὶ Περὶ τοῦ παντός,[18] as well as with the title in the longest extant fragment (Fr. 353 Holl, *T. U.* XX.2, 1899, pp. 137-143, preserved in *Sacra Parallela* 2.801, *P.G.* 96, 542 f., of John Damascene): ‹Κατὰ› Πλάτωνος περὶ τῆς τοῦ παντὸς αἰτίας καὶ κατὰ Ἑλλήνων.[19]

---

[18]The best text of the three inscriptions on the chair of the Vatican statue is in Margherita Guarducci, *Epigrafia Greca*, IV, Rome, 1978, 535-547.

[19]In John Philoponus, *De Opificio Mundi* 3.16, the title of the treatise is, Περὶ τῆς τοῦ παντὸς αἰτίας; Hippolytus himself, in *Refut.* 10.32.4, refers to the work as Περὶ τῆς τοῦ παντὸς οὐσίας; while Photius (cod. 48) knows both titles, Περὶ τοῦ παντός, ὃ ἐν ἄλλοις ἀνέγνων ἐπιγραφόμενον Περὶ τῆς τοῦ παντὸς αἰτίας, ἐν ἄλλοις δὲ Περὶ τῆς τοῦ παντὸς οὐσίας. Finally, in cod. Coislinianus 305 saec. XI (see note 20) the title is Κατ' Ἑλλήνων (sic). On the problem of the authorship of *De Universo* compare Marcovich, *Hippolytus, Refutatio* (supra, note 12), 12-15.

Now, the entire Fr. 353 Holl (running some 137 lines) deserves a separate study: it gives a vivid description of Hades and deals with the resurrection of the body. On this occasion, I shall limit myself to making a few remarks on the text and content of four shorter fragments of the lost *De Universo*.

(a) Fr. I Malley[20] should read:

Οὐ συγχωρητέον οὖν οἷς τὸ πολὺ τῶν δαιμόνων σκοτοφυὲς[21]
πνεῦμα ἐνείρκται ἐν ψυξαῖς, πολλὴν ‹τῶν› θεῶν γένεσιν καὶ
ἀναρίθμητον φανταζομένοις οὖσαν, κατά γε τὴν Ἡσιόδου
θεογονίαν καὶ Ὁμήρου ματαιολογίαν·[22] οἷς, εἰ ‹καὶ› μὴ θέλοιεν
5 δοκεῖν πείθεσθαι οἱ καθ' Ἕλληνας φιλόσοφοι ἐπαγγελόμενοι,
ἀλλά γε διὰ τὸ σέβειν τὰ ὑπ' αὐτῶν μεμυθευμένα[23] συνῄραντο.[24]

---

2 ἐνείρκται Malley : ἐνῄρκται P Ι τῶν addidi Ι 3 οὖσαν scripsi :
οὐσίαν P Ι 4 καί² addidi Ι 4-5 θέλοι ἐνδοκεῖν P, corr. Malley Ι 6 τὸ
scripsi : τοῦ P Ι συνῄραντο P

"One should not therefore agree with those who, following Hesiod's theogony and Homer's idle talk, imagine that there is[25] a manifold, even countless, generation of the gods, for the mighty spirit of the demons, born out of darkness, is shut up in their minds. The self-proclaimed philosophers among the Greeks, even if they did not want to appear following Hesiod and Homer,

---

[20]See W. J. Malley, "Four unedited fragments of the *De Universo* of the Pseudo-Josephus found in the *Chronicon* of George Hamartolus (Coislin 305)," *Journal Theol. St.*, N.S., 16 (1965) 13-25.

[21]σκοτοφυής is a *hapax*. Cf. δενδροφυής in the poem quoted by Hippolytus in *Refut.* 5.7.4. For πνεῦμα, in such a derogatory sense, compare my *Index verborum* in *Refutatio*, p. 501, col. 3.

[22]Cf. ματαιοπονία in *Refutatio* 4.7.4; 6.43.5.

[23]Cf. *Refutatio, Index*, p. 487, col. 2.

[24]The verb, συναίρεσθαί τινι, in the sense of "*join* somebody (either in his opinion or in his party)," is employed five times by Hippolytus in *Refutatio*: 5.20.1 (Λέγουσι δὲ καὶ Μωσέα αὐτῶν συναίρεσθαι τῷ λόγῳ); 5.16.5 (οἱ μὲν πατρικοὶ ἄγγελοι τῷ πατρὶ συναίρονται); 10.15.3; 9.7.3 (διὰ τὸ συναίρεσθαι αὐτοῖς τὸν Ζεφυρῖνον καὶ τὸν Κάλλιστον); 9.12.14 (ὡς› συναράμενον αὐτὸν ‹θέλων ‹ἔχειν› πρὸς τὴν κατάστασιν τοῦ κλήρου). Cf. Lampe, *A Patristic Greek Lexicon*, s. v. συναίρω.

[25]An ἀναρίθμητος οὐσία cannot be paralleled. Hence my reading, οὖσαν (sc. ‹τῶν› θεῶν γένεσιν) for P's οὐσίαν -- an easy emendation.

nevertheless ended up by joining them, for the simple reason that they cherished the fables the former had invented."

As pointed out in footnotes 21-24, the lexicon coincides with that of Hippolytus' *Refutatio*. Add to this Fr. II Malley: Ἀλλ' ἐπειδὴ πολλοὶ λίαν οἱ παρ' Ἕλλησι περὶ θεοῦ λέγειν ἐπαγγελόμενοι, θεὸν δὲ τὸ καθ' ὅλου μὴ ἐγνωκότες... The idea recurs three times in *Refutatio*: 1.26.3; 4.43.2; 10.32.5: τὰ μέρη τῆς κτίσεως ἐδόξασαν, τὸν κτίσαντα ἀγνήσαντες, and the source of inspiration is *Rom.* 1:25.[26]

(b) Fr. III Malley should read:

Εἷς δὲ τούτων ὁ παρὰ πᾶσι σοφώτερος κριθεὶς νενόμισται Πλάτων· ὃς καὶ περὶ θεοῦ καὶ ψυχῆς καὶ κτίσεως ἐπεχείρησε λέγειν. Πρὸς τοῦτον ἡμῖν ἡ ἅμιλλα γινέσθω τῶν λόγων, τὸν καὶ πάντων νομιζόμενον παρ' Ἕλλησι θεοσεβέστατον [τε] καὶ
5 ἀληθέστερον. Οὗ φανέντος <δὲ> ἠγνοηκέναι θεὸν καὶ τὴν τούτου δημιυοργίαν, ἀνάγκη «καὶ» τοὺς λοιποὺς συγχωρεῖν εἰς μορμολύκ«ε»ια <σύμπαντα> συμφύρεσθαι καὶ τερατεύεσθαι· καὶ οὕτως <ἔπειτα> ἡμεῖς ἐπιδείξομεν τίς θεὸς ἀληθινὸς καὶ ἡ τούτου δημιουργία.
10   Θεὸν μὲν γὰρ ἐπεχείρησεν εἰπεῖν εἰς πάντας ἄρρητον[27] Πλάτων, ἀεὶ ὄντα, γένεσιν δὲ οὐκ ἔχοντα·[28] ὃν ἐξ ἀκοῆς ὑπονοήσας, μὴ μαθὼν <δὲ> ἐπεξείρησε διηγήσασθαι. Οὗ τὴν μὲν προαίρεσιν ἀποδεχόμενος θεὸν ζητήσαντος, τὴν ὑπερηφανίαν δὲ καὶ αὐταρέσκειαν οὐκ ἐπαινῶ, μαθεῖν μὴ θελήσαντος. Ὅς,
15 <ὡσὰν> ὑπὸ τῆς ἀληθείας βιασθείς, παρ' οὗ ταῦτα ἦν ἀκηκοὼς ἱερέως ἐν Αἰγύπτῳ, ἀπήγγειλε τοῖς ἰδίοις ἐπανήξας εἰς τὴν ἀλαὸν Ἑλλάδα ὡς ἴδια, οὐκ ἐπιζητήσας <δὲ> πόθεν παραλαβὼν ὁ Αἰγύπτιος ἱερεὺς ἀπήγγειλε Σόλωνι τῷ φιλο- σόφῳ (καθὼς ἐν τῷ Τιμαίῳ διαμέμνηται).[29] <Ὅς δὲ
20 εὐλαβούμενος> καὶ ταῦτα φάμενος ὅσα ἐκ παρακουσμάτων ἦν εἰληφώς, <ὡς> τοῖς τὰ πρῶτα περὶ θεοῦ μανθάνουσιν, ὡς μεγάλα τῷ Σόλωνι διηγήσατο περί τε κατακλυσμοῦ τοῦ πρώτου καὶ ἐκπυρώσεως μερικῆς, <τῆς> ἐν Σοδόμοις. Οἷς καταπλαγεὶς[30] ὁ Σόλων ὡς μεγάλα καὶ θαυμάσια κατὰ

---

[26]Cf. Malley 23.

[27]Cf. Plat. *Tim.* 28 c 3; Athenag. *Legat.* 6.2; 23 s.f.

[28]Cf. *Tim.* 27 d 6: τί τὸ ὂν ἀεί, γένεσιν δὲ οὐκ ἔχον...

[29]*Tim.* 21 e -- 25 d.

[30]Καταπλήσσεσθαι, in the sense of "being highly impressed or amazed," is typical of Hippolytus -- thirteen instances are listed in *Index* to *Refutatio*, p. 474, coll. 2-3.

25 πᾶσαν τὴν Ἑλλάδα κηρύσσει κατὰ τὴν τοῦ ἱερέως καὶ τοῦ
Πλάτωνος ὑπόθεσιν. Οἷς ‹δὲ› εἰ ἐβούλετο Πλάτων μὴ
φιλοδόξως ἀλλὰ θεοσεβῶς ‹προσέχειν›...³¹

1 ὁ τούτων P, transposui I 4 τε delevi I 5 δὲ addidi I 6 τούτων P,
corr. Malley I καὶ addidi I 7 μορμολύκια P I σύμπαντα supplevi I 8
ἔπειτα addidi I 12 δὲ addidi I 14 ἐπαινῷ P I 15 ὡσὰν addidi I 17 ἀλαὸν
(i.e. ΑΛΑΟΝ) scripsi : λάλον (i.e. ΛΑΛΟΝ) P I δὲ addidi I 19-20 ὃς (sc. ὁ
ἱερεὺς) δὲ εὐλαβούμενος supplevi I 21 ὡς addidi I 23 τῆς addidi I 26
δὲ addidi I ἐβούλετω P I 27 προσέχειν supplevi

Hippolytus' intention, expressed in line 3 (πρὸς τοῦτον ἡμῖν ἡ
ἅμιλλα γινέσθω τῶν λόγων), to engage in a real *Agon* with Plato, only
confirms what has been suggested above, on p. 11. In line 7, the
addition of σύμπαντα is necessary; the word refers to τὰ περὶ θεοῦ καὶ
ψυχῆς καὶ κτίσεως (of line 2), and the sense is: ". . . then of necessity
one will have to agree that the rest of Greek philosophers too have
engaged in reducing *everything* to disfigured comic masks and in
devising fantastic theories (just as Plato did)." In line 17, we learn that
the Greeks were *blind* when believeing Plato. They were not *babblers*,
but blind in their minds (*Refut*. 8.8.1 τυφλώττοντες). Hence the need to
change P's λάλον into ἀλαόν — an old Homeric adjective (*Odyssey*
8.195; 10.493; 12.267).

In lines 19-23, Hippolytus comes to his real point. While Plato
proved to be a κλεψίλογος by claiming other peoples' wisdom as his
own (ἀπήγγειλε τοῖς ἰδίοις... ὡς ἴδια, 16-18), in his turn the Egyptian
priest displayed *caution and discretion* in revealing the full truth to
such obvious *beginners* in matters of Theology as Solon and Plato and
all the Greeks were. Accordingly, he revealed to Solon only the first
flood and the small conflagration of Sodom (*Gen*. 19:24). The full
truth, however, about the *priority of the Hebrew religion*, the priest
kept for himself.

The need for the supplement εὐλαβούμενος (in line 20) is confirmed
by Strabo 17.1.29 (806 Cas.): allegedly, Plato had spent thirteen years in
Heliupolis without gaining much from the *secretive* Egyptian priests,
slow to impart knowledge — περιττοὺς γὰρ ὄντας κατὰ τὴν ἐπιστήμην
τῶν οὐρανίων (sc. τοὺς ἱερέας), μυστικοὺς δὲ καὶ δυσμεταδότους. As a
result, τὰ πολλὰ δὲ ἀπεκρύψαντο οἱ βάρβαροι. The motif of the Greeks as
mere beginners in matters of Theology recurs in *Refutatio* 6.22.1: Ἡ

---

³¹Προσέχειν τινί is common in Hippolytus, *Index* to *Refut*., p. 507, col. 1.

μὲν οὖν ἀρχὴ τῆς ὑποθέσεώς ἐστιν ἐν τῷ Τιμαίῳ τῷ Πλάτωνι σοφία
Αἰγυπτίων· ἐκεῖθεν γὰρ ὁ Σόλων τὴν ὅλην ὑπόθεσιν περὶ τῆς ‹τοῦ›
κόσμου γενέσεως καὶ φθορᾶς ... τοὺς Ἕλληνας ἐδίδαξε, παῖδας νέους
ὄντας (Tim. 22 b 4) καὶ πρεσβύτερον ἐπισταμένους μάθημα θεολογούμενον
οὐδέν. And, of course, the thesis of the priority of the Hebrew people
and their religion is visible enough in Refutatio (e.g., 10.31.4: πῶς οὐ
προγενέστεροι ἦσαν ‹οἱ› θεοσεβεῖς πάντων Χαλδαίων, Αἰγυπτίων,
Ἑλλήνων;).

(c) The fragment quoted by Photius (Cod. 48):

Δοξάζει δὲ συγκεῖσθαι τὸν ἄνθρωπον ἐκ πυρὸς καὶ γῆς
καὶ ὕδατος, καὶ ἔτι ἐκ πνεύματος, ὃ καὶ ψυχὴν ὀνομάζει.
Περὶ οὗ πνεύματος αὐταῖς ‹ταῖς› λέξεσιν οὕτω φησίν·
"Τούτου (sc. τοῦ πνεύματος) τὸ κυριώτερον ἀνελόμενος
5 (sc. ὁ θεὸς) ἅμα τῷ σώματι ἔπλασε, καὶ διὰ παντὸς μέλους
καὶ ἄρθρου πορείαν αὐτῷ παρεσκεύασεν· ὃ τῷ σώματι συμ-
πλασθὲν καὶ διὰ παντὸς διϊκνούμενον τῷ αὐτῷ εἴδει τοῦ
βλεπομένου σώματος τετύπωται, τὴν οὐσίαν δὲ ψυχρότερον
ὑπάρχει πρὸς τὰ τρία, δι' ὧν τὸ σῶμα συνήρμοσται."

3 ταῖς addidi | 6 παρεσκεύασεν A : κατεσκεύασεν M | 9 τὸ σῶμα A :
τῷ σώματι M

This is a gem of the syncretism of Platonism and Stoicism. In
Hippolytus' Theology in Refutatio 10.32-34, we learn that prior to the
Creation God first created "four primary bodies" or elements — fire
and air, water and earth (Refut. 10.32.2; 33.4), just as the Demiurge in
Timaeus did (48 b 4; 53 c 4; 55 d 7 ff.; 57 c 7). And the same as in
Timaeus (42 e - 43 a; Albinus Didaskal. 17.1), we learn from Hippolytus
that Man was created out of all four elements (both in Refut. 10.33.7
and in Photius' fragment, lines 1-2).

Enter Stoicism. Unlike Plato, Hippolytus calls the fourth element
pneuma, not air. This is repeated five times in Refutatio (10.32.1; 32.2;
33.4; 33.5 bis), and is present here as well (2 καὶ ἔτι ἐκ πνεύματος). The
reason becomes clear from our fragment — to equate the cosmic spirit
with the human soul (line 2), just as the Stoics did (e.g., S.V.F. II Nr.
785: πῦρ ἢ πνεῦμα λεπτομερές ἐστι (sc. ψυχή), διὰ παντὸς διῆκον τοῦ
ἐμψύχου σώματος). Lines 4-5 of the fragment I understand as follows:
"Taking the superior (part) of the (cosmic) spirit, God formed it (cf.
Gen. 2:7) along with the (human) body..." Possibly, this κυριώτερον (sc.
μέρος) τοῦ πνεύματος hints at the Stoic τὸ ἡγεμονικόν (animae
principale). For it is by preference this part of the soul that reaches

every corner of the human body, and hence Chrysippus' famous simile about the spider and its web (*S.V.F.* II Nr. 879).[32] But one cannot be sure enough.

The point is that the Stoic explanation of the human soul as being no other thing than the *cooled* cosmic spirit is present in our fragment. For the Stoic etymology, ψυχὴ παρὰ τὴν ψῦξιν,[33] is implied by Hippolytus' expression of lines 8-9: τὸ πνεῦμα (=ἡ ψυχή) τὴν οὐσίαν δὲ ψυχρότερον ὑπάρχει πρὸς τὰ τρία (sc. στοιχεῖα). Compare *S.V.F.* II, Nrr. 804-808 (*Anima refrigeratione orta*), e.g., Plut. *De Stoicorum Repugn.* 1052 F: ... ψυχόμενον ὑπὸ τοῦ ἀέρος καὶ στομούμενον τὸ πνεῦμα μεταβάλλειν καὶ γίγνεσθαι ζῷον· ὅθεν οὐκ ἀπὸ τρόπου τὴν ψυχὴν ὠνομάσθαι παρὰ τὴν ψῦξιν; 1053 C.

(*d*) Plato in Fr. 353.47-56 Holl:[34]

Οὗτος ὁ περὶ "Αιδου λόγος, ἐν ᾧ αἱ ψυχαὶ πάντων κατέχονται ἄχρι καιροῦ, ὃν ὁ θεὸς ὥρισεν, ἀνάστασιν τότε πάντων ποιησό-μενος· οὐ ψυχὰς «δὲ» μετενσωματῶν, ἀλλ' αὐτὰ τὰ σώματα ἀνισ-τῶν. "Α ἀεὶ λελυμένα ὁρῶντες ἀπιστεῖτε, Ἕλληνες· μάθετε «δὲ»
5 μὴ ἀπιστεῖν. Τὴν γὰρ ψυχὴν γενητὴν καὶ ἀθάνατον ὑπὸ θεοῦ γεγονέναι πιστεύσαντες κατὰ τὸν Πλάτωνος λόγον, μὴ ἀπιστήσητε «ὅτι» χρόνῳ καὶ τὸ σῶμα, ἐκ τῶν αὐτῶν στοιχείων σύνθετον γενό-μενον, δυνατὸς ὁ θεὸς ἀναβιῶσαν ἀθάνατον ποιεῖν. Οὐ γὰρ τὸ μὲν δυνατός, τὸ δὲ ἀδύνατος ῥηθήσεται περὶ θεοῦ.

2 ποιησόμενος M et Baroccianus : ποιησάμενος cett., Holl | 3 δὲ addidi | 4 δὲ addidi | 7 ὅτι addidi | χρόνῳ hoc loc M (μὴ ἀπιστεῖται χρόνῳ) : post 6 λόγον cett. | καὶ : καὶ γὰρ M : <ὡς> καὶ Hoeschell | 8 ἀναβιῶσαν M : ἀναβιώσας cett., Holl

A soul "subject to generation but immortal" according to Plato (5 τὴν γὰρ ψυχὴν γενητὴν καὶ ἀθάνατον) puzzled the learned Dr. Gerard Langbaine (long before 1720), and he suggested the change of γενητὴν into ἀγέννητον while referring to *Phaedrus* 246 a 1: ... ἐξ ἀνάγκης

---

[32]Cf. M. Marcovich, *Eraclito: Frammenti,* Florence, 1978, Fr. 115 (pp. 393-397) = B 67a Diels-Kranz.

[33]The source of inspiration seems to have been Aristotle, *De Anima* A 2, 405 b 28 (οἱ δὲ τὸ ψυχρὸν διὰ τὴν ἀναπνοὴν καὶ τὴν κατάψυξιν καλεῖσθαι ψυχήν), not Plato's *Cratylus* (399 d 10 -- e 3), where ἀναψῦχον means "reviving," not "cooling."

[34]In addition to Holl's MSS (*T.U.* XX.2, p. 137), compare H. Cherniss, in *Class. Philol.* 24 (1929) 346-350.

ἀγένητόν τε καὶ ἀθάνατον ψυχὴ ἂν εἴη; (compare also 245 d 1: ἀρχὴ δὲ ἀγένητον).

The change is, however, unwarranted. For, first, Hippolytus is here having in mind *Timaeus* alone, and there he found Psychogony in 34 c 4: . . . ὁ δὲ (sc. ὁ θεὸς) καὶ γενέσει καὶ ἀρετῇ προτέραν καὶ πρεσβυτέραν ψυχὴν σώματος ... συνεστήσατο ἐκ τῶνδε...; 36 d 8: ἡ τῆς ψυχῆς σύστασις. The contradiction between *Phaedrus* and *Timaeus* as for the Psychogony is an old problem, maybe best summed up by Plutarch (*De Animae Procreatione in Timaeo*, 1016 A), who stated that only a "drunken sophist," and not a Plato, could produce such a λόγων ταραχὴν καὶ ἀνωμαλίαν as to say, ἀγένητον μὲν ἐν Φαίδρῳ τὴν ψυχήν, ἐν δὲ Τιμαίῳ γενομένην (cf. also Proclus *In Plat. Tim.* II, p. 119.29 f. Diehl; Chalcidius *Plat. Tim.* pp. 76.10-12; 77.13-20 Waszink). *Timaeus* (43 a 4; 69 c 5) will be Hippolytus' source here also for the ἀθάνατος ψυχή, and in line 3 (οὐ ψυχὰς ‹δὲ› μετενσωματῶν) there is another obvious attack on Plato, inspired by *Tim.* 42 b-d, in the first place (cf. *Refut.* 1.19.12 with apparatus).

And second, Hippolytus is here making the following point. "You, the Greeks, believe Plato when he says that God was able first to *create* the soul, and then to make her *immortal*. But soul is composed of the *same* elements as *body* [compare Fr. *c*]. Consequently, you should believe that God is *equally* capable first of *making* the body, and then resurrecting it and making it *immortal*." The motif of the resurrection and immortality of the body recurs in *Refutatio* 10.34.3: ἕξεις δὲ ἀθάνατον τὸ σῶμα καὶ ἄφθαρτον ἅμα ‹τῇ› ψυχῇ. Here again, Hippolytus' expression is close enough to that of Theophilus of Antioch, *Ad Autol.* I.7 s.f.: Ἀνεγείρει γάρ σου τὴν σάρκα ἀθάνατον σὺν τῇ ψυχῇ ὁ θεός.

In conclusion, the fragments of *De Universo* complement the Theology outlined in *Refutatio* 10.32-34, while pointing to one author alone — St. Hippolytus (not "Josephus"). But the point is that in both works Hippolytus stood under an undeniable spell of Plato (particularly *Timaeus*), Middle Platonism, and Stoicism.

The Alien God in Arius[*]

RAOUL MORTLEY

It was particularly the subordinationism of the system of Arius which caught the attention of the orthodox. (I use the word "system" deliberately, since there is something very tight about the way it is expressed in the various summaries, something which suggests a strongly disciplined body of thought such as we see very clearly with the later Arian, Eunomius. Another example of such extremely rigorous writing may be found with Proclus' *Elements of Theology*, and the "system" of Arius has something of the same deductive power. Unlike the credal statements, there is a syllogistic character about Arius' statements).

It was the diminution of the Son; that he should be seen to be of a lesser essence, which offended orthodoxy, and the orthodox therefore claimed him to be *homoousios*, of the same essence. The inferiority of the Son was more or less inevitable given the involvement of Arius with the monism of the Neoplatonists: any emanationist system of thought such as this tends to produce continuingly inferior beings as part of the outflow from the point of origin. And the inferiority of the Son did constitute a grave problem for essential themes such as the idea of revelation. If the Word is a lesser god, then what is the value of his revelation? He only excites the curiosity further; the desire to go beyond comes into being, and the face of God in Christ is seen as but a mask. This is a principle grasped very clearly in the Tripartite Tractate, a Valentinian text which has the Word as a principle of decline: a lesser being creating even lesser beings. The monism of the system forces a decline on all its parts.

---

[*]It is a great privilege to be able to contribute to a volume in honour of Fr. des Places, whose work has instructed all historians of Greek and Christian thought in the last generation.

There is another element of this which deserves attention. Not only did the Son emerge as subordinated in the Arian system, but also alienated. This has not been much emphasized, but it did catch the imagination of Athanasius and does indeed represent a peculiarity of the Arian system and vocabulary. God was foreign (ξένος) to the Son: ξένος τοῦ Ὑίοῦ κατ᾽ οὐσίαν in Athanasius' summary.[1] And this is repeated in the *Depositio Arii*, in which Alexander summarises Arian views from a different angle: that of the Word, who is said to be "foreign, alien from, and separated from the essence of God" (ξένος τε καὶ ἀλλότριος καὶ ἀπεσχοινισμένος ἐστὶν ὁ λόγος τῆς τοῦ θεοῦ οὐσίας).[2] This is peculiar language: the word "foreign", ξένος, in particular is striking; ἀλλότριος "other", "alien", is not so unfamiliar given that otherness is an established theme of Greek philosophy.

There seems to be a radical perversity in proclaiming that God is foreign to the Son, especially since the Son is the revealer. Arius' position is virtually revisionist; the role of the Son as revealer is contradicted. How can what we know of the Son be useful for knowing what is alien to him? The revelation of the Word is a non-revelation. Not only that but there is a distinct religious shift: the spirituality of the appreciation of the deity is markedly altered. God is no longer cast in terms of sameness, but of absolute difference. These are words which echo strangely in the tradition of Christian spiritual sentiment: this is a point almost unconsciously recognized by Athanasius when he says: "They who separate the Son and alienate the Word from the Father, ought themselves to be separated from the Catholic Church and to be alien from the Christian name". (Τοὺς γὰρ χωρίζοντας τοῦ Ὑὸν, καὶ ἀπαλλοτριοῦντας τοῦ Λόγον ἀπὸ τοῦ Πατρὸς, χωρίζεσθαι τῆς καθολικῆς ἐκκλησίας προσῆκει, καὶ ἀλλοτρίους εἶναι τοῦ χριστιανῶν ὀνόματος).[3] Subordinating the Son to the Father is not so strange; indeed the very image of Fatherhood almost seems to require it. But saying that the Father and the Son are foreign to each other, or alien—this is terminology which is both curious and thought-provoking. It sounds like the tip of an iceberg, a sign of the deliberate taking up of an elaborate position.

---

[1] *De Synodis* 15.3 (Optiz II,7). I take it that Arius must himself have used the word ξένος, because of Athanasius' great concern with defining it and denouncing it.

[2] *Depositio Arii* 2; Migne, PG 18, 571-578, Opitz Urkunde 4b,8.

[3] *Apologia Contra Arianos* 49, Migne PG 18, 336.

Turning to Platonist sources (since we are certainly not dealing with a Biblical image) does not shed a great deal of light on the matter. There is no mention of God as "foreign" in Festugière's fourth volume of *La Révélation d'Hermès Trismégiste*, and this is surely the most comprehensive study of the language of transcendence in Middle Platonism. Festugière collects all the negative epithets, all the positive epithets, and indeed any epithet whatever which applies to God in the Middle Platonists Numenius, Apuleius, Albinus, and Atticus. Looking further afield, to the texts of Valentinian Gnosticism, one finds no enlightenment either. The Tripartite Tractate[4] even has the Word as "brother" to the Father (58); his essence is like that of the Father. This is quite the opposite to Arius' position: it is precisely the essence (οὐσία) which is alien. [It may be that in the course of the saga of emanation described by the Tripartite Tractate, the Son does decline to an alien position, undergoing a loss of substance as he moves downwards].

If we look to Plotinus, we find that he scarcely used the word ξένος[5], yet it is Plotinus who will help elucidate the matter. While foreignness is not a major theme for Plotinus, that of alienation (ἀλλοτριότης) is very prominent. This word and its cognate form are used very frequently by Plotinus; it is a specific characteristic of his language. Despite what we have said above about the Gnostics, it is they who, Plotinus claims, refer to the world as "this foreign land" (ἡ γῆ ξένη). They see a radical discontinuity between the divine and the world, and against this sense of otherness Plotinus argues for continuity: there must be a rational design in the world that comes from soul, its maker. An *image* of soul, something coming down from it, so to speak, would "correspond to its maker and remain in close connection with it" (παρακολουθοῖ ἂν τῷ ποιήσαντι καὶ συνηρτημένον ἔσται).[6] Plotinus focusses on difference, on discontinuity, and tries to do away with it in his ontology; he prefers rather to move towards, not sameness, but contact, proximity, mediation, association. The One is not totally lost in what follows it. (It should be noted that this kind of sameness between the One and what follows it could conceivably be reconciled with Arius' position: Stead notes that all the

---

[4]See J.M. Robinson (ed.) *The Nag Hammadi Library* (Harper and Row, San Francisco 1977).

[5]This is based on J.H. Sleeman and G. Pollet, *Lexicon plotinianum* (Leiden, Brill 1980).

[6]II.9.11.12.

titles of God allowed by Arius are given καταχρηστικῶς, according to the unsympathetic account given by Alexander.[7] "But although the Father has conferred on him these dignities, he has not surrendered anything that belongs to himself...."[8] Such an idea is probably compatible with that of Plotinus enunciated above. The Father may not be diminished by what comes after him, but he may still be "in close connection" with it, in Plotinus' words.)

In general, the alienation of the world from its maker is an idea which Plotinus condemns as part of his critique of Gnosticism. The term otherness, ἀλλοτριότης, is also part of Plotinus' vocabulary, and if we accept the idea of allowing Plotinus to elucidate the thought of Arius for a while longer, we may find food for thought. Otherness is generally used by Plotinus in a pejorative sense: for example, multiplicity in the world is said to create the alienation of the parts of it from each other. Thus they war with each other.[9] Or alternatively, take the use of ἀλλότριος in iv.4.22.21: one must not suppose that the world is held together by an alien soul—it has its own soul. Or vi.4.4.43: souls are separate from each other, but not so that there are gaps or intervals. They are, in some sense, *in* each other, without being alienated (οὐκ ἀλλοτριωθεῖσθαι). In each of these cases, and in general in Plotinus, the state of alienation is a matter for regret: there is an element of difference which in the best of all possible worlds, will be overcome.

We can assert, then, that the separation between Father and Son envisaged by Arius would have been a disturbing otherness for Plotinus. He would concede no doubt that such a degree of otherness could exist, but would regret it, and probably consider it to constitute a separation only between principles which are very distant from each other. But that such alienation should intervene between the One and its first offspring, would no doubt have appeared very curious to Plotinus. We are dealing here with a mode of thought which is, in this respect, quite markedly different from that of Plotinus and his school. Perhaps Plotinus points us in the right direction when he speaks of the Gnostics and their sense of the foreignness of the world from its maker: but more likely, we should look further into the lesser-known documents of Neoplatonism—the Aristotelian

---

[7]*Depositio Arii*, Opitz, Urkunde 4b.

[8]G.C. Stead, *The Platonism of Arius*, 'Journal of Theological Studies' 15 (1964) 16-37.

[9]III.2.2.4

commentators such as Dexippus, Syrianus and Alexander of Aphrodisias. Arius' Platonism, if such it is, strikes a new note here.

It is precisely this sense of creation as alienation which Plotinus objects to in the Gnostics: the whole thrust of his case against them is to show that this world was not a result of decline. It is not a νεῦσις (ii.9.4.7), or downward gravitation, and the system of Arius sounds suspiciously like a case of νεῦσις. In a play on negatives, Plotinus says in this passage: the world is not a case of decline; rather it's a non-decline. He negates the noun, not the verb, and this is part of his *via negativa*. "Non-decline" means that we may temporarily use the notion of decline, to provide an angle of vision for our seeing of the issue, but then we must negate the concept: we must remove all the essential features of the notion "decline", in order to re-see the issue.

This reminds us of Arius' negative theology, and one wonders whether the radical otherness he envisages between Father and Son was in fact postulated in order to underpin the use of the negative descriptions in relation to God the Father. Of course the foreignness of the Father and the Son is not absolute: there is *some* relation between them, and this is expressed usually by the term participation, μετόχη. And the negative theology of Arius appears to imply a relation between the two: he says that "we call God unbegotten because of the nature of the begotten" (ἀγέννητον δὲ αὐτόν φαμεν διὰ τοῦ τὴν γεννητόν).[10] Not enough attention has been paid to the "because" (διά): God is named "unbegotten" *because* of the begotten. Where is the causal relationship: why not two independent assertions? God, unbegotten, the Son begotten. There is an echo here of a phrase of Plato's *Phaedrus*, ἡ...ἀρχὴ ἀγένητος: the unbegotten beginning.[11] This phrase is echoed deliberately in Plotinus v.4.1.18, in exactly the same context as Arius: the first principle is unbegotten. Whatever has no beginning in time is unbegotten (ii.4.5.26): this may be another conscious echo of the *Phaedrus*, though it is less clear than the former passage (ii.4.5.26: ἀγένητα δέ, ὅτι μὴ χρόνῳ τὴν ἀρχὴν ἔχει). There is therefore a link between the ἀρχή and the ἀγένητον in the language of Platonism, based on this slogan from the *Phaedrus*; just as God is described as ἀγένητον, the negation of the begotten, so we will expect to find him described as ἄναρχος, the negation of the beginning. And the

---

[10]*De Synodis* 15, Migne PG 26,705, Opitz II.7.

[11]254d 1

two are closely linked in the *De Synodis* passage cited above, just as they are in Plotinus.

Returning now to the "because": we say "unbegotten" *because* of the begotten. The only explanation here can be that by a deployment of the *via negativa*, or of the negative method, one reasons from the positive state to the negative. That the lower order is begotten *shows* that the higher order is non-begotten: by an act of abstraction, *aphairesis*, of conceptual removal, the true nature of the higher order is revealed. We say "non-begotten", and in that way we remove an element which enables us to achieve an insight into the purer form of being which lacks this element. Plotinus does say that negations such as this "teach us" (6.7.38.36): more exactly, he says that abstractions (*aphaireseis*) teach us, but this is his word for what we see throughout his work to be the negative process. We look at the positive, given, evident nature of a thing, and negate systematically its central aspects, until a new perception is possible. This must lie behind Arius' "because": the positive character of the begotten allows the negation to teach us the nature of the higher principle. We know about the one through the negation of the other.

There is nevertheless here a kind of rigidity about this reasoning which seems foreign to Plotinus, for whom the negative imagination always seems to have an exploratory, or aporetic quality. There is no certainty about the results of the negative. But the Arians do feel that they have demonstrated something; that they have created a watertight logical argument. This sounds more like the demonstrative negative theology of Proclus: negation as a demonstrative method emerges clearly in Proclus' commentary on Euclid's Elements. Proclus thinks that Euclid uses negations to define the abstract elements of geometry, and says about this, in commentary: "Every originating-principle has a being other than that of the things which flow from it, and the negations of these show us the specific character of the former."[12] I have commented on this in my *From Word to Silence* (II, 104), but here we may note that Proclus is attracted by the apodeictic power of the negative: he does, after all, say elsewhere that negation is the mother of affirmation. Both Arius and the later Arians seem to think that there is something specifically important about this term unbegotten: it has a privileged status. They seem to feel that there is something special about this term alone, and

---

[12]Comm. Elements I, Def I, ed. Friedlein, p. 94.

that its use can be validated. The negative involved sounds more like a negation which is "demonstrative of essence", to use the language of Dexippus (see my *From Word to Silence II*, 91-2), and not an abstraction which singly unshackles the intellect, as sometimes seems to be the case with Plotinus.

The question of analogy might cast some further light here. As well as negation, says Plotinus, analogies teach us. But Eusebius of Emesa explicitly rules out comparing created beings to the uncreated.[13] one can conclude nothing about the nature of God from what he created, from dewdrops, or rebellious sons, or other creatures.[14] This letter of Eusebius of Nicomedia is preserved in Theodoret, and Gregg and Groh seem to me to interpret it rightly when they say that in Eusebius' accounts of Arian doctrine there is no *analogia entis*; nor of concept, one might add. Eusebius does not use the word ἀναλογία here, it should be noted, but what makes it all the more plausible that this is the issue, is the fact that the neo-Arians do explicitly reject arguments from analogy. Aetius argues in Thesis 4 (see my *From Word to Silence II*, 129) that God and his offspring are "incomparable in essence": I take the word "incomparable" (ἀσύγκριτος) to indicate the impossibility of arguments from analogy, and this is based on the rigid dichotomization of metaphysical reality. A word is appropriate to its own reality, and no other. A word is real; it has an ontic base which does not allow it to be flexible, or in any way transposable. There is a very unusual philosophy of language among the Neo-Arians which needs further study, though I have made some suggestions in the above work (II, Chapters 6-10). This leads to a rejection of analogy, and after Aetius, Eunomius does so quite clearly. In Thesis 26 (see *From Word to Silence II*, 134) Aetius indicates further disquiet about applying all sorts of terms to God: the essence of God cannot be embellished (καλλωπίσασα) by the language of men. This would be a failure of logic, since it would mean that the language generated by God's own substance, which is the language which is founded in that substance, and appropriate to that substance, is inferior to the language generated by the imaginative capacities (the ἐπίνοιαι) of human beings, which are themselves inferior to God! Language cannot enhance God's being, unless it is the language which emerges from that being.

---

[13]Optiz, Urkunde 8, 7-8.

[14]See R.C. Gregg and D. Groh, *Early Arianism--a view of salvation* (Fortress Press, Philadelphia 1981).

Names for God are just empty sounds, says Eunomius later on[15] (Migne PG 30, 841D-844B), and he is reported as saying that argument by analogy, and the introduction of verbal correspondences into the human attempt to picture God, is the work of the over-eager intelligence, an intelligence whose eagerness outstrips its judgment.[16] Eunomius attacks Basil for comparing God to all sorts of things, even corn, and for the use of certain analogies and relations (ἀναλογίας τινὰς καὶ σχέσεις).[17]

In sum, it appears that the passage of Eusebius has rightly been interpreted as refusing arguments by analogy. The later Arians confirm that this was a preoccupation, and it must be characteristic of Arianism as a whole. It is clear also that a certain group of later Platonists contested the value of analogy, despite its appearance of being a permanent part of the Platonist edifice in the writings of the Middle Platonists such as Albinus, Atticus and in Plotinus himself. The rejection of analogy finds its clearest expression in Damascius in the 6th century, but appears to be a view known to Proclus also.

The assertion of the alienness of God underpins this rejection of analogy, as it also supports the negative theology implied in the use of the term unbegotten. Indeed it is concerns such as this that prompt Damascius' later rejection of both negation and analogy: it seems that his extreme emphasis on the transcendence of the One undermines such cognitive activity as is directed towards the One. The otherness of God from his Son, and his other children, can only ever be relative of course: there can never be any absolute separation, any uncrossable gulf. There must remain some link, and whilst he does stress the otherness of God, Arius does use the word μετόχη. The son *participates* in the Father. This word of ancient connotation—it is one of the words Plato uses to describe the relation between an object and the transcendent form which is its source—is used insistently by Arius. And in Plato it raises the whole question of the relationship of substance between the model and its instantiation: where Plato talks about the copy/model approach to the problem, using words like "mimetic" to describe the relationship, we are not yet at the nub of the problem. The problem is: what does the form *share* with its particular, and the word μετόχη gets at this.

---

[15]Migne Pg 30, 841D-844B.

[16]Attributed to Eunomius by Gregory, in the *Contra Eun.* II, 305J.

[17]*Contra Eun.* II, 362J.

It appears frequently in Arius, and has the status of a technical term,[18] and is objected to by Athanasius who argues for a relationship based on *ousia*, essence. Scriptural usages of the word are of course brought into the discussion, such as the τοὺς μετόχους of Ps.44:7 (LXX), but this veneer of meaning should not disguise the basic Platonic architecture which underlies the discussion. The word could be the subject of a whole study in itself, but let us note Plotinus' usage in vi.7.33.3, and vi.6.13.39, where it is clearly indicated that to have a quality by participation is to have it in a lesser way: "when we speak of beauty," says Plotinus, "we must get any from beauty of shape, placed before the eyes, in order not to fall from beauty itself into things called beautiful because they have a faint participation in beauty" (vi.7.33.3). Participation is part of the mechanics of Platonism; it assures the continuity of the structure, but is also associated with ontological inferiority. The beautiful object has beauty by ἀμυδρᾷ μετοχῇ or "tenuous" participation in the beautiful. If Plotinus is any guide here, the word participation is intended to conjure up an image of remoteness, while at the same time asserting a functional link of a specific type. The term is clearly a technical term from Greek metaphysics, disguised as a Biblical term by the Arians, and suspected as such by Athanasius, who then chooses to reply with another technical term of Greek metaphysics, *ousia*, also disguised as a Biblical term, but taking on a life of its own with its Biblical investiture of meaning. It must not be forgotten that Plotinus, and Neoplatonist metaphysics in general, has a hard and rigid quality about it: its terminology will tend to cut through that of any looser system of thought, such as that called Biblical.

It would be useful to study Plotinus' doctrine of grace, χάρις, and compare it to that of the Arians in general. One particular passage on this is of interest for our theme of continuity and otherness: Plotinus associates grace with giving, and he compares the principle whereby a higher being imparts life to a lesser being as a "grace". The Good has an enhancing power, which brings to life that which is below it: it imparts the breath of life to that which is inert (vi.7.22.7), as if "giving graces". But more importantly for our subject, the grace giving process is not to be thought to imply the separateness (χώρις) of the higher principle and the lesser. Matter participates in the source of goodness, and takes that degree of goodness which it is capable of receiving. But

---

[18]See Gregg and Groh, *op. cit.*, 57.

the source and the product are not separate, he says, as if that which gives by grace had suddenly become stationary through lack of power.[19]

Here one may make the casual observation that where Plotinus talks of grace, he also talks of giving; and the verb δίδωμι is particularly noticeable in the language of Arius.

A last point should be made concerning the will. It is clear that Arius places great emphasis on the *will* of God, to the point of unsettling Athanasius. One would expect a Christian thinker to be able to talk about God's will without it being in any way extraordinary, but clearly enough, in this case, it is. Arius' insistence on the will of God obviously began to sound suspicious, and so we have Athanasius' rejoinder that God created the Son by necessity, and not out of willing (ἀνάγκῃ καὶ μὴ θέλων).[20] Albrecht Dihle has discussed this in relation to Gregory of Nazianzus in his Sather lectures *The Theory of Will in Classical Antiquity*,[21] and his analysis of the alternative philosophies is very instructive. That God creates the lower orders out of his will and wish (βούλημα and θέλημα) is a theme which runs across the whole Arian tradition. Arius, Astorius and Eusebius of Nicomedia[22] all have the same emphasis. Athanasius, and probably Plotinus too for that matter, prefer an image of creation which involves an outflowing of a natural kind: hence Athanasius' somewhat surprising use of the term "necessity", which really refers not to some hypothetical bondage imposed on God, but to the consistency of his nature: his nature is what it is, and does what it does, in the ordinary course of events.

The voluntarist emphasis of the Arians psychologizes the act of creation, to put it in the realm of whim, or even of wilfulness. In terms of the theme of this paper, it also underlines the distance of the Father from the Son. The creative act is seen more as an arbitrary one, a matter of psychological autonomy, and not of nature. The creative outflowing need not have happened, necessarily. Only an uncaused choice, an act of will, brought the Son into being along with his fellow creatures. The alien character of God both requires this emphasis on will, and explains it. An exercise of will involves overcoming resistance, bridging a gap, perhaps even doing the unpalatable. No natural evolution is envisaged, but a leap of a uniquely intentional

---

[19]iv.8.6.23

[20]Athanasius C.Ar. 3.59.

[21]University of California Press 1982, 117 ff.

[22]See Gregg and Groh, *op. cit.*, 5.

kind. The alien God can only act in our interests out of his will: the natural expression of his essence would simply lead him away from us, further into the unbridgeable difference. The emphasis on difference, at the expense of identity in the Arian system, leads to a God of magnificent existential freedom, an autonomous being pivoting within an infinite range of choices, among them being concern with us lower beings. It is, after all, an image capable of reinforcing a strong sense of piety and religious sentiment.

In conclusion. This paper has toyed with a comparison between Plotinus and Arius, with some other Neoplatonist allusions, in order to bring out a picture of Arius' thought on a contrasting background. At first sight it would appear that Plotinus is not so much a model for understanding Arius, as an anti- model: Plotinus wants to get away from, or moderate, the otherness which is thought to separate higher and lower beings in his ontology. No foreign Gods for him. And there is no emphasis like this in the less developed Platonists such as Atticus or Albinus, for example. Festugière's classic study of primitive Neoplatonism *La Révélation d'Hermès Trismégiste* has no ξένος in any of the indices of its four volumes. The puzzle remains: Arius' language is strikingly different.

It is true that the *language* is different, but the thought may not be. We have shown at various points how ontological discontinuity sits side by side with continuity in Platonist thought. As Platonism develops, a move away from ontological continuity becomes clear, accompanied by an abandonment of the linguistic tools which were predicated upon it. The epistemological pessimism of later Platonism matches its sense of the remoteness of the First Principle. This sounds more like Arius than the school books of Atticus and Albinus, the early generation.

We have seen that Arius has participation just like any Platonist, and it must at bottom be a matter of emphasis. Arius' system is much like that of Plotinus, but Plotinus stresses the continuity in it, whereas Arius stresses discontinuity: they may indeed have been able to agree with each other in the end, on fundamentals at least.

It is probably the case that Arius' Platonism was radical for his time, anticipating developments in Proclus and others. He chose to differentiate himself by using shock vocabulary, and thus created the impression that he was outside the Platonist mould. But this impression is misleading.

«Image d'image», «Miroir de miroir»

(Grégoire de Nysse, *De hominis opificio* xii, PG 44, 161 C - 164 B)

JEAN PÉPIN

Dans le chapitre XII de son traité *Sur la création de l'homme*, Grégoire de Nysse en vient à rejeter la localisation, proposée par les philosophes, du *noûs* ou *hēgemonikón* dans une partie déterminée du corps humain (160 D); il préfère comparer le corps tout entier à un instrument de musique, dont le bon état général conditionne la performance de l'artiste; or, le bon état du corps, c'est son respect de l'ordre de la nature (161 AB)[1]. Vient ensuite, à la faveur de cette référence à la «nature», un essai assez concentré d'anthropologie et d'ontologie spirituelles. En voici un essai de traduction:

«En outre, me semble-t-il, il y a lieu de considérer dans cette partie un point de nature plus physique, qui permet d'apprendre une doctrine du meilleur aloi. Comme en effet le Bien de tous le plus beau et le plus éminent est la divinité même, vers laquelle inclinent toutes choses qui ont le désir du Beau, pour cette raison nous affirmons que, puisqu'il est né à l'image du Beau suprême, l'intellect lui aussi, aussi longtemps qu'il aura part, dans la mesure du possible, à la ressemblance avec ce modèle, demeure lui-même dans le Beau, tandis que, s'il vient à se trouver hors de celui-ci, le voilà dépouillé de la Beauté où il était. Tout de même que, venons-nous d'affirmer, c'est par l'assimilation de la Beauté originelle qu'est mis en ordre l'intellect, tel un miroir qui prend figure par l'effigie de qui s'y réfléchit: c'est selon le même rapport que, d'après notre

---

[1]Sur le début de ce chapitre, voir K.Gronau, *Poseidonios und die jüdisch-christliche Genesisexegese* (Leipzig-Berlin 1914), p.179 et p.191, n.2.

raisonnement, la nature administrée par l'intellect se situe vis-à-vis de lui et reçoit à son tour, de la beauté proche d'elle, sa mise en ordre, devenue elle-même comme un miroir de miroir; (161 D) par elle est dominée et régie la partie matérielle de notre substance, à laquelle on voit qu'est commise la nature.

Aussi longtemps donc que l'une de ces réalités se situera ainsi vis-à-vis de l'autre, la Beauté véritable se communiquera à travers tous les degrés selon ce rapport, donnant, par le moyen du degré supérieur, beauté au degré suivant. Mais quand il vient à se produire, de cette parfaite cohésion, une déchirure, ou si, tout à l'envers de l'ordre, le supérieur se met à la remorque de l'inférieur, alors la matière même, isolée de la nature, lâche la bride à son indécence (car d'elle-même la matière manque de figure et de structure), et son informité ruine du même coup la beauté de la nature, qui tient sa beauté de l'intellect. Ainsi c'est l'intellect lui-même (164 A) qu'atteint de proche en proche, par le relais de la nature, la laideur de la matière, en sorte que l'image de Dieu cesse d'être visible en effigie dans la créature. Car l'intellect, qui en use vis-à-vis de l'Idée des biens comme un miroir qui tournerait le dos, rejette les rayons que darde l'éclat du Bien, tandis qu'il imprime en soi-même l'informité de la matière. C'est de cette façon que se produit la genèse du mal, qui tire sa constitution de la subversion du Beau. Est beau tout ce qui se trouverait être en situation appropriée par rapport au Bien premier; mais ce qui serait avec lui hors de tout rapport et de toute assimilation, cela n'a aucunement part au Beau. Si donc, pour la raison considérée, le Bien véritable est un: l'intellect, c'est au fait d'avoir été créé à l'image du Beau qu'il doit lui-même d'être beau; la nature, quand elle est régie par l'intellect, est comme une image d'image; (B) de ces énoncés il ressort que ce que nous avons de matériel obtient sa constitution et son encadrement quand la nature l'administre; mais sa dissolution et, redisons-le, sa chute surviennent quand cette matière se sépare de ce qui l'encadre et la régit, et qu'elle déchire sa connaturalité avec le Beau»[2] .

_____

[2] Grégoire de Nysse, *De hominis opificio* XII, PG 44, 161 C - 164 B:

Καί μοι δοκεῖ φυσικώτερον εἶναί τι κατὰ τὸ μέρος τοῦτο θεώρημα, δι' οὗ μαθεῖν ἔστι τι τῶν ἀστειοτέρων δογμάτων. Ἐπειδὴ γὰρ τὸ κάλλιστον πάντων καὶ ἐξοχώτατον ἀγαθὸν αὐτὸ τὸ Θεῖόν ἐστι, πρὸς ὃ πάντα νένευκεν, ὅσα τοῦ καλοῦ τὴν

Le lecteur aura perçu que l'essentiel de cette page réside dans une vision hiérarchique des composants de l'homme dans son rapport à

ἔφεσιν ἔχει, διὰ τοῦτό φαμεν καὶ τὸν νοῦν, ἅτε κατ᾽ εἰκόνα τοῦ καλλίστου γενόμενον, ἕως ἂν μετέχῃ τῆς πρὸς τὸ ἀρχέτυπον ὁμοιότητος, καθόσον ἐνδέχεται, καὶ αὐτὸν ἐν τῷ καλῷ διαμένειν, εἰ δέ πως ἔξω γένοιτο τούτου, γυμνοῦσθαι τοῦ κάλλους ἐν ᾧ ἦν. Ὥσπερ δὲ ἔφαμεν τῇ ὁμοιώσει τοῦ πρωτοτύπου κάλλους κατακοσμεῖσθαι τὸν νοῦν, οἷόν τι κάτοπτρον τῷ χαρακτῆρι τοῦ ἐμφαινομένου μορφούμενον· κατὰ τὴν αὐτὴν ἀναλογίαν, καὶ τὴν οἰκονομουμένην ὑπ᾽ αὐτοῦ φύσιν ἔχεσθαι τοῦ νοῦ λογιζόμεθα, καὶ τῷ παρακειμένῳ κάλλει καὶ αὐτὴν κοσμεῖσθαι, οἷόν τι κατόπτρου κάτοπτρον γινομένην· κρατεῖσθαι δὲ ὑπὸ ταύτης καὶ συνέχεσθαι τὸ ὑλικὸν τῆς ὑποστάσεως, περὶ ἣν θεωρεῖται ἡ φύσις. Ἕως ἂν οὖν ἔχηται τοῦ ἑτέρου τὸ ἕτερον, διὰ πάντων ἀναλόγως ἡ τοῦ ὄντως κάλλους κοινωνία διέξεισι, διὰ τοῦ ὑπερκειμένου τὸ προσεχὲς καλλωπίζουσα. Ἐπειδὰν δέ τις γένηται τῆς ἀγαθῆς ταύτης συμφυΐας διασπασμὸς, ἢ καὶ πρὸς τὸ ἔμπαλιν, ἀντακολουθῇ τῷ ὑποβεβηκότι τὸ ὑπερέχον· τότε αὐτῆς τε τῆς ὕλης, ὅταν μονωθῇ τῆς φύσεως, διηνέχθη τὸ ἄσχημον (ἄμορφον γάρ τι καθ᾽ ἑαυτὴν ἡ ὕλη καὶ ἀκατάσχευον) καὶ τῇ ἀμορφίᾳ ταύτης συνδιεφθάρη τὸ κάλλος τῆς φύσεως, ἣ διὰ τοῦ νοῦ καλλωπίζεται. Καὶ οὕτως ἐπ᾽ αὐτὸν τὸν νοῦν τοῦ κατὰ τὴν ὕλην αἴσχους διὰ τῆς φύσεως ἡ διάδοσις γίνεται, ὡς μηκέτι τοῦ Θεοῦ τὴν εἰκόνα ἐν τῷ χαρακτῆρι καθορᾶσθαι τοῦ πλάσματος. Οἷον γάρ τι κάτοπτρον κατὰ νώτου τὴν τῶν ἀγαθῶν ἰδέαν ὁ νοῦς ποιησάμενος, ἐκβάλλει μὲν τῆς ἐκλάμψεως τοῦ ἀγαθοῦ τάς ἐμφάσεις, τῆς δὲ ὕλης τὴν ἀμορφίαν εἰς ἑαυτὸν ἀναμάσσεται. Καὶ τούτῳ γίνεται τῷ τρόπῳ τοῦ κακοῦ ἡ γένεσις, διὰ τῆς ὑπεξαιρέσεως τοῦ καλοῦ παρυφισταμένη. Καλὸν δὲ πᾶν, ὅπερ ἂν τύχῃ πρὸς τὸ πρῶτον ἀγαθὸν οἰκείως ἔχον· ὅ τι δ᾽ ἂν ἔξω γένηται τῆς πρὸς τοῦτο σχέσεώς τε καὶ ὁμοιώσεως, ἄμοιρον τοῦ καλοῦ πάντως ἐστίν. Εἰ οὖν ἓν μὲν κατὰ τὸν θεωρηθέντα λόγον τὸ ὄντως ἀγαθόν· ὁ δὲ νοῦς τῷ κατ᾽ εἰκόνα τοῦ καλοῦ γεγενῆσθαι, καὶ αὐτὸς ἔχει τὸ καλὸς εἶναι· ἡ δὲ φύσις ἡ ὑπὸ τοῦ νοῦ συνεχομένη, καθάπερ τις εἰκὼν εἰκόνος ἐστί· δείκνυται διὰ τούτων, ὅτι τὸ ὑλικὸν ἡμῶν συνέστηκε μὲν καὶ περικρατεῖται, ὅταν οἰκονομῆται ὑπὸ τῆς φύσεως · λύεται δὲ, καὶ διαπίπτει πάλιν, ὅταν χωρισθῇ τοῦ περικρατοῦντός τε καὶ συνέχοντος, καὶ διασπασθῇ τῆς πρὸς τὸ καλὸν συμφυΐας.

Les historiens d'aujourd'hui ne se sont pas passionnés pour ce texte de Grégoire; à peine peut-on signaler J.Daniélou, *Platonisme et théologie mystique. Essai sur la doctrine spirituelle de saint Grégoire de Nysse*, collect. «Théologie», 2 (thèse Paris 1944), p.231; J.T.Muckle, «The Doctrine of St.Gregory of Nyssa on Man as the Image of God», dans *Mediaeval Studies*, VII (1945), p.73-77: «The Mirror of the Soul»; R.Leys, *L'image de Dieu chez saint Grégoire de Nysse*, collect. «Museum Lessianum. Section théologique, 49» (Bruxelles-Paris 1951), p.50-51; G.B.Ladner, «The Philosophical Anthropology of Saint Gregory of Nyssa», dans *Dumbarton Oaks Papers*, XII (1958), p.92-96; E.Corsini, «Plérôme humain et plérôme cosmique chez Grégoire de Nysse», dans M.Harl, éd., *Écriture et culture philosophique dans la pensée de Grégoire de Nysse* (Leiden 1971), p.112. En revanche, la même page connut la célébrité à l'époque carolingienne, puisque Jean Scot, qui connaît le *De hominis opificio* sous le titre de *Sermo de imagine* (voir par exemple *Periphyseon* IV 11, PL 122, 788 AB), en cite (sous le nom de chapitre XIII) une bonne partie du chapitre XII, 161 C - 164 B, en *Periphyseon* IV 11, PL 789 A - 790 A; cf.Éd.Jeauneau, *Études érigéniennes* (Paris 1987), p.41, sur quoi M.Luc Brisson a bien voulu attirer mon attention.

Dieu; dans la ligne stoïcienne, cette question est dite ressortir à la
«physique». Le nom même de Dieu intervient remarquablement peu:
une seule fois, et une autre fois sous les espèces de τὸ θεῖον, «le divin»;
bien plus souvent, Dieu est désigné comme la transcendance du Bien
et du Beau, traités constamment comme interchangeables. Les trois
composants de l'homme sont, en dignité décroissante, l'intellect (νοῦς),
la nature (φύσις), la partie matérielle (τὸ ὑλικόν). Entre eux d'une part,
entre eux et le niveau divin qui les dépasse d'autre part, différents
rapports hiérarchiques sont possibles. De haut en bas, la Beauté
originelle se communique de palier en palier: son cheminement
produit de proche en proche (pour énumérer en vrac, dans l'ordre
d'apparition des notions) mise en ordre (κατακοσμεῖν), administration
(οἰκονομεῖν), domination (κρατεῖν), maintien (συνέχειν[3]), etc.; toutefois le
principal est la diffusion ordonnée de la beauté. Mais il arrive que cette
consécution bienfaisante soit exactement inversée: suite à la rupture
de l'intellect avec la Beauté divine, c'est la matière qui prend
l'initiative d'envahir de son influence tout ce qui la précède; de proche
en proche également, sa laideur infecte successivement la nature et
l'intellect, se substituant à la beauté de naguère qui empruntait, dans
l'autre sens, le même trajet; telle est la genèse du mal.

La diffusion graduelle de la beauté, en quoi se résume la première
perspective, a ceci de remarquable qu'elle est décrite systématiquement
selon le rapport de l'image au modèle: on lit en 161 C que l'intellect a
été créé «à l'image» de la Beauté, dite elle-même dans le texte grec
«archétype» et «prototype» (les versets de la Genèse 1, 26-27 sont à
l'arrière-plan, d'autant plus certainement que le mot ὁμοίωσις,
«ressemblance» [mais traduit ici par «assimilation»] figure dans les
parages); le thème revient à la fin de 164 A, avec une addition
importante aux termes de laquelle, l'intellect ayant été créé à l'image
du Beau, la nature, tenant sa beauté de l'intellect, est par rapport au
Beau initial comme une «image d'image», εἰκὼν εἰκόνος. Cette formule
redoublée est attestée assez largement dans la théologie juive et
chrétienne d'Alexandrie, également en relation avec la création de
l'homme «à l'image» de Dieu, mais dans une perspective très particu-
lière: c'est le Logos qui est l'image directe de Dieu créateur; l'homme
est fait conforme «à l'image», c'est-à-dire conforme au Logos, image du

---

[3] Ce verbe, qui signifie «contenir» aux différents sens (voisins) d'«enfermer», de
«maintenir uni», de «régir», revient ici à trois reprises, chaque fois, me semble-t-il, dans
le dernier sens; l'alliance, pratiquée par Grégoire, de συνέχειν et κρατεῖν trouve un
précédent chez Posidonius, fgt 149, 9-11 Edelstein-Kidd, p.137.

Logos, et donc, par rapport à Dieu, image relayée, «image d'image».
Cette représentation tout à fait spécifique ne semble pas avoir jamais
été partagée par Grégoire de Nysse[4] ; en tout cas, ce n'est absolument
pas elle que l'on voit à l'oeuvre dans la page en question de *De
hominis opificio*; nulle mention ici de la situation intermédiaire du
Logos, à la fois image et modèle, dont le nom n'est même pas
prononcé. Un détail permet de toucher du doigt combien les deux
points de doctrine sont différents, en dépit de leur formule commune
«image d'image»: il arrive aux Alexandrins de désigner par cette
expression, non plus l'homme dans sa totalité, mais ce qu'il y a de
meilleur en lui, l'intellect; or chacun aura compris que c'est tout le
contraire ici, où l'intellect humain est l'image directe de Dieu, et la
nature humaine son image relayée, l'«image d'image». Même dans
l'usage de cette formule connue, Grégoire ne manque donc pas
d'originalité.

Mais il en montre davantage encore quand on le voit, pour exposer
ses vues sur la relation hiérarchique, ne pas se satisfaire de manier la
notion d'image, mais appeler en renfort le schéma, plus différencié, du
miroir. Dans son effort de s'assimiler la Beauté divine, écrit-il en 161 C,
l'intellect ressemble à un miroir où elle se réfléchit, et auquel de ce fait
elle donne sa propre figure; il y a là l'idée remarquable, dont on verra
plus d'une attestation, que le miroir, instrument familier de la magie,
capte quelque chose de l'objet qui s'y mire. Encore le miroir auquel est
comparé l'intellect n'est-il pas fixe, mais tournant: si sa surface
réfléchissante s'offre normalement à la Beauté, en revanche la
subversion de l'ordre fait qu'il lui présente au contraire son revers,
repoussant le rayonnement du Bien, pour recevoir sur sa face
l'empreinte de la matière informe; la comparaison rend à merveille le
retournement de l'intellect (164 A). Il n'est pas jusqu'à la formule
«image d'image» qui ne soit transposée en «miroir de miroir» (fin de
161 C), pour désigner semblablement la nature dans son rapport à ce
premier miroir qu'est normalement l'intellect. Cependant, en rigueur
de termes, l'image n'est pas le miroir, mais *dans* le miroir; dès lors,
même si elles semblent souvent employées de façon interchangeable,
la comparaison du miroir n'est pas identique à celle de l'image; l'étude
que l'on va lire se propose justement de commenter la substitution
qu'opère ici Grégoire de la première à la seconde, et de le faire à la
lumière de la réflexion religieuse contemporaine, où cette métaphore

---

[4] En raison de son orthodoxie antiarienne, comme l'a très bien montré E.Corsini, *art.
cit.*, p.112-113.

rencontra le succès dans des applications d'ailleurs sensiblement différentes.

* * * * *

La première démarche doit être d'interroger, sur ce point, Grégoire lui-même en d'autres de ses pages. La plus notable de celles-ci se lit dans le commentaire du *Cantique des cantiques,* autour de l'idée suivante: il est impossible de fixer le regard sur le Dieu Logos, de même que l'on ne peut fixer le soleil: mais on peut regarder le soleil dans un miroir, et Dieu dans le miroir que l'on est soi-même (ἐν ἑαυτῷ δὲ καθάπερ ἐν κατόπτρῳ); vient peu après, pour rendre la même idée, la formule concourante «grâce au miroir que nous sommes» (τῷ ἡμετέρῳ κατόπτρῳ); puis voici que reprend ses droits le schéma plus usuel de l'image et du modèle: à l'aide des vertus naît en nous la connaissance du Bien q u i d é p a s s e t o u t e p e n s é e, «de la même façon que l'on peut, à partir d'une image, conjecturer la Beauté archétype»[5]. Une formule très proche de celle-ci apparaît dans le traité du même auteur *Sur l'âme et la résurrection,* quand on voit l'âme humaine orientée vers la transcendance grâce au reflet de celle-ci qu'elle discerne en elle-même: «faisant retour à soi-même et se voyant soi-même exactement telle qu'elle est de par sa nature, c'est comme dans un miroir et une image (ἐν κατόπτρῳ καὶ εἰκόνι) que, par le moyen de sa propre beauté, elle a regard à la Beauté archétype»[6].

Si l'on veut bien, à l'âme, substituer ici l'intellect qui en est l'*hē gemonikón*, on reconnaît aisément, plus dépouillé, le point de doctrine que l'on vient de relever dans le *De hominis opificio* : c'est grâce à l'effigie qui s'en dépose en lui comme dans un miroir que l'intellect de l'homme peut assimiler la Beauté transcendante. On trouverait, à cette façon de penser et de parler de Grégoire, bien des parallèles dans l'esprit du temps. «La pensée du sage est un miroir de

---

[5] Grégoire de Nysse, *Comment. in Canticum cantic.* (1, 12), Orat. III, éd. Langerbeck, p.90, 10-91, 4; l'éditeur rapproche avec raison, pour l'exaltation du Bien et l'analogie solaire, Platon, *Républ.* VI 508 e-509 b; mais il oublie de signaler la citation textuelle de *Philippiens* 4, 7 sur la paix de Dieu «qui dépasse toute pensée». Même comparaison du soleil que l'on voit dans un miroir, même présentation de la pureté personnelle comme l'image où l'on perçoit son archétype en *De beatitudinibus,* Orat. VI, PG 44, 1272 B.

[6] *De anima et resurrect.,* PG 46, 89 C.

Dieu (θεοῦ ἔνοπτρον)»; cette célèbre sentence de Sextus[7] énonce le fondement en quelque sorte statique de la thèse. Les théologiens ne manqueront pas d'en exploiter les ressources pour la connaissance de Dieu: si l'âme humaine reflète celui-ci comme un miroir, elle doit pouvoir, en se regardant elle-même, saisir indirectement quelque chose de Dieu. Parmi les enseignements incomparables communiqués par Origène dans son école, son disciple Grégoire le Thaumaturge signale vers 238 que ce maître voulait que l'âme de chacun ait souci de soi-même, se détourne intérieurement vers soi-même, se rende à soi-même, se tende vers soi-même; mais, poursuit Grégoire, cet appel répétitif à l'intériorité ne se fermait pas sur la connaissance de soi, proposée en fait comme le moyen d'une autre connaissance: «l'âme s'exerce à se voir comme dans un miroir (ὥσπερ ἐν κατόπτρῳ), dans ce miroir, si toutefois elle est digne de cette société, elle voit (κατοπτριζομένης) en soi-même l'Intellect divin, et la voici qui s'engage dans une voie secrète, celle de la divinisation»[8] ; sans doute ne faut-il pas trop serrer la comparaison: un miroir ou deux miroirs? il est difficile d'en décider; l'auteur veut probablement dire en tout cas que, l'âme étant un miroir où Dieu se reflète, la connaissance qu'elle a d'elle-même lui permet de voir Dieu et de s'unir à lui; à l'exception peut-être de cette dernière notation, le panégyriste d'Origène anticipe, on le voit, pour le fond et la forme, les exposés de Grégoire de Nysse.

Il n'est pas le seul. Un siècle plus tard environ, Athanase, par une association toute naturelle, met en rapport la pureté de l'âme et le privilège qu'elle a d'être elle-même le miroir grâce auquel elle peut voir (κατοπτρίζεσθαι) Dieu[9]. Plus loin dans le même pamphlet *Contre les païens*, il reprend la même idée en la reliant, comme fera Grégoire, au verset de *Genèse* I 26 sur l'homme fait «à l'image» (comme la plupart des théologiens alexandrins, il voit dans cette image le Logos, lui-même image du Père): si l'âme dépose la souillure du péché et «ne garde que sa pure conformité à l'image, il est à croire que, dans l'éclat de cette ressemblance, elle contemple comme dans un miroir (ὡς ἐν

---

[7] *Enchir. Sexti* 450, éd. Chadwick, p.62; ailleurs (190, p.34; cf. *Recueil de Clitarque* 9, p.76), le sage est appelé «image vivante de Dieu».

[8] Grégoire le Thaum., *Panégyrique d'Origène* XI 140-142; il n'y a, pour ce passage, aucun éclaircissement à attendre d'un autre, très incertain, du même écrit (IX 119) sur l'âme qui se contemple comme dans un miroir.

[9] *Contra gentes* 2, éd. Camelot, p.56, 5-6

κατόπτρῳ) l'image du Père qu'est le Logos, et en lui se représente le Père, dont le Sauveur est effectivement une image»[10].

Les philosophes païens eux-mêmes partagent ce qu'ils peuvent de cette conception. Au Ve siècle, Hiéroclès d'Alexandrie, chez qui l'on a d'ailleurs subodoré certaines influences chrétiennes, affirme, dans des termes proches de ceux qu'avait employés auparavant Grégoire de Nysse, que, pour l'âme dépourvue de vertu, il est impossible de «voir comme dans un miroir» (ἐνοπτρίσασθαι) la beauté de la Vérité[11]. Mais le texte profane le plus étonnant dans cette perspective a pour auteur, c'est bien connu, Porphyre, dans une page de la *Lettre à Marcella* relative à la prière; il vient d'être question du soin extrême que l'on doit apporter au choix de l'objet et du moment des prières de demande; Porphyre enchaîne alors: «C'est surtout moyennant ces précautions que Dieu en personne se montre comme dans un miroir (ἐνοπτρίζεσθαι)»; après diverses autres considérations, la même idée revient bientôt de la façon suivante: «Que l'intellect (νοῦς) suive donc Dieu, qu'il voit comme dans un miroir parce que Dieu lui ressemble (ἐνοπτριζόμενος τῇ ὁμοιώσει θεοῦ), et que l'âme (ψυχή) suive l'intellect; que l'âme à son tour ait à son service le physique (σχῆμα), pur autant qu'il se peut au service d'une âme pure. Car s'il est souillé par suite des passions de l'âme, en retour il lui ramène ses souillures»[12]. Sans doute ces lignes ne sont-elles pas aussi claires qu'on le souhaiterait; mais voici ce que l'on peut en dégager touchant l'enquête actuelle: dans certaines conditions, Dieu consent à se laisser voir par l'intellect humain comme dans un miroir parce que cet intellect lui ressemble; bien que cela ne soit pas dit expressément, on ne voit pas de quel autre miroir il pourrait s'agir que l'intellect lui-même. Cette conception de l'intellect humain comme un miroir lui permettant, regardant en soi,

---

[10] *Ibid.* 34, p.164, 21-24; «se représente», λογίζεται; on a rencontré le même verbe en *De hom. opif.* 161 C fin.

[11] *In Aureum carmen comment.*, prol., éd.Koehler, p.6, 9-10, sur quoi cf.Th.Kobusch, *Studien zur Philosophie des Hierokles von Alexandrien.* Untersuchungen zum christlichen Neuplatonismus, collect. «Epimeleia», 27 (München 1976), p.114-115 et n.33, qui rapproche beaucoup de textes, souvent peu pertinents.

[12] Porphyre, *Ad Marcellam* 13, éd. des Places, p.113, 6-7 et 18-23. Je ne suis pas entièrement la traduction du P.des Places: à la suite de LSJ, *s.u.*, je vois dans ἐνοπτρίζεσθαι un passif; mais ἐνοπτριζόμενος est un moyen; d'autre part, ὁμοιώσει θεοῦ (ce dernier mot étant d'ailleurs une correction de Mai) ne signifie pas «par l'assimilation à Dieu», mais «par la ressemblance de Dieu», comme dans *Epist. Iacobi* 3, 9 citant *Gen.* 1, 27.

de voir Dieu qui s'y reflète rejoint de façon étonnante le *De hominis opificio*[13], où elle était également fondée, avec allusion à la *Genèse* 1, 27, sur la ressemblance de Dieu. Mais il y a davantage: la comparaison du miroir, on s'en souvient, débordait chez Grégoire le niveau de l'intellect pour s'étendre à celui, immédiatement inférieur, de la «nature», et c'est même cette extension qui suscitait l'éclosion de la singulière formule «miroir de miroir»; or qui ne voit que cette hiérarchie (Dieu, l'intellect, la nature) est également présente chez Porphyre, qui simplement, sans doute par fidélité à son maître Plotin, l'étoffe par l'adjonction d'un degré intermédiaire, celui de l'âme (on a d'ailleurs repéré cette entité dans d'autres textes de Grégoire); que le σχῆμα, qui chez Porphyre suit l'âme, ne soit guère différent de la φύσις du *De hominis opificio*, c'est ce que montre sa traduction par le P.des Places, certainement mû par d'autres considérations: «le physique». Non seulement, enfin, les deux auteurs associent à la comparaison du miroir une hiérarchie normative à peu de chose près identique, mais ils envisagent l'un et l'autre l'inversion catastrophique de cet ordre; de ce funeste renversement, Grégoire donnait une description dramatique que l'on n'a pas oubliée; Porphyre est plus succinct dans l'évocation de la même éventualité, lorsque «le physique», au lieu de servir l'âme, fait remonter vers elle son impureté. Il y a là, on en conviendra, sur toute une constellation de thèmes[14] une coïncidence étonnante; nul ne sait si Grégoire de Nysse a jamais lu la *Lettre à Marcella* [15]; mieux vaut sans doute expliquer leur rencontre par leur commune perméabilité à l'esprit du temps.

* * * * *

---

[13] Aussi bien les harmoniques chrétiens de ce chapitre de la *Lettre à Marcella* ont-ils si fort impressionné Reitzenstein qu'il l'a rapproché d'un verset paulinien que l'on retrouvera bientôt, *II Cor.* 3, 18; cf. P.Corssen, «Paulus und Porphyrios (Zur Erklärung von 2 Kor 3, 18)», dans *Zeitschrift für die neutestam. Wissenschaft*, 19 (1919 / 20), p.2-10.

[14] Il pourrait y en avoir d'autres encore; par exemple l'opposition de la beauté de Dieu et de la laideur du vice ou de la matière (Porphyre, p.113, 9 et 11; *De hom. opif.*, passim et 162 D fin-164 A début); d'autre part, il n'est pas exclu que Porphyre ait voulu dire, à la manière de Grégoire, que, tout comme l'intellect est miroir de Dieu, l'âme l'est de l'intellect, etc.

[15] Le problème n'est pas abordé par P.Courcelle, «Grégoire de Nysse lecteur de Porphyre», dans *Revue des Études grecques*, LXXX (1967), p.402-406.

Touchant le même domaine des rapports de l'âme avec Dieu, il arrive à Grégoire de Nysse de donner un tout autre sens à la comparaison du miroir. Il s'agit maintenant d'une page de son sermon *De mortuis*. La comparaison elle-même est organisée un peu différemment de ce que l'on a vu dans le commentaire du *Cantique* ; le cercle dont la perception exige l'emploi du miroir n'est plus, comme alors, celui du soleil, mais celui de l'oeil même: ne pouvant, de par leur nature, exercer leur fonction visuelle sur eux-mêmes, les yeux découvrent leur aspect dans un miroir, par le moyen de leur image; comme eux, l'âme qui veut se connaître doit passer par le détour de son image, où elle rencontre, non pas évidemment son aspect physique, mais son «caractère» propre. Toutefois, poursuit Grégoire, les deux cas diffèrent sur un point: quand l'oeil aperçoit son reflet dans le miroir, «l'image est configurée d'après l'archétype», entendons plus simplement qu'elle a l'oeil pour modèle; mais c'est l'inverse pour l'âme; ayant pour «caractère» l'image de Dieu, c'est quand elle a regard à son divin archétype qu'elle se découvre elle-même avec exactitude[16].

Les précédents éventuels que les éditeurs proposent pour ce texte en demeurent fort éloignés; le plus proche semblerait tenir dans la célèbre page du *I*[er] *Alcibiade*, 132 d-133 c, surtout si l'on y inclut l'extrait controversé reproduit par Eusèbe; mais Grégoire aurait alors négligé l'essentiel de la comparaison platonicienne, à savoir que le miroir où l'oeil s'aperçoit n'est autre qu'un autre oeil. Ce qui éclate en revanche, c'est la différence avec les passages de Grégoire examinés plus haut touchant l'objet précis qui, dans la réalité, est l'homologue du miroir dans la comparaison: c'était, tout à l'heure, le sujet humain (ἐν ἑαυτῷ καθάπερ ἐν κατόπτρῳ, commentaire du *Cantique* cité), âme ou intellect (τὸν νοῦν, οἷόν τι κάτοπτρον, *De hom. opif.* 161 C); c'est maintenant, à l'évidence, Dieu même, qui s'offre au regard de l'âme comme son modèle et lui permet, par ce détour, de se connaître. Voir Dieu dans le miroir de notre âme où il se reflète, connaître notre âme en en découvrant l'original, comme dans un miroir, en Dieu qui l'a faite à son image, deux démarches spirituelles en quelque sorte inverses, mais également fondées sur le thème biblique de l'homme «à l'image».

Moins attestée peut-être que la première d'entre elles, la seconde est loin d'être inconnue, dans le christianisme et hors du

---

[16] *De mortuis*, éd.Heil, p.41, 9-19; en *Comment. in Canticum cantic.*, Orat. VII, éd. Langerbeck, p.218, 20-219, 1, Grégoire applique la comparaison du miroir à la pupille de l'oeil, qui reçoit sur elle l'image des objets visibles et en compose la forme.

christianisme. L'auteur du roman pseudo-clémentin met en oeuvre un schéma plus simple que celui de Grégoire, mais en son fond de même nature, quand il oppose, à la femme futile, la femme chaste «qui se voit dans un beau miroir (καλῷ ἐσόπτρῳ) quand elle porte son regard vers Dieu»[17]. On aurait peine à imaginer un auteur plus éloigné de celui-là que l'alchimiste Zosime (IIIe-IVe siècle de notre ère); ils se rejoignent néanmoins sur le thème de Dieu miroir de l'âme: «Alexandre de Macédoine et ses successeurs — écrit Zosime — eurent dans leur maison un miroir, qui représentait l'esprit divin; l'âme qui s'y regarde voit ses turpitudes et les rejette»[18].

* * * * *

Voici, tout proche de celui-ci, un autre texte de Zosime, où le même miroir reçoit une signification un peu différente: «Ce miroir est le Fils de Dieu, le Verbe, et l'Esprit-Saint. L'homme qui s'y regarde voit Dieu qui est en lui, par l'intermédiaire de l'Esprit-Saint»[19]. L'auteur alchimiste se fait ici le véhicule d'une représentation de grande conséquence, dont, malgré son absence dans les textes considérés de Grégoire de Nysse (et peut-être dans toute son oeuvre?), il faut dire un mot en finissant. Il s'agit d'attribuer la fonction de miroir, non plus à Dieu sans autre précision, mais, dans l'optique trinitaire, à deux personnes divines, le Fils de Dieu et l'Esprit-Saint, avec l'idée qu'à regarder dans ce miroir-là, l'on se voit et l'on voit Dieu en soi.

Or il faut savoir que (mis à part pour le moment l'Esprit-Saint) cette comparaison de Jésus à un miroir (magique chez Zosime) où l'homme, en se voyant, voit Dieu qui est en lui n'est pas non plus sans exemple dans l'ancienne tradition chrétienne. Peut-être le Nouveau Testament lui-même, avec l'*Épître de Jacques* 1, 23-24, en offre-t-il une attestation en quelque sorte négative quand les auditeurs inertes de la

---

[17] *Homil. ps. clement.* XIII 16, 2, éd. Rehm, p.201, 4-5.

[18] Texte traduit par M.Berthelot, *La chimie au Moyen âge*, t.II: *L'alchimie syriaque* (Paris 1893), p.262.

[19] *Ibid.*, p.263. L'attention a été attirée sur les passages de Zosime par N.Hugedé, *La métaphore du miroir dans les Épîtres de saint Paul aux Corinthiens*, collect. «Bibliothèque théologique» (Neuchâtel-Paris 1957), p.56; pour le thème qui va être abordé maintenant, cf. p.22, n.1; 66; 68; 100; 112; 113, n.1; plusieurs des textes examinés *supra* (mais non pas ceux de Grégoire) ont été également produits par cet historien, pour tenter d'éclairer les deux versets pauliniens *I Cor.* 13, 12 et *II Cor.* 3, 18, cf. *supra*, p. 225, note 13.

Parole sont dits ressembler à un homme qui considère dans un miroir son visage originel et s'empresse d'oublier ses propres traits (ἐπελάθετο ὁποῖος ἦν); il n'est pas invraisemblable que ces «traits» reçus dès sa naissance, scrutés avec plus d'application, lui eussent révélé plus qu'eux-mêmes, ce qui expliquerait le jugement sévère porté sur sa désinvolture; aussi bien la «Parole implantée» (ἔμφυτον λόγον) salvatrice du verset 21 pourrait-elle bien désigner le Verbe de Dieu. On approche davantage de la formule de Zosime avec un apocryphe tardif (IIᵉ siècle de notre ère) de l'Ancien Testament, les *Odes de Salomon*, qui accordent à Jésus valeur de miroir:

«Behold, the Lord is our mirror
«Open <your> eyes and see them in him»[20].

De la même époque approximativement datent les *Actes* apocryphes *de Jean*, où une formule très voisine est mise sur les lèvres mêmes de Jésus: «Je suis un miroir pour toi qui as regard à moi»[21].

L'obscur passage de l'*Épître de Jacques* est plus riche de virtualités qu'immédiatement utilisable. Quant aux deux apocryphes, s'ils disent en effet de Jésus qu'il est un miroir tendu aux hommes (métaphore plus que comparaison), ils ne précisent pas ce que ces derniers pourraient y découvrir hors de leur propre aspect. Clément d'Alexandrie offre une réponse de niveau, si l'on ose dire, encore modeste: suivre le Sauveur, écrit-il en écho à *Marc* 10, 28, c'est aspirer à sa perfection , c'est «s'en rapporter à lui comme à un miroir (πρὸς ἐκεῖνον ὥσπερ κάτοπτρον) pour donner à notre âme l'ordre et la mesure»[22]; la comparaison du miroir revient ici à conférer à Jésus le simple rôle d'une norme en vue d'un arrangement du domaine de la vie spirituelle; elle ne transcende pas véritablement le propos, rencontré plus haut dans les *Homélies* pseudo-clémentines, sur la femme chaste qui compose son visage devant un miroir qui n'est autre que Dieu.

Mais l'assimilation de Jésus au miroir fut parfois le tremplin d'un enseignement d'une tout autre portée. C'est ce qu'en quelque sorte l'on découvre avant même l'éclosion du christianisme, dans un texte

---

[20] *Odes de Salomon* 13, 1, trad. Charlesworth («The Old Testam. Pseudepigrapha» 2), p.747; le traducteur rapproche avec raison *Epist. Iacobi* 1, 23 rappelé à l'instant; on doit penser également au *De mortuis* de Grégoire de Nysse examiné plus haut, où il était question des yeux qui ne se découvrent que dans un miroir.

[21] *Actes de Jean* 95, éd. M.Bonnet (R.A.Lipsius et M.Bonnet, *Acta Apostolorum apocrypha* II 1), p.198, 12.

[22] *Quis diues saluetur* 21, 7, éd. Stählin, p.174, 7-10.

judéo-hellénistique comme la *Sagesse de Salomon* ; les affinités sont bien connues entre cette entité dite Sagesse et celle que les Évangiles nommeront Verbe, Fils de Dieu, incarné en Jésus; or voici un élément de la description que ce texte offre de la Sagesse: «Elle est le reflet (ἀπαύγασμα) de la lumière éternelle, le miroir (ἔσοπτρον) sans tache de l'activité de Dieu et l'image (εἰκὼν) de sa bonté»[23]; le miroir est le terme central; sur le miroir se produisent le reflet et l'image; tous trois, si l'on y porte le regard, révèlent des attributs de Dieu, c'est-à-dire Dieu même. Le thème réapparaît, appliqué cette fois à Jésus, dans l'un des plus anciens documents de la littérature chrétienne, l'*Épître aux Corinthiens* de Clément de Rome: «Par lui nous tendons nos regards vers les hauteurs des cieux; par lui nous voyons comme dans un miroir (ἐνοπτριζόμεθα) le visage immaculé, plein de noblesse de Dieu; par lui les yeux de notre coeur se sont ouverts»[24]; par lui (διὰ τούτου, complément d'instrument trois fois répété) nous voyons comme dans un miroir, la formule invite à comprendre: dans le miroir qu'est Jésus-Christ, nous voyons Dieu. La théologie la plus traditionnelle frayait ainsi la voie aux intuitions aventureuses de l'alchimiste Zosime.

---

23 *Sagesse* 7, 26, trad. Guillaumont.

24 *Clementis Epist.* 36, 2, trad.Hemmer.

Osservazioni sull'*Epistola 140* di Sinesio

ANTONIO GARZYA

Negli anni fra il 393 e il 399 il giovane Sinesio indirizzò a Erculiano, già suo sodale alla scuola d'Ipazia, un gruppo di lettere d'occasione (137-146)[1] nelle quali s'insinuano qua e là spunti personali e pensieri di ordine generale.

Le leggi dell'antica epistolografia avevano vietato, com'è noto, che nella lettera privata entrasse il ragionamento filosofico: εἰ γάρ τις ἐν ἐπιστολῇ σοφίσματα γράφοι καὶ φυσιολογίας, γράφει μέν, οὐ μὴν ἐπιστολὴν γράφει (ps.—Demetr., *de eloc.* 231). Vi fu un certo mutamento di prospettiva nella tarda antichità e al συμφιλοσοφεῖν fu fatto posto anche in tale genere letterario: *epistulare convivium . . . doctrinae quoque sale condiatur* (Hieron, *ep.* 29, 1 Lab.). Un posto, tuttavia, limitato, a evitare che s'invadesse il campo di altre discipline: πληρώσει τε τὴν ἐπιστολὴν χάρις ἱστοριῶν καὶ μύθων μνήμη . . . καὶ φιλοσόφων δογμάτων χρῆσις, οὐ μέντοι γε ταύτην διαλεκτικῶς προσενεκτέον (Procl., *de forma epistolari* p. 15 Weich.).

Un esempio di lettera filosofeggiante è appunto la 140 di Sinesio, nella quale questioni di peso vengono svolte con tocco lieve, per accenni rapidi che presuppongono non solo un destinatario, ma anche un certo pubblico ben al giorno della materia. Si sa che l'epistola tardoantica era destinata alla pubblicizzazione: passava di mano in mano, veniva mandata a memoria, era oggetto di lettura negli *auditoria*, come attesta fra altro lo stesso Sinesio;[2] contribuiva

---

[1]Edizione: Synesii Cyrenensis, *Epistolae.* A. Garzya recensuit ("Scriptores Graeci et Latini consilio Academiae Lynceorum editi"), Romae 1979; traduzione: *Le Opere di Sinesio di Cirene* a cura di A. Garzya ("Classici greci UTET": testo, traduzione e note), Torino 1988.

[2]Ved. *ep.* 101 = p. 169, 5ss. Gar.: "Ho letto la tua lettera insieme con diletto e ammirazione: merita e l'uno e l'altra per il suo tono affettuoso e per la bellezza dello stile. In tuo onore ho súbito predisposto una riunione (θέατρον) di Libici di lingua greca,

insomma all'intrattenimento della comunicazione letteraria e a una certa divulgazione culturale, retorica o poetica o filosofica che fosse.

Quanto a un'epistola come la presente, essa è anche testimonianza preziosa di quel che poteva essere in ambiente africano all fine del IV secolo il tenore medio della formazione intellettuale. Un'analisi del testo permetterà di additarne gli agganci storico-culturali.

—P. 244, 4-14 Gar.

> Degli amori, quelli che hanno vita terrena e origini umane sono detestabili e efimeri, commisurati soltanto, e se pure, alla presenza degli amanti; quelli, invece, ai quali la divinità presiede fondendo insieme gli amanti stessi con l'arte sua—come dice il divino Platone—e facendone di due uno, sono tali da aver la meglio sulla distanza e di tempo e di luogo. Niente invero può impedire che delle anime che sentono reciproca attrazione si avvicinino per segreti sentieri e si congiungano. La nostra amicizia deve dipendere da questo modello, se non vogliamo recare disdoro all nostra educazione filosofica dimostrando attaccamento ai sensi e non dando accesso all'anima quando quelli non sieno risvegliati dal corpo.

E il primo tèma dell'epistola: prevalenza dei legami spirituali su quelli terreni anche perché essi prescindono dalla presenza fisica. L'articolazione è duplice: filosofica e epistolografica.

Con l'esplicito riferimento a Platone (*symp.* 191d θέλω ὑμᾶς συντῆξαι καὶ συμφῦσαι)[3] viene rilevata la natura del primo punto, il quale verte propriamente sull'amicizia. La teoria relativa (varî tipi, varî modi di realizzarla, ecc.) aveva un posto nella ricezione recente delle antiche dottrine. Ad esempio, la si trova accennata in quel grande bacino di raccolta di tradizioni che sono gli *Stromata* di Clemente Alessandrino[4] e, con maggiore pertinenza all'opposizione

---

invitandoli a venire per ascoltare la lettura d'una dotta epistola: cosí Pilemene, l'autore della divina lettera, è ora famoso nelle nostre città; cfr. A. Garzya, L'epistolografia letteraria tardoantica, in *Il mandarino e il quotidiano*. Saggi sulla letteratura tardoantica e bizantina ("Saggi BIBLIOPOLIS", 14), Napoli 1983, pp. 14422.

[3]Sinesio ritorna sul luogo platonico, variandolo di poco, in *ep.* 152 = p. 270, 14s.

[4]Ved. *strom.* II 19 = p. 168, 18ss. St., in cui l'autore si rifà a precedenti stoico-pitagorici e cristiani: Τριττὰ δὲ εἴδη φιλίας διδασκόμεθα, καὶ τούτων τὸ μὲν πρῶτον καὶ ἄριστον τὸ κατ᾽ ἀρετήν· στερρὰ γὰρ ἡ ἐκ λόγου ἀγάπη· τὸ δὲ δεύτερον καὶ μέσον <τὸ> κατ᾽ ἀμοιβήν· κοινωνικὸν δὲ τοῦτο καὶ μεταδοτικὸν καὶ βιωφελές· κοινὴ γὰρ ἡ ἐκ χάριτος φιλία· τὸ δὲ ὕστατον καὶ τρίτον ἡμεῖς μὲν τὸ ἐκ συνηθείας φαμέν, οἱ δὲ τὸ καθ᾽ ἡδονὴν τρεπτὸν καὶ μεταβλητόν. καὶ μοι δοκεῖ παγκάλως Ἱππόδαμος ὁ Πυθαγόρειος

fra spirituale e corporeo, in Basilio, *ep.* 133 (a. 373) = p. 47, lss. Court. Τῆς μὲν σωματικῆς φιλίας ὀφθαλμοὶ πρόξενοι γίνονται καὶ ἡ διὰ μακροῦ χρόνου ἐγγινομένη συνήθεια βεβαιοῖ. τὴν δὲ ἀληθινὴν ἀγάπην ἡ τοῦ Πνεύματος δωρεὰ συνίστησι συνάπτουσα μὲν τὰ μακρῷ διεστῶτα τῷ τόπῳ, γνωρίζουσα δὲ ἀλλήλοις τοὺς ἀγαπητούς, οὐ διὰ σωματικῶν χαρακτήρων, ἀλλὰ διὰ τῶν τῆς ἀρετῆς ἰδιωμάτων. Abbiamo in Basilio in veste cristiana quanto in Sinesio figura in veste profana (ἀγάπη/ἔρωτες, Πνεῦμα/θεός, ecc.). Ma è il séguito che permette di meglio precisare la collocazione dei due testi. Basilio continua, 7ss.: ὃ δὴ καὶ ἐφ᾽ ἡμῶν ἡ τοῦ Κυρίου χάρις ἐποίησε παρασχομένη ἡμᾶς ἰδεῖν σε τοῖς τῆς ψυχῆς ὀφθαλμοῖς καὶ περιπτύξασθαί σε τῇ ἀγάπῃ τῇ ἀληθινῇ καὶ οἱονεὶ συμφυῆναί σοι καὶ πρὸς μίαν ἐλθεῖν ἕνωσιν ἐκ τῆς κατὰ τὴν πίστιν κοινωνίας. Affiora anche qui, in quel συμφυῆναι rilevato da οἱονεί, il precedente del *Simposio* platonico e c'è poi il motivo della ἔνωσις, che c'è pure in Sinesio, ma a garantirla è la πίστις, nel senso cristiano del termine, mentre il Cirenese parla di ἄρρητοι σύνοδοι. Eccoci dunque in terreno neoplatonico: non aveva già Plotino formulato lo stesso divario quando, poste le due categorie di 'viventi' (ζῷα), il 'complesso comune' mescolato d'anima e corpo (τὸ κοινόν/μικτόν) e ὁ ἀληθὴς ἄνθρωπος, si chiedeva Φιλίαι δέ τινος; rispondendo αἱ μὲν τούτου (sc. τοῦ κοινοῦ), αἱ δὲ τοῦ ἔνδον ἀνθρώπου (*enn.* I 1, 5, 2; 7, 20; 10, 14s.)? E quanto all' 'ineffabilità' delle σύνοδοι, è forse il caso di ricordare qual posto abbia la categoria concettuale dell'ἄρρητον nella storia del platonismo,[5] senza per questo attribuirle qui il valore ristretto alla sfera propriamente iniziatica che pur ebbe a acquisire in ambienti misterici?[6] Che peraltro una sfumatura misticheggiante non fosse del tutto estranea a codesto filosofare non è certo da escludere. Il concetto di ὁμοίωσις θεῷ, entrato nella coscienza ellenica con Platone (*Theaet.* 176b), aveva finito con l'essere assunto e esser vissuto, a partire da

---

γράφειν τᾶν φιλιᾶν ἃ μὲν ἐξ ἐπιστάμας θεῶν, ἃ δ᾽ ἐκ παροχᾶς ἀνθρώπων, ἃ δὲ ἐξ ἀδονᾶς ζώων. οὐκοῦν ἡ μέν τίς ἐστι φιλοσόφου φιλία, ἡ δὲ ἀνθρώπου, ἡ δὲ ζώου.

[5] A partire da Platone; cfr. H. Dörrie, Spätantike Symbolik und Allegorese, in *Platonica minora* ("Studia und Testimonia Antiqua," VIII), München 1976, p. 114s.; ved. anche Id., Die Erneuerung des Platonismus im ersten Jahrhundert vor Christus, *ibid.*, p. 162, Die Frage nach dem Transzendenten im Mittelplatonismus, *ibid.*, p. 214.

[6] I precedenti filosofici di Sinesio sono da ricercare piuttosto, anche se forse non esclusivamente, nel filone porfiriano che in quello giamblicheo e caldaico; cfr. Garzya, Ai margini del neoplatonismo: Sinesio di Cirene, in *Il mandarino* cit., p. 238s.

Plotino (preceduto almeno da Eudoro), come ἐνωθῆαι (θεῷ),[7] come *unio mystica*, il grado piú alto del superamento—sul versante ancóra una volta e pagano e cristiano[8]—del divario ἀπεῖναι/παρεῖναι. Il commercio amicale, a sua volta, finí col far da tramite in tale ascesa: lo avverte espressamente Simplicio nel suo lungo *excursus* sugli *officia amicitiae*: ...μεγάλα καὶ θαυμαστὰ φιλίας ἀγαθά...ἀνθρώπινα τά γε πλεῖστα αὐτῶν...τὸ δὲ μέγιστον καὶ μάλιστα θεῖον αὐτῆς... · ὅτι ἡ καθαρὰ φιλία, τὰς φιλας ψυχὰς εἰς ἕνωσιν συνάγουσα, μελέτη καλλίστη γίνεται τῆς πρὸς θεὸν ἐνώσεως (*in Epict. enchir.* 30 = p. 89, 8ss. Dübn.).

Veniamo al secondo punto. L'impianto filosofico dei pensieri relativi all'amicizia fa contestualmente da supporto alla motivazione teorica della lettera: è questa il mezzo piú adatto per ottenere quell'unione degli spiriti al di fuori della presenza fisica ch'è appunto il segno piú alto della φιλία. Alla rielaborazione dell'antica dottrina epistolografica il IV secolo sia pagano che cristiano diè contributo non piccolo, e vi ebbe la sua parte anche Sinesio (paradigmatica l'*ep.* 138 Gar.). Basteranno due esempî: uno dal cosí detto 'corrispondente di Giamblico,' che aduna un ricco campionario della topica epistolare del tempo (ps.—Iulian., *ep.* 183 [a. 320/325] = p. 243, 8 ss. B.-C. εἰ <δὲ> δή μοι καὶ κατ' ἐμαυτοῦ τὴν κρίσιν ἐθέλοις πιστεῦσαι καὶ διδοίης ἐνεγκεῖν ἣν βούλομαι, ἐμαυτόν, ὦ γενναῖε, τῷ σῷ χιτωνίσκῳ προσάφαιμι ἂν ἡδέως, ἵνα σου κατὰ μηδὲν ἀπολειπόμην, ἀλλὰ συνείην ἀεὶ καὶ πανταχῆ προσφεροίμην, ὥσπερ οὕς οἱ μῦθοι διφυεῖς ἀνθρώπους πλάττουσιν· εἰ μὴ κἀκεῖνο οἱ μῦθοι λέγουσι μέν ὡς παίζοντες, αἰνίττονται δὲ εἰς τὸ τῆς φιλίας ἐξαίρετον, ἐν τῷ τῆς κοινωνίας δεσμῷ τὸ δι' ἑκατέρου τῆς ψυχῆς ὁμογενὲς ἐμφαίνοντες), e uno da Ambrogio, il quale esegue un po' la stessa operazione nell'*ep.* I 47 (=*PL* XVI 1151a ...*epistolis, quarum eiusmodi usus est, ut disiuncti locorum intervallis, affectu adhaereamus: in quibus inter absentes imago refulget praesentiae, et collocutio scripta separatos copulat: in quibus etiam cum amico miscemus animum, et mentem ei nostram infundimus)*

---

[7]Cfr. H. Dörrie, Plotin, Philosoph und Theologe, in *Platonica minora* cit., p. 370s; e come non ricordare quanto Porfirio racconta sull'esperienza "ineffabile" del πλησιάσαι καὶ ἐνωθῆναι ...τῷ ἐπὶ πᾶσι θεῷ che occorse al maestro ben quattro volte (*vit. Plotin.* 23, 13ss.)?

[8]Pensiamo al *De Isaac vel anima* di Ambrogio e al suo retroterra porfiriano quale ha illustrato H. Dörrie, Das fünffach gestufte Mysterium: Der Aufstieg der Seele bei Porphyrios und Ambrosius, in *Platonica minora* cit., pp. 477ss. Il tèma rimarrà in voga a lungo in Oriente (anche islamico) e in Occidente, anche col richiamo al luogo del *Simposio* e all'epistola 140 di Sinesio; cfr. G. Karlsson, *Idéologie et cérémonial dans l'épistolographie byzantine* (Stud. Gr. Upsaliensia," 3), Uppsala 1962, p. 65.

richiamandosi da un lato all'autorità degli scrittori latini (*maiorum nostrorum exempla*) dall'altra a quella dell'Apostolo santo (1 Cor. 5, 3).
—P. 245, 1-14

Perché dunque ti lamenti e inondi le lettere di lacrime? Se è per pietà di me che non sono ancora un filosofo pur avendone l'apparenza e il nome, riconosco la fondatezza della lamentela; ma se è perché la sorte insensata ci ha fatto il torto di separarci (tale il senso delle tue lettere), trovo femmineo e infantile il tener tanto a cose che possono fornire al dèmone il destro di frustrare la riescita dei nostri piani. Io vorrei invece che il sacro capo di Erculiano sia rivolto verso l'alto, tutto nella contemplazione delle essenze e della origine delle cose mortali, dopo aver da tempo oltrepassato le virtù che rivolgono il loro corso verso la terra per regolarne la vita. Per questo motivo alla fine delle mie lettere io adopro la formula: «Sii molto saggio», non «Salve» né «Stai bene», ch'è la più comune. Alle azioni infatti presiede l'intelletto inferiore, non quello puro che immagino nascosto in te.

Anche qui due punti: 1) portante, anzi essa può interferire negativamente sulla loro 'ascesa'; 2) mèta prima dev'essere la contemplazione piuttosto che l'azione. La variazione nella *formula valetudinis*[9] suggellerà tale prospettiva. L'orizzonte si è ora allargato con la chiamata in causa dell'altro grande tèma del dibattito culturale contemporaneo—sul posto eventuale della πρᾶξις, sui modi del suo trascorrere nella θεωρία,[10] ecc.,—tèma caro e Sinesio, che vi ritorna nel *Dione* e in molte delle lettere.
- - - , 15-246, 8.

Di tutto ciò avevo discorso ampiamente in due mie lettere precedenti, ma nessuna delle due i latori ti recapitarono. Con questa è la quinta lettera che ti scrivo, speriamo che non sia anche questa volta invano. Invano non sarà stato, anzi tutto, se ti giunge; poi, cosa ancor più importante, se ti consiglierà, insegnerà, persuaderà a trasferire la vigoria corporea alla

---

[9]La *pointe* insita nella *variatio* risalterà ove si ponga mente non tanto al neutro (Πολλά) χαίρειν e sim. quanto al platonico Εὖ πράττειν e all'epicureo Εὖ διάγειν (in alternanza con Σπουδαίως ζῆν) già essi di per sé innovatívi (cfr. Diog. Laert., III 61 e X 14). Anche Seneca ha una *pointe* consimile: *ep. 15 Recte nos dicimus: "Si philosopharis, bene est." Valere autem hoc demum est.*

[10]Cfr. A. Garzya, Sul rapporto fra teoria e prassi nella grecità tardoantica, in *Il mandarino* cit., pp. 199-219.

fortezza dell'anima, non quella che procede dalla prima e terrestre tetrade delle virtù, ma quella che è proporzionata nel terzo e quarto grado. Ne entrerai in possesso quando nessuna delle cose di quaggiù ti moverà ad ammirazione. Che se non ti è ancora chiaro quanto ho detto sulla distinzione fra virtú primigenie e ultime nella serie, quando sarai al punto da non lamentarti per nulla ma da disprezzare a buon diritto le cose di quaggiù, avrai già ottenuto uno stabile criterio di discernimento quanto al possesso delle virtù prime. Cosí potrò di nuovo scriverti nelle mie lettere «Sii molto saggio».

Si sviluppa il concetto precedente con il riferimento alle virtú. Sinesio ha introdotto poc'anzi la distinzione fra νοῦς ἐλάττων e νοῦς ἀνακεχωσμένον—come dire 'esterno' e 'interiore'—la quale si può rapportare a quella tra visione esterna e visione interiore vigente per tutto il corso del platonismo.[11] Ora accenna alla scala delle virtú, anzi a piú tetradi disposte in ordine crescente, dal primo gradino del primo βαθμός in su, fino al corrispondente nel quarto. Ematerla plotiniana (enn. I 2), ovviamente, ma filtrata attraverso il Porfirio dell'ἀφορμή 32,[12] a parte la locuzione τετρακτὺς τῶν ἀρετῶν che sembra essere un πρώτως εἰρημένον, o quasi, se si consideri la concorrenza del piú giovane contemporaneo Evagrio Pontico (de orat., prooem. = PG LXXIX 1165c).

La gradazione delle virtú dà l'avvio alla conclusione dell'epistola.

«Possa tu viver sano», ammirevole signore, e la filosofia ti concili una vita lieta e serena. Se la filosofia sa come garantire l'apatia, e se gli stadî intermedi conducono alla metriopatia, dove mai dovremo collocare l'estremo della passione (ἀπειροπάθειαν) e l'estremo della umiliazione? Non forse lungi da quella filosofia della quale auspicammo che tu divenissi sacerdote? E tu, a me fra tutti carissimo, non altro mostrarmi in te che un amico virile.

---

[11]Ved. il celebre Plat., resp. VII 533d (la dialettica che innalza τὸ τῆς ψυχῆς ὄμμα); Plotin., enn. I 6, 9, 1 (...δυιν ἄλλην ..., ἣν ἔχει μὲν πᾶς, χρῶνται δὲ ὀλίγοι.) Τί οὖν ἐκείνη ἡ ἔνδον βλέπει; e 25s. οὗτος γὰρ μόνος ὁ ὀφθαλμὸς τὸ μέγα κάλλος βλέπει; ecc. In Sinesio si può ricordare fra altro l'ep. 137 = p. 239, 9s. Ἔρρωσο καὶ φιλοσόφει καὶ διατέλει τὸ ἐν ἡμῖν κατακεχωσμένον ὄμμα ἀνορύττων.

[12]Cfr. la discussione in Porfirio, Introduzione agli intelligibili. Trad., comm. e note a cura di A.R. Sodano ("Quaderni di KOINΩNIA," V), Napoli 1979, pp. 36ss., e piú in generale O. Schissel von Fleschenberg, Marinus von Neapolis und die neuplatonischen Tugendgrade, Atene 1928; Helen F. North, Canons and Hierarchies of the Cardinal Virtues in Greek and Latin Literature, in The Classical Tradition Ythaca-New York 1966, pp. 165-183.

La filosofia può garantire nel suo stadio perfetto, in quanto filosofia teoretica, l'impassibilità, nell'avvicinarsi a quello stadio, in quanto, diremmo, filosofia politica, la moderazione nelle passioni; cadono al di fuori della filosofia e il travalicamento nell'irrazionale per sfuggire alla materia e il soggiacimento al suo dominio. Per Erculiano Sinesio auspica dunque la φιλοσοφικὴ προαίρεσις. Non precisa se la sua preferenza vada a una scelta rigorista o a una moderata, si limita a dire che entrambe rientrano nel dominio della filosofia. Sarà piú chiaro, forse piú disincantato, qualche anno dopo, nel *Dione*,[13] quando, nel riprendere la distinzione fra ἀπάθεια e μετριοπάθεια (ἀπάθεια μὲν γάρ ἐν θεῷ φύσει· ἀρετῇ δὲ ἄνθρωποι κακίαν ἀμειβόμενοι μετριοπαθεῖς γίνονται, 6 = p. 250, 10ss. Terz.), dichiarerà, per un verso, di non esser "lo spirito puro, ma spirito calato nell'anima d'un essere vivente" (οὐ ... ὁ ἀκήρατος νοῦς, ἀλλὰ νοῦς ἐν ζῴου ψυχῇ, 6 - p. 249, 13s.), e definendo cosí le ragioni della sua scelta moderata, per un altro, di rifiutare l'atteggiamento di chi intenda attingere il sommo dell' "esperienza conoscitiva" (ἐπιστασία γνώσεως) per via iniziatica e non razionale (τοὺς τελουμένους οὐ μαθεῖν ..., ἀλλὰ παθεῖν καὶ διατεθῆναι, δηλονότι γενομένους ἐπιτηδείους· καὶ ἡ ἐπιτηδειότης δὲ ἄλογος, 8 = p. 254, 8ss.), cosí precisando il valore dell'*hapax* ἀπειροπάθεια che ricorre in questa fine dell'*ep.* 140.[14]

Ma sul divario impassibilità/moderazione non fu solo Sinesio a prender partito. Sette secoli prima l'accademico Crantore aveva cominciato con l'opporre la μετριοπάθεια come *Stichwort* meno severo di fronte a quello di ἀπάθεια venuto in voga con la Stoà. Filone aveva poi risolto l'opposizione in gradazione gettando un ponte fra le due condotte di vita.[15] La questione giunse a Porfirio, il quale collocò

---

[13]Gli anni 404-405 ai quali l'operetta viene comunemente datata saranno stati quelli dell'elaborazione definitiva, ma essa avrà avuto una prima redazione piú antica; cfr. A. Garzya, in *Gnomon* XXXII (1960), p. 505s.

[14]Ved. anche il séguito della citazione dal *Dione*, p. 254, 14-16 τούτοις οὖν (*sc.* τοῖς τελουμένοις) καὶ ἡ κάθοδος (nel senso, s'intende, dell'ottavo trattato della quarta *Enneade* plotiniana, Περὶ τῆς εἰς τὰ σώματα καθόδου τῆς ψυχῆς) εὐθὺς ἐπὶ σμικράν τινα πρᾶξιν, ἄμεσος αὕτη καὶ πολὺ πόρρω, καὶ ἔοικε πτώματι, καθάπερ τὴν ἀναδρομὴν (neoplatonismo anche questo: cfr. Porphyr., *ep. Marc.* 7 εἰς θεόν, *de abst.* I 29 εἰς τὸν ὄντως ἑαυτόν; Procl., *inst. th.* 209 εἰς τὸ οἰκεῖον εἶδος) εἰκάζομεν ἅλματι; cfr. A. Garzya, Synesios' Dion als Zeugnis des Kampfes um die Bildung im 4. Jahrhundert nach Christus, in *Storia e interpretazione di testi bizantini* ("Variorum Reprints" CS 28), Londra 1974, II, p. 11s.

[15]Cfr. M. Pohlenz, *Die Stoa. Geschichte einer geistlichen Bewegung*, I, Göttingen 1959;2, p. 376.

anch'egli la metriopatia sulla via delle καθάρσεις di colui che vuole "elevarsi alla contemplazione" (πρὸς θεωρίαν προκόπτειν) e l'apatia in cima a quella via: non alternativa, quindi, ma complementarità.[16] In posizione analoga non rigorista è il pur cosí sensibile all'influsso stoico Clemente, col suo platoneggiante ἐξομοιοῦσθαι θεῷ κατὰ τὸ δυνατόν,[17] e per contro meno aperto un Marino di Neapoli, il quale nel suo maestro e eroe ammira l'aver saputo "non limitare soltanto le passioni, ma esserne completamente immune."[18] Ma non si vuol qui seguire una vicenda complessa e suggestiva la quale richiederebbe trattazione apposita. Si vuol soltanto rilevare la posizione di Sinesio in quanto contraddistinta da atteggiamento, nell'epistola e nel *Dione*, non univoco. Dall'uno scritto all'altro, due protrettici in certo senso e l'uno e l'altro, c'è stato un approfondimento dei modi della (βίου) διαγωγή: la filosofia ha acquisito una divisa meno aspra; la metriopatia è sembrata una ragionevole mèta, confacentesi all'ideale, che Sinesio rivendicherà poi anche da vescovo, d'un umanesimo sofferto e senza entusiasmi.

Concludendo, speriamo di aver offerto un convincente esempio del come di tra la *routine* che presiede alla composizione dei testi tardoantichi possano ricavarsi, ove li si accosti con attenzione, notazioni che trascendono l'episodico e sono atte a lumeggiare la condizione spirituale non solo dei loro autori, ma anche del loro pubblico.

---

[16]Ved. *sent*. 32 = p. 25, 6-9 Lamb. ἡ μὲν οὖν κατὰ τὰς πολιτικὰς ἀρετὰς διάθεσις ἐν μετριοπαθείᾳ θεωρεῖται, τέλος ἔχουσα τὸ ζῆν ὡς ἄνθρωπον κατὰ φύσιν, ἡ δὲ κατὰ τὰς θεωρητικὰς ἐν ἀπαθείᾳ, ἧς τέλος ἡ πρὸς θεὸν ὁμοίωσις (e la ripresa in Psello, *de virt.*, ed. Rita Masullo, Un trattatello di Michele Psello sulle virtú, in *Atti Acc. Pontaniana* XXXVII [1988],); cfr. Pohlenz, *op. cit.*, p. 397 (e nota II, p. 192).

[17]Cfr. M. Pohlenz, Klemens von Alexandreia und sein hellenisches Christentum, in *Kleine Schriften*, I, Hildesheim 1965, p. 542s., il quale riconosce in ciò, nell'Alessandrino, "ein unstoischer Ton."

[18]*vit. Procl.* 21 = p. 78, 2s. Masullo (Napoli 1985).

"παθὼν τὰ θεῖα"

YSABEL DE ANDIA

INTRODUCTION: "οὐ μόνον μαθὼν ἀλλὰ καὶ παθὼν τὰ θεῖα"
(*Noms divins* 648B)

Dans l'éloge que le pseudo-Denys fait, au second chapitre des *Noms divins*, de son maître Hiérothée, il écrit que celui-ci "non seulement savait, mais aussi pätissait les choses divines" (DN 648 B).

L'excellence de Hiérothée comme "connaisseur" des choses divines vient du fait que sa connaissance de Dieu est inséparable d'une expérience de Dieu.

Cette relation entre la connaissance et l'expérience, ou même la souffrance, est présente dans la littérature grecque, surtout chez les tragiques, mais, à travers Denys, elle est aussi devenue la caractéristique du mystique chrétien qui "souffre les choses divines." Entre le topos de la littérature grecque: μαθεῖν¬παθεῖν[1] et la formule-clé

---

[1] Chez les tragiques grecs, il n'y a pas d'opposition entre la connaissance et la souffrance, bien au contraire, la souffrance est un moyen de connaissance.

Le choeur de l'*Agamemnon* d'Eschyle fait l'éloge de Zeus en ces termes: "τὸν φρονεῖν βροτοὺς ὁδώσαντα τῷ πάθει μάθος θένταικυρίως ἔχειν: il a ouvert aux hommes les voies de la prudence en leur donnant pour loi: souffrir pour comprendre" (176-177).

"Etre instruit par la souffrance" est la grande leçon de la Tragédie d'Eschyle et le choeur des Euménides répétera encore: "il est bon d'apprendre à être sage à l'école de la douleur" (*Euménides* 519-520).

"Souffrir pour comprendre" est la loi de la condition humaine, la voie pour atteindre la sagesse que les dieux tracent aux hommes. La souffrance humaine est référée par Eschyle à une intention divine qui n'est pas seulement jalousie ni vengeance, mais aussi "violence bienfaisante" (χάρις βίαιος)" (*Agamemnon* 182-183).

Cf. H. Dörrie, *Leid und Erfahrung. Die Wort-und Sinnverbindung* πάσχειν¬μαθεῖν *im griechischen Denken*, AAWLM. G 1966, 5 (5) - (41).

de la mystique chrétienne occidentale: *pati divina*, la phrase de Denys sur Hiérothée: οὐ μόνον μαθὼν ἀλλὰ καὶ παθὼν τὰ θεῖα montre encore une fois l'importance de l'énigmatique auteur du *Corpus Dionysiacum* comme point de transition de la culture grecque dans la tradition chrétienne.

I. μαθεῖν–παθεῖν

L'antécédent du παθὼν τὰ θεῖα dionysien serait la phrase fameuse d'Aristote sur les Mystères:

"τοὺς τελουμένους οὐ μαθεῖν δεῖ ἀλλὰ παθεῖν:"

"les initiés ne doivent pas apprendre quelque chose, mais éprouver des émotions."

C'est un fragment du Περὶ Φιλοσοφίας rapporté par Synésius de Cyrène[2] en *Dion* (10. 48a) qui porte le nº 15 de l'édition des *Aristotelis Fragmenta*[3] par Ross.

Ce passage est un bref jugement d'Aristote sur la nature de l'activité exigée de ceux qui sont initiés aux mystères d'Éleusis. Il est cité par Synésius dans son livre sur Dion, le rhéteur philosophe, qu'il propose comme modèle à son fils, dans le cadre d'une comparaison entre l'attitude bizarre des moines égyptiens, qui ne connaissent pas de milieu entre la contemplation (θεωρία) et de grossières occupations, et la modération (μετριοπάθεια) de l'idéal grec qui, entre la contemplation et les occupations matérielles, développe l'activité rationnelle.

Synésius oppose la "science (qui) est une marche de l'esprit (ἐπιστήμη δὲ νοῦ διέξοδος) qui passe d'un raisonnement à un autre et progresse à travers ces raisonnements," au "transport bacchique" qui ressemble à un "bond d'insensé et d'inspiré (ἄλματι μανικῷ δή τινι καὶ θεοφορήτῳ)."

Ces deux manières d'avancer correspondent, d'un côté, à l'attention à la connaissance (ἐπιστασία τις γνώσεως) et, de l'autre, à l'expérience sacrée (τὸ χρῆμα τὸ ἱερόν).

Car l'expérience sacrée ne ressemble en rien à une attention de la connaissance, ni à une marche de l'esprit; elle ne ressemble pas non plus à ce qui varie dans ces situations; mais,

---

B. Snell, "Wie die Griechen lernten, was geistige Tätigkeit ist," *The Journal of Hellenic Studies* 93 (1973): 172-184: 6) "μανθάνειν."

[2]N. Terzaghi, *Synesii Cyrenensis opuscula*, Rome 1944, p. 254.

[3]W.D. Ross, *Aristotelis Fragmenta Selecta*, Oxford 1958 2, p. 84 (Rose, *Aristotelis Fragmenta*, Leipzig 1886).

pour comparer une grande chose à une petite, il en va de cela
*comme de ce que dit Aristote de ceux que l'on initie, qu'ils ne
doivent pas apprendre* (μαθεῖν) *quelque chose, mais éprouver
des émotions* (παθεῖν) *et être mis dans certaines dispositions,*
évidemment après être devenus aptes à les recevoir.[4]

L'opposition classique "μαθεῖν-παθεῖν," reprise par Aristote,
correspond, selon Synésius de Cyrène, à celle de la science et de
l'initiation mystérique où l'émotion donne la force d'adhésion aux
mytères représentés.

Le court fragment d'Aristote cité par Synésius a pu être plus
amplement interprété grâce à la publication par Bidez[5] dans son
VIème volume du *Catalogue des manuscrits alchimiques grecs*, d'une
Scolie de Michael Psellus à la *Scala Paradisi* de Jean Climaque.

Dans cette *Scolie*, Psellus oppose *"les impressions* (cf. παθεῖν)" que
doit éprouver celui qui contemple et *"le fait d'apprendre* quelque
chose par le moyen de la démonstration ou de la recherche dialectique
(δι' ἀποδείξεως ἢ διαλεκτικῆς)."

L'opposition "μαθεῖν-παθεῖν" est celle de deux éléments, l'un
didactique (τὸ διδακτικόν) et l'autre initiatoire (καὶ τὸ τελεστικόν).

Or le premier—ajoute Psellus—c'est par l'ouïe qu'il
parvient aux hommes, tandis que le second, c'est quand l'esprit
lui-même a éprouvé l'illumination.   C'est ce dernier
qu'Aristote a appelé *"du type des mystères"* (μυστηριῶδες) et
semblable (à ce qui se passait) aux Éleusinies; car, dans ces fêtes,
*celui qui était initié recevait, à partir des spectacles, des
impressions, mais non un enseignement."*[6]

Ainsi l'enseignement passe par la médiation de la parole et
parvient aux hommes par l'ouïe, tandis que l'initiation est une
illumination que l'esprit lui-même éprouve (αὐτοῦ παθόντος τοῦ νοῦ
τὴν ἔλλαμψιν). L'initié est "impressioné" par les spectacles initiatiques
ou les contemplations (τυπούμενος ὁ τελούμενος τὰς θεωρίας).

Psellus emprunte vraisemblablement le terme "τυπούμενος" à
Aristote qui définit la sensation: "une empreinte (τύπος) dans l'âme

---

[4]Synesius, PG 66, col. 1133, cité et traduit par J. Croissant, *Aristote et les Mystères*, Liège-Paris, 1932, p. 140-142.

[5]J. Bidez, *Catalogue des manuscrits alchimiques grecs*, VI *Michael Psellus*, Bruxelles 1928, p. 171.

[6]Traduction modifiée de J. Croissant, *Aristote et les Mystères*, Liège-Paris, 1932, p. 146.

comme celle d'un cachet dans la cire."[7]   En ce sens la sensation, qui
s'oppose à la raison et à la science, est comparable à la contemplation.[8]

L'initiation n'est pas de l'ordre de la parole ou de l'enseignement,
mais du spectacle ou de la contemplation.   C'est pourquoi
l'enseignement (μάθησις) s'oppose à l'initiation (τελείωσις) comme
l'activité à la passivité et la parole à l'ineffable.

1. Activité et passivité

Prenant l'exemple de l'immortalité de l'âme, Psellus montre la
différence entre "l'instruction didactique (ἡ διδασκαλικὴ μάθησις)" qui se
fait par un automouvement de l'intellect ayant acquis la conviction de
l'immortalité de l'âme, et l'initiation où l'on voit l'âme elle-même
"grâce à une vision perçue par les yeux mêmes de l'intellect
(αὐτοπτήσας τῷ νῷ εἶδεν αὐτὴν τὴν ψυχήν)."

La conception de l'activité discursive comme mouvement
spontané (αὐτοκίνησις-αὐτοκινησία) de l'intellect appartient à l'école néo-
platonicienne.[9] L'expression "αὐτοπτήσας τῷ νῷ" fait allusion aux
mystères de la théurgie néoplatonicienne.

Le cadre de pensée de Psellus est néoplatonicien, mais s'il se refère
à l'autorité d'Aristote pour expliquer le mécanisme psychologique de
la contemplation de saint Jean Climaque, c'est qu'il trouve dans
Aristote la source de cette conception de l'illumination de l'intellect
dans la contemplation.

Dans le De Anima, Aristote a comparé l'intellect agent à la lumière
et c'est ainsi qu'il a pu considérer l'acte intellectif comme une espèce
d'illumination de l'intellect passif:

> On distingue, d'une part, l'intellect qui est analogue à la
> matière par le fait qu'il devient tous les intelligibles, et, d'autre
> part, l'intellect <qui est analogue à la cause efficiente> parce
> qu'il les produit tous, attendu qu'il est une sorte d'état (ἕξις)

---

[7]Aristote, De memoria 450 a 31-b5. C'est un lieu commun de l'Antiquité. Le Pseudo
Denys utilise l'image des différentes empreintes du sceau dans la cire pour montrer les
différences de réceptivité dans le même chapitre des Noms divins (DN II, 6, 644 B-C).

[8]Aristote, De Sensu, 1. c: "οὐ γὰρ κατὰ τὸ μανθάνειν ἀλλὰ κατὰ τὸ θεωρεῖν ἐστι τὸ
αἰσθάνεσθαι."

[9]cf. Plotin, Ennéade VI, 2, 18: "ἡ ἐπιστήμη ἐστὶν αὐτοκίνησις." Et Ennéade VI, 6, 6. Sur
ce sujet voir S. Gersh, KINHSIS AKINHTOS. A Study of Spiritual Motion in the
Philosophy of Proclus, Leiden, 1973.

analogue à la lumière: car, en un certain sens, la lumière, elle aussi, convertit les couleurs de la puissance à l'acte.[10]

Les couleurs existent en puissance dans l'obscurité et c'est la lumière qui les actualise; de même l'intellect agent (νοῦς ποιητικός) est nécessaire pour faire passer à l'acte les intelligibles en puissance dans l'intellect passif.

L'analogie aristotélicienne de l'intellect agent et de la lumière et la distinciton entre le νοῦς ποιητικός et le νοῦς παθητικός indique une voie très profonde pour chercher le fondement de la passivité dans l'esprit lui-même.

Mais ce n'est pas cette voie qui a été retenue par ceux qui interprètent la passivité du παθεῖν à partir d'une théorie des passions.

2. La parole et l'ineffable

Or cette conception de l'illumination de l'intellect dans la contemplation va permettre à Psellus[11] de penser l'extase mystique:

Dans le second cas—poursuit-il—la vision est ineffable (ἄρρητος ἡ θέα), les organes des sens restant sans éprouver aucune sensation; c'est de cette façon que Paul a vu et entendu ce qui ne peut être contemplé ni exprimé (καθ' ἣν Παῦλος εἶδέ τε καὶ ἤκουσε τὰ ἀθέατα καὶ τὰ ἀπόρρητα).

L'extase paulienne ne passe pas par les organes des sens. La vision est ineffable, car c'est une vision de choses invisibles (τὰ ἀθέατα) et inexprimables (τὰ ἀπόρρητα). On reconnaît l'allusion à I Co 2, 9: "C'est ce que l'oeil n'a pas vu, ce que l'oreille n'a pas entendu, et ce qui n'est pas monté au coeur de l'homme, tout ce que Dieu a préparé pour ceux qui l'aiment."

La référence à saint Paul ne fait qu'illustrer le "second cas," c'est-à-dire le cas de "celui qui a éprouvé des impressions et est initié" (οὗτος πεπονθώς ἐστι καὶ τελούμενος).

Par conséquent il faut dire que l'extase, ou l'initiation mystérique qui lui sert de modèle, est une "impression," un παθεῖν, mais qui ne

---

[10]Aristote, De Anima III, 430 a 15ss.

[11]A travers Psellus tout pénétré de platonisme et de néo-platonisme et à travers le Fragment 15 d'Aristote lui-même, c'est à Platon qu'il faudrait revenir.

Dans la Lettre VII (341 c-d), Platon déclare totalement inexprimable (ῥητὸν γάρ οὐδαμῶς ἐστιν) la science du réel et compare la connaissance suprême qui naît de longs efforts à l'étincelle qui jaillit du frottement et à la lumière qui brille soudain en nous (οἶον ἀπὸ πυρὸς πηδήσαντος ἐξαφθὲν φῶς).

passe ni par les organes des sens, ni par la raison, et à cause de cela, ne peut être enseignée.

Le παθεῖν du monde tragique est une souffrance qui engendre la connaissance et cette expérience de la souffrance est la meilleure école pour l'homme pour "apprendre" ce qu'est la destinée humaine.

Le παθεῖν des mystères est une expérience initiatique qui s'oppose à la démarche rationnelle de la science. Ce sont les représentations mystériques qui provoquent des émotions fortes ou des "impressions" emportant l'assentiment.

Cet élément de représentation (θέαμα) ou de contemplation (θεωρία) ôte au παθεῖν son caractère de souffrance et l'intellectualise: il s'agit de l'illumination de l'intellect dans la contemplation, illumination qui "impressionne" directement l'intellect.

Le pseudo-Denys reprendra ce caractère à la fois direct et ineffable de la contemplation des choses divines qui s'apparente à l'initiation: le παθεῖν dionysien a un sens plus mystérique que tragique.

II. παθὼν τὰ θεῖα

1) Hiérothée

Lorsque le Pseudo-Denys reprend, au second chapitre des *Noms divins*, le topos grec "μαθεῖν-παθεῖν" pour caractériser son maître Hiérothée, il ne le reprend pas sous forme d'opposition absolue: "οὐ μαθεῖν, ἀλλὰ παθεῖν τὰ θεῖα," comme dans le fragment d'Aristote que nous venons d'étudier, mais sous forme d'opposition atténuée: "οὐ μόνον μαθὼν ἀλλὰ καὶ παθών τὰ θεῖα" Il y a un "μόνον" de plus qui modifie le sens.

Hiérothée, en effet, mieux que tout autre, a loué les mystères de la nature merveilleuse de Jésus. Toutes "ces choses,"

> notre illustre maître, dit Denys, les a célébrées dans ses *Éléments Théologiques* d'une façon tout à fait prodigieuse, soit que ce personnage les ait reçues des saints théologiens, soit qu'il les ait considérées au terme de son investigation savante des *Oracles*, après y avoir consacré beaucoup de temps et d'exercices, soit qu'il ait été initié par une inspiration plus divine, *non seulement connaissant mais patissant les choses divines.* et, par suite de cette "sympathie,"[12] si on peut ainsi parler, envers elles,

---

[12]"οὐ μόνον μαθὼν, ἀλλὰ καὶ παθὼν τὰ θεῖα" . . ."συμπάθεια."

Le terme "sympathie" est un terme de la théurgie néo-platonicienne: "Chaque dieu a sa représentation "sympathique" dans le monde, animal, végétal et minéral" (cf. E.R.

il a été rendu parfait dans une mystérieuse union et foi en ces choses qu'on ne peut enseigner (DN 648 A-B).[13]

Il ne s'agit pas ici d'une initiation cultuelle de Hiérothée comparable aux initiations aux mystères païens, mais de sa connaissance du mystère de l'Incarnation, de la formation de Jésus (ἡ καθ' ἡμᾶς Ιησοῦ θεοπλαστία) qui est indicible pour tout discours (καὶ ἄρρητος ἐστι λόγῳ παντί) et de toutes les choses qui touchent à sa nature merveilleuse (καὶ τὰ ἄλλα ὅσα τῆς ὑπερφυοῦς ἐστιν Ιησοῦ φυσιολογίας) (DN 648 A2 et 10).

1. Enseignement et initiation

Or "ces choses" (ταῦτα δέ) Hiérothée les a connues de trois manières différentes. (La répétition "εἴτε . . . εἴτε . . . εἴτε" n'indique pas trois possibilités, mais plutôt la succession de trois activités différentes).

a) *"soit qu'il (les) ait reçues des saints théologiens (εἴτε πρὸς τῶν ἱερῶν θεολόγων παρείληφεν)."*

Il y a d'abord une réception des Oracles divins par le moyen des écrivains sacrés (θεολόγοι). C'est le moment de la tradition des livres saints.

b) *"soit qu'il les ait considérées[14] au terme de son investigation savante des Oracles, après y avoir consacré beaucoup de temps et d'exercices."*

(εἴτε καὶ ἐκ τῆς ἐπιστημονικῆς τῶν λογίων ἐρεύνης συνεώρακεν, ἐκ πολλῆς τῆς περὶ αὐτὰ γυμνασίας καὶ τριβῆς).

Cette vision synoptique de l'Ecriture ou de la théologie vient au terme d'une savante recherche (ἐπιστημονικὴ ἔρευνα) après beaucoup d'exercice (γυμνασία) et de temps (τριβή).[15]

C'est le moment de l'activité intellectuelle de l'exégèse.

c) *"soit qu'il ait été initié par une inspiration plus divine."*

(εἴτε καὶ ἐκ τινος ἐμυήθη θειοτέρας ἐπιπνοίας)

Dodds, "Theurgy," in PROCLUS, *The Elements of Theology*, p. 292; voir également Andrew Smith, *Porphyry's Place in the Neoplatonic Tradition: A Study in Post-plotinian Neoplatonism*, The Hague, M. Nijhoff, 1974, pp. 90-94.

[13]Traduction des *Noms divins* par Y. de Andia, à paraître dans un volume de *Sources chrétiennes* sur les *Noms divins et la Théologie mystique de Pseudo-Denys l'Aréopagite*.

[14]"Συνεώρακεν": "il a vu ensemble": s'agit-il de la vision synoptique qui caractérise la science de Hiérothée? ou d'une vision commune à celle des "théologiens"?

[15]cf. MT *, 997 B.

Mais il y a aussi une initiation par une inspiration plus divine (θειοτέρα ἐπιπνοία). Le mystagogue est l'Esprit-Saint qui inspire les Écritures et qui, par sa puissance et non par la sagesse humaine, fait adhérer aux réalités ou aux mystères révélés dans la théologie.

Telle est la règle (θεσμός) que Denys propose au début des *Noms divins:*

> Que pour nous, maintenant encore, la loi des *Oracles* soit
> bien établie à l'avance: lier la vérité de ce que nous disons sur
> Dieu "*non avec les raisons convaincantes de* l'humaine *sagesse,
> mais avec une démonstration de la puissance*"[16] des
> théologiens, inspirée par l'Esprit, puissance grâce à laquelle
> nous sommes unis, d'une manière ineffable et inconnaissable,
> à ce qui est ineffable et inconnaissable, selon une union
> supérieure à notre puissance et activité rationnelle et
> intellectuelle" (DN 585 B-588 A).

C'est la puissance de l'Esprit qui meut les théologiens (ἡ πνευματοκινήτη τῶν θεολόγων δύναμις) par laquelle nous adhérons (καθ' ἣν συναπτόμεθα) aux choses ineffables selon un mode ineffable, unis à elle "selon une union au-delà des puissances de la raison et de l'intellect."

La puissance (δύναμις) n'est pas ici la "δύναμις λογικὴ καὶ νοερά," mais la "δύναμις θεοῦ" dont parle saint Paul en I Co 2, 5. C'est elle qui cause l'union[17] de l'homme et des réalités mystérieuses qui sont signifiées par les paroles des théologiens. Dans l'union s'achève l'initiation.

2. *La sympathie*

C'est au terme de ces trois moments de la réception de l'Écriture, de la recherche et de la vision de son sens et de l'initiation par l'inspiration divine que Denys dit de Hiérothée que "*non seulement il connaissait, mais également il pâtissait ces choses divines.*" Or ce "pâtir" est immédiatement expliqué comme une "sympathie."[18]

---

[16]I Co 2, 4: "humaine" ne se trouve pas dans le texte de saint Paul qui est paraphrasé.

[17]"ἔνωσις" et "συνάπτω" sont ici les expressions clés du vocabulaire de l'union.

[18]La sympathie intervient dans la divination, comme Jamblique le montre dans le *De Mysteriis* (II, 15-16) "Les dieux font signe par l'intermédiaire de la nature qui est à leur service pour la production des phénomènes, la nature en général et celle des êtres particuliers, ou par les démons générateurs" (133, 10 55). Ces démons revèlent symboliquement l'intention du dieu. "En outre l'union et la sympathie du tout (καὶ ἡ ἔνωσις δὲ καὶ ἡ συμπάθεια τοῦ παντός), le mouvement simultané, comme en un seul

Par la sympathie envers celles-ci (πρὸς αὐτά), c'est-à-dire envers les choses divines (τὰ θεῖα), l'union mystique qui ne s'enseigne pas et la foi sont accomplies d'une manière parfaite.

De même que c'était la "puissance" de l'Esprit qui opérait l'union avec les réalités ineffables, de même c'est la sympathie avec les "choses divines" qui rend parfaite la foi en elles et l'union avec elles.

Pour mieux exprimer l'union, Denys emploie des termes composés du préfixe: "συν-": "συν-άπτω": être con-joint, uni, adhérer à-, et "συμπάθεια": souffrir avec. "Toucher" et "souffrir" sont des sensations ou des passions qui ne sont pas de l'ordre de la rationalité ou du discours, mais qui, par là même, traduisent l'immédiateté de l'expérience vécue. C'est cette immédiateté qui seule peut correspondre à l'union avec l'Un, le discours ou la science étant encore de l'ordre de la multiplicité[19] et de la médiation.

Le "παθεῖν" indique ici un mode de connaissance des choses divines qui ne passe pas, comme la μάθησις, par la médiation du discours; en ce sens, il marque davantage l'immédiateté de l'union ou la passivité de l'homme face à Dieu que la souffrance comme telle.

Mais on peut se demander si la passion humaine, qui est toujours caractérisée d'une manière négative par le Pseudo-Denys, ne prend

---

être, des parties les plus éloignées, comme si elles étaient voisines, font descendre des dieux sur les hommes la procession de ces signes (τὴν τῶν σημείων τούτων πομπὴν ἐκ θεῶν ἀνθρώποις καταπέμπει), qui se manifeste aux hommes d'abord par le ciel, puis par l'air, avec le plus d'éclat possible" (137, 20-185, 5).

Ce passage de Jamblique est cité par K. Reinhardt dans son chapitre sur *Poseidonios et Jamblique* pour montrer que l'unité organique du tout permet la communication des signes. Cf. K. Reinhardt, *Kosmos und Sympathie*, Munich 1926, p. 252-256.

On retrouve la même idée de l'univers comme un "tout sympathique à lui-même" (συμπαθὲς δὴ πᾶν τοῦτο τὸ ἕν) chez Plotin, *Ennéades*, IV, 4, 32, trad. É. Bréhier, Paris 1927, p. 137-138. Cette sympathie qui existe entre toutes choses comme entre les parties d'un animal unique, comme l'univers, est renforcée par la similitude du patient et de l'agent: "Quand le patient est semblable à l'agent, il subit une influence qui n'est pas étrangère à sa nature; quand il ne lui est pas semblable, la passion qu'il subit lui est étrangère, et il n'est pas porté à la subir." (p. 138).

En *Enn.* IV, 4, 40, Plotin reconnaît à la sympathie une puissance magique ("comment expliquer les charmes de la magie? Par la sympathie. . . . La vraie magie c'est "l'Amitié et la Dispute" qui sont dans l'Univers." En *Enn.* IV, 4, 41 il affirme que "la prière produit ses effets, parce qu'une partie de l'univers est en sympathie avec une autre partie comme dans la corde tendue (d'une lyre) où la vibration venue d'en bas se propage jusqu'en haut."

[19] cf. Plotin, *Ennéade* VI, 9, 4.

pas, comme "pâtir," une valeur positive en relation avec la passion du Christ.

2) La passion du Verbe

Les "choses divines" dont il est question en DN 648 B sont l'Incarnation et la nature merveilleuse de Jésus. C'est donc dans un contexte christologique que Denys affirme que Hiérothée "*non seulement connaissait mais aussi pâtissait les choses divines.*" Or il dit plus haut:

> Seul le Verbe suressentiel assuma pour nous notre propre *substance* de façon entière et vraie; par son action comme par sa passion (καὶ δρᾶσαι καὶ παθεῖν), c'est lui seul qui proprement et singulièrement assuma la totalité de l'opération humano-divine (DN 644 C).

Le "παθεῖν" est ici la passion du Verbe "selon notre propre substance."

Certes ce "παθεῖν" n'affecte pas sa propre nature. Car dans sa "philanthropie," la Bonté théarchique "s'unit à notre bassesse sans rien perdre de sa propre nature, *sans subir* aucun mélange, sans souffrir aucun dommage" (EH 441 B) ou encore: "*sans que fût diminuée* la transcendance de sa plénitude (μηδὲν πεπονθὼς εἰς τὸ ὑπερπλῆρες αὐτοῦ)" (DN 649 A).

Ce "παθεῖν" est rédempteur. Jésus "*pendant sa passion*, implore le pardon du Père" (EP 8, 1096 B): et il dit, dans une vision, à Carpos: "*me voici de nouveau prêt à souffrir pour le salut des hommes* (ὑπὲρ ἀνθρώπων ἀνασωζομένων παθεῖν) *et je le ferais avec grande joie, si je devais ainsi empêcher d'autres hommes de pécher*" (EP 8, 1100 C).

Enfin c'est la Rédemption qui "*rachète les passions*" (DN 897 B).

Cependant les passions humaines sont toujours mêlées de corruption et l'attitude de l'homme divin, comme celle des anges, est l'impassibilité.

3) Les passions humaines et l'impassibilité

La vie humaine est située entre la vie animale et la vie angélique. Des animaux, il partage les passions, des anges, l'impassibilité.

1. les passions animales

Les passions sont liées à la concupiscence, attachées aux "voluptés destructrices" (EH 556 A). "Nous nous livrons nous-mêmes à la mort—dit Denys—en succombant aux passions corruptrices" (EH 444

B). Nous sommes "agités en tous sens par le tumulte des passions" (DN 953 A).

Les passions s'opposent à la raison, "contre la raison s'était déjà élevée la révolte des passions" (DN 717 A), et les "passions animales" aux "vertus divines."

Si l'on commence soit à pratiquer l'injustice à l'égard d'autrui, soit à pratiquer le bien, n'eut-on pas réalisé pleinement ce qu'on a voulu, il reste qu'on a pris ainsi l'habitude, soit de la malice, soit de la bonté, et qu'on possédera dorénavant la plénitude ou des vertus divines ou des passions animales. (EP 8, 1097 A).

Selon ce choix, l'homme marchera "sur les traces des bons anges," ses "compagnons," soit il sera en proie aux cruels démons. Les passions le livrent aux démons, la vie angélique le rapproche de l'impassibilité.

2. L'impassibilité angélique

A l'opposé, l'impassibilité est le propre des anges. Ainsi les Trônes ont une "aptitude à recevoir dans une totale impassibilité (ἐν ἀπαθείᾳ πάσῃ) toutes les visions de la Théarchie" (CH 205 D); et les Puissances angéliques "reçoivent *impassiblement* les illuminations théarchiques en toute simplicité, avec souplesse, sans résistance, dans un envol rapide et pur" (CH 332 A).

Mais comment alors attribuer l'éros qui est une passion à des esprits impassibles?

Chaque fois que, par l'application des similitudes dissemblantes aux êtres intelligents, nous les douons figurativement de concupiscence (ἐπιθυμίαν), il faut entendre par là un *amour divin* de l'immatérialité qui est au-dessus de la raison et de l'esprit, le désir stable et constant de la contemplation suressentiellement pure et *impassible* (καὶ ἀπαθοῦς θεωρίας) et de la communion réellement éternelle et intelligible avec cette pure et sublime transparence de là-haut et avec l'invisible splendeur qui est source de beauté (CH 144 A).[20]

Le pseudo-Denys nous donne, dans ce passage, des précisions sur le vocabulaire de l'amour et de la passion et une distinction entre le désir passionnel (ὄρεξις) des êtres sans raison et le désir impassible (ἔφεσις) des êtres intelligents.

---

[20]Denys l'Aréopagite, *La Hiérarchie céleste*, SC 58 bis, Paris, 1970, p. 83.

La concupiscence (ἐπιθυμία) est, chez ceux qui sont privés de raison, "un penchant inconsidéré et tendant vers la matière." Elle se manifeste par "l'empire irraisonné du désir corporel (τὴν ἄλογον τῆς σωματικῆς ὀρέξεως ἐπικράτειαν) qui précipite l'animal tout entier vers les objets que la sensation lui fait désirer."

L'amour angélique, au contraire, n'est pas un "désir passionnel," mais un "amour divin" (θεῖος ἔρως) qui est un "désir" ou une "tendance" (ἔφεσις) vers la contemplation pure et impassible de la réalité divine, au-delà de tout intellect.

La contemplation, en effet, exige un *intellect impassible* et le rayonnement intelligible de la très divine Transfiguration ne peut être participé que par un "intellect libre de passions et dématérialisé (ἐν ἀπαθεῖ καὶ ἀύλῳ τῷ νῷ)" (DN 592 C).

L'impassibilité nécessaire à la contemplation sera donc le propre de l'ange et du θεῖος ἀνήρ. Elle est le fruit de l'illumination baptismale (EH 404 C) et de la déification:

> L'homme parfaitement divin, celui qui est digne d'entrer en communion avec les réalités divines, celui que des déifications intégrales et perfectionnantes ont élevé au plus haut degré de conformité avec Dieu qui lui soit accessible ... ayant atteint la plus haute déification qu'il puisse obtenir, sera tout ensemble le temple et le compagnon de l'Esprit théarchique, fondant sa similitude en Celui-là même dont il est devenu le semblable, *loin de subir* jamais l'effet des phantasmes et des épouvantails de l'adversaire, il s'en moquera bien, et s'ils se présentent, il les repoussera et les poursuivra. Il sera donc plus *actif* que *passif*, et lui qui a fait de l'*impassibilité* et de la fermeté (ἀπαθεῖ καὶ ἀνενδότῳ) la loi constante de sa nature, on le verra aussi, tel un médecin, aider les autres dans leur lutte contre de pareilles tentations" (EH 433 C).

Ce texte accumule des expressions de la connaissance des choses divines et de la déification:
—"entrer en *communion* avec les réalités divines,"
—"être élevé au plus haut degré de *conformité* avec Dieu,"
—"atteindre la plus haute *déification* possible,"
—"être le *temple* et le *compagnon* de l'Esprit théarchique,"
—"fonder sa *similitude* en Celui-là même dont il est devenu semblable."

Il s'agit bien de celui qui "éprouve les choses divine." Celui-là est à la fois "plus actif que passif" vis-à-vis de l'adversaire et "impassible" dans son esprit, l'impassibilité de l'esprit étant la condition même pour "pâtir des choses divines," sans confondre ce "pâtir" avec les passions humaines.

En effet le "pâtir les choses divines" suppose l'impassibilité (ἀπάθεια) et la déification (θέωσις) de celui qui pâtit. Hiérothée[21] que Denys nomme "saint mystagogue ou initiateur (ἱερομύστης[22] et ἱεροτελεστής[23])" est aussi un "θεῖος ἀνήρ."

3. Le possible et l'impassible

Si le "παθὼν τὰ θεῖα" suppose une doctrine de la connaissance de Dieu et de la déification de l'homme, celle-ci suppose à son tour toute une anthropologie.

Dans la *Lettre* IX à Tite sur la signification des métaphores employées à propos de la Sagesse: sa "maison", son "cratère," sa "nourriture" et sa "boisson", Denys distingue deux parties de l'âme: la "partie impassible" et la "partie passionnelle":

> Ainsi la partie impassible de l'âme est destinée aux spectacles simples et intérieurs des images qui ont la forme divine, tandis que la partie passionnelle de cette même âme tout ensemble se guérit comme il sied à sa nature et s'élève vers les réalités les plus divines à travers les figurations bien combinées des symboles allégoriques" (EP 9, 1108 A).

a) *La partie impassible de l'âme est définie par son intentionalité ou sa finalité: elle est "destinée aux spectacles simples et intérieurs des images qui ont la forme divine."*

Cette partie impassible est l'intellect (νοῦς) qui contemple les spectacles simples des images, c'est-à-dire la θεωρία (IIIème partie) qui achève, dans chaque chapitre de la *Hiérarchie ecclésiastique*, la description du *mystère* (IIème partie) du sacrement envisagé (Ière partie).

A propos de chaque sacrement, la méthode d'analyse est la même: elle consiste à passer de la multiplicité des symboles à la contemplation simple de l'Un:

> Quand nous aurons examiné de façon systématique les saintes images qui nous le représentent, la multiplicité de ces

---

[21] Sur Hiérothée voir I.P. Sheldon-Williams, "The ps. Dionysius and the Holy Hierotheus," *Studia Patristica*, vol. VIII, Part II, Berlin 1966, p. 108-117. L'auteur rapproche d'une manière très suggestive la doctrine de Hiérothée, telle qu'elle apparaît dans le *Corpus Dionysiacum*, et la pensée de Jamblique.

[22] *Hieromustès*: DN III, 2, 681 A 5.

[23] *Hierotelestès*: DN IV, 14, 713 A 2; X, 2, 937 B 13-14; CH VI, 2, 200 D 2-3.

symboles nous élèvera par des contemplations hiérarchiques jusqu'à l'Un (EH 472 D).

Cette élévation de la vue des images multiples, contemplation simple du signifié qui est lui-même simple et Un, s'accompagne d'une unification de l'âme. C'est pourquoi la *Hiérarchie ecclésiastique* s'achève par ces mots:

> Tels sont, mon enfant, les beaux spectacles capables d'unifier nos âmes que j'ai découverts dans notre hiérarchie (EH 568 D).

b) *Cette unification de l'âme est en même temps une guérison de sa partie passionnelle.*

Il y a à la fois un rôle thérapeutique ou cathartique des symboles et des rites.

C'est ce que Jamblique avait déjà montré dans *les Mystères d'Égypte*[24] où il reprend la doctrine de la "catharsis"[25] et présente le culte comme une "imitation de l'ordre des dieux" où "l'indicible s'exprime en symboles mystérieux."[26]

L'initiation (μύησις), le culte (θεραπεία) ou les "saintes mystagogies" (ἱεραὶ μυσταγωγίαι) (EH 369 D) à la fois guérissent la partie passible de l'âme et l'élèvent vers la réalité impassible à travers les symboles mystérieux où la vérité simple et indicible s'exprime.

Les rites ou les sacrements ont donc cette double fonction *cathartique* et *anagogique*.

Or le pseudo-Denys cite de nouveau son "illustre précepteur," Hiérothée, dans la *Hiérarchie ecclésiastique*, à propos de la communion que celui-ci nommait "le sacrement des sacrements (τελετῶν τελετή)"; et il ajoute:

---

[24]Jamblique, *Les Mystères d'Égypte*, texte établi et traduit par É. des Places, Paris 1966, cf. I, 11: la catharsis, 12: les dieux restent impassibles, p. 61-62, et I, 21: l'Impassibilité divine, où Jamblique défend "la distinction entre la passible et l'impassible (διαίρεσιν τὴν τοῦ ἐμπαθοῦς ἀπὸ τοῦ ἀπαθοῦς)" (p. 76).

[25]cf. Aristote, *Poétique* 6 1449 b 27-28; *Politique* VIII, 1341 b 38-40.

[26]"Le culte (θεραπεία) ... imite l'ordre des dieux, l'intelligible et celui du ciel. Il comporte des mesures éternelles de ce qui est et des signes admirables, vu qu'ils ont été envoyés ici-bas par le démiurge et père de tous les êtres: grâce à eux, l'*indicible s'exprime en symboles mystérieux* (οἷς καὶ τὰ μὲν ἄφθεγκτα διὰ συμβόλων ἀπορρήτων ἐκφωνεῖται), les êtres sans forme sont maîtrisés dans les formes, ceux qui sont supérieurs à toute copie sont reproduits au moyen de copies, et toutes choses s'achèvent par une seule cause divine, qui est tellement *séparée des passions* qu'à la raison même il n'est pas possible de l'atteindre." (Jamblique, *Les Mystères d'Égypte*, p. 61).

Après avoir exposé, grâce à la science divine que nous dispensent Écriture et hiérarchie, les saintes allégories qui la concernent, il nous faudra donc nous élever sous l'inspiration de l'Esprit théarchique jusqu'à la sainte contemplation de ce qu'elle est en vérité (EH 424 C).

Nous retrouvons à propos des sacrements les trois moments que nous avions vus dans le passage des *Noms divins* où Denys disait que Hiérothée *"non seulement connaissait mais aussi pâtissait les choses divines:"*

a) les "allégories" ou les "symboles,"

b) la *"science divine"* que nous dispensent Écriture et hiérarchie—c'est le moment du "μαθεῖν."

c) et le mouvement anagogique vers la contemplation *"sous l'inspiration de l'Esprit théarchique"*[27]—c'est le moment qui correspond au "παθεῖν" en DN 648 B.

Dans les deux cas il s'agit de "l'inspiration de l'Esprit théarchique" qui "élève" l'esprit dans la contemplation et fait "éprouver les choses divines."

La question qui se pose alors est celle-ci: n'est-ce pas "sous l'inspiration de l'Esprit théarchique" que l'homme déifié, que ce soit Hiérothée (DN 428 A), le "θεῖος ἀνήρ" (EH 433 C) ou le Grand Prêtre (EH 428 A), peut "éprouver les choses divines" (παθεῖν τὰ θεῖα)? Et dans ce cas, le "παθεῖν" n'est-il point une "inspiration" de l'Esprit qui touche et élève l'intellect?

Ce qui est en question, c'est la divinisation de l'homme.

III. PATI DIVINA

Les scoliastes et les traducteurs de Pseudo-Denys vont être à l'origine d'une nouvelle compréhension du "παθὼν τὰ θεῖα," d'une part en donnant un sens christologique au παθεῖν qui réintroduira la signification de souffrance que Denys avait écarté, d'autre part en glissant du sens passif d'impression de l'intellect par une "illumination" dans l'initiation ou l'exégèse,—illumination qui, chez Denys, est une "inspiration de l'Esprit-Saint,"—au sens de connaissance affective.

---

[27]Voir aussi EH 428 A: "Cependant que la foule ne prend garde qu'aux seuls symboles divins, (le Grand Prêtre), au contraire, inspiré par l'Esprit théarchique ne cesse d'élever son âme vers le saint principe du rite sacramentel grâce à des contemplations bienheureuses . . ."

1) *Les scolies de Jean de Scythopolis ou de Maxime le Confesseur proposent trois explications de la phrase "*οὐ μόνον μαθὼν ἀλλὰ καὶ παθὼν τὰ θεῖα*" (DN 648 A).*

1. La première se refère à Hb 5, 8: *le Christ "apprit de ce qu' il a pâti l'obéissance (*καίπερ ὢν υἱὸς ἔμαθεν ἀφ' ὧν ἔπαθεν τὴν ὑπακοήν*)."*[28]

Le Christ apprend par la souffrance et il est rendu parfait (καὶ τελειωθείς) (5, 9) par elle.

2. La seconde évoque certains textes pauliniens comme Rm. 6, 4 et Ga. 6, 17:

> Nous avons été ensevelis avec le Christ afin de ressusciter avec lui et de régner avec lui; celui qui a crucifié sa chair porte les stigmates du Christ dans son corps. A bon droit, il règne avec le Christ et peut contempler ses mystères.

3. La troisième, qui est peut-être de Maxime, est plus mystique:

> Pâtir les réalités divines, (c'est) non pas recevoir par mode d'enseignement et par un discours l'initiation à ces réalités, mais en recevoir l'empreinte (ἐντυποθῆναι) par l'illumination divine, comme si était imprimée dans son esprit la

---

[28]J. Coste, "Notion grecque et notion biblique de la souffrance éducatrice (à propos d'Hébreux V, 8)," *RSR* 43 (1955): 481-523.

L'auteur montre les thèmes de la souffrance éducatrice dans l'Ancien Testament où il y a une "pédagogie paternelle" de Dieu qui châtie Israël, comme un père corrige son fils (pr 3, 11-12; 15, 5). Israël *apprend* à travers tous ses maux que Yahvé est Dieu (Ez 13, 14) et il revient vers lui (Ps 78, 34; Jr 31, 18).

L'expérience du prophète Jérémie est celle des *anawim* qui se laissent instruire par la souffrance.

On retrouve la même idée dans tant de "psaumes de pauvres:"

"Avant d'avoir été *éprouvé* ('è'enèh) je m'égarais,

Maintenant je garde ta parole.

Il est bon pour moi d'avoir été *éprouvé* ('unnêtî)

Afin que j'*apprenne* tes préceptes." (Ps 118, v. 67 et 71).

Ce que la souffrance enseigne, c'est que l'homme, à travers ses limites et son échec, voit se dissoudre en lui sa dureté de coeur qui l'éloignait de Dieu et des hommes;

L'auteur de l'*Épître au Hébreux* a pu être influncé par l'usage très fréquent de l'expression "ὃ ἔμαθεν ἀφ' ὧν ἔπαθεν" chez Philon, bien que le sens soit très différent. La Christologie de l'*Épître aux Hébreux* ne peut laisser place à l'idée d'une vertu acquise chez le Christ, ce qui supposerait un état d'imperfection initiale.

Jean Coste conclut: "Au lieu de déclarer avec le P. Spicq "l'accent de la phrase porte sur l'enseignement de l'obéissance, ὃ ἔμαθεν τὴν ὑπακοήν,' nous serions portés à nous demander si l'insistance ne serait pas à mettre plutôt sur l'ἔπαθεν, sur l'expérience douloureuse que le Christ, dans son sacrifice, a faite de l'obéissance" (p. 521).

connaissance de ce qui est au-dessus de la nature, et il appelle cette initiation aux réalités divines *sympathie* (συμπάθειαν) ou *connaturalité* (συνδιάθεσιν).[29]

Nous retrouvons l'image de "l'empreinte"[30] par l'illumination divine. La connaissance de ce qui est au-dessus de la nature est "imprimée" sur l'intellect qui "reçoit" l'illumination divine.

2) Ce sont les traductions latines du *Corpus dionysiacum* et des *Scolies*[31] qui ont été à l'origine de la formation de la formule "*pati divina*" qui devient un des critères de l'expérience mystique.

Le "οὐ μόνον μαθών ἀλλὰ καὶ παθὼν τὰ θεῖα" a été traduit en latin par:

—"non tantum discens sed et *patiens divina*" (Hilduin, Sarrazin, Robert Grossetête),

—"non solum discens sed et *affectus divina*" (Jean Scot Erigène),[32]

—Thomas Gallus, Abbé de Verceil, écrit dans sa paraphrase (achevée en 1238):

Sed et Hierotheus in theologicis obscuris commentis de eis supernaturaliter tractavit; quae ipse didicit sive per aliorum doctrinam sive per studium scripturarum sive per divinam inspirationem et *divinorum experientiam*, ad indocibilem et mysticam ipsorum unitionem et fidem \<perfectus\>.[33]

Jean Scot Erigène parle donc d'un "*affectus divina*" et Thomas Gallus d'une "*divinorum experientia*." On assiste à un glissement de sens "affectif" ou "expérimental" de la formule "παθὼν τὰ θεῖα."

---

[29]PG 4, 228 BC. La *Paraphrasis* de George Pachymère conserve cette dernière formule et l'explique en s'inspirant de la troisième scolie (PG 3, 673 A).

[30]Cf. Jamblique, *Les mystères d'Égypte* III, 15, éd. É. des Places, p. 119-120.

"Les démons révèlent symboliquement l'intention du dieu, "sans dire ni cacher," comme s'exprime Héraclite (*Fragm.* 93, Diels-Kranz) ces prémonitions de l'avenir, mais "en les signifiant, puisqu'ils frappent (ἀποτυποῦσι) le mode de la démiurgie par la prémonstration."

n° 2: Ils "frappent" comme une monnaie ou "impriment," comme sur une cire. Voir aussi *Les Mystères* I, 11; 37, 11).

[31]Les scolies attribuées à Jean de Scythopolis ou Maxime le Confesseur figuraient dans les mss utilisés au XIIIème siècle, par exemple le *Parisinus Lat.* 17341; cf. H.F. Dondaine, *Le Corpus dionysien de l'Université de Paris* 13ème siècle, Rome, 1953, p. 15-20 et 67-28.

[32]Cf. Ph. Chevallier, *Dionysiaca*, t. 1, Paris, 1937, p. 104.

[33]Cf. Ph. Chevallier, *Dionysiaca*, t. 1, Paris, 1937, p. 679.

Thomas d'Aquin, dans son *Commentaire des Noms divins* (en 1261), utilise la version de Sarazzin, mais l'explique en recourant, semble-t-il, à celle de Jean Scot:

> Non solum discens, sed et *patiens divina,* id est non solum divinorum scientiam in intellectu accipiens, sed etiam diligendo eis unitus *per affectum.* Passio enim magis ad appetitum quam ad cognitionem pertinere videtur, quia cognita sunt in cognoscente secundum modum cognoscentis et non secundum modum rerum cognitarum, sed appetitus movet ad res, secundum modum quo in seipsis sunt, et sic ad ipsas res quodammodo afficitur.[34]

Il rattache le *patiens divina* à "l'appétit" qui se meut vers les choses *"prout sunt in seipsis,"* tandis que l'intelligence les saisit *"secundum modum cognoscentis."*

La distinction *"discens"*—*"patiens divina"* correspond maintenant à la distinction de deux principes de connaissance, l'*intellect* et l'*affectus.* Le *"patiens divina"* est le propre du *diligere*[35] qui est affecté par les choses en ce qu'elles sont en elles-mêmes, tandis que l'intelligence ne les reçoit que selon son propre mode de connaître.

L'opposition grecque "μαθεῖν-παθεῖν" devient maintenant, dans la scolastique médiévale, celle de la connaissance et de l'amour.

Mais la charité établit un autre type de connaissance des choses divines: la "connaissance par connaturalité," et c'est à propos de la sagesse, don du Saint-Epsrit, que saint Thomas évoque le *"pati divina"* dans la *Somme théologique.*

> Avoir un jugement correct sur les choses divines par mode de connaturalité relève de la sagesse en tant qu'elle est un don du Saint-Esprit. Denys, parlant d'Hiérothée, dit de lui qu'il est parfait en ce qui concerne les choses divines non seulement parce qu'il les connaît, mais parce qu'il les éprouve (*non solum discens, sed et patiens divina*). Ce sens des choses divines (*compassio*), cette connaturalité avec elles (*connaturalitas ad res divinas*) est donnée par la charité qui nous unit à Dieu, selon I Co 6, 17: Celui qui s'unit à Dieu n'est avec Lui qu'un seul Esprit (*Qui adhaeret Deo unus spiritus est*). Ainsi donc, la sagesse qui

---

[34]Thomae Aquinitatis, *In librum Beati Dionysii De divinis nominibus expositio,* II, 4, nº 191; éd. C. Pera, Turin-Rome, 1950, p. 59.

[35]"La passion des chose divines signifie ici l'affection aux choses divines et l'union à elles par l'amour, ce qui se fait cependant sans modification corporelle" *Somme Théologique,* Ia IIae, Q. 22, a. 3, ad 1.

est un don a pour cause la volonté, c'est-à-dire la charité; mais elle a son siège dans l'intellect (*in intellectu*), dont l'acte est de juger correctement, comme on l'a vu plus haut.[36]

Trois remarques sur ce texte permettent de mesurer la distance entre la phrase de Denys sur Hiérothée dans les *Noms divins* et sa réception dans la *Somme théologique:*

a) "συμπάθεια" est traduit par deux termes: "*compassio*" et "*connaturalitas,*" dont le second définit le mode de connaissance de la *sapientia Spiritus,*

b) l'"ἕνωσις" mystique est référée au passage de I Co 6, 17 qui a servi de fondement à toute la mystique cistercienne de l'*unitas Spiritus.*

c) la sagesse a son siège *in intellectu* alors que, pour Denys, l'union à Dieu est une union *au-delà* de l'intellect (ἕνωσις ὑπὲρ νοῦν).

"Pâtir les choses divines" suppose une connaturalité avec elles grâce à la charité qui nous unit à Dieu, dans l'unité de l'Esprit.

CONCLUSION: LE DÉSIR, LA PASSION ET LA PASSIVITÉ

Que signifie ce "pâtir" les choses divines?

Le sens s'éclaire dans la double opposition "μαθεῖν-παθεῖν" et "παθεῖν-ἀπάθεια" qui permet de définir le "παθεῖν" par rapport à la "συμπάθεια" et à l'"ἀπάθεια."

1) C'est à propos des mystères qu'Aristote, dans le fragment 15 du Περὶ Φιλοσοφίας qui nous est conservé, oppose la connaissance rationnelle et l'émotion provoquée par l'initiation rituelle; tandis que c'est à propos de l'exégèse de l'Écriture ou de l'explication de la théologie que le Pseudo-Denys reprend ces deux termes qu'il n'oppose plus, mais hiérarchise.

La recherche et la connaissance scientifique progressent par raisonnements, mais ne peuvent atteindre Celui qui est au-delà de tout discours et connaissance. Le pâtir, au contraire, est une relation immédiate de Dieu à l'homme—et non de l'homme à Dieu, qu'elle s'ébauche dans la "sympathie" ou s'achève dans "l'union."

2) Ce pâtir, s'il est un "pâtir des choses divines," doit être purifié. La passion des choses divines n'est pas une passion sensible. Les "passions" (πάθη) ont toujours un sens négatif chez le Pseudo-Denys: ce sont des passions "animales," "corruptrices." Cependant la Rédemption "rachète" les passions (DN 717 A) et la contemplation

---

[36]*Somme théologique* IIa IIae, Q. 45, a. 2, *Resp.*

(θεωρία) des symboles bibliques ou liturgiques "guérit" et "élève" la partie passible de l'âme (EP 9, 1108 A).

Il y a un double aspect "cathartique" et "anagogique" de la θεωρία qui, en purifiant les symboles et découvrant la simplicité de leur vérité, élève les intellects, les purifie et les unifie.

La contemplation exige une limpidité ou une impassibilité de l'intellect contemplatif semblable à celle des anges, l'ἀπάθεια devient alors la condition du "παθὼν τὰ θεῖα."

3) Mais alors ce "παθὼν τὰ θεῖα" peut-il être dit un πάθος?

Il faut distinguer dans le παθεῖν la passion et la passivité.

a) L'éros est une passion. Platon, dans le *Phèdre* (265 a) parle de la "passion amoureuse" (τὸ ἐρωτικὸν πάθος). Pourtant le Pseudo-Denys ne définit pas l'éros comme une passion, mais comme une "puissance" (δύναμις);[37] et lorsqu'il parle de l'amour angélique, il dit que l'éros des anges est "sans passion," c'est une tendance (ἔφεσις), un désir.

b) L'initiation (μύησις) comme l'inspiration (ἐπίπνοια) est une expérience des choses divines. C'est l'aspect de passivité. Mais le sens d'"affect" ou d'"affection" est moderne et c'est ce sens qui sera retenu dans la "mystique affective."

Il y a deux éléments dans l'amour: le désir qui naît de la connaissance, donc d'une illumination, et demeure à distance de l'objet désiré, et l'affect, plus obscur, à la fois connaissance par contact et ignorance de celui qui le touche.

C'est cette ignorance de Celui qui est au-delà de tout, alors même qu'il s'unit à l'âme, qui donne au "παθεῖν" son sens le plus juste: le "pâtir" est le mot le plus suggestif pour signifier que l'âme, au-delà de tout raisonnement et discours, est saisie en elle-même par Celui qu'elle ne peut saisir et portée hors d'elle-même, dans le mouvement extatique de l'amour.

---

[37]DN IV, 17, 713 D.